HISTORY OF LAN NA

Sarassawadee Ongsakul

Translated by

Chitraporn Tanratanakul

Edited by

Dolina W. Millar

Sandy Barron

I0891898

SILKWORM BOOKS

This publication was made possible by a grant from
The Toyota Foundation.

Thai text © 2001 by Sarassawadee Ongsakul
English text © 2005 by Silkworm Books

All rights reserved.
No part of this publication may be reproduced,
stored in a retrieval system, or transmitted, in any form or by any means, electronic,
mechanical, photocopying, recording or otherwise,
without the prior permission in writing of the publisher.

ISBN 974-9575-84-9

First published in 2005 by
Silkworm Books
6 Sukkasem Road, T. Suthep
Chiang Mai 50200, Thailand
E-mail: silkworm@silkwormbooks.info
Website: www.silkwormbooks.info

Cover: Mural, Chiang Man Temple, Chiang Mai
Set in 10 pt. Janson Text by SilkType
Printed by O. S. Printing House, Bangkok

1 3 5 4 2

CONTENTS

MAPS

PHOTOGRAPHS

FOREWORD

Associate Professor Sarassawadee Ongsakul has expressed her hope that this work "will be an early milepost on a long road . . . in the study of Lan Na history." Although only an early milepost, her work has taken us quite far along the path. It is appropriate to review the things we have gained through the vehicle of this work.

Many decades ago, anyone who wished to begin the study of Lan Na history was advised to read the Yonok Chronicle of Phraya Prachakitkorachak because it gave a unified and detailed chronological account of the Lan Na region. Although other studies might be of better quality, they only discussed a particular period or some events without a chronological sequence from the beginning to the end like the Yonok Chronicle. Parts of this well-known chronicle were published for the first time in the Wachirayan collection in 1898–1899, or about a century ago. Over this period there have been quite a few local materials collected, transliterated, and published, or gathered and indexed in the archives. There have also been other materials available about Lan Na published in foreign languages. Yet there was no one who tried to use these materials for wide-ranging research on the history of Lan Na from beginning to end like the Yonok Chronicle until this work of Sarassawadee Ongsakul. Unlike her earlier edition of Lan Na history, this work does not emphasize any particular period of history.

Therefore, this is the first time we can advise those who begin to study Lan Na history that this book is indispensable. The century between the Yonok Chronicle and this book has created significant differences.

The *History of Lan Na* explains quite clearly Lan Na's economic, social, and political development. As a result, this history is not an account of what various kings did or did not do but the history of "periods" that are very different from those periods named after capital cities. For example, the Lan Na kingdom did not originate only because Phaya Mangrai founded Chiang Mai. The author is able to clearly explain the specific differences in society and culture during the periods before and after the establishment of Lan Na. Thus, Lan Na history has been developed to another level, not just referring to the name of the kingdom as is usually the case with other histories.

Every period mentioned in this book contains details based on sources scarcely used in other studies of Lan Na history. These details derive from the author's diligence in collecting documentation as well as from the orientation of her analysis, which does not narrowly concentrate on the deeds of kings but utilizes a collection of sources other historians have largely overlooked. For this reason, even those who have long studied the history of Lan Na will likely be very excited by the unfamiliar data and analysis when they read this book.

Of all the periods that show advances in the study of Lan Na history, one that stands out is the period when Lan Na was under the kingdoms of the Tounggu and Alaungphaya dynasties of Burma. There are very few mentions in Lan Na histories about the more than two centuries under Burmese rule, but this book contains a separate chapter on this topic with sufficiently clear details and analysis of the system of administration and politics in Lan Na at that time.

The success of such a clear presentation of this period arises from the author's extensive research. Her efforts show in every chapter and are the main reason this book has advanced the study of Lan Na history to such an extent.

It is said that if we know a topic in depth, we will be able to see a lot of conflicts pertaining to that topic. Extensive details in this study of Lan Na history show these conflicts and a multi-faceted "Lan Na." For example, a great many ethnicities and cultures played important roles in its history. Lan Na did not remain static but changed according to the period. There were many conflicts between different *mueang* and different river valleys, between nobles, between *phrai* (commoners) and nobles, between monks, between *phrai*, between Lua and Tai, Tai and Lao, etc. These conflicts became factors contributing to change in Lan Na history, similar to the history of other regions. Lan Na in this book becomes lively, not static or a string of singular occurrences such as generally appear in other histories.

The author analyzes the levels of structure of Lan Na resulting in in-depth explanations. The loss of independence to Burma was not due to the weakness of any particular king but to weaknesses in the structure of the Lan Na kingdom. For example, the author mentions various evidence pointing to the disintegration of the Lan Na kingdom prior to the fall of Chiang Mai to Burma.

The author's use of extensive materials and her historical analysis of structures result in an orderly arrangement of Lan Na's historical periods from beginning to end, a clearer and more credible periodization of the Lan Na kingdom than those of previous historians of Lan Na. Periodization is the strongest point of this book and is an important advance in the study of Lan Na history as a whole.

The arrangement of periods is that of change, which is the core of historical study. Besides the historical periodization that shows differences in substance, each individual period is also connected to another in a line of change from one period to another. If the *History of Lan Na* has some weaknesses, it is because of the unclear process of this line of change. However, as the author mentions, there are many materials that have yet to be collected and meticulously analyzed, and this book is only an early milepost on a long road in the study of Lan Na history.

The author humbly mentions her work as being a mere milepost, but I believe this book is sure to be the focus of the study of Lan Na history for many years to come, and one must point out whether scholars of Lan Na history wrote before or after this landmark book.

Nidhi Eoseewong
April 14, 1996

PREFACE

The *History of Lan Na* was first published in November 1986 under the auspices of the Institute for the Promotion of Arts and Culture of Chiang Mai University. The one thousand copies printed were well received by the public and sold out in less than a year. A large number of people still wanted the book, and some publishing houses were interested in a second printing because of this demand. However, I turned them down because I wished to improve the text. It took me about a decade to do this, and as a result of many improvements, this revised edition of the *History of Lan Na* has become an almost totally new book, very different from the original text.

The first edition of the *History of Lan Na* emphasized the modern period from the restoration of Lan Na by the Chao Chet Ton clan in 1774 to the termination of the *thesaphiban* system of provincial administration in 1933. This was because my academic life started with my research on this period. The first stage of my research was with documents in the National Archives as well as in the Wachirayan Archives. I did extensive research with these materials until there were no new challenging questions. Thus, I began to be interested in the early history of Lan Na going back from the time of King Kawila to its beginning. This interest in ancient Lan Na led me to study *tua muang* script and to research palm-leaf and *phap nang sa* manuscripts. I intended to read these manuscripts as thoroughly as I had previously read the materials in the National Archives and Wachirayan Archives. I was confident that I could obtain more extensive data, so I worked hard to read these *tua muang* mansucripts. I knew from the time of the first edition of the *History of Lan Na* that it would require much time and effort to check and verify the early writings on the history of Lan Na.

The second edition of the *History of Lan Na* makes extensive textual improvements on history prior to 1774, emphasizing the use of palm-leaf and *phap nang sa* manuscripts, both those that have been transliterated as well as those that have not. A number of secondary sources were also used. The content of this book shows the development of the Lan Na state, beginning with chapter 2, which covers the era of various domains and city-states scattered along the river valleys, including Hariphunchai,

Khelangkhanakon, Yon (Yonok), Phayao, Phrae, and Nan. This section has been expanded from its original emphasis on the Hariphunchai and Yon domains. Chapter 3 concentrates of the development of Lan Na into a kingdom in the period 1296–1558 with expanded coverage of administration, the economy, and relations with neighboring states. An analysis of the decline of the Mangrai dynasty and the fall of the kingdom that led to Burmese rule in the period 1558–1774 is given in chapter 4. This chapter has been expanded to include more details and analysis of this period, but there are still limitations concerning sources from Burma. The material on the period 1774–1993 has also been enlarged and improved.

Nevertheless, I consider this *History of Lan Na* to be only a preliminary effort because it is the first scholarly book that gives an extensive and in-depth history of Lan Na. That this is a trail-blazing work in the field is already a limitation. I hope that this book will be an early milepost on a long and complicated road in the study of Lan Na history.

This second edition includes 119 additional illustrations, mostly old and hard-to-find photographs. These are photographs that I have collected from many sources, such as the National Archives, Payap University archives, and Mr. Bunserm Satraphai. The aerial photographs are also old and very difficult to find; for example, the aerial photgraph of Chiang Mai which Dr. Volker Grabowsky of Hamburg University discovered in London, for which I am very grateful.

I would like to express my deepest respect to "Mae Khru" [Mother Teacher] Thanphuying Warunyupha Snitwong na Ayuthaya, who has untiringly supported me ever since I became interested in research on Lan Na history twenty years ago right up to the present. I dedicate this book to "Mae Khru."

Thanks also are due to Professor Nidhi Eoseewong, who has been very supportive in strengthening my academic work. His advice to study *tua muang* was very important for me. Thanks also go to Dr. Chayan Vandhanaphuti, the former director of the Social Research Institute, who provided support and inspiration and promoted my work to the public on several occasions. I am grateful to Achan Pathom Phuaphansakul, who gave me permission to use his slide for the book cover.

Thanks are due to the personnel of the Wachirayan Archives, including those responsible for microfilm who made copies of the chronicles and of the palm-leaf manuscripts. Their assistance facilitated my research in Chiang Mai. Thanks also go to the people at the Social Research Institute of Chiang Mai University and the people at the Institute for the Promotion of Arts and Culture also at Chiang Mai University who assisted in microfilming. I am also grateful to people at the National Archives and at Payap University archives who assisted in making copies of photographs. Thanks go to the director of the Ratchamankhalaphisak Archives in Chiang Mai, who assisted in making the index.

Finally, I thank Achan Somchot, Nua, and Maenam, who provided me with great moral support.

Sawassawadee Ongsakul

The Department of History
Faculty of Humanities
Chiang Mai University
November 1995

MAP 1. MAP OF LAN NA

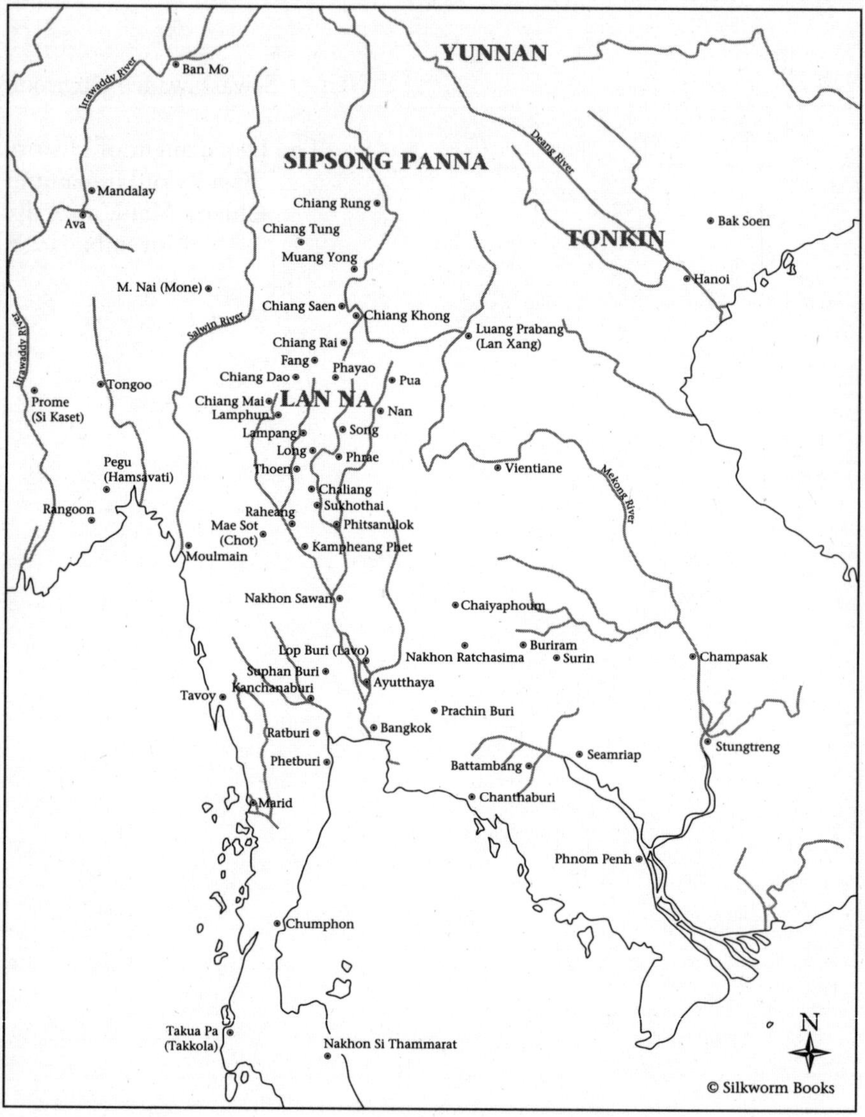

CHAPTER 1

THE STUDY OF LAN NA HISTORY

THE STATE OF LAN NA HISTORICAL STUDIES

The study and writing of Lan Na history started about six hundred years ago, when local scholars and monks began composing chronicles on palm-leaf manuscripts. The tradition they pioneered lasted until the mid-twentieth century. Today, the chronicles still retain a strong foothold in local popular consciousness, and they are a rich source of information for modern historians.

OVERVIEW OF THE HISTORICAL RECORDS

Lan Na's oldest written historical records date back to before the chronicles and are mainly records of dynastic succession recorded in steles. The Wat Phra Yuen stele, inscribed in 1370, is considered the region's oldest stone inscription. It says, "This stele records the fact that Chao Thao Songsaenna Anthammikarat [Phaya Kuena], who is the beloved son of Phaya Phayu, is the grandson of the great Phaya Khamfu and the great-grandson of Phaya Mangrai."[1]

Another stele of dynastic succession (LP. 9), considered to be the oldest stone inscription in Fak Kham script, was inscribed in 1411 during the reign of Phaya Samfangkaen, for the purpose of claiming his legitimacy as the eighth king of the Mangrai dynasty. It reads:

> From the time Mangrai reigned over the kingdom and the time of kings Khram [Chaisongkhram], Thao Saenpu, Khamfu, Phayu, Kuena, Chao Saenmueangma, after the reign of these seven kings, King Samfangkaen became very powerful, a credit to the glory of his line, a sacred person had been born.[2]

Stele gave way to palm-leaf manuscripts. These chronicles were incised on palm leaves with a sharp instrument and then soot was rubbed into the incisions, where it combined with sap. Bundles of leaves were stitched together and sometimes bound between decorated wooden covers.

The chronicles were a mix of religion, fact, and folklore; they were not intended as strict records of historical fact. Thus in one chronicle we read

"All the lords [and] lord professors have created [this] as a tale and recitation and the customary lore . . ."[3] They followed oral conversational style, for example, "Here, we will speak of all the kings who changed the era, in succession."[4]

The earliest chronicles, written in the fifteenth and sixteenth centuries, are now generally considered "classical chronicles." Important texts from this period, including the Mulasasana, Camadevivamsa, and Jinakalamali chronicles, became the models for all others over the next centuries. The classical chronicles were written during the prosperous golden age of Lan Na, when the society was undergoing much change and its boundaries were being extended. In all of the loosely connected *mueang*, or city-states, large or small, people found it necessary to explain Lan Na's developing unity. Expansion acted as a stimulus to the composition of chronicles. The texts reflected and fostered a sense of awareness of the past, an awareness that had earlier found oral rather than written expression. Chronicle writing became so common that the North came to have a reputation as the repository for more written history than any region of Thailand. Many Lan Na chronicles have yet to be studied. A wealth of information remains hidden in palm-leaf manuscripts.

The production of chronicles dipped slightly under Burmese rule (1558–1774), and revived dramatically during the reign of King Kawila, ruler of Chiang Mai from 1782 to 1816. The revival continued during the reconstruction of *mueang* that had been deserted after years of warfare. Keen to construct a sense of heritage around itself, the ruling Chao Chet Ton dynasty encouraged the writing of its dynastic history. This heralded a "second wave" of new chronicles written in the traditional style, as well as the copying of many older texts. (Palm-leaf manuscripts are not very durable; most of those that survive today were copied during the Ratanakosin (Bangkok) era). Leading chronicles written during this period include the Chao Chet Ton Chronicle and the Chiang Mai Chronicle (Prime Minister's Office edition, bundle numbers 6, 7, 8).

Chronicle writing continued to flourish during the reign of King Rama V (1868–1910) or the reign of King Inthawichayanon, ruler of Chiang Mai. Western influence in Siam during the reigns of King Rama IV and King Rama V contributed to new trends in the study and writing of history in central Thailand, such as the writing of the Yonok Chronicle, but traditional chronicle writing continued to be as important as ever in the Lan Na region. Well-known texts reproduced around King Rama V's reign include the Chiang Saen (Singhonti or Singhanawatikuman) Chronicle, the Mueang Ngoen Yang Chiang Saen Annals, the Ratchawongpakon Annals, and Mueang Nan Chronicle (*Prachum phongsawadan phak thi sip*).[5]

In the reign of King Rama VI, the study of the Central Thai language spread to the Lan Na region. The practice of copying chronicles into palm-leaf manuscripts declined but continued during the period from the People's

Party coup in 1932 until around 1957. Texts included the Wat Buppharam Chronicle at Pa Heo Temple, San Kamphaeng village, Chiang Mai province, inscribed in 1933; the Wat Luang San Kamphaeng Chronicle at Wat Luang San Kamphaeng Temple, San Kamphaeng district, also inscribed in 1933; and the Mueang On Chronicle at Pa Sak Noi Temple, San Kamphaeng district, inscribed in 1952. These new chronicles continued in the classical tradition. Each begins with the arrival of the Lord Buddha to the location, follows with a prophecy for the area, and goes on to give an account of the history of the temple or town. Older chronicles copied on to palm leaf included the Mueang Nan Annals, the palm-leaf manuscript of the Hia Temple, Nan, inscribed in 1933; and the Mueang Nan Chronicle, a palm-leaf manuscript owned by the Siam Society (bundle number 50, running number 504), inscribed in 1964.

OVERVIEW OF THE CHRONICLES

The Lan Na chronicles were inspired in style by Buddhist chronicles in Sri Lanka, notably the Mahavamsa manuscript. Buddhism was always at the center of the chronicles. The purpose of writing the texts was principally to support the religion and to make merit. All such chronicles begin with the history of Buddhism. Events throughout, including historical events, are generally explained in religious terms; for example, in terms of karma and punishment, or of supernatural powers, or of Buddhist prophecy. The main texts were divided into two types: *wat* (temple) or Buddha-sasana (Buddhist) chronicles, and *mueang* (town or city-state) chronicles.

Early classical Buddhist chronicles, such as the Mulasasana, Camadevivamsa, and Jinakalamali, were presented in two parts.[6] The first part contained a general history of Buddhism, beginning with the story of Buddha when he was a Boddhisatta and determined to become enlightened as the Lord Buddha, and continuing with the birth of Buddhism. The second part drew on local folklore that had been passed down for generations to give a chronological history of local kings and dynasties, generally also describing their role in Buddhism. Examples include accounts of Queen Chamathewi establishing Buddhism in the city of Hariphunchai; Phaya Athittarat founding Phrathat Hariphunchai; and Phaya Kuena establishing the Raman branch of Buddhism. Such accounts were drawn from ancient oral histories of local heroes such as Lao Chok, Khun Chuang, Phaya Ngammueang, and Khun Nun Khun Fong.

The Mulasasana Chronicle, the earliest of the texts, was put together by the monks Buddhañana and Buddhabukama. The writers of the Camadevivamsa and Jinakalamali chronicles followed their lead, using similar structures, and even using some identical stories. A tale that relates the birth of man from an animal footprint is found in the three chronicles, with slight variation in the details. Current scholars of Lan Na history, for whom the chronicles are a key resource, must be conscious of this sort of borrowing. It was the normal practice of the times. The synthesis of indigenous folk history with the new Buddhist writing influences from Sri Lanka resulted in something distinct and new, and was an indication of an advanced level of intellectual activity and awareness.

The temple chronicles, *(tamnan wat)* can be sub-divided into four kinds—Phrathat, Phraphuttharup,[7] Wat,[8] and Phrabat.[9] These are chronicles of, respectively, stupas that contain a relic of the Lord Buddha, Buddha images, Buddhist temples, and Buddha footprints. Chronicles of these kinds are scattered throughout the Lan Na region.

The Phrathat chronicles contain first sections similar to the already mentioned general Buddhist chronicles. They go on to explain how the Buddha came to help the people of the region, his prophecy for the area, the area's acquisition of a Buddha relic, the founding of the local town, and the construction by a king of a stupa to house the holy relic. These kinds of chronicles have remained very popular. Prominent versions are now icons of their communities; for example, the Phrathat Cho Hae Chronicle in Phrae province; the Phrathat Chae Haeng Chronicle in Nan province; the Phrathat Lampang Luang and the Phrathat Kaeo Dontao chronicles in Lampang province; the Phrathat Doi Tung Chronicle in Chiang Saen district; the Phrathat Hariphunchai Chronicle in Lamphun province; and the Phrathat Doi Suthep and Phrathat Chom Thong chronicles in Chiang Mai province. After the tradition of copying manuscripts disappeared, local people remained keen to read printed copies of Phrathat and Phrabat. Printed versions of temple chronicles, such as the Wat Phrathat Chom Thong Chronicle in Chiang Mai province, and the Wat Phrathat Lampang Luang Chronicle in Lampang province, are also very popular.

Mueang chronicles, the second of the two main types, are also known as *phuen*, meaning "history" in the Lan Na language. The term *tamnan*, also often used, means "chronicle" and comes from the Khmer language. The terms *phuen* and *tamnan* are often used interchangeably and are sometimes combined, as in *Tamnan Phuen Mueang Chiang Mai*. The term *phuen* is mainly used in *mueang* chronicles, while the term *tamnan* is used both in temple chronicles and *mueang* chronicles.[10] There are many *phuen*, for example, *Phuen Mueang Nan* (History of Nan) and *Phuen Mueang Chiang Rai* (History of Chiang Rai). The term *phuen* emphasizes the chronicle's importance to the history of the area, particularly the history of kings and their dynasties. Some chronicles are called Ratchawongpakon or texts about dynasties, such as the *Prachumphongsawadan phak thi sip*, called "Ratchawongpakon, Chronicle of Nan." Some versions of the *Tamnan Phuen Mueang Chiang Mai* (hereafter called the Chiang Mai Chronicle) are given the name *Tamnan Ratchawongpakon*.[11]

Mueang chronicles are of a variety of types, and they draw on hero chronicles, miscellaneous chronicles, and folklore. The hero chronicles emphasize a single leader who was prominent or who was the founder of a family line, for example, the Phaya Chuang, the Phaya Ngammueang, the Pu Chao Lao Chok, the Chao Suwankhamdaeng, the Phaya Mangrai, the Khun Nun Khun Fong, and the Thao Phanong chronicles. The chronicle of dynastic succession, or dynastic chronicle, developed from the chronicle of heroes.

Mueang chronicles are very important evidence in the study of Lan Na history. Leading examples include the chronicles of Chiang Mai, Chiang Rai, Phayao, Nan, Chao Chet Ton, Singhonti, Mueang Suwankhomkham, and Lamdap Saisakun Chao Luang Tuen Chao Mueang Nan.

There were also "miscellaneous" (*pakinaka*) chronicles, which generally contain short accounts about an area. It is likely that many more of the sorts of stories they contain were circulated orally than were written down. When the author was transliterating the Phuen Mueang Nan, Wat Phra Koet version, she found several such chronicles, including the Tamnan Tang Mueang Khwang (The Founding of Mueang Khwang), the Nang Klua, the Tit Suai Ho, the Kaeo Ma Tok Suk, and the Ubai Hai Hai Khro Mueang Tai chronicles.

Gazettes or *pum* were brief chronological writings on important annual historical events. Scribes usually detailed the year, the position on the astrological twelve-year cycle, the month, the day regarding the waxing or waning of the moon, the day and *horakhun*, or the number of days since the first year of Chulasakarat (639 C.E.). These were generally written for personal use and they thus discuss many aspects that are not found in the town chronicles. *Pum* tend not be very structured in content. As personal stories, they tend to provide little in the way of hard historical evidence.[12]

WRITING IN LAN NA

Three writing systems were used in Lan Na: Lan Na Tham script, Fak Kham script, and Thai Nithet or Khom Mueang script. For various reasons, including political ones, they gradually declined in importance and are now known by only a circle of academics.

The Northern Thai script known as Lan Na Tham script (*tua Tham* or Dhamma script) was widely used in the region. George Cœdès, a scholar of ancient scripts and author of *The History of Thai Scripts*, hypothesized in a theory now generally accepted that Tham script originated from Mon script, also the precursor of other writing systems in the region such as Burmese, Tai Yai or Shan, Ahom Tai, Lue, Khoen, and Isan Tham script. Mon script does not have tone marks. When the people of Lan Na first adopted Mon writing, they did not use tone marks, though Lan Na Tham was a tonal language. The use of tone marks only began in the sixteenth century, and usage was not strict.

Like other languages, Lan Na Tham script evolved by making improvements on an earlier system, in this case Mon. The oldest form of Lan Na Tham script discovered is the Lan Thong inscription found in Sukhothai. It is dated 1376 and contains four lines. The first three are in Sukhothai script and Thai language, while the fourth line is in Pali, written in Lan Na Tham script, and shows close similarity to other Mon writing in inscriptions.[13] It is clearly different in origin from the Sukhothai script of King Ramkhamhaeng.

This inscription suggests that Lan Na Tham script probably originated in the Lan Na region many decades before 1376 and later spread to Sukhothai, which then began to use Lan Na Tham script instead of Khom (Cambodian) script to write Pali.

Lan Na Tham script arose from religious necessity. It was used to write Dhamma texts to communicate with the general public. Therefore, it was first used mainly for the writing of Pali and was later adapted for writing the Northern Thai dialect.[14] Lan Na Tham script was considered sacred writing, and was thus generally called Dhamma (or Tham) script. Later, Dhamma script was needed for writing about topics such as medicine and astrology.

Lan Na Tham script accompanied the spread of Buddhism into the Lan Xang kingdom and then into the Isan region. There is evidence that King Bodhisalarat of Lan Xang sent an envoy to Lan Na asking for the Tipitaka and a group of Buddhist monks from Chiang Mai.[15] It is likely that the use of Lan Na literature increased in Lan Xang during the reign of King Sethathirat (Chaiyachettha). It is also possible that Lan Na Tham script spread to Sipsong Panna. Indeed, Prasert Na Nagara believes that Lan Na Tham script spread to Sipsong Panna during the time of King Tilokarat with the Langkawong sect of Buddhism, particularly after the Buddhist Tipitaka Council in 1477.[16]

The second writing type is Fak Kham script, which originates from and closely resembles King Ramkhamhaeng's Sukhothai script. The Sukhothai script spread to Lan Na with the Raman sect of Buddhism and underwent some variations influenced by Lan Na Tham script before becoming known as Fak Kham script.[17] It is possible that the stone inscription at Wat Phra Yuen (inscription number 62), inscribed in 1370, was a precursor of Fak Kham script. It has been accepted as the oldest Sukhothai script in the North. Fak Kham was used mainly for writing stone inscriptions, a practice which may have come from Sukothai before it was replaced by the more popular Lan Na Tham. More than one hundred stone inscriptions in Fak Kham have been found.[18] As mentioned above, the oldest discovered is LP. 9, inscribed in 1411. Fak Kham script also spread to Chiang Tung and was similarly used in stone inscriptions there.

Fak Kham was in wide use for about two hundred years, but it survived for a further two centuries. The latest inscription found was inscribed in 1827. Just four inscriptions in total have been found dated in the nineteenth century.[19]

Thai Nithet script, or Khom Mueang script, was adapted from the Lan Na Tham and Fak Kham scripts. Previously, it was believed that it emerged during the reign of King Kawila, but later evidence has shown that it probably appeared earlier. Thai Nithet script was widely used in poetry relating to worldly matters, such as "*Nirat Hariphunchai*" and "*Mangthra Rop Chiang Mai*" [Mangthra Fought Chiang Mai], and the poetry in "*Phromathat*."

THE MODERN STUDY OF LAN NA HISTORY

The pioneer of the modern study of history in Thailand was Phraya Prachakitkorachak (Chaem Bunnag), who produced a renowned study of Lan Na, the Yonok Chronicle, (*Phongsawadan Yonok*), first published in 1898–1899. The founding of Chiang Mai University in 1964 saw the introduction of local history classes based mainly on the Yonok Chronicle. Interest was rather modest, but a small number of outstanding local history articles were presented at a 1967 seminar on history and archaeology arranged by the Department of History, Faculty of Humanities.

Activity has increased since the late 1970s, due to a nationwide and local resurgence of interest in history, a wider variety of study areas being offered, and influences from the social sciences.[20] The widespread interest in local history is reflected in the emergence of cultural centers and public events about local history around the country.

A growing number of courses on Lan Na history have been offered at the Rajabhat Institute (formerly the Chiang Mai Teacher's College) since 1978 and at Payap University. Since 1988, the Department of History at Chiang Mai University has offered Lan Na history at the graduate level. Since 1991, the new curriculum for history majors at the undergraduate level has included two compulsory courses: Lan Na History and Problems in Lan Na History, in response to interest among students and faculty.

However, there is still a shortage of research. The topics covered so far have lacked diversity and depth, and many aspects of Lan Na history have not been studied at all. Evidence from palm-leaf manuscripts has not been utilized as much as it could. Research opportunities thus remain wide open.

It is also worth noting that the modern approach to the study of history is still the preserve of a closed circle of local academics. Their knowledge has yet to penetrate into the wider consciousness, where the traditional texts still hold sway.

PROBLEMS IN THE STUDY OF LAN NA HISTORY

The modern study of Lan Na history is hampered by the nature and availability of the historical materials and the challenges in interpreting them. Written materials from Lan Na comprise chronicles, inscriptions, gazettes, and other literature inscribed on palm-leaf and *pap sa* (mulberry paper) manuscripts.

THE MATERIALS

There are hundreds of thousands of bound palm-leaf manuscripts still scattered in *ho tham* (temple depositories) around the region. Countless others have been lost to fire, insects, or age. Palm-leaf manuscripts lost their importance and were neglected after educational reforms during the period of King Rama V to VII, when the study of Central Thai script was introduced to Lan Na.

Concern over the preservation of the old manuscripts led the Social Research Institute at Chiang Mai University to establish a program to survey and collect them, and place them on microfiche. A collection of more than fifteen thousand bundled palm-leaf manuscripts is now in a repository.[21] The Center for the Promotion of Arts and Culture, also at Chiang Mai University, has a similar program and has catalogued, cleaned, restored, and microfilmed many manuscripts. However, both institutes have focused on important temples; a large number of manuscripts remain uninspected.

Other historical material was written with a pen on *pap nang sa*, or *pap sa* paper documents, which are less durable than the palm-leaf manuscripts. *Pap nang sa* documents were folded accordion style into long, narrow books. The writing tended to fade over time and the documents were vulnerable to insect damage. The content of *pap nang sa* usually related to nonreligious matters such as history, astrology, medicine, rites, and law. In the past, historians paid relatively little attention to these documents. The author feels they merit more study.

Students face a number of problems using palm-leaf manuscripts and *pap nang sa*. First, very many are written in Lan Na Tham script. Academic institutions in the North should encourage the study of Lan Na Tham script as well as transliteration of the texts into the Central Thai (Siamese) script. This would widen the availability of the material and encourage further study.

Palm-leaf manuscripts were written with no spaces between sentences, with no paragraphs, and sometimes with little consideration of chronology. Sometimes two or three different texts were grouped together, without regard to subject matter, so that one bound volume could contain both a *mueang* chronicle and a medicinal reference. To survey such documents means having to read the entire content. A further difficulty lies in the fact that there is no standardization for Lan Na Tham script (standardization for the Thai language only originated during the reign of King Rama V); a single scribe might sometimes write the same word differently on the same line. Transliteration of these documents should at least organize the material into paragraphs.

Students also need to be familiar with inscriptions on materials like sandstone, wood, and metal. These are now scattered in various temples and in deserted temple ruins, as well as in museums. The Social Research Institute at Chiang Mai University has a collection of some 1,300 inscriptions and continues to study and collect them.[22] The Department of Archaeology has registered 207 Lan Na inscriptions, most of them from Phayao province.[23]

The inscriptions generally consist of a limited amount of ad hoc detail, often concerning donations of people and materials to temples. Details might include the names of the temple, names of donated persons, names of officials dealing with rents donated for temple upkeep as memorials to the dead, and the names of the kings who permitted such donations.[24] More inscriptions are still being found, and the new finds also tend to cover the same topics. A number of inscriptions contain just a few letters. Most were inscribed during the golden age of Lan Na. Despite their limitations, inscriptions are important historical evidence because they are contemporaneous with the events they describe.

Covering the later period, government materials pertaining to the administration of the provinces are useful. The National Library contains material on Lan Na from the time of King Rama I up to King Rama V. The National Archives house material from King Rama V until the present. The documents cover administrative materials and official documents sent between the Lan Na provinces and the central government in Bangkok. There are records on Chiang Tung (or Keng Tung) and Chiang Rung (today known as Jinhong, in Yunnan, PRC), and of the relationships between Burma, Bangkok, Chiang Mai, etc.

There is also material written in Chinese, English, and Shan or Greater Tai. Materials in Chinese, which are mainly dynastic annals, are extremely useful due to their accuracy with regard to dates, as well as their contemporaneity with events. They should be used to check the content in chronicles and will contribute to confidence in the use of chronicles. The dynastic history of the Yuan dynasty (*Yuan-shih*) is considered an important source. The Commission for the Study of Chinese Records on Thai History published an old Chinese history of Ba Bai Xifu / Ba Bai Dadian (Chiang Mai) as part of the celebration of the seven hundredth anniversary of the founding of Chiang Mai. The English materials are the result of the English role in the Lan Na region in the nineteenth century. In 1837, Dr. David Richardson traveled from British-held Moulmein in Burma to Lan Na, and his findings were later published (and are now available in *The Gold and Silver Road of Trade and Friendship, The McLeod and Richardson Diplomatic Missions to Tai States in 1837*, Silkworm Books, 2003). There is also material in English from Christian missionaries in the archives of Payap University. A number of people are now transliterating Shan or Tai Yai materials, including materials in Lue, Khoen, and Thai Yai, into the Central Thai language. Thawi Sawangpanyangkun, for example, has transliterated the Chiang Tung, the Phuen Mueang Sipsong Panna, and Mueang Yong chronicles.

Other evidence useful for the study of Lan Na includes materials from the fields of archaeology, art history, aerial photography, and oral history. Archaeological excavations are very useful because they can provide concrete evidence of the past of a kind that cannot be obtained from historical documents. Archaeological materials can also be used to check the evidence of chronicles. However, the high cost of excavations mean few have taken place. Art, such as stupas, Buddha images, and murals, can help date a period and can reveal much about people's culture and beliefs.

Aerial photography, which can show traces of earthen ramparts and moats, old waterways, landscape, and settlements, can also be very useful. Oral history, which became part of general history study only about twenty years ago, is helpful mainly for the study of villages and minority groups.

THE INTERPRETATION

The old practice of copying material from one palm-leaf manuscript to another had some limitations. Omissions and revisions were common, for example. This has resulted in several versions for many of the chronicles. At least sixteen versions have been found of the Phrathat Doi Tung Chronicle and there are several versions of the main Chiang Mai Chronicle (including the Sip Ha Ratchawong and the Ratchawongpakon chronicles). This means that students of the chronicles need to develop expertise in comparative reading, which takes much time and effort, not to mention proficiency in the *tua mueang* or local script.

It is no easy task to use the chronicles as historical evidence. The information they contain on periods prior to the fifteenth century was written long after the events described. Details about key figures such Queen Chamathewi, Phaya Mangrai, Phaya Kuena, and Phaya Samfangkaen, for example, were based on oral accounts and were mixed in with folklore and religious and spiritual matters. Students need to study the tradition and the writing styles carefully, and to familiarize themselves with the assumptions and worldview of the writers, in order to be able to undertake a critical evaluation of the material.[25]

Students will find little in the chronicles that sheds light on the lives of ordinary people. The chronicles aimed to relate the stories of kings and their dynasties.

Finally, the government materials relating to Lan Na dating from the time of Rama I are in the Central Thai language, which is convenient for research. However, the bulk of this material reflects the views of the central government, which may not accord with local sources. Thus certain documents may need to be weighed against other evidence.

CHAPTER 2

THE ERA OF DOMAINS AND CITY-STATES BEFORE THE BEGINNING OF THE LAN NA KINGDOM

LAN NA: MEANING AND BOUNDARIES

MEANING

Over the centuries the term Lan Na has appeared in two versions using different tone marks, as either Lán Nã, "the land of a million rice fields" or Lãn Nã "the land of many rice fields." Tone marks first began to appear in Lan Na Tham script in the sixteenth century,[1] but there was no strict system for how they were used. By the early Ratanakosin era there was widespread acceptance of the version Lãn Nã (many rice fields). During the twentieth century this version spread throughout Siam, in textbooks and other academic materials.[2] Still, the issue remained unresolved and in 1967 a group of academics contended that the other version, Lán Nã (land of a million rice fields) was the correct term. In 1980 Hans Penth presented an article confirming that this term appears in the 1553 Chiang Sa stone inscription from Chiang Rai province (now in Chiang Mai Museum). This was a decisive piece of evidence, as stone inscriptions are contemporaneous with the events they describe. The other term has not been found on any stele. Later, the Historical Commission of the Prime Minister's Secretariat, chaired by Prasert Na Nagara, also investigated the Chiang Sa inscription. It concluded in 1987 that the term Lán Nã was correct. The term should be seen as paralleling the name for the old Lao kingdom, Lan Xang, "land of a million elephants," the commission held. In 1983 Chiang Mai's academic circle used the term Lán Nã Thai in the title of a book commemorating the royal opening of the Three Kings Monument in the city. Since the Commission's ruling on the matter the term Lan Na (million rice fields) has been widely, though not universally, accepted.

The term *panna* is also pertinent to the discussion. In the past, large areas of agricultural land were measured in units called *panna*, meaning "a thousand rice fields." Chiang Rai had thirty-two *panna*, Phayao thirty-six, Chiang Saen sixty-five, and Fang five. To combine all the *panna* of the kingdom would amount to a huge number—hence, perhaps, "a million rice fields."

Further support for the now accepted version of Lan Na may be found in

MAP 2. LAN NA AND ITS SURROUNDINGS

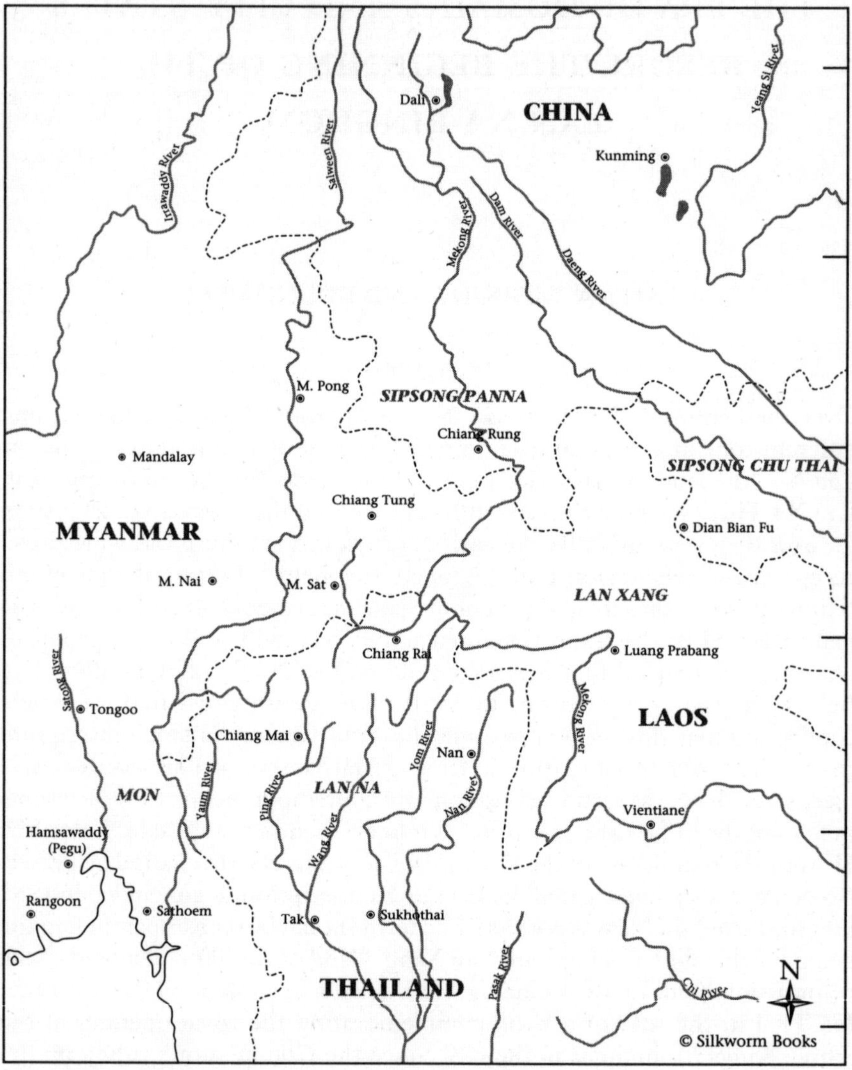

(Drawn after Sarassawadee Ongsakul, *Prawatsat Lan Na*, p. 24)

the name of Phaya Kuena (1335–1385), the sixth king of the Mangrai dynasty, which means "lord of a hundred million rice fields."[3]

Lastly, there is support for the term in the form of the royal title bestowed by King Rama V on Chao Chiwit Ao of Chiang Mai: "King Kawilorotsuriyawong Damrong Naphisinakhon Sunthon Thosalakkaset." The term *thosalakkaset* means ten hundred thousand rice fields or Lan Na.

The term Lan Na appears to have been first used during the reign of Phaya Kuena, not during the reign of Mangrai.[4] It was widely used during the reign of King Tilokarat (1441–1487), when kings were called "Thao Lan Na" or "Thao Phaya Lan Na," and the general populace was called "Chao Lan Na."[5] There was also a tradition of prefixing the names of towns with Lan Na. In the reign of Phaya Samfangkaen (1402–1441), we find references to Lan Na Chiang Saen[6] and Lan Na Chiang Mai.

BOUNDARIES

Neither Siam nor Lan Na had clear boundaries prior to the beginning of absolute monarchy in the reign of King Rama V, but there is more or less sufficient evidence for the existence of approximate boundaries. Lan Na referred to an area comprising a group of principalities whose southern boundary extended as far as Tak (Ban Tak district) and the top part of the Sukhothai kingdom. To the west, Lan Na reached the Salween River; to the east, it extended to the Mekong River; and to the north, Chiang Rung. Lan Na was made up of *mueang*, autonomous or semi-autonomous principalities or city-states, that varied greatly in size and influence. Western Lan Na was the most important area and included Chiang Mai, Lamphun, Lampang, Chiang Rai, and Phayao. These were connected in the early Mangrai dynasty and developed a common history. Eastern Lan Na's most prominent *mueang* were the small, culturally linked river valley states of Phrae and Nan. They had been independent, with close relations with the Sukhothai kingdom, until the reign of Tilokarat, when they were incorporated into Lan Na. They did not develop very close ties with Chiang Mai. The southern section of Lan Na included the upper part of Tak and Uttaradit provinces. Lan Na's peripheral areas, where it had fluctuating influence, included Chiang Rung, and Chiang Tung, Mueang Yong, Mueang Pu, Mueang Sat, and Mueang Nai in the Shan (Thai Yai) states.

Today, Lan Na is understood to cover the area comprising eight provinces in northern Thailand: Chiang Mai, Lamphun, Lampang, Chiang Rai, Phayao, Phrae, Nan, and Mae Hong Son. Chiang Mai city, which celebrated its seven hundredth anniversary in 1996, has always been the center of Lan Na.

The Chiang Mai Chronicle mentions that there were fifty-seven *mueang* within Lan Na,[7] but it does not provide names. It is probable that this number includes a large number of small *mueang*, as the important territories alone would not reach fifty-seven.

MAP 3. THE TOPOGRAPHY OF LAN NA

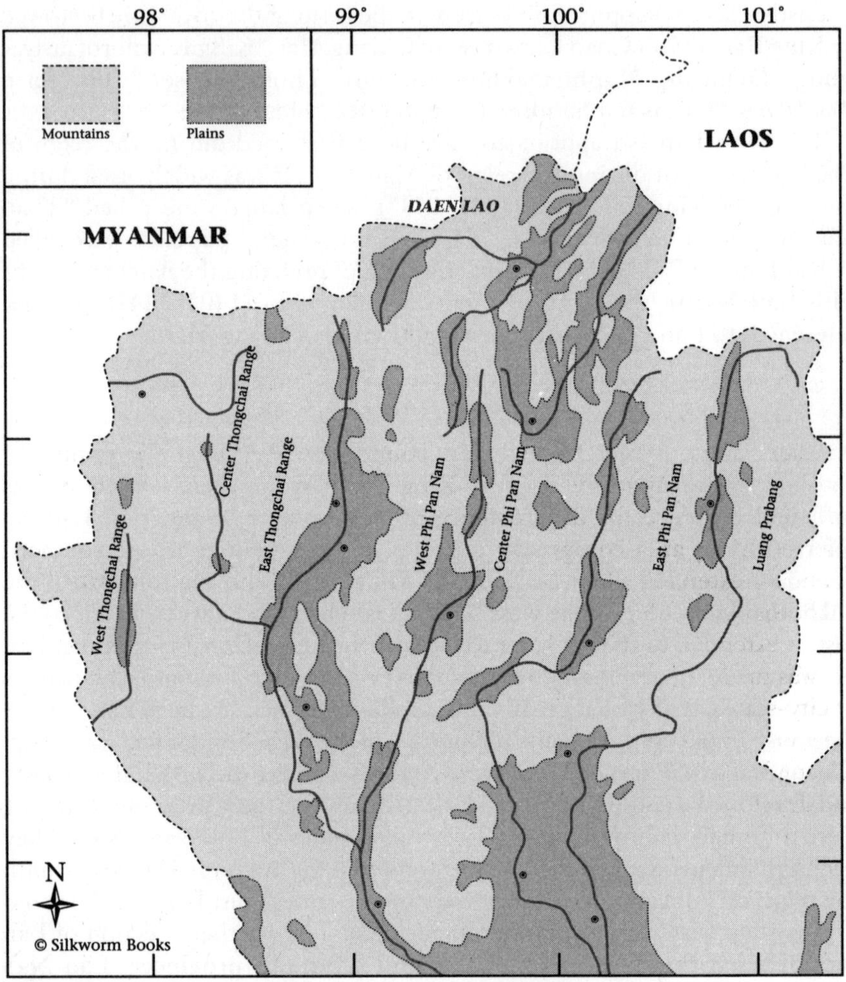

(Drawn after Sarassawadee Ongsakul, *Prawatsat Lan Na*, p. 26)

THE INFLUENCE OF GEOGRAPHY ON LAN NA HISTORY

Lan Na was a mountainous territory studded with river valleys in the landlocked heart of the Asian continent. The topography of the region led to the rise of independent city states. Under Lan Na, many of these small states were united into a kingdom for 262 years. Others in the upper regions such as the Shan States and Sipsong Panna, retained their status as separate city states.

The region's lack of direct access to the sea limited the extent of external trade and political power that could be achieved. Goods transported to and from the river valley states had to pass through neighboring as well as distant territories. Any expansionist activity by these areas rendered the river valley states vulnerable.

The physical characteristics of Lan Na are markedly different from other areas in Thailand. Central Thailand is composed of large plains. The Lan Na region is an extension of the Himalayas and of the mountains of China's Yunnan province. The northern mountain ranges are mostly long, running north to south in parallel fashion. They include the Daen Lao Mountains in the far north, the Thongchai Range in the west, the Phipannam Mountains in the center, and the Luang Prabang Mountains to the far east.[8]

The area's northernmost rivers, including the Kok, Ing, Fang, and Lao, are short, fast-running, and empty into the Mekong River. Below them are several rivers that mostly flow north to south, into the Chao Phraya River. These include the Ping, Wang, Yom, and Nan. The Ping was always the region's most important river for communication purposes. In the west, the Pai, Yuam, and Moei rivers flow into the Salween River.

Lan Na can also be thought of in terms of an east-west division. Western Lan Na comprises Chiang Mai, Lamphun, Chiang Rai, Phayao, and Lampang. These are located on three plains—the Chiang Mai–Lamphun basin, the Chiang Rai basin, and the Lampang basin.[9] Eastern Lan Na has the Nan and Phrae basins.

The plains, deep basins surrounded by peaks, were the region's most important areas, though they make up only a quarter of the total territory. They tend to be long and narrow, running north to south, parallel to the flow of important rivers.

The key plains area was the Chiang Mai–Lamphun basin, or the Ping River valley, located between the central Thanon Thongchai and the Western Phipannam Mountains. The second most important plains were in the Chiang Rai basin in the Kok River valley. The Lampang plain in the Wang River valley covered Lampang, Hang Chat, and Ko Kha districts. In a narrower plains area were the districts of Wang Nuea, Sop Prap, and Thoen. Step plains in this area were unsuitable for agriculture.

The plains of the Nan and Phrae basins were small and produced low rice yields.

MAP 4. THE MAIN RIVERS IN LAN NA

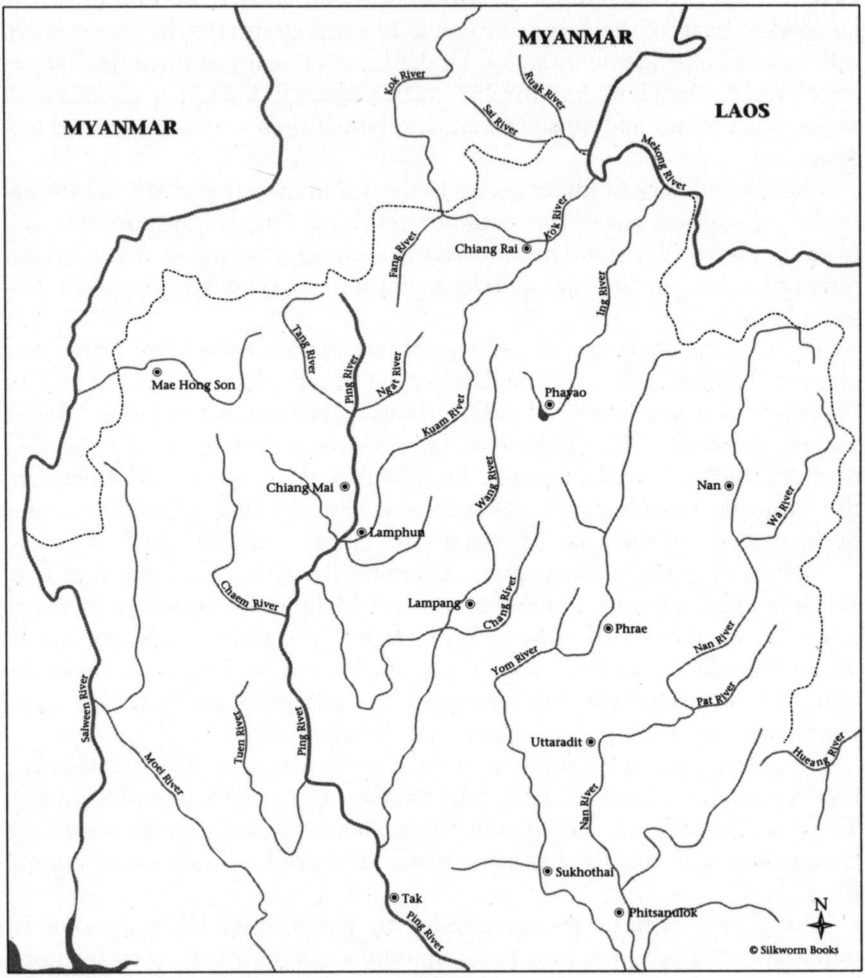

(Drawn after Sarassawadee Ongsakul, *Prawatsat Lan Na*, p. 28)

Settlement in Lan Na was concentrated in river valley areas. The sparsely populated highland areas contained mainly Lua and Yang people who produced highland rice and seasonal products. Lowlanders and highlanders had different ways of life but lived together peacefully. The topography meant intra-regional communication was difficult. Each *mueang* developed its own cultural characteristics, such as a local dialect or language.

The Thai Yuan considered three main features when selecting a site for a city. Selection of auspicious sites was undertaken by experts using local lore called "*chaiyaphum*." A large river was important and auspicious. They also checked the quality of the soil by looking at its color. The Chao Suwankhamdaeng Chronicle states that the area around the Chiang Mai basin was so fertile that the rice yield for one year could provide sustenance for seven years. Finally, it was considered auspicious for towns to have mountains close by, to the west. Chiang Mai and Chiang Saen had this auspicious feature. Chiang Mai had seven auspicious landmarks and Phayao had three. It was felt that to choose an inauspicious location was to invite a fate such as that suffered by Mueang Suwankhomkham and Wiang Nong. Both were submerged.

THE KOK RIVER VALLEY

The communities of the Kok, Lao, Kham, Chan, and Sai river valleys occupied territory that was peripheral to large powers such as Cambodia, Dvaravati, Yunnan, and Pagan. It is likely that the population grew fast in the twelfth century. The most important of the communities was in the Kok valley, which had fertile plains and a long history of settlement, with different *mueang* such as Ngoen Yang, Roi, and Chiang Saen occupying overlapping areas over time.

Archaeological evidence in the area, mostly from Buddhist sites, sheds little light as the great majority of it appears to go back no further than the fourteenth century. Aerial photography has helped identify traces of moats and earthen walls in more than one hundred locations, but the sites cannot be dated without additional supporting archaeological or other evidence. An abundance of stone utensil fragments has been found in the region, which some believe date back to prehistoric times. Others, including Srisak Vallibhodhama, believe the utensils are contemporaneous with Hariphunchai and Lan Na, though they are culturally less developed.[10] This interesting hypothesis needs further study.

The main evidence for the history of the region comes from local chronicles. Written long after the events they describe and featuring a mix of historical "fact" and folklore, they pose great challenges to the historian. The chronicles are perhaps best understood as reflections of the memories of the Thai Yuan people, and of their efforts to explain the history of the land

MAP 5. LOCATION OF ANCIENT *MUEANG* IN CHIANG RAI AND ITS VICINITY

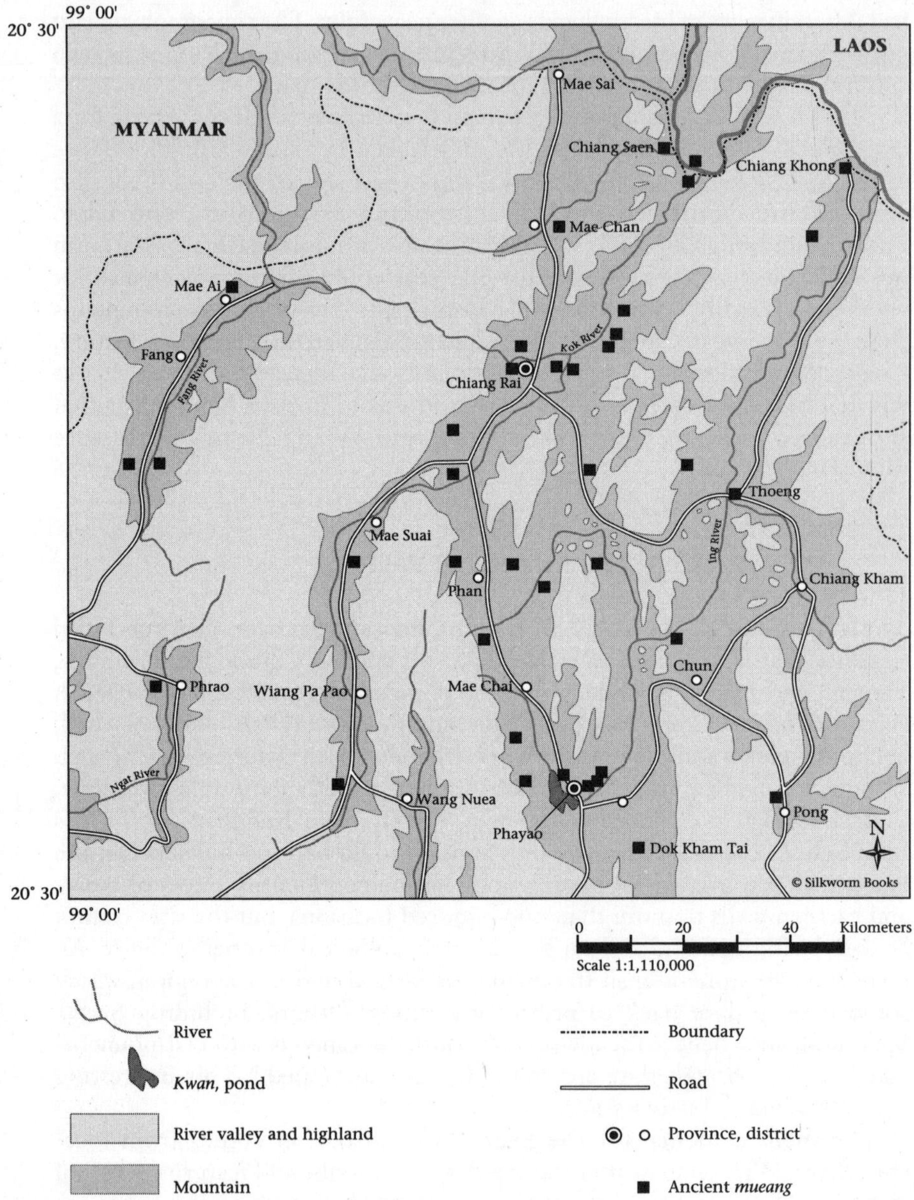

(Drawn after Sarassawadee Ongsakul, *Prawatsat Lan Na*, p. 32)

they came to live in. Despite the chronicles' limitations, when approached with due care, they are a rich source of information.

The evidence from these early texts suggests that the long early history of settlement in the Kok valley may most usefully be divided into the earlier "period of the people in the chronicles" and the later "Ngoen Yang period."

THE PERIOD OF THE PEOPLE IN THE CHRONICLES

Two important early chronicles refer to the early history of the region: the Mueang Suwankhomkham and the Chiang Saen (Singhanawatikuman or Singhonti) chronicles.

The chronicles suggest that the Thai movement into this area was a gradual process, involving small groups of people who were looking for fertile land. They had a wet-rice culture and were knowledgeable about the construction of irrigation canals. They founded towns in the lowlands. They were led by "princes," such as "Prince Singhonwat, Prince Suwankhamdaeng, etc.[11] The Chiang Saen Chronicle refers to Prince Singhonwat as the son of King Ho, which has contributed to the belief that these early Thais probably came from Yunnan province. It is believed that they migrated across the Mekong River in a southeast movement, which makes them appear to be a group of the Shan (Thai Yai) people. The thrust of the chronicle suggests that they moved down to the Chiang Rai basin, though all locations are speculative.

They founded Wiang Yonok, which the Chiang Saen Chronicle locates in the area around what was later called Wiang Nong in Chiang Saen district, Chiang Rai province. It is possible that Wiang Yonok lies under what is now Chiang Saen Lake. Eventually, they also founded towns such as Wiang Phangkham and Wiang Chainarai. The chronicle dates Wiang Yonok to about the first century.[12] It places the demise of Wiang Yonok in about the eleventh century. "Forty-five kings of the Singhonti dynasty ruled Wiang Yonok until it disintegrated into swamp in about the eleventh century."[13] Nuansiri Wongthangsawat, who investigated the location of Wiang Yonok / Wiang Nong from satellite and aerial photographs, thought it possible that the town disintegrated because it was located directly over a geographical fault line. (All dates pertaining to this era are as still entirely speculative and contradictory. The Chiang Mai Chronicle, for example, dates the history of the Lao dynasty to a ruler in Mae Sai in 639 up to Mangrai at the end of the thirteenth century.[14] There have been no conclusive archaeological excavations in the area. The Thais moved on to a site at Mueang Suwankhomkham, originally home to the Krom (Khom or Khmer, whose center was in present-day Cambodia), [15] who had expanded along the Mekong River to found the town at "a location that was an island with a sandbank next to the mouth of the Ram River, the body of water to the west."[16] This indicates that Mueang Suwankhomkham was on an island in the Mekong River, south of the mouth of the Kok River.

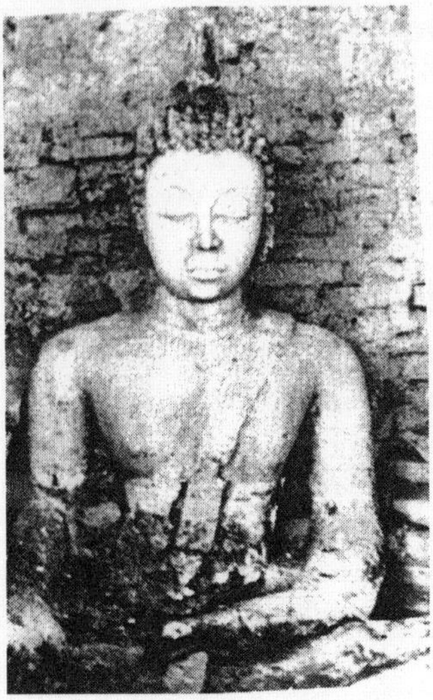

1. Ancient Buddha image at Phrathat Pha Ngao Temple, excavated in 1976. (Phrathat Pha Ngao Temple, c. 1980)

The chronicles suggest that at some point, the old Mueang Suwankhomkham had disintegrated. According to the Suwankhomkham Chronicle, "The Mekong tore into the bank and cut towards the east. Mueang Suwankhomkham then fell apart."[17]

Describing the movement of the Thai community towards the old Mueang Suwankhomkham site, the Chiang Saen Chronicle states:

> The population then divided and set up a new town to the southeast. This settlement was on high ground on a big island that had formed, the site of the old Mueang Suwankhomkham . . . The king of Mueang Yonok sent his son Chainarai to found the town on a hill. He lived there and called it Wiang Chainarai Mueang Mun.[18]

Jit Phumisak has concluded that the town was located on a large island on the Lao side of the Mekong River at Don Mun, diagonally opposite the mouth of the Kok River and opposite Ban Suan Dok, Chiang Saen district, Chiang Rai province.[19]

Aerial photographs back up this hypothesis. They show that the Don Mun site is relatively large, suitable for the founding of a town. In Laos today it can be seen that the area to the west of Don Mun was the old course of the Mekong River, and clear traces of a town have been found there.[20]

The Suwankhomkham Chronicle also refers to the Krom founding of another town, U-mongkha Sela, believed to have been near the mouth of the Kok River. The Krom expansion along the Mekong River possibly extended to Yunnan province. The records of a Chinese emissary in the eighth century mention the expansion of Upper Chenla. "The territory of this state seemed to stretch as far as Yunnan to the north."[21]

This is only a very preliminary study of Mueang Suwankhomkham and other old towns of the area. Further study is necessary.

The chronicles indicate that the Thais quickly established dominance over the indigenous Lua people of the Kok River valley. The Chiang Saen Chronicle says that a Thai leader "ordered all leaders of the Milakkhu (Lua) to accept his control."[22] In turn, the Lua were given the power to control smaller communities.[23] According to the chronicles, relations between the minority Thais and the earlier occupants were relatively smooth.[24] There is mention of mutual assistance. The Chiang Saen Chronicle states that a Thai prince, Singhonwat, had a native wife. The Suwankhamdaeng Chronicle refers to a prince, Suwankhamdaeng, also having a native wife whose culture was inferior to his own. The indigenous people were encouraged to become Thai. In the long run, the increase in Thai numbers in the Kok River valley was probably partly a result of this process of Thai-ization.[25]

The Thais called their towns Yonok or Yuan. Sometimes they used the term Mueang Yuan, which meant the home of the Thai Yuan people.

The terms Yuan, Yon, Yonok, or Yun went on to develop two main meanings. One referred to the *mueang* in the Chiang Rai basin that were united by Mangrai into what he called the Yon domain or Yon state. After seizing Hariphunchai, Mangrai ordered the raising of the *sawetthachat*, the nine-tiered white umbrella symbolic of royalty, to show the unity of all the Yon domain.[26] It is possible that Mangrai's entire kingdom was first called Yon or Yonok.

The second meaning of the term Yon or Yuan meant a group of Thai people. In the past, the Siamese Thai called the northern Thai people Yuan. The Burmese called them Yon. They called the Chiang Mai people Yon Chiang Mai; the Lampang people, Yon Lakhon; and Chiang Mai lacquerware, *yon the*. [27]

The Chiang Saen Chronicle uses the disintegration of the Wiang Yonok in the eleventh century to symbolize the end of the old Singhonwat dynasty in the Kok River valley and its replacement by the Lao Chong group.

THE NGOEN YANG PERIOD

The chronicles suggest that the communities of the Kok River valley developed into *mueang* during the Ngoen Yang period, which was ruled by kings of the "Lao" dynasty. The founder of the dynasty was originally named Lao Chong or Lao Chok.

There are two hypotheses regarding the meaning of the term "Lao" in relation to the dynasty that later became known as the Lawachangkarat. The first theory is that they were originally from the Lawa or Lua group (which would make Mangrai a descendant of the Lua). The Chiang Saen Chronicle describes Puchao Lao Chok as Khun Lawa, who established a settlement in the foothills of Doi Tung.[28] The Lua had long played an important role in establishing early settlements in the Chiang Rai and Chiang Mai basins. Srisak Vallibhodhama has stated, "Phaya Mangrai was not Thai, neither by his lineage nor ethnicity, because the chronicles clearly mentioned that he was Lao Chok, who were a group of highland Lua."[29]

The second hypothesis contends that the dynasty was possibly from a section of the Thai race known as Aî Lão or Ai Lão;[30] thus the kings used the term Lao in front of their names. Prakhong Nimmanhemin feels that the old names for the dynasty, such as Lao Chong and Lao Chok, were later changed in error, via translation into Pali, into Lawachangkarat, with its misleading intimations of the word "Lawa."

It is impossible to be conclusive about early ethnicity in the region. The area had a multitude of ethnic groups, and intermarriage was not uncommon. The key issue was the wide adoption of Thai culture, the use of the Thai language, and Thai-ization.[31]

In its explanation of the origins of the Lao dynasty, the Chiang Mai Chronicle refers to an invitation sent out to the kings of several *mueang* to attend a meeting to discuss the creation of a new calendar. The people of Chiang Lao at Doi Tung near the Sai River did not have a king to send (this coincides with descriptions of the disintegration of the Singhonwat dynasty around the early eleventh century.)[32] Lord Indra then sent his son, Lao Chong, and one thousand followers to descend silver stairs from heaven to the area of Doi Tung.[33] The people of Chiang Lao proclaimed Lao Chong their first king, and thus began what the Jinakalamali Chronicle calls the Lao dynasty.[34]

The Chiang Mai Chronicle refers to Lao Chong's birth as "*oppatika*," meaning "born by itself, without parents," and gives no further indication of his origin. (The Jinakalamali Chronicle suggests the seventh century as the origin for the dynasty; the more likely reality was that the period of this group, or Ngoen Yang period, began around the eleventh or twelfth century.)

2. View of Doi Tung. (SO, 1989)

The Chiang Saen Chronicle mentions that the husband and wife Puchao Lao Chok believed in Buddhism.[35]

The Doi Tung Chronicle says that the leader of the Milakkhu (Lua) was Lord Lao Chok. He was a farmer at Doi Tung and traded with lowland Thai at the foot the mountain. In the period before Buddhism Doi Tung had been called Doi Din Daeng and later Doi Pu Chao.[36]

The Lao Chong group was centered in Chiang Lao, in the areas around Doi Tung and the Sai River, which by Mangrai's time were joined together as Panna Chiang Lao.[37] The group founded several new towns. Lao Chong nominated Lao Khrop, his eldest son, to rule Chiang Khong; Lan Xang, his second son, to rule Mueang Yong; and Lao Kao, the youngest son, to rule Chiang Lao.[38] Other areas included Chiang Kham and Phayao. By the time of Mangrai's rise to power in the thirteenth century, the dynasty's descendants had scattered throughout the region. Mangrai claimed direct descent from Lao Chong when he joined the various areas together as Panna Chiang Lao. Eventually the dynasty's center of power moved to Ngoen Yang on the bank of the Mekong River, during the reign of Lao Khiang, the ninth king mentioned in the Chiang Mai Chronicle. The area was called Mueang Tha Sai Ngoen Yang or Mueang Ngoen Yang Tha Sai, according to the Nan Chronicle.[39] [*Tha sai* means sandy landing.] Ngoen Yang was probably located near what later (after 1328) became Ngoen Yang Chiang Saen. Its location reflected a trend of political expansion along waterways. Ngoen Yang Chiang Saen was on an important trade route linking Yunnan and *mueang* in the upper Southeast Asian mainland.[40] Towns in this area built before the fourteenth century were usually located along the Mekong River. Later towns were located on tributaries deep inland.

A great expansion of the Lao dynasty occurred during the reign of the nineteenth king, Khun Chuang, who lived around the twelfth century, according to the Chiang Mai Chronicle. (The Phayao Chronicle says that Khun Chuang was previously the king of Phayao. He protected Ngoen Yang from the Kaeo (Vietnamese) and later ruled this town.[41] Both chronicles describe Khun Chuang as a brave and heroic king who was victorious in a war with the Kaeo, took the daughter of the Kaeo king as his consort, and ruled over the Kaeo town. Khun Chuang expanded Ngoen Yang's territory and power. He died on a battlefield in Yunnan in a war with Phaya Ho Maentatok Khokfatayun.

Khun Chuang's five sons were said to have ruled Ngoen Yang, Chainarai, Lan Xang, Kaeo, and Chiang Rung. The story of the hero-king Khun Chuang was handed down and retold over a very long time in the areas of Sipsong Panna, Ngoen Yang, Phayao, and Lan Xang, each of which claimed him as their own. This suggests that the peoples of these areas were once members of the same ethnic group and were politically linked. The Thais of Ngoen Yang became the Lan Na line.

MAP 6. WIANG PHANG KHAM, AN ANCIENT WIANG IN MAE SAI

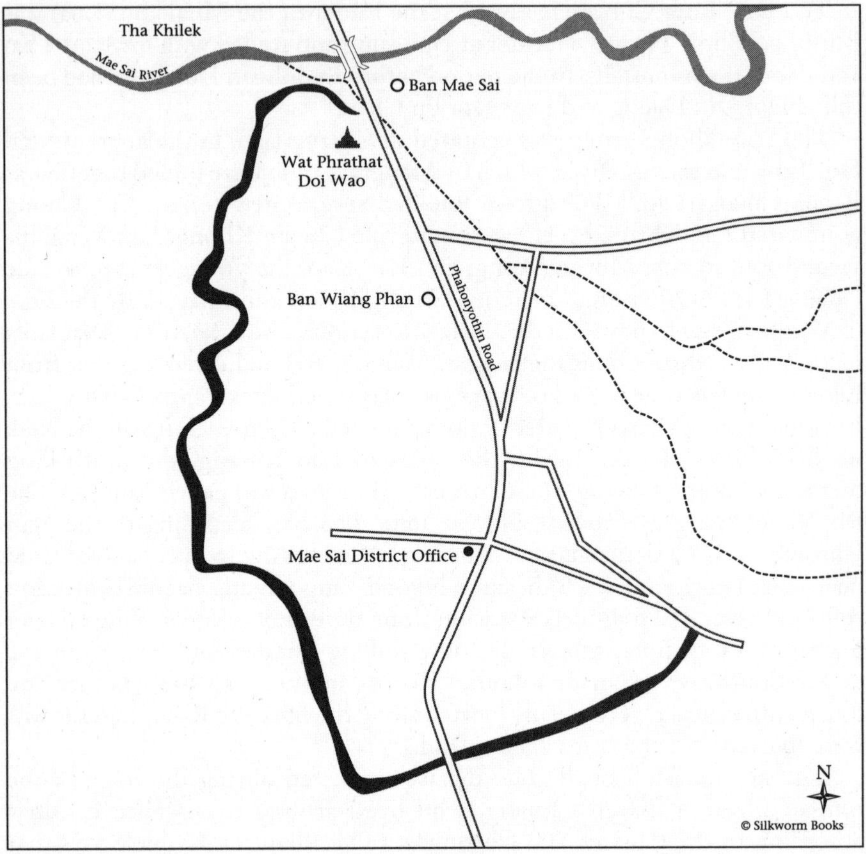

(Drawn after Sarassawadee Ongsakul, *Prawatsat Lan Na*, p. 39)

At the beginning of the thirteenth century Ngoen Yang was probably an important center whose political power had been built up through a system of lineage links. For example, Phaya Lao Meng of Ngoen Yang was betrothed to Nang Ua Ming Chommueang (Nang Thepkhamkhai or Khamkhayai), the daughter of King Rungkaenchai of Chiang Rung, the parents of Mangrai.[42] This was a reflection of Ngoen Yang's relative power. Around the same time, Ngoen Yang sent a king's daughter, Nang Ua Chiang Saen, to Phayao to be married to Phaya Ngammueang as a way of building friendly political relations. Kinship ties were a key way to build political relationships. Chinese records called Ngoen Yang Chiang Saen "Ba Bai Xifu" or "the state where the king had eight hundred consorts." The Chinese annals during the Yuan dynasty mention that Ba Bai Xifu called the indigenous people Chingmai (Chiang Mai). In the distant past there was a story mentioning that the ruler of that people had eight hundred consorts. Each consort was responsible for one community and that was where the name came from.[43]

The society at the time was made up of diverse tribal cultures. Control over commoners in the Kok River valley around the thirteenth century was probably based on methods described in the Mangraisat legal code:

> Every ten commoners had one leader (*nai sip*) and one man who acted as interpreter and announced routine work (*khomkwan*). Five leaders of ten (*nai sip*) had one leader of fifty (*nai hasip*) with two assistants. Two leaders of fifty had one leader of a hundred (*nai roi*). Ten leaders of a hundred had one leader of a thousand (*chao phan*). Ten *chao phan* had one leader of ten thousand (*chao moen*). Ten *chao moen* had one leader of one hundred thousand (*chao saen*).[44]

The early social hierarchy was divided into lords, nobles, commoners or *phrai*, and slaves. The Mangraisat states that commoners were drafted to work for the state for ten-day periods, alternating with ten-day periods when they returned home and worked for themselves.[45] This method of recruitment suggests that the society was small, and lords and commoners probably knew each other. Labor given to the lords could be for either personal or public use, such as the construction of irrigation canals or wartime duties. It is possible that besides providing corvée labor for "public works," commoners were required to send tribute in kind to their lords. (The system continued for a very long time—in 1852, Chao Anantaworaridet, the ruler of Nan, proclaimed the laws of the Lakkham kingdom, which contained an order that "the head of ten controls the group's members."[46]

Thai society at the time practiced spirit worship. There were a multitude of spirits. The spirit of a village was called *phisuea ban*. It had the duty of protecting the locality and providing happiness and prosperity to its inhabitants. A shrine was erected for this spirit within the village compound, usually near a big tree. There was probably also a *chai ban*, or "Heart of the Village," a pillar or edifice placed in the center of a settlement. At the *mueang* level, there was a *phisuea mueang*, the guardian spirit of the *mueang*, located at a *suea mueang* tree, possibly often the *yang*, a tall, resinous, tropical tree.[47] (Later, Chiang Mai people also probably worshipped the *yang* tree, which was planted, for example, in the grounds of Sadue Mueang and Chedi Luang temples.)[48]

Gradually the old beliefs merged with Buddhism. Worship of Doi Suthep had many similarities with that of the old Doi Tung site, for example.[49] There is some doubt over whether Buddhism was practiced in Thai society in the Kok River valley before the fourteenth century, because ancient Buddhist sites are no older than that. However, Buddhist buildings were often

3. Pa Sak Temple, Chiang Saen. (NAT, c. 1927)

4. Chedi Luang Temple, Chiang Saen. (NAT, c. 1927)

constructed over older sites to the point that no traces of the earlier sites remained. Buddhism may well have arrived in the Kok River valley before the fourteenth century, but the issue needs further study. At the very least, it seems certain that Mangrai practiced Buddhism in the area. He was not a recent convert to the religion by the time he seized Hariphunchai.

The Chiang Saen Chronicle refers to the ordination of Buddhist hermits from the time of a Phaya Achutarat, of unknown date, who was married to the daughter of a hermit, who according to the chronicle lived at Doi Din Daeng or Doi Tung.[50] It is possible that the hermit was a Lua.

The Kok valley area is also believed to have been the production site for beautiful old Buddha images known as "the first group of Chiang Saen Buddha images." Santi Leksukhum feels that the first group of images were produced around the beginning of the thirteenth century or earlier and were influenced by the Pala style, via the Pagan style.[51]

One can surmise that early Buddhist beliefs had characteristics of folk Buddhism; that is, there was a blending of Buddhism, belief in spirits, and supernatural worship.[52] This continued up to the time of Mangrai, who blended early beliefs with Buddhism in both Wiang Kumkam and Chiang Mai.[53]

PHAYAO IN THE ING RIVER VALLEY

The historical study of Phayao owes much to Phra Thamwimonmoli, an important local scholar who has studied the area's history, archaeology, and culture for several decades and who founded the Center for Cultural Exhibitions at Si Khomkham Temple. Phayao contains more historical evidence than most Lan Na *mueang*. A large number of damaged sandstone Buddha images are housed at Si Khomkham and Li temples. Most of the area's Buddha images are probably no older than the thirteenth century.[54] Most of the area's archaeological and art history evidence comes from the fifteenth and sixteenth centuries, when Lan Na prospered. Phayao has Lan Na's largest collection of stone inscriptions.[55] Most were inscribed during the fifteenth and sixteenth centuries, and they describe the donation of people and goods to monasteries.

The Mueang Phayao Chronicle is an important source of historical evidence. However, since its purpose was clearly to present an image of the heroic nature of the local kings, it has to be used with some caution. It mainly describes the activities of two kings, Khun Chuang (who later became ruler of Ngoen Yang) and Phaya Ngammueang. It does not mention Phayao's defeat in war and incorporation into Chiang Mai. As a result, it has been called the "big-headed chronicle."[56]

Phayao is situated in the southern Chiang Rai basin, on a plain at the foothills of the mountain that the chronicle calls Phuyao, or long mountain. This name was later changed to Phyao and ultimately became Phayao. Phuyao, or Doi Duan, runs north-south, starting at Phan district and continuing down to the center of Phayao proper. According to the chronicle, Phayao was founded by the Lao dynasty. The area was selected because of three auspicious factors. First, there was the Ing River, whose watershed area is in the central Phi Pan Nam Mountains. It flows southward to Kwan Phayao, and then northeasterly past Thoeng district, emptying into the Mekong River at Chiang Khong district, a length of 240 kilometers.[57] The riparian area is flat and relatively fertile and was therefore suitable for the founding of important *mueang*, namely, Phayao, Thoeng, and Chiang Khong. Second there was the lake, Kwan Phayao, or Nong Iang. Finally, there was Doi Chom Thong, the mountain to the north, which would later be the site for the Phrathat Chom Thong temple.[58]

Phayao also had limitations. It was surrounded by high mountains. Situated on the southern Chiang Rai basin, it could communicate conveniently only with Chiang Rai to the north and Chiang Khong to the northeast. The west abutted a high mountain range where Wang Nuea district is now located. In the south beyond Ngao district was another high mountain range. To the east, it adjoined Nan, which was also very mountainous. Phayao was hemmed in.

Phaya Lao Ngoen of Ngoen Yang sent his son, Khun Chomtham, to establish Phayao in around the twelfth century. The Mueang Phayao Chronicle says that the location had high ground to the west, sloping down

MAP 7. CLUSTER OF PHAYAO'S ANCIENT MUEANG

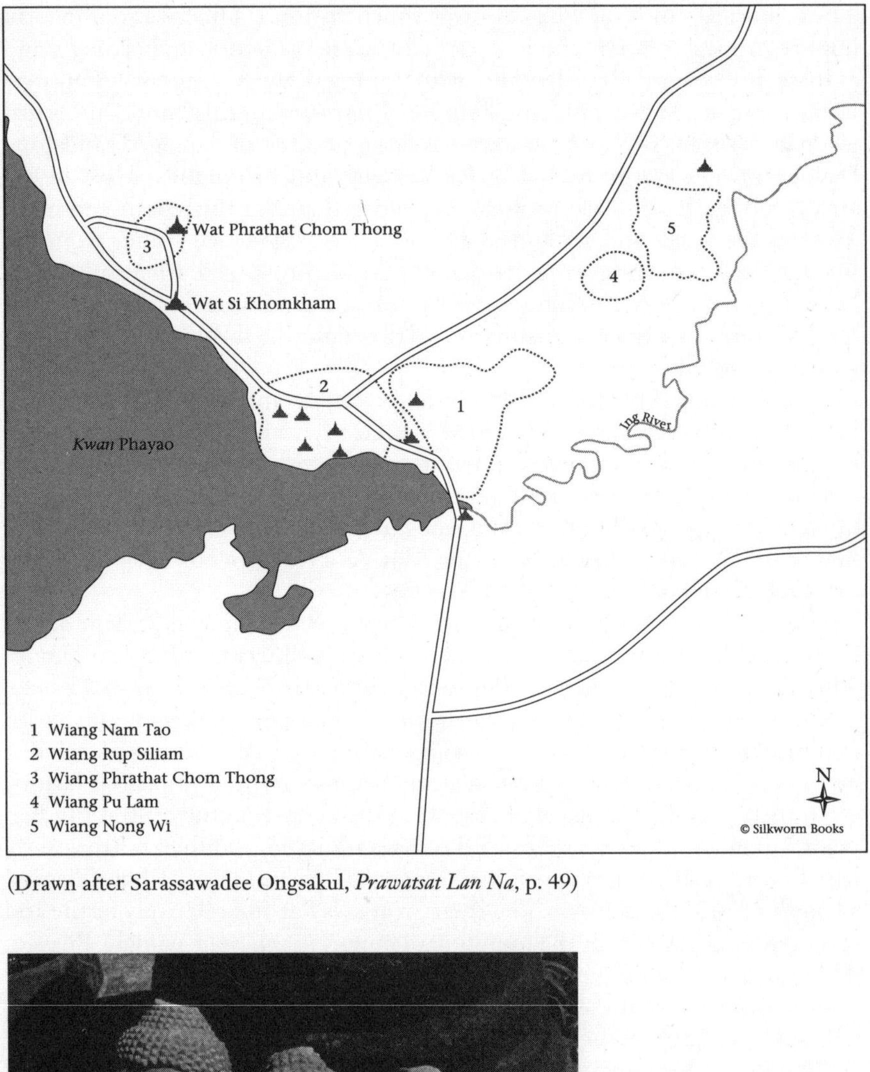

(Drawn after Sarassawadee Ongsakul, *Prawatsat Lan Na*, p. 49)

5. Sandstone Buddha heads, Phayao style. (SS, 1989)

to the east. There were swamps to the northwest and northeast. The first town established was called Nam Tao, and it was constructed in the shape of a bottle gourd. Though the area was deserted then, there had been towns there at an earlier period.[59]

The Nam Tao community expanded toward the banks of the nearby lake, Kwan Phayao. In 1174, in the reign of Phaya Singharat, a rectangle-shaped western town was built by Bunmueang, according to the chronicle.[60] Satellite *mueang* such as Phrathat Chom Thong, Pulam, Nongwi, and Tom began to appear. Phrathat Chom Thong was located in foothills north of the principal *mueang*. Since a Buddha relic was deposited there it became known as Wiang Phrathat. Pulam and Nongwi were small twin *mueang* located northeast of Phayao. Tom was west of the lake. These principal and satellite *mueang* made up the city-state of Mueang Phayao.[61] Khun Chomtham ruled Phayao as an independent state, with close ties to Ngoen Yang. There were eleven kings of the Phayao dynasty from Khun Chomtham Phaya Khamlue, after which Phayao was incorporated into the Lan Na kingdom.[62]

The history of the area becomes clearer in the mid-thirteenth century when it was ruled by Phaya Ngammueang, a historical figure. The ninth king of the dynasty, Ngammueang was born in 1238. When he was fourteen years old, he went to study under a hermit at Doi Duan. At sixteen, he went to Lawo, or Lop Buri, where he became friends with fellow student Pho Khun Ramkhamhaeng. Ngammueang became ruler of Phayao in 1258. His wife was Nang Ua Chiang Saen, her name an indication that she was a daughter of that *mueang*. Relationships between Phayao and Ngoen Yang continued to be consolidated through marriage ties.

The Mueang Ngoen Yang Chiang Saen Annals refer to Ngammueang and Mangrai as friends, like their grandfathers before them.[63] Friendship among the three kings of the Thai states, Mangrai, Ngammueang, and Ramkhamhaeng, led them to join together against a Mongol invasion, in the signing of the Three Kings Accord in 1287. Before this agreement Mangrai had had his eye on Phayao. In 1276, he had sent troops there, but the two sides ended up negotiating instead of fighting.[64]

Ngammueang also avoided territory held by his friends, turning eastward instead to seize the territory of Pua in what was later called Nan, and sending his wife and son to rule there for many years. Pua eventually became independent. The Nan Chronicle describes the difficulties experienced during war with Phayao, indicating that Phayao was relatively strong during the time of Ngammueang.[65]

Ngammueang was succeeded by Thao Khamdaeng, the tenth king, who developed good relations with Chiang Mai. For example, he sent an army to help Phraya Chaisongkhram subdue Khun Khrua, who had seized power in Chiang Mai from Chaisongkhram's son, Thao Saenphu. Khamdaeng then asked for Chaisongkhram's daughter, Nang Kaeophota, for his son, Thao Khamlue, the eleventh and last independent king of Phayao.[66]

Phayao was incorporated into the Lan Na kingdom during the reign of Khamlue's successor, Phaya Khamphu (1334–1336). The Chiang Mai Chronicle states that Chiang Mai succeeded in seizing Phayao at least partly as a result of support from Nan.[67] By seizing Phayao, Chiang Mai neutralized any sense of threat to itself from this direction, and also gained a power base for later expansion into Phrae and Nan.

Phayao was relatively important during the Lan Na period, and it was ruled by high-ranking princes. For example, Chiang Mai's Phaya Samfangkaen (r. 1402–1441) sent his uncle, who had assisted him to become king, to rule the territory. He also designated the ruler of Phayao to be *chao simoen*, lord of forty thousand. King Tilokarat (r. 1441–1487) rewarded Phaya Yuthithira, the former ruler of Song Khwae who had submitted to him, by sending him to rule Phayao.[68] Still, Phayao had no particularly important role in Lan Na after it had served as a base for the capture of Phrae and Nan.

THE UPPER PING RIVER

The upper Ping River area developed and grew faster than other river valleys in northern Thailand. The land was fertile and suitable for the founding of large *mueang*. The area's early history can be divided into two periods: a) the period of the indigenous Lua, and b) the Hariphunchai period.

THE INDIGENOUS LUA PERIOD

The Lawa or Lua were indigenous people of the northern region. In the Chiang Mai–Lamphun area, their center was in the foothills of Doi Suthep, where they had a shrine to their ancestors, the Phi Pu Sae and Ya Sae (Grandfather Spirit and the Grandmother Spirit). The Suwankhamdaeng Chronicle says that Lua settlements were scattered out from Doi Suthep towards the plain of the Ping River.[69] The Lua believed that prominent figures such as the hermit Wasuthep, and the leader of the last Lua period, Luang Wilangkha, were descendants of the grandparent spirits.

The Lan Na chronicles fall into three groups in their attitudes towards the Lua. The Phrathat chronicles, the first group, usually simply describe the Lua as people who had lived in the region for a long time. The chronicles sometimes refer to the Buddha coming to the area and being presented with food by a Lua. The Phrathat Lampang Luang Chronicle says that the Lua Ai Kon gave honey to Lord Buddha. The Phrathat Cho Hae says that Khun Lua Ai Khom offered the Buddha betel nut.[70]

The classical Lan Na chronicles of the second group, i.e., the Mulasasana, Jinakalamali, and Camadevivamsa, say that the area's indigenous people were born in the footprints of animals such as elephants, rhinoceroses, cattle, and deer. However, the chronicles do not specifically name the Lua. The classical chronicles were written by high-ranking monks at a time when Buddhism was flourishing, and they looked upon the non-Buddhist Lua as uncivilized.

The third group, including the popular Chao Suwankhamdaeng and Sao Inthakhin chronicles, were written in the early Ratanakosin period. They emphasize the importance of the Lua, stating that they constructed Wiang Chet Lin, Wiang Suan Dok, and Wiang Nopburi or Chiang Mai and that a large number of Lua lived in these areas. The chronicles also emphasize the cultural blending of the Lua and the Thai. The Phrabat Don Klang Chronicle, Chom Thong district, an extended version of the Suwankhamdaeng Chronicle written during the reigns of kings Rama V and VI, emphasizes the importance of the Lua. It says that Phaya Lua moved down from Doi Suthep to build Chiang Mai. After ruling there for a long time, he fled back to the mountain and left Chiang Mai deserted.[71]

All the chronicles agree that a Lua community had lived in the area for a long time and were influenced by outside cultures. According to a palm-leaf manuscript called "*Awahan 25*," Phi Pu Sae and Ya Sae and their descendants began to practice Buddhism by not killing animals, by paying respect to Buddha images, and by ordaining their sons as hermits.[72] This is in agreement with the chronicles that mention the hermit Wasuthep, who lived at Doi Utchubanphot or Doi Oi, later named Doi Suthep. Wasuthep also built Lamphun, according to the Jinakalamali Chronicle. He had the status of a sage, a cultural leader, and was possibly the king of a tribal state.[73]

The acceptance of outside cultural influences reflected a willingness on the part of Lua society to change. It seems likely that certain groups of Lua people were relatively advanced. For example, the Lua were making iron tools long before the Lan Na period. Kings of the Mangrai dynasty ordered the Lua to send tribute in the form of iron tools.[74] The leader of Lua tribal society was called *samang*.

We also know of the Lua from a story, believed to have dated from around the ninth century. The Lua leader at the foothills of Doi Suthep, Khun Luang Wilangkha, went to war with Queen Chamathewi of Lamphun over Lua dissatisfaction with outsiders intruding into their localities. He lost and groups of Lua then scattered into hills and forests. Others submitted to Queen Chamathewi, marking the end of Lua unity. The queen appointed a *khun Lua* to rule the Lua community and ordered him to send tribute regularly. The Lua continued to live around Doi Suthep. They were friendly with Mangrai and helped him to attack Hariphunchai. It is notable that Mangrai had several high-ranking Lua close to him. For instance he nominated Ai Fa, a Lua, to rule Lamphun. The Lua leader Mangkhum Mangkhian was appointed to rule Chiang Tung, and Khun Chaisena was appointed to rule Lampang. Gradually these people lost their tribal characteristics and became like the Tai.

The Chiang Mai Chronicle indicates that Chiang Mai was a Lua territory before Mangrai arrived. The elders of the domain are supposed to have told King Mangrai that "the area used to be the place of Thao Phaya,"[75] meaning that old Lua rulers had lived here. The Nopburi Mueang Phing Chiang Mai Chronicle says that after Mangrai founded Chiang Mai he checked with Sikhunchuk, a Lua noble, about an auspicious gate for the entrance. After consulting with other Lua leaders Sikhunchuk said that Mangrai should enter through the Hua Wiang Gate, meaning "head of the city" (now Chang Phueak Gate).[76] It was the custom in coronation rites thereafter for the king to enter the city through that gate. That the Lua were accepted as the original owners of the land can be seen in the coronation procession, in which a Lua walks with a dog ahead of the king into the city.[77] The coronation ritual of the rulers of Chiang Tung, who were related to the Mangrai dynasty, also involved the Lua. But in Chiang Tung the ceremony involved enacting the driving out of the Lua. The ritual involved cooking a meal and putting it on a stage for the Lua to eat. After the meal, the Lua were chased away.

The influence of Lua beliefs can still be seen in Chiang Mai today. An important example is the belief in the Inthakhin Pillar—earlier located at Sadue Mueang Temple in the center of Chiang Mai until it was moved by King Kawila into Chedi Luang Temple. The city pillar has long been regarded as a sacred object, an icon of Chiang Mai. There are also ritual offerings to Pu Sae and Ya Sae, revered as the spirits protecting Chiang Mai. An annual ceremony for this purpose is carried out by the people of Tambon Mae Hia, Mueang district, Chiang Mai province.

THE HARIPHUNCHAI PERIOD

Hariphunchai (Lamphun) was founded around the second half of the eighth century and was the northernmost point of Lawo (Lop Buri) culture, itself an extension of the Dvaravati kingdom. The expansion to Hariphunchai was enabled principally by the Ping River, an important avenue of communication since ancient times. Later, Hariphunchai became separate and independent.

The Central Plains had become densely populated as the old Dvaravati *mueang* of Nakhon Pathom, U-thong, Suphan Buri, Lop Buri, Ratchaburi, Petchaburi, Chai Nat, and Prachin Buri spread out. The Hariphunchai area offered a number of favorable prospects. The Chiang Mai–Lamphun basin was a large, fertile river valley suitable for growing rice. There was good potential for trade.[78]

Queen Chamathewi, the daughter of the king of Lawo, founded the Chamathewi dynasty in Hariphunchai around 767–768.[79] An old Chinese source refers to Hariphunchai as Ni Wang Kok, which means the kingdom with a female monarch.[80] Queen Chamathewi arrived in the new territory with experts such as monks, scholars, and skilled artisans. Her arrival amounted to the transference of a complete Lawo state to the area.[81] She and her people were initially regarded as "a new group of outsiders."

6. Phrathat Hariphunchai. (NAT, 1907)

7. *Ho trai* (library), Phrathat Hariphunchai Temple. (NAT, 1907)

8. Flat gong, Phrathat Hariphunchai Temple. (NAT, 1907)

The Development of Buddhism. Theravada Buddhism also arrived with Queen Chamathewi. According to the Mulasasana Chronicle, "She built chambers for the five hundred monks who had come with her from Lawo. She patronized these monks with the four requisites of monks [food, clothing, shelter, and medicine] and paid daily respect to them without fail."[82] The religion subsequently flourished.

> The people in the villages had faith in Buddhism. They helped each other construct two thousand temples . . . The area was full of temples everywhere. There were five hundred monks who lived in Lawo and came together with Queen Chamathewi. This number only included monks, but their disciples were much more numerous. Queen Chamathewi brought Buddhism and five hundred monks to help Hariphunchai prosper.[83]

Successive kings all patronized Buddhism, particularly during the golden age of Hariphunchai (approximately 1157–1292). Sources suggest that the kings built a great quantity of temples and religious objects. The Jinakalamali Chronicle says that Phaya Athittarat constructed Phrathat Hariphunchai Temple in the heart of Hariphunchai.[84] Inscriptions in old Mon script from the time of Phaya Sapphasit tell of his constructing Chetawan Temple and three stupas in front of it, donating servants to the monks, and later entering the monastery with his two sons.[85] He also copied the Tipitaka,[86] and restored Ku Kut Temple, which had collapsed from a big earthquake.[87] He built Mahawan Temple and donated servants and goods to the monks. He also added to the stupa that Phaya Athittarat had built so that it reached a height of twelve meters, thus accumulating much merit.[88] Artifacts in the Hariphunchai style, such as Buddha images and terra cotta votive tablets, also show the area's close connection with Buddhism.[89]

Hariphunchai was still an important religious center when Mangrai captured it around 1292. The new ruler did not stay long, saying "Hariphunchai is a Phrathat town; I cannot stay."[90] He later made Hariphunchai the center of Buddhism in Lan Na.

The Society. Hariphunchai society was organized into the domain and the *mueang*. The domain was the entire territory, comprising several *mueang*. The Hariphunchai domain first comprised a cluster of *mueang* within the Chiang Mai–Lamphun basin. The first and principal *mueang* was called Hariphunchai. It later expanded across the Khun Tan Mountains to Khelang, (Lampang) which probably became the second most important *mueang*.

Each *mueang* comprised a central *wiang* or town, and the surrounding village communities were called *ban*. Mueang Hariphunchai was probably composed of numerous village communities as well as the center. The Mulasasana Chronicle mentions seven thousand villages.[91]

The Hariphunchai period introduced urban society into the region. Towns were based on rivers, particularly in river valleys that flooded, as these were good for wet-rice agriculture. There are no traces of Hariphunchai settlements in the highlands, where the Lua tribe continued to live quite separately.

Towns were generally surrounded by an earthen wall and moat. In the event of an invasion, people who lived scattered outside the town would gather within its walls. The *wiang* was the center of Hariphunchai society. It had Buddhism, art, and culture. Kings normally lived in *wiang*. In Hariphunchai society, royal succession was handled peacefully. Administration was both orderly and complex. For example, different areas were set aside for different groups of people. The ruling class was literate, judging from inscriptions about the Hariphunchai kings. Learned men likely gave counsel. The ruling class could raise corvée labor and the relatively large population of town society was probably tightly controlled.

Hariphunchai towns were similar to their Dvaravati counterparts in the Central Plains, for example, in their river valley locations and their earthen walls and moats. Most towns used a loop in a river as a natural moat.[92] There were several types of town plans: circular, oval, oblong, rectangular, and polygonal, and of overlapping shapes.[93] Hariphunchai town, the center of power, was built in an oval or conch-shell shape. It was 450 meters wide on a north-south axis and 825 meters long on an east-west axis. The plan probably followed the bend of the river. The Mulasasana Chronicle says the hermit Wasuthep planned the town's conch-shell shape.[94] The shape was probably in style at the time, because Khelang and Phrae were built in the same way. An oval-shaped town plan was quite advantageous because it was adaptable and did not need a lot of scientific technique. It had a short radius out from the town center. The plan placed the palace in the center of the town, according to the Jinakalamali. This may have made it easier for the kings to keep peace and order. The palace of Phaya Athittarat was torn down in around 1157 to make way for the Phrathat Hariphunchai temple.[95]

A satellite community, Wiang Tha Kan, was located at what is now Ban Tha Kan in Tambon Ban Klang, San Pa Thong district, Chiang Mai province. Its town plan was rectangular, 490 by 740 meters. Water was plentiful, with the Kan River to the west and the Ping River to the east. Wiang Tha Kan had probably been an important rice-growing area since ancient times. It is believed that the town proper was built during Hariphunchai's golden age. An octagonal stupa in the town center was built around the twelfth century. The author found clear traces of an old earthen wall and moat. There are ruins in adjacent communities and Hariphunchai art objects scattered within a radius of two to three kilometers, in centers such as Ban Phrachao Song-ong, Ban Phrachao Thongthip, Ban San Kong Ket, and Ban San Kawan.

Wiang Mano, the northernmost Hariphunchai town, was located at what is now Tambon Nong Thong, Hang Dong district, Chiang Mai province, just eight miles northwest of Lamphun.[96] The town plan was rectangular, 750 by 900 meters. There are abundant traces of the town having been destroyed. Only parts of an earthen wall and moat remain. The important Mae Hin Bot Wiang Mano stele, twenty-one centimeters wide by thirty-seven centimeters high and three centimeters thick, was inscribed in ancient Mon, Mon, and ancient Burmese scripts, during, it is believed, the twelfth century.[97] The Mon inscription indicates that the town had Mon rulers during the Hariphunchai period. Terra cotta votive tablets similar to Hariphunchai and Pagan art works were also found.[98]

Wiang Tho was located at what is now Tambon Song Khwae, Chom Thong district, Chiang Mai province, and is considered the southernmost Hariphunchai town. It had a rectangular plan and was located near the western bank of the Ping River, close to the entry point of the Khan River. The town had a long north-south axis along the Ping, similar to Hariphunchai. The author's field research suggests that Wiang Tho was likely destroyed by Ping river currents, which destroyed half the area in front of Song Khwae Temple in the center of the town.

The western city wall was almost totally destroyed; only the base of the earthen wall remains. Important evidence found at Wiang Tho includes a stone inscription in ancient Mon found behind the *wihan*, the Buddha image hall, of Song Khwae Temple. The inscription has yet to be read and translated. The principal Buddha image in the *wihan* of Song Khwae Temple is made of stone, in the Hariphunchai style.

Later Hariphunchai towns had more geometric rectangular forms and were surrounded by two earthen walls, divided by a moat that was used as a reservoir.

Most Hariphunchai towns were located on the south side of the Chiang Mai–Lamphun basin. No Hariphunchai town and little trace of the art style has been found in the northern part of the Chiang Mai–Lamphun basin, which is believed to have been lightly populated. North of Mae Rim the plains are narrow and were probably not suitable for towns.

Hariphunchai probably controlled village communities in the areas of what are now Mae Taeng, Mae Rim, San Sai, San Kamphaeng, and Mueang districts of Chiang Mai. Evidence for this is the "Ai Fa irrigation canal" built in the late thirteenth century to deal with a water supply problem in the areas of "Phanna Thuan" and "Phanna Pu Kha."[99] Corvée labor was used to to build the canal north of Sob Nam Mae Tang, where the Taeng River meets the Ping River. The Ai Fa canal skirted the foothills for 17,000 wa (34,000 meters) and connected the Ping River with the Kuang River.[100]

The author's field research in 1985 indicates that the canal began at the right bank of the Ping River, approximately one kilometer north of the Sinthukitpricha irrigation canal. It is about thirty-four kilometers from the city of Chiang Mai and is now under the Mae Faek irrigation program at Tambon Mae Faek, San Sai district, Chiang Mai province. Clear traces of the canal are still visible.

It is believed that the northernmost perimeter of Hariphunchai reached Doi Ang Salung (Doi Chiang Dao) in Chiang Dao district, Chiang Mai province. An auspicious elephant of Queen Chamathewi came from the foothills of Doi Ang Salung.[101] The scholar who wrote *Phuttha Tamnan Phrachao Liap Lok* accepted the idea that Mueang Chiang Dao was under Hariphunchai.[102]

Hariphunchai was threatened in the early eleventh century, according to the Munlasasana and Jinakalamali chronicles, when the Cambodian kingdom expanded west, capturing Lop Buri. This meant that only two important Dvaravati kingdoms remained—Hariphunchai and Sathoem (Sudthamwadi).

Cambodia later invaded Hariphunchai but was unable to seize it. According to George Cœdès, it is likely that the attack was led by King Suriyavarman I (1002–1050).[103]

War erupted again in the early twelfth century, instigated by Phaya Athittarat, the ruler of Hariphunchai. It is believed that at least part of the war was conducted during the reign of the Cambodian leader Suriyavarman II (1114–1150).[104] Hariphunchai lost, and Lawo retaliated by attacking Hariphunchai on three occasions. The first occasion was known as a "Thammayut War," actually a contest, when the two sides vied over the digging of a reservoir and Hariphunchai emerged the victor. The second time Hariphunchai won again, and Phaya Athittarat ordered prisoners captured from Lawo to build Chedi Mahaphon. The third time, the Lawo troops tried extremely hard to capture Hariphunchai but were defeated. Hariphunchai was then at peace for a time.[105]

The Hariphunchai domain flourished especially strongly over a peaceful period of about 130 years (approximately 1157–1292).[106] This period's most prominent leaders were Phaya Athittarat and Phaya Sapphasit. Phaya Athittarat ruled the kingdom by 1150,[107] and began to build Phrathat Hariphunchai around 1157. Queen Phathumwadithewi later built a stupa named Suwannachedi[108] in the same compound. Phaya Sapphasit, who lived in around the thirteenth century, has already been mentioned as contributing much to the development of Buddhism during the period.

Hariphunchai had seven more kings before the reign of Phaya Phantonya, who was assassinated in a coup in around 1258 led by Thaiya Ammat, one of his nobles, who was likely a Thai.[109] Five descendants of Thaiya Ammat then ruled for thirty-four years. The last king was Phaya Yiba. Prasert Na Nagara says that Phaya Yiba was probably Thai. The Thai term "yi" in his name indicated that he was a second son.[110]

Mangrai captured Hariphunchai in 1292, and it was incorporated into the Yon domain. Mangrai stayed at Hariphunchai for only two years. He then promoted Ai Fa to the title Khun Fa and appointed him to rule the area. Mangrai probably did not want to have the small walled city of Hariphunchai as the capital of his new kingdom. He decided to keep it as a Buddhist center.

The Mulasasana Chronicle states, "Phaya Mangrai then said, 'I will leave Khun Fa to live in that town and rule it. I am Khun Yuan, Khun Roidok, and my works are not as important as those of the monks. Khun Fa and you and the monks can deal with affairs together.' "[111]

Mangrai then built a residence at Wiang Kumkam, probably in 1294. Two years later he moved to Chiang Mai.[112]

KHELANG IN THE WANG RIVER VALLEY

The study of Khelang (Nakhon Khelang or Lampang) is hampered by a lack of chronicles. There are no chronicles concerning Lampang town among the microfilmed palm-leaf manuscripts at the Social Research Institute, Chiang Mai University. Seven chronicles at the institute, including the Phuen Nakhon, Lampang, Mueang Lakhon, and Mueang Thoen chronicles, are named as though they were town chronicles but all are actually Phrathat texts. Among the area's most popular manuscripts of this sort are the Phrathat Lampang Luang, the Phrathat Kaeo Don Tao, and the Phrathat Chumphit Nakhon chronicles.[113] These texts have important limitations. For example, the narrative of the Phrathat Lampang Luang Chronicle jumps from a section on Queen Chamathewi to a section on King Tilokarat, with no mention of the interim period. This is probably because these chronicles focus almost exclusively on the role of the Phrathat supporters. The Phrathat Kaeo Don Tao Chronicle contains mainly folk stories and gives few dates. The chronicles give little information about the Khelang city state of the twelfth and thirteenth centuries. For Khelang history, one has to rely on the scant information in the general Buddhist chronicles, the Mulasasana and Jinakalamali.

There is also little in the way of early archaeological evidence in the area. Four steles from Lampang are included in the *Prachum silacharuek* (Corpus of Stone Inscriptions), part 3, prepared in 1965 by the Commission for Historical, Cultural, and Archaeological Publications of the Prime Minister's Office. The oldest, stone inscription number 65, was inscribed in 1476; number 70, the inscription at the *wihan*, or Buddha image hall, of Phrathat Lampang Luang Temple was inscribed in 1496; and number 78 from the *wihan* of Phrathat Lampang Luang Temple was inscribed in 1796. The fourth inscription is not dated. The content of the inscriptions focuses on merit-making activities, which limits their informational value.

It is possible that there were existing communities, possibly of Lua, in the Wang River valley before the founding of Nakhon Khelang, but the chronicles provide little information. The Phrathat Lampang Luang Chronicle mentions the area at the time the Buddha was supposed to have visited it. There was a village named Amphakariwan inhabited by the Lua Ai Kon. After the hermit

9. Khong Gate, Phrathat Lampang Luang Temple. (NAT, c. 1927)

10. Phra Kaeo Don Tao Temple. (NAT, c. 1927)

Phraphrom founded Khelang for Phaya Anantayot, there were "forest dwellers who were Lawa and Karen living around this village. Their numbers had increased in the area around the town because of King Anantayot's power and the hermit's magical power."[114] The Muang Thoen Chronicle refers to the Lua community in the southern Lampang plain but uses the term "Yak" (ogre) instead of Lua.[115] The Jinakalamali says that after the seizure of Khelang from Phaya Boek and Phaya Yiba, Phaya Mangrai appointed the "Milakkhu" (Lua) people to rule.[116] The ruler, Khun Kin Mueang Khelang, was likely a Lua local. It has already been noted that Mangrai often received assistance from indigenous people.

According to the Mulasasana Chronicle, Khelang was built in about the ninth century during the time of Queen Chamathewi. The queen sent her son Phaya Anantayot to rule it. The original location was situated at what is now Tambon Wiang Nuea, Mueang district, Lampang. The town had an oval conch-shell plan, "like Hariphunchai's capital"[117] and measured 600 by 1,400 meters. Judging from aerial photographs and field research, the town's shape was even more like a conch shell than that of Hariphunchai. The town was built on the western bank of the Wang River and had a twin city to the south, Wiang Alamphang Khanakhon, built as the population expanded. Both cities adopted Hariphunchai culture.[118] (The third *wiang*, Wiang Khelang, may have been built in the Lan Na period. The Jinakalamali says that in

1301, after seizing Nakhon Khelang, Phaya Mangrai appointed a noble to rule it. He left the old town deserted and built the new town of Mueang Khelang.)[119]

Phra Kaeo Don Tao Suchadaram Temple was an important site in the original location. The old city gates were called Ma, Phabong, Thanang, Nokkot, and Tan. Outside the town, to the west, were Phanchoeng Temple and Ku Khao Temple. During a survey at the Phanchoeng Temple, Srisak Vallibhodhama found a stucco head of a Buddha image in the Hariphunchai style,[120] which could confirm the chronicle's authenticity. There are very few traces of archaeological finds in the Hariphunchai style within Khelang, compared with other *mueang*.

Wiang Khelang was the residence of the king and the ruling class. Satellite towns had a variety of functions, including as defensive outposts. They included Wiang Chai; Wiang Hi at Ban Mae Tha, Tambon Thung Fai, Mueang district; and Wiang Tan at Hang Chat district. Its twin to the south, Wiang Alamphang Khanakhon, was built to accommodate an expanding population and to hold a palace for Queen Chamathewi. Shards of Hariphunchai-style pottery were found by Phasakon Thonawanik on the bottom level of an excavation at the satellite town of Wiang Phrathat Lampang Luang, and this settlement probably dated from the twelfth century.[121] The three rings of the city wall were possibly constructed in the Lan Na period.[122]

The territory was in the Wang River valley, which is elongated north to south. The Western Phi Pan Nam Mountains (Khun Tan) were to the west, stretching from Wang Nuea district to Mae Phrik district, and the Central Phi Pan Nam Mountains were to the east. There were three separate plains—northern, central, and southern.

To the north was a relatively expansive plains area, including Chae Hom district and the settlements of Ban Sop Mon, Ban Mai Pha Khao, and Ban Wat Akkho Chai Khiri. They have not yet been dated and need additional study and analysis.[123]

The central plain was home to the largest communities, including the Mueang, Hang Chat, and Ko Kha districts. There appears to have been continuous settlement in this area. In the southern plain, strategically located at an entry into the territory, Mueang Thoen was made up of four old settlements; Ban Wiang, Wiang Pom, Wiang Peng, and Wiang Phaya Kan. Wiang Phaya Kan was sturdily built and had a plan in the shape of a bird stretching its wings.[124]

For further information on Khelang, we must rely on a scant scattering of clues. Townspeople in the areas around the Pong Yang Khok Temple, and in Wiang Tan in Hang Chat district, have long believed that Queen Chamathewi visited and built several constructions in these areas, including the town well and the Chamathewi Wihan at Pong Yang Khok Temple. They believe that Wiang Tan in Hang Chat district was a rest stop for the queen.

11. Wang River, Lampang. (NAT, c. 1907–1914)

12. Lampang city wall. (PUA, c. 1882–1927)

Describing events after Queen Chamathewi's reign, the Mulasasana and the Jinakalamali chronicles say that Thaiya Ammat of Khelang assassinated the king of Hariphunchai and then ruled the conquered territory. The account then skips to the time of Mangrai.

Saeng Monwithun believes that the term Khelang comes from the Mon word *halang* or *khalang*, meaning bowl or basin. A nearby mountain was called Doi Khelang. The name suggests that the dynasty that built Khelang was Mon. It continued to be used during the time of Mangrai.[125] By 1476, the name Mueang Khelangkhanakhon had been abbreviated to Mueang Nakhon. Evidence for this is stone inscription number 65, which states, "Chao Moen Khamphet came to rule Mueang Nakhon and to revitalize the religion of the Phrathat in Lampang."[126] The shortened name continued to be used through to the early Bangkok period. "Nakhon" was generally written as "*lakhon*" and the indigenous pronunciation was "*lakon.*" Written material from the early Bangkok period uses both *nakhon* and *lakhon*. Stone inscription number 78 inscribed in 1796 refers to Mueang Nakhon properly, as Nakhon Khelang.[127]

Towards the end of the reign of King Rama IV (1855–1868), documents from the Ho Wachirayan library show that the term Mueang Nakhon Lampang was also used, to refer to both Mueang Nakhon (or Khelang) and Lampang Luang. Lampang was an old community located at Phrathat Lampang Luang Temple. It was of lesser importance than Wiang Khelang. Stone inscription number 65 refers to the area as "Lamphang" but the place-name was pronounced as "Lampang." The Phrathat Lampang Luang Chronicle called the Lampang community "Lamphakappanakhon." Stone inscription number 78 used the term "Lamphakaburi." By the time of King Rama V, the term Mueang Nakhon Lampang was in general use. Later the area became Lampang province.

The Chiang Mai Chronicle details Mangrai's victories over Khelang and Hariphunchai. It states that Phaya Yiba of Hariphunchai fled to his son Phaya Boek in Khelang. Boek then surrounded Wiang Kumkam and fought on elephant-back with Phraya Chaisongkhram. He lost, and was executed. Yiba fled to Mueang Song Khwae.[128]

MUEANG PHRAE IN THE UPPER YOM RIVER VALLEY

There is a dearth of local evidence for the early history of Phrae. The only local texts are temple chronicles, including the Phrathat Cho Hae, Phrathat Doi Pu Phu Thap, Mueang Long, and Laem Li chronicles.

The Phrathat Cho Hae Chronicle is directly concerned with Mueang Phrae, but its contents are quite limited. Only two transliterated versions exist: the Phrathat Cho Hae Mueang Phrae Chronicle, printed in the *Prachum*

13. Phra Maechao Chamathewi's Buddhist assembly hall at Pong Yang Khok Temple. (SO, 1989)

14. Phrathat Sadet Temple, Lampang. (NAT, c. 1927)

tamnan phrathat (Collection of Phrathat Chronicles), part 1, published in memory of Ms. Khae Fusak for her funeral in 1942; and the Phrathat Cho Hae Chronicle of Phrae province, printed in the *Prachum tamnan Lanna Thai* (Collection of Lan Na Thai Chronicles), volume 2, transliterated by Sa-nguan Chotisukharat in 1972.

The Social Research Institute has microfilmed three chronicles that have not yet been transliterated. The Phrae Chronicle, Mueang Mo Temple in Tambon Thung Si, Rong Kwang district, has ten palm-leaf pages. It was titled the "Mueang Phrae Chronicle," but it is a Phrathat chronicle. The Phrathat Cho Hae Chronicle at Sung Men Temple, Tambon Sung Men, Sung Men district, has twelve palm-leaf pages, inscribed in 1895. The Phrathat Cho Hae Mueang Phrae Chronicle at Luang Temple, Tambon Nai Wiang, Mueang district, has ten palm-leaf pages, inscribed in 1909. These three palm-leaf manuscripts are similar in content and are also very similar to those chronicles that have been transliterated.

The main purpose of the chronicles was to explain the deposit of a holy relic at Cho Hae Hill in Mueang Phon Nakhon, (an early name for Phrae), but no dates are given and there is no information on the history of the town. We must thus rely on evidence from other regions, with reservations.

Phrae was small city-state in the Yom River valley. Elongated plains ran from north to south, passing Song, Rong Kwang, Mueang, Sung Men, Long, and Wang Chin districts and on to Sukhothai province.[129] The northern plain, within the Yom's watershed area, included Mueang Song, which was ringed with three sets of earthen walls and moats. It is believed that this was Mueang Song of Phra Phuan and Phra Phaeng mentioned in the ancient Thai poem "*Lilit Phra Lo*." Mueang Thep was also in this area. Wiang Thep was located on the western bank of the Yom and had only one earthen wall and moat.[130]

The central plain cluster, the largest, had only one city, Wiang Phrae, which was built in a conch-shell plan on the Yom River. It had only one earthen wall and moat, traces of which remain. Phrae's current provincial government offices are located in what was the old city. The Phrathat Cho Hae Temple was located on a hill eight kilometers east of the town.

The southern plain cluster comprised Mueang Long and Mueang Trok Salop. It is believed that Mueang Long was a very old site, with an ancient continuous royal lineage that originally referred to the area as Kukkutkai-ek (the town where the rooster crows).[131] The Phrathat Wat Si Don Kham Chronicle (Huai-O) says the name was changed from Mueang Kukkutkai-ek to Mueang Long in the time of Queen Chamathewi. It says that the queen got lost on the journey from Lawo to Hariphunchai. After an inconclusive argument with her nobles about which direction to take, she said, "Kho long du kon" (Let's try this way first). They arrived at this town, which was then named Long (try).[132] The chronicle says that Mueang Long contained important and venerated places, including Phrathat Kuai Pu, Phu Thap, Laem Li, and Si Don Kham.

15. Conch-shell shape of Wiang Phrae on the bank of the Yom River. (AP, 1943)

Mueang Trok Salop in Wang Chin district was an old town with an irregular earthen wall and moat. It was located on the right bank of the Yom River near the mouth of Salop Stream.[133] An inscription, probably written in 1339, states that Mueang Trok Salop was ruled by a low-ranking noble. It is regrettable that damage to the inscription has obscured his name. It refers to "Khun U…w, the ruler of Troksal (op)"[134]

External chronicles refer to this area as Mueang Phonlarat, or Mueang Phon Nakhon, in around the twelfth century. The Phrathat Lampang Luang Chronicle mentions a Phaya Samantarat, also named Phaya Phala, ruler of Mueang Phonlarat. The chronicle says that he knew that there was a holy relic in Mueang Lamphakappa and came to search for it, without success. When Queen Chamathewi came to Mueang Lamphakappa, the holy relic miraculously appeared to her.[135] No dates are given for either Mueang Phonlarat or Phaya Phonlarat. The Phrathat Cho Hae Chronicle mentions the relationship between Phrathat Cho Hae and Phrathat Hariphunchai.[136]

It is believed that the name Mueang Phonlarat was gradually replaced with the name Phlae. Stone inscription number 1 refers to areas north of the Sukhothai kingdom as Mueang Phlae, Mueang Man, Mueang N..., and Mueang Phlua.

The name Mueang Phlae was written with a tone mark in the Pu Sabot inscription, believed to have been inscribed in 1392. It read, "All our towns, Mueang Phlae, Mueang Ngao . . ., (N)an, Mueang Phlua . . ."

Various stone inscriptions use Phlae, Phae, and Phlâe; the spelling sometimes even differs in the same inscription. The Si Bunrueang Temple inscription dated 1497, uses Phãe (in lines 2, 14, 16, and 17) while line 6 uses Phlae. The Wat Buppharam inscription dated 1529 uses Phlãe in line 4 and uses Phlâe in line 5.

It appears that the name Phlae came into use after the construction of the highly venerated stupa on Doi Cho Phrae. The Phrathat Cho Hae Chronicle says:

> At that time the Buddha's holy relic continued to produce miracles. The rulers of Mueang Phon Nakhon went to worship the holy relic of the Buddha at Doi Cho Phrae. And thus that hill had been named Kosiyathatcha Banphot or Doi Cho Phrae and the town was named Mueang Phrae just as the Lord Buddha had predicted.[137]

The oldest use of the term Phrae appears in the stone inscription of Phra Kanchana Mahathera, the monk who had a copy of the Tipitaka made in 1837.[138] The Yonok Annals refer to Khun Chuang of Ngoen Yang going to Mueang Phrae to capture elephants. There, a Phaya Phrae, named Phromwong, presented the visitor with his daughter.[139] The Mueang Ngoen Yang Chiang Saen Annals in the *Prachum phongsawadan* (Corpus of Annals), part 61, contains similar details. It says that a certain Phaya Phrae named Phromwangso gave his daughter and fifty elephants to Khun Chuang.[140]

The acceptance of the name of this town as Phrae, meaning to expand, became widespread during the reign of King Rama V, and it has been used ever since.

Phrae was always surrounded by larger states, i.e., Lan Na, Sukhothai, and Nan. It was able to maintain its independence for most of the period from the twelfth to the early fifteenth century. At this time, it had close links with Sukhothai, which was also in the Yom River valley. From time to time Phrae came under the influence of Sukhothai, including during the reign of King Ramkhamhaeng (1279–1298). It came under Sukhothai once more in the reign of Phaya Lithai (1347–1368). He took his troops to Mueang Phlae and stayed there for seven months.[141] It is possible that Phaya Lithai built the Phrathat Cho Hae and Phrathat Chom Chaeng.

Whenever the opportunity arose, Phrae would attempt to expand into neighboring Nan. For example, from 1398–1399, the brothers Phaya Thera and Phaya Unmueang captured Nan.[142]

In 1340, Phrae was attacked by Lan Na's Phaya Khamfu. According to the Chiang Mai Chronicle:

> In the *kot si* year, s. 702 (1340 / 41), when Phraya Khamfu was thirty-eight years of age, he led his forces to take and plunder M. Phrae, but failed and returned by way of Nakhon Khelang, appointing Saen Mai to head the rear guard. The Phrae people sent an army intending to cut off the tail of the elephant of Phraya Khamfu. Khamfu and Saen Ta Chuai and Saen Mai fight the Phrae force, but they failed and withdrew. Cao Phraya Khamfu brought his forces back to Chiang Saen.[143]

A hundred years later, when Lan Na was at its height, King Tilokarat made another bid for Phrae, sending troops to the area. In 1443, Phrae's Thao Maenkhun pledged his allegiance to Lan Na, and the city-state's independence came to an end. It took Tilokarat six more years to capture Nan.[144]

MUEANG NAN IN THE UPPER NAN RIVER VALLEY

A number of basic historical studies of Nan have been undertaken, including some by the government. In 1935, Nan civil servants collaborated in the publication of the useful book *Nakhon Nan*, which covered the area's geography, history and conditions, and characteristics of the Nan people. In 1987, the Fine Arts Department published three books on the occasion of the opening of the Nan National Museum in 1987— *Mueang Nan: Boranakhadi prawatisat lae silapa* (Mueang Nan: Archaeology, History and Arts); *Mueang Nan*; and *Chao Nan* (People of Nan). In the same year the

Office of Nan Province published *Prawat mahathai suan phumiphak changwat Nan* (The History of the Ministry of Interior of Nan Province).

Most of the archaeological evidence from Nan is deposited in the Nan National Museum. Inscriptions on the bases of Buddha images, on *dhamma* box lids, and on doors have been deciphered by linguists from the Department of Fine Arts.[145] Nan stone inscriptions have been collected into a book, *Charuek Lanna* (Lan Na Stone Inscriptions), part 1, book 1. Stone inscriptions from Chiang Rai, Phayao, and Phrae are also useful sources for the study of Nan history.

There are several Mueang Nan chronicles, and several versions of the Phrathat Chae Haeng chronicles. These appear in *Prachum tamnan phrathat* (Collection of Phrathat Chronicles), part 2; *Prachum tamnan Lanna Thai* (Collection of Lan Na Thai Chronicles), translated by Sa-nguan Chotsukarat; and *Tamnan Phrathat Chae Haeng* (Phrathat Chae Haeng Chronicle), Phra Samuhaphrom version, translated by Somchet Wimonkasem.

The author has transliterated and analyzed the Nan Chronicle, or the Phuen Mueang Nan, Phra Koet Temple Version.[146] The Nan and the Phrathat Chae Haeng chronicles also appear in the Ratchawongpakon Mueang Nan Annals, in *Prachum phongsawadan* (Corpus of Annals), part 10, composed in 1894 by Saenluang Ratchasomphan on orders from King Suriyaphongpharitdet of Nan. It is divided into two parts. The first, Ratchawongpakon, covers Lan Na history. Interestingly, it says that the Lawachangkarat dynasty sent a crown prince to rule Nan. However, there is no link with the following section, which begins with the birth of Khun Nun and Khun Fong and continues until the time of King Suriyaphongpharitdet.

The first *mueang* in Nan were founded towards the middle of the thirteenth century in the Upper Nan River valley, which is composed of small and discontinuous plains between the Eastern Phi Pan Nam and the Luang Prabang mountain ranges.

The Nan plains are divided into two parts. The northern part, the watershed area of the Nan River, is comprised of Thung Chang, Chiang Klang, Pua, and Tha Wang Pha districts.[147] There is evidence of four old settlements in the Nan River valley at Pua, and more research is needed on them.[148]

The Nan Chronicle says that Phaya Phu Kha, the founder of the Kao, or Phu Kha, dynasty, ruled the small Mueang Yang in the lower valley of the Yang River, a tributary of the Nan River in the area that is today Tha Wang Pha district. Phaya Phu Kha had two sons, Khun Nun and Khun Fong. When they reached adulthood, they each wished to rule a territory. The elder son was sent to build Mueang Lao, or Luang Prabang, where he would rule over Lao people, while the younger son was sent to build Mueang Pua and rule over Kao people.[149]

The chronicle portrays Mueang Pua and Luang Prabang as enjoying a close relationship. There is mention of the Kao and Lao as tribal people in Sukhothai stone inscription number 1, side 4; "The Ma, Kao, Lao, and the

16. Scorpion-tail boat on the Nan River. (PUA, c. 1882–1927)

17. Phrathat Chae Haeng, Nan. (SO, 1991)

Thai from the south . . . Tai, Chao U, Chao Khong came under [Sukhothai]."

The Nan Chronicle, Phra Koet Temple version, calls Mueang Pua a Kao town—Mueang Kao or Mueang Kao Thet. It further states that the Kao were a group of Tai people, referring to the "Kao Tai people." In another passage, it states, "In the year 727 [1365 C.E.], the Year of the Pig, the Kao Tai people helped each other build a palace."[150]

The Chiang Mai Chronicle refers to the rulers of Nan as "Phaya Kao Nan." Nan people in general are called Kao Nan. Sukhothai stone inscription number 45 of 1392 refers to the ancestor spirits of the Nan dynasty as "Dam Phong Kao," confirming that the Nan kings were Kao.[151]

The Wat Burapharam inscription, side 1, in the *Prachum silacharuek* (Corpus of Stone Inscriptions), part 7, says that in 1396 the king of Sukhothai in 1396 expanded his territory in several directions, specifying several *mueang*, including Mueang Kao. It states, "He subdued the Kao state." The Wat Burapharam inscription, side 2, used the Pali term and called it "Kao Ratta" and said that the Kao state was located north of the Sukhothai domain.[152]

Mueang Pua and Mueang Yang continued to enjoy a close relationship. A chronicle says that Phaya Kaokluan, a grandson of Phaya Phukha, left Pua in the hands of his wife while he ruled Yang.

In the late thirteenth century, Pua was a small, new and vulnerable city-state. Around it were the three strong and allied states of Lan Na, Sukhothai, and Phayao. Pua's weakness gave Phaya Ngammueang, the ruler of Phayao, an opportunity for plunder. The ruler of Pua, Nang Phaya Mae Thao Khamphin, fled and during the flight gave birth to a son, Phaya Phanong. Phaya Ngammueang sent his wife, Nang Ua, and his son, Chao Ampom, to rule Pua. According to the Nan Chronicle, he controlled the territory for almost twenty years until Phanong grew up, regained his family's old territory, and took Ngammueang's wife for himself. Phanong was the fourth king of the Kao dynasty and he ruled between 1322 and 1352. During his reign, Pua began to gain stability and it expanded to include new areas such as Mueang Khwang. Phanong assisted Phaya Khamfu of Lan Na to plunder and incorporate Phayao. Still, the relationship between Nan and powerful Lan Na was always uneasy, and Nan cultivated ties with Sukhothai.

In 1359, Phaya Khranmeuang of Pua led an expansion into the southern Nan valley. To encourage his people to make the move, Khranmueang appealed to their spiritual beliefs. With the help of Phaya Lithai of Sukhothai, he sent an invitation to a monk from that kingdom, Phra Dharmapanthera, who arrived with a holy relic. The site chosen to house the relic was named Wiang Phu Phiang and was located along the Thian and Ling rivers.

The Nan Chronicle says that there was trouble over wood destined to be soaked in the rivers before being used for a palace for Khranmueang. "The water had dried up and the rain did not fall. So it was called Chae Haeng . . ."[153] Thereafter the name Wiang Phu Phiang was linked with the word Chae Haeng (literally, dry soak), meaning a very dry *mueang*. The holy relic was called Phrathat Chae Haeng.

The lack of water eventually made it necessary to move Wiang Phu Phiang to a site on the western bank of the Nan River. The new town, Nan, was founded in 1368 during the reign of Phaya Phakong. It became the administrative center of the area.

The relationship between Nan and Sukhothai remained strong. In 1376, Phaya Phakong sent troops to assist Phra Mahathammaracha II of Sukhothai to fight against Phra Boromaracha I of Ayutthaya.

Soon after, when Nan was seized by Phrae, its nobles fled to Sukhothai, which helped them regain the *mueang*. Power struggles within the ruling family meant the kingdom was unstable.

During the reign of King Tilokarat, Dai Viet (Kaeo) from Vietnam invaded Luang Prabang and Nan, which resisted strongly and forced the invaders to retreat.[154]

In 1438, when Sukhothai was defeated by Ayutthaya, Nan became more vulnerable. The Nan Chronicle states that Lan Na besieged Nan during the reign of King Tilokarat. "[They] shot their artillery in the direction of the royal garden gate, shouted, entered, and seized it." Thao Inthakaen fled. King Tilokarat appointed Thao Phasaeng, the son of Thao Phaeng of the Kao dynasty, to rule Nan. He was the last ruler of the Kao dynasty. After his death, "there was no ruler . . ."[155] Nan was incorporated into Lan Na in 1448.[156]

18. Nan city wall. (PUA, c. 1882–1927)

CHAPTER 3

HISTORY OF THE KINGDOM (1296–1558)

By the thirteenth century, a new historical situation had arisen in the upper region of Southeast Asia. The decline and disintegration of once prosperous old domains like Cambodia, Dvaravati, Hariphunchai, and Pagan were providing new opportunities for the Thai people. By the following century the important new kingdoms of Lan Na, Sukhothai, and Ayutthaya had emerged. Theravada Buddhism of the Langkawong (Sri Lankan) sect was widely practiced. Common religious beliefs helped cement good relations between the kingdoms. But competition between kings for prestige and grandeur also led to wars.

Lan Na developed when a loose collection of domains and city-states were integrated into a single kingdom. The kingdom was not akin to a modern nation-state. Rather, the capital at the center held a shifting and often limited degree of power and influence over the wider territory. Lan Na's rulers worked to extend their influence in several ways, including by establishing lineage connections throughout the territory, and through the propagation of Buddhism.

The historical development of early Lan Na can be divided into three periods: the formative period (1296–1335), the period of prosperity (1335–1525), and the period of decline and fall (1525–1558).

The formative period was set in motion by the determination of Phaya Mangrai of Ngoen Yang to expand his territory. After first incorporating together *mueang* in the Chiang Rai basin, Mangrai moved into the Chiang Mai–Lamphun area, establishing the city of Chiang Mai in 1296. Eventually, the incorporated *mueang* included centers such as Chiang Rai, Chiang Saen, Chiang Mai, Lamphun, Lampang, and Phayao. Four more kings ruled during the fifty-nine-year formative period.

Lan Na began to flourish during the reign of Phaya Kuena (1335–1385). Its prosperity reached a height during the reign of King Tilokarat (1441–1487), known later as the golden age, which continued until the reign of Phaya Kaeo (1495–1525). During this period, the kingdom expanded greatly, incorporating Phrae and Nan and consolidating its influence over the Shan (Tai Yai) states, including Chiang Tung, Mueang Nai, Mueang Sipo, and Mueang Yong, as well as in Chiang Rung in Sipsong Panna and even Luang Prabang in Mueang Lao.

Lan Na's decline began during the reign of Phaya Khetchettharat (1525–1538), at the end of the Mangrai dynasty. There was a thirty-three year period of chaos before Lan Na became a dependency of Burma in 1558.

THE FORMATIVE PERIOD (1296–1355)

THE UNIFICATION OF MUEANG IN THE YON DOMAIN

Mangrai was born in Ngoen Yang around 1239.[1] He was the son of Phaya Lao Meng and Nang Ua Ming chommueang (Nang Thepkhamkhai or Khamkhayai), daughter of Thao Rungkaenchai of Chiang Rung. By 1261, Mangrai was the ruler of Ngoen Yang and was also known as the twenty-fifth king of the Lao dynasty. At the beginning of Mangrai's reign, the once-united *mueang* in the Kok River valley had become divided. Inter-state invasions and struggles over manpower caused great distress to the population. Mangrai set out to unify the *mueang* under Ngoen Yang. He claimed direct descent from Lao Chong to justify his right to rule. In his coronation ceremony, he received regalia such as a sword of victory, spear, and the Sikanchai dagger that had once belonged to Lao Chong and had been handed down to every king of the Lao Chong dynasty. The rulers of other principalities were only distant descendants of the dynasty, Mangrai claimed.

Mangrai tried to persuade the leaders of other *mueang* to join him, in which case he allowed them to continue to rule.[2] When territories such as Mueang Mop, Mueang Lai, and Mueang Chiang Kham refused, he attacked and installed his own nobles as rulers. Mangrai also cultivated friendly relations with powerful leaders such as Phaya Ngammueang of Phayao, who had close ties with Sukhothai.[3]

Mangrai's next step—propelled in the immediate sense by fear of a Mongol invasion—was to expand southward. By 1262, when the Mongols had already captured Yunnan, Burma, and Tonkin, he moved his capital to Chiang Rai. Chiang Rai served as a base for the incorporation of many additional *mueang*, and there was a period of consolidation from 1262 to 1273, when he founded Mueang Fang. In 1276 Mangrai led his troops to Phayao, but ended up renewing his friendship with that area.[4] By now, he was the leader of territories that together were called the Yon domain.

One stimulus for Mangrai's ambition was the growth of trade in the region since the twelfth century, when there was a decline in the southern Srivijaya kingdom and its monopoly on trade.[5] The decline heralded a shift in Chinese and Asian trading practices, according to O. W. Walters.[6] Srivijaya's decline meant that Chinese ships began to trade directly with ports around the South China Sea. The number of merchants increased markedly, supported by the development in China of large junks that could carry a large volume of goods.[7]

This change began in the Sung dynasty (1127–1279) and likely continued through the Yuan dynasty (1279–1368) and early Ming dynasty (1368–1506). It helped make port cities wealthy and it also created wealth in the inland areas that traded with the ports, setting the stage for the establishment of new political entities.[8] Economic factors were very important in Mangrai's seizure of Hariphunchai in the upper Ping River valley. The river was an important trade route; it allowed goods from as far north as Fang to be traded all the way down to the southern port city of Ayutthaya. As a result, Hariphunchai was relatively wealthy.[9] According to the Chiang Mai Chronicle,

> Commerce was thriving. At that time, many parties of traders from Haribhunjaya came to conduct commerce in Fang. King Mangrai therefore summoned the traders and asked them. "This Haribhunjaya where you live: How prosperous is it?" A trader replied, "The Haribhunjaya where I live is far away, and is replete with all kinds of good things. Traders of all countries frequent it both by land and by water to trade. By water, one can reach Yodhiya [Ayutthaya], and traders from there come. In trade, the people of the domain are very prosperous."
>
> Again the king asked, "Is the ruler [of Haribhunjaya] richly endowed with troops, elephants and horses, and retainers? Is the country rich?" A trader replied, "The king of my yonder domain is richly endowed with elephants and horses and retainers, and he has all kinds of wealth." King Mangrai upon hearing that Haribhunjaya was wealthy was consumed with a desire to obtain it for his own, so he consulted with his generals thusly: "We have heard the news that Haribhunjaya is very rich—richer than our own domain. How can we make it our own? . . ."[10]

THE SEIZURE OF HARIPHUNCHAI

The move to capture Hariphunchai was a big step and had to be carefully planned. Mueang Fang adjoined the northern part of Hariphunchai and could be used as a base for expansion.[11] It had easy access routes to the southern territory. While he prepared to seize Hariphunchai, Mangrai fed large numbers of nobles and brave soldiers.[12]

His next move was to send a spy, Ai Fa, to Hariphunchai. In 1287 he also signed the friendship pact, called the Three Kings' Accord, with Phaya Ngammueang of Phayao and King Ramkhamhaeng of Sukhothai. The pact meant that Mangrai could feel secure that his expansion into Hariphunchai would not meet with opposition from the two others.

After Ai Fa sent the word, Mangrai attacked and captured Hariphunchai in 1292.[13]

19. Ku Kut stupa (on the right) showing the original remains of the rectangular stupa with fifteen Buddha images on each side, a total of sixty Buddha images. (NAT, c. 1932–1947)

20. Rectangular stupa or *ku kham* at Wiang Kumkam, influenced by the Ku Kut stupa. (NAT, c. 1927–1947)

THE FOUNDING OF WIANG KUMKAM

Mangrai stayed in Hariphunchai for only two years and in 1294 appointed Ai Fa to rule there.[14] In the same year he moved on to build Wiang Kumkam. The Jinakalamali Chronicle offers 1303 as an alternate date for the founding of Wiang Kumkam.

Archaeological evidence as well as the Chiang Mai Chronicle indicates that an original village on the site dated to about the twelfth century. Situated on the banks of the Ping River, the site was well placed for trade and travel, and the surrounding plains supported rice-growing and other forms of agriculture. It thus had the potential to develop into an urban society.

Mangrai's town plan for Wiang Kumkam was influenced by Hariphunchai culture. The town's location on a flood plain was a distinctive Hariphunchai feature. Traditionally, the Thai Yuan had built towns in the foothills. Wiang Kumkam was built in a rectangular shape, whereas Thai Yuan towns normally followed geographical contours.

The Lan Na state would go on to incorporate and build upon many aspects of the more highly advanced Hariphunchai culture. The Lan Na Tham script was derived from Mon Hariphunchai script. The Lan Na Sangha originated in a sect from Hariphunchai. Art works also followed Hariphunchai style. The Hariphunchai stupa at Ku Kut (Chamathewi) Temple was the original model for the stupa at Ku Kham (Chedi Liam) Temple. The octagonal form of Haripunchai stupas was the influence for the stupas in Wiang Kumkam and at Kumkamthiparam, Pu Pia, and Mai Song Temples. The blend of Hariphunchai culture with the influences of other ethnic groups combined to create the distinctive characteristics of what would become Lan Na culture.

Mangrai did not remain in Wiang Kumkam for long. After traveling to the foothills of Doi Suthep and finding an auspicious site, he founded Chiang Mai in 1296. Wiang Kumkam continued as a satellite town of Chiang Mai, a residence of nobles, and a defense outpost.[15]

THE FOUNDING OF CHIANG MAI

Chiang Mai was founded in "the year 658, the Year of the Monkey, the eighth day of the waxing moon in the eighth month at an auspicious early hour." This information appears on a stele at Chiang Man Temple, and corresponds with 4 A.M. on April 12, 1296 in the solar calendar.[16] The date was set by the Committee on the Verification and Study of the Town's Horoscope, appointed by the Chiang Mai Administration Office.

In the process of founding the city, Mangrai had invited Ngammueang of Phayao and Ramkhamhaeng of Sukhothai to examine both the site and town plan, which was influenced by that of Sukhothai. Its geometric style, not a Thai Yuan tradition, would not appear again in Lan Na.

When first built, Chiang Mai had walls measuring 900 *wa* by 1,000 *wa* (1 *wa* = 2 meters).[17] The walls as they appear today are composed of two sections:

a rectangular brick inner wall, and an earthen outer wall. The question of whether the inner and earthen walls were built contemporaneously remains unsolved.[18] The author believes that a rectangular inner wall, probably made of earth, was built during Mangrai's reign, while an outer wall was built during the reign of Thao Maeku (Phaya Maekut).[19]

Chiang Mai was well situated. First, it was located between the Kok and the Ping river valleys and was in a position to control the *mueang* of the Yon and Ping domains.[20] Second, it was well situated for trade. The Ping River was a communications route with the south and it was also relatively easy to trade with *mueang* in the north such as Chiang Saen and Yunnan.[21] Third, the fertile Ping River valley, particularly the area around the city, was the largest expanse of plains for agriculture in the region. Finally, the site was located between the foothills of Doi Suthep, ensuring a fine water supply. There was a large reservoir northeast of the city, another important water source.[22]

With a lessening of the threat from the Mongols, Chiang Mai was also suitable for political reasons. The Mongols had taken Pagan in Burma in 1287.[23] Three years later Mangrai had helped the leaders of the Greater Tai, three brothers, to expel them. In 1290, according to the Chiang Mai Chronicle, Mangrai "raised an exceedingly numerous army and by stages reached the southeastern frontier of Ava, where he encamped."[24] Two years later, in 1292, Kublai Khan sent an army to attack Mangrai in Lan Na (known as Ba Bai Xifu).[25] They were expelled.[26] In 1296 Mangrai's troops set out to recapture Chiang Rung from the invaders, who by this time had probably been weakened due to the death of Kublai Khan two years earlier. The death

21. Chiang Mai city wall. (PUA, c. 1937)

probably eased the way for Mangrai's plans for Chiang Mai. The new city would create stability and help the region to be in a position to mount a strong response to any further problems with the Mongols.

CHIANG MAI'S SIGNIFICANCE

The founding of Chiang Mai opened up a new era for the Thai Yuan people. From the beginning, the city was deliberately created to be the political, economic, social, and cultural center of the new kingdom.

Its significance was multifaceted. First, it was a permanent capital, a new idea in Thai Yuan culture. Previously, Mangrai had repeatedly changed residences and whichever town he happened to be living in was known as "the city of the king." He had built several temporary capitals, including Chiang Rai, Fang, and Wiang Kumkam. These were simple constructions, with moats and earthen walls for defense. Chiang Rai, for example, was quite small, and was mostly made up of the king's residence. Capital cities were not an important idea or an important political institution for what was essentially a tribal society.[27] The sites for some of the capitals that appear in the chronicles, such as Chiang Lao and Ngoen Yang, have never been identified.

But the creation of the Lan Na kingdom, a much larger proposition, heralded many changes. The blending of several ethnic groups would lead to a new, relatively unified, culture. Hariphunchai influences were important from the beginning, in the author's opinion, especially in relation to the idea of establishing a permanent capital to serve as a political institution offering continuity to the state. Hariphunchai had had a permanent capital city of the same name for almost five hundred years. Though the capital had encountered troubles, such as a cholera epidemic in the eleventh century which forced residents to flee for a time to Mueang Sutthamnakhon, it was never changed. At times the Hariphunchai domain came under the control of rulers from other areas, but they too ruled from the traditional capital.[28]

Such continuity was clearly in Mangrai's mind when he founded the city that he wanted to become the permanent center of the Lan Na kingdom. He stated, "I will build a truly large city."[29] Mangrai ordered Chiang Mai to be built, 2,000 *wa* on each side, which would have been very large, twice the size of the present-day city of Chiang Mai proper, the area within the old city walls. Phaya Ngammueang opposed that plan. King Ramkhamhaeng considered it too big. Finally, it was reduced by half. The result was a well laid-out city in a good location.

Chiang Mai was a new city, built on vacant land, and so, unlike centers like Hariphunchai, Khelang, and Chiang Saen, it had no heritage. For its importance to be recognized, it would have to acquire one. From the beginning, Mangrai proclaimed the city's greatness to other Thai states. The invitation to Phaya Ngammueang and King Ramkhamhaeng to consult in the city's planning helped gain their acceptance. Mangrai sought an auspicious date for the

MAP 8. MAP OF CHIANG RAI

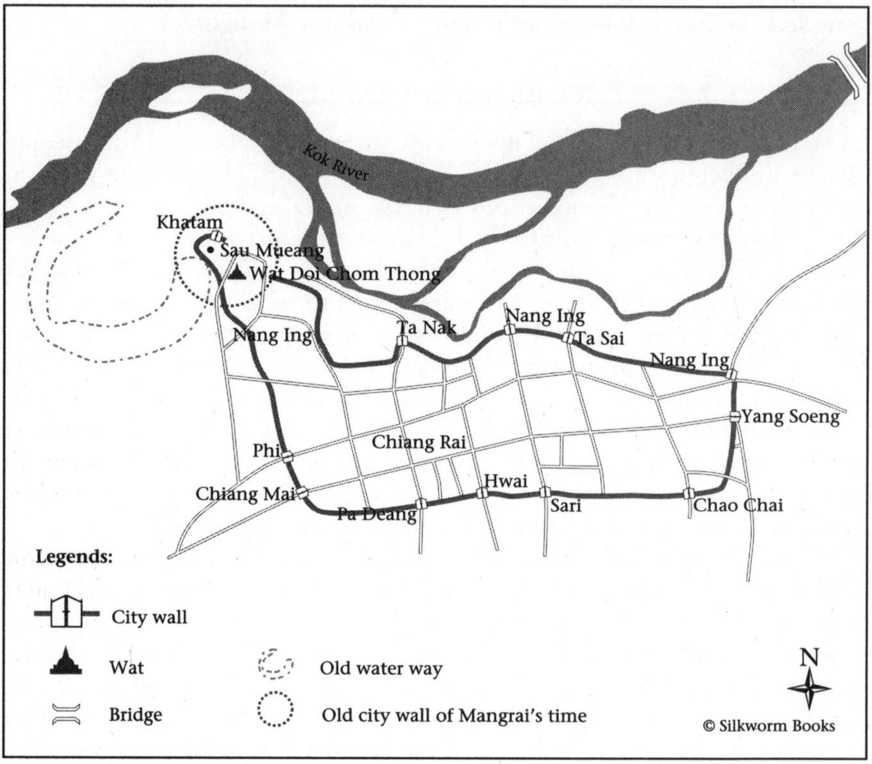

(Drawn after Sarassawadee Ongsakul, *Prawatsat Lan Na*, p. 116)

city's founding, and identified the special characteristics that would determine its destiny. The details of the founding date were carefully recorded, enabling modern scholars to identify the exact date on the solar calendar, a first for a Lan Na town. The city was regarded as very modern at the time.

Mangrai lived in Chiang Mai until his death, by which time he had certainly built a sense of political importance around the city. We know that from the reign of Phaya Chaisongkhram (1311–1325) onwards, the key element in any battle for the throne was seizure of the capital city.

Mangrai built Chiang Mai according to cosmological principles; that is, the city, surrounded by satellite towns, was likened to the center of the universe. The Chedi Luang Temple, or "Mount Meru," was sited, in accordance with cosmological traditions, in the center of the town, or the center of the universe, and it was also regarded as the city's spiritual center. It was surrounded by eight satellite temples—Chiang Yuen, Chai Si Phum, Buppharam, Chai Mongkhon, Nantharam, Tapotharam, Suan Dok, and Chet

Yot—which were analogous with eight planets of cosmological lore.[30] Many other sites in the center of the city were considered powerful and sacred, including the Inthakhin City Pillar, the *yang* tree, Kumphan Asura [an ogre who was the protector of the city], and the palace. All of these helped to build a sense of heritage for Chiang Mai and to give it a much higher status than satellite towns.

Today, it is recognized that the founding of Chiang Mai was highly successful. The city has always been recognized as the center of Lan Na, even after the kingdom's disintegration during Burmese rule. King Kawila, founder of the Chao Chet Ton dynasty, regarded the then deserted and ruined Chiang Mai still as the center of Lan Na and he restored the city to its former glory. It has remained the center of northern Thailand ever since.

CHIANG MAI'S CITY PLANNING

When founding a city, people had to consider elements such as climate, water availability, and soil conditions. Traditional knowledge about such matters developed into lore known as *chaiyaphum*, or auspicious characteristics for settlement. Mueang chronicles in Lan Na mention the *chaiyaphum* of several cities. Chiang Mai, for example, had seven auspicious characteristics. Phayao had three.

The choice of Chiang Mai's location indicates the Tai Yuan knowledge of the environment. The city "turned its back to the hill and faced the water"; that is, Doi Suthep was at its back and the Ping River at its front, with a west to east slope ensuring that the community had a constant flow of water, and from a variety of sources, which meant it was known as a "water town." Of the seven auspicious factors, four involved water. The seven factors were:

1. Two white deer, a doe and her fawn, came out of the big forest in the north to live at this auspicious location, and the people worshipped them.
2. Two white barking deer, a doe and her fawn, came to live at this auspicious location. The dogs couldn't bite them and fled.
3. People saw a white rat with four attendants that came to this auspicious location.
4. The western topography was high and sloped down towards the east. (Doi Suthep was the water source.)
5. The Mae Kha Stream flowed down from Doi Suthep, circled the town, and flowed towards Wiang Kumkam.
6. There was a large reservoir in the northeast where the animals could drink.
7. The Ping River flows to the east of the city of Chiang Mai.

Forested Doi Suthep was the source of streams such as the Mae Kha, Mae Tha Chang, Huai Chang Khian, Huai Kaeo, and others which ensured that Chiang Mai had plenty of water year-round. The water was stored in the city moat as well as distributed to households.

In the past, the Mae Kha Stream, which originates at Doi Suthep and is adjacent Doi Pui, flowed down to Nong Bua Chet Ko, (also known as Nong Khiao or Nong Pa Phaeng) a year-round reservoir to the northeast that ceased to exist in the middle of the twentieth century. From there, the stream flowed on to more or less embrace the city, serving as an outer moat. Originally, the Mae Kha flowed in an easterly direction beside the earthen wall and on in a southern direction to meet the Wai Stream. Later it was extended to reach the city wall at Ku Hueang Corner. Any overflow from the Mae Kha was released into the Ping River, helping to prevent floods. City residents also constructed ponds and irrigation canals. The author found an ancient pond in the shape of a trapezoid, and an irrigation canal, on the grounds of the Faculty of Agriculture, Chiang Mai University.[31] They were used to trap water from Doi Suthep and distribute it to Wiang Suan Dok and agricultural fields. Such reservoirs helped prevent Chiang Mai from flooding. The people placed great importance on water resources. Obviously, a shortage of water would mean doom for the town. The Phuen Mueang Lan Na Chiang Mai states, "In any year that Nong Bua Chet Ko lacked water, the city suffered. If Huai Kaeo had no flowing water that emptied into the city moat and one couldn't hear the roar of waterfalls at night, the city suffered."

Chiang Mai was also a *mueang wananakhon*, a forest town. Before the founding of the city, the indigenous people who lived in the foothills believed that Doi Suthep was the sacred residence of the spirits of their ancestors. During the Lan Na period when Buddhism prospered, holy relics were deposited at Doi Suthep. Doi Suthep Temple at the peak of the mountain symbolized its sacredness. The mountain was also of course respected as a water source.[32]

The forest area, much larger then than it is today, consisted of Doi Suthep and its foothills. It started at the Suan Dok Gate. Wiang Suan Dok was then the garden of the king and was known as the Phayom Flower Garden, after a type of flower found in Thailand and Laos. There were few residences in this area. Suan Dok, Pa Daeng, Fai Hin, and Umong temples were located in the foothills of Doi Suthep. The area stretched to Chet Yot Temple.

Land use within the city followed the original rectangular town plan. The old city was composed of a rectangular inner wall. An L-shaped outer wall was probably added later. The residences of the king, nobles and local commoners, and prominent temples, were inside the rectangular wall, the center of the *mueang*'s wealth. The L-shaped outer wall was less important, judging from the many small, winding roads and lanes it encompasses. The temples in this area were small and less important and it was inhabited by a mix of locals and people from other ethnic groups, such as the Khoen, Mon, Burmese, and Ho.

Population settlement in the city was related to beliefs about the importance of direction. The Yuan believed the cardinal directions represented concealed

22. Aerial view of Chiang Mai, c. 1932. The rectangular city wall is located in the center, to the left is Nong Bua, an ancient reservoir in the northeastern part of town. The white sections in the photograph are Nong Bua, showing how extensive the reservoir was. (MT, c. 1932)

23. Ku Tao Temple, with Doi Suthep in the background. Nong Bua reservoir appears in the foreground. The water level was low in summer. (NAT, c. 1932–1947)

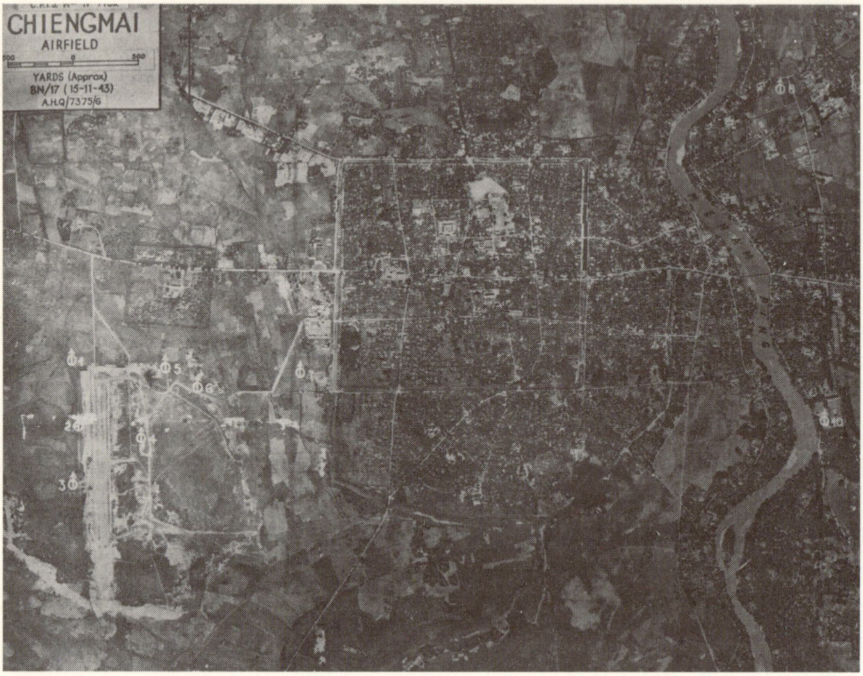

24. Aerial view of Chiang Mai in 1943, with clear evidence of inner and outer walls. Wiang Suan Dok is on the west; northwest of Wiang Suan Dok is the irrigation ditch and trapezoidal ancient reservoir, now located in Chiang Mai University. (NAT, 1943)

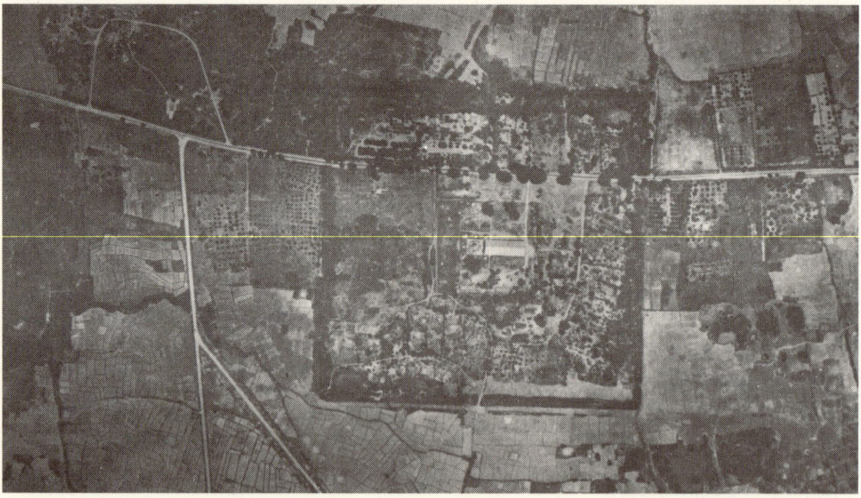

25. Enlargement of Wiang Suan Dok, appearing as a square, with Suan Dok Temple in the center. (NAT, 1943)

26. Aerial view of Wiang Chiang Mai. (Hunting Aerosurveys Ltd., 1952)

MAP 9. LOCATION OF CHIANG MAI, IN AN AREA OF PLENTIFUL WATER

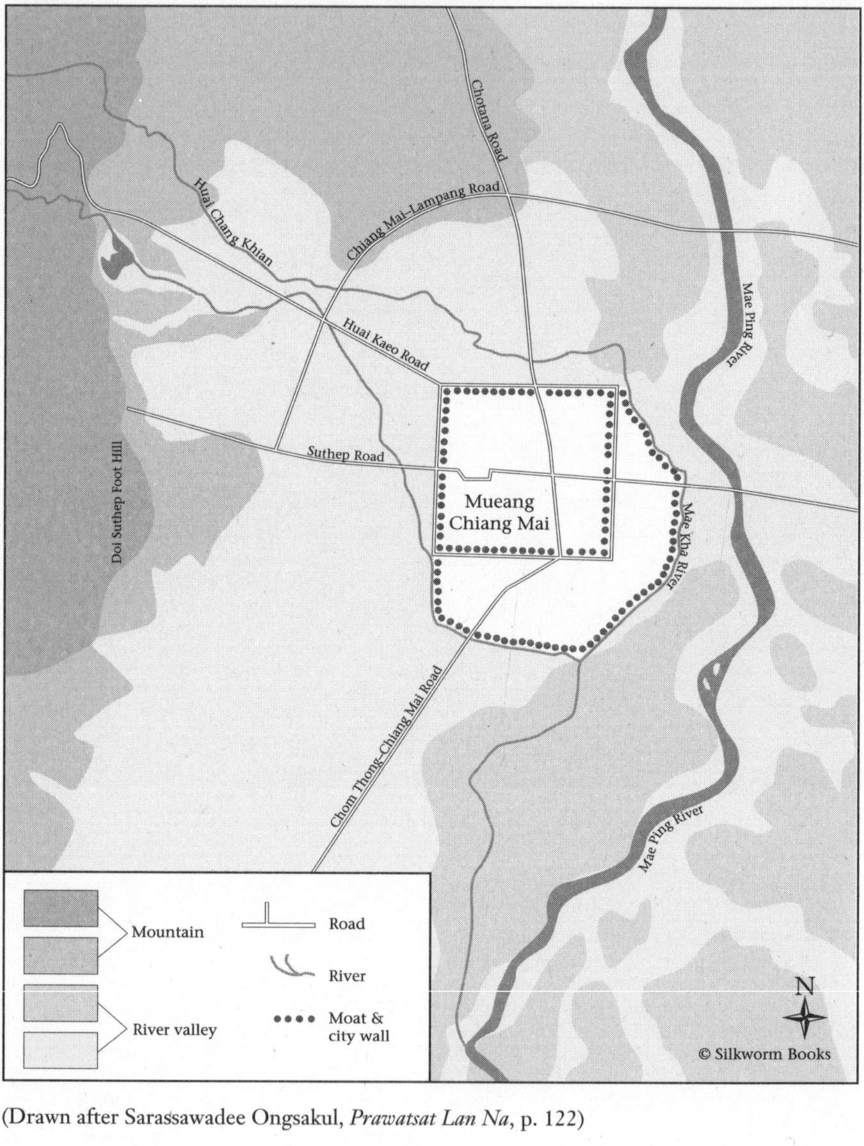

(Drawn after Sarassawadee Ongsakul, *Prawatsat Lan Na*, p. 122)

meanings that could be both auspicious and inauspicious. They also believed that a city, *wiang*, or *mueang* was a living thing with a body and a soul.[33] The head was the important part of the body, and the head of the city should be in the north. Lan Na kings would enter the city through the gate at its head, Hua Wiang Gate (called White Elephant Gate since 1400) for coronation ceremonies. It was forbidden for anything inauspicious to enter through this gate. Wiang Kaeo, the royal residence, was in the north, as well as the homes of other nobles and prominent temples such as Chiang Man Temple and Chedi Luang Temple. Settlement was dense in this area. There were a total of fifteen temples from the Hua Wiang Gate to Khuang Singh Temple.

The center or "navel" of the city was the location of the Inthakhin City Pillar, which dates back to the founding of the city. It is believed that the pillar had to be in place before the city was actually built. Residents regarded it as the *suea mueang*, or spirit of the city, and worshipped it.[34] Ceremonies to strengthen the city's destiny involved worship of the eight directions, the city's navel, the Inthakhin City Pillar, the *yang* tree (a tall resinous tree), Kumphan Asura (the ogre that protected the city from anything inauspicious), and the five gates.[35]

The foot of the city, to the south, was an elongated strip of land from Hua Lin Corner to Ku Hueang Corner, edging towards the Khatam and Siphum corners. This was an unimportant, inauspicious, peripheral area, and its temples and houses were usually small. The land level was also lower. This was a place for funeral processions and anything inauspicious or evil. It was stipulated that the dead should exit through Saen Pung and Hai Ya gates. After Khun Khrua was captured following his revolt, he was imprisoned in the southwest around Ku Hueang Corner. Beliefs around the inauspiciousness of the south continued for a long time. Early in the twentieth century a Siamese commissioner who did not know local customs ordered the nobles to move the market from the center of the town to Saen Pung Gate. The new location was unpopular and the market was soon moved back to its old location.

To the west was the forest area which contained mainly forest temples. Settlement was light.

The front gate of Chiang Mai faced east. This was seen as a suitable area for trade and communication. Settlement was dense around Tha Phae and Chang Moi roads.

The important axis of the city was the horizontal line, along the main road from Tha Phae Gate to Phra Singh Temple. The vertical axis was the road from Hua Wiang Gate to Chiang Mai Gate. The roads met at the Klang Wiang intersection. The center of the city was a wide, multi-purpose plaza called Khuang Luang, which was designed in the original plan. It was located on both sides of what is now Phra Pokklao Road, from in front of the Chedi Luang Temple through the Klang Wiang intersection, extending past the Chiang Mai market, the stupa containing Mangrai's ashes, the old city

MAP 10. MAP OF CHIANG MAI

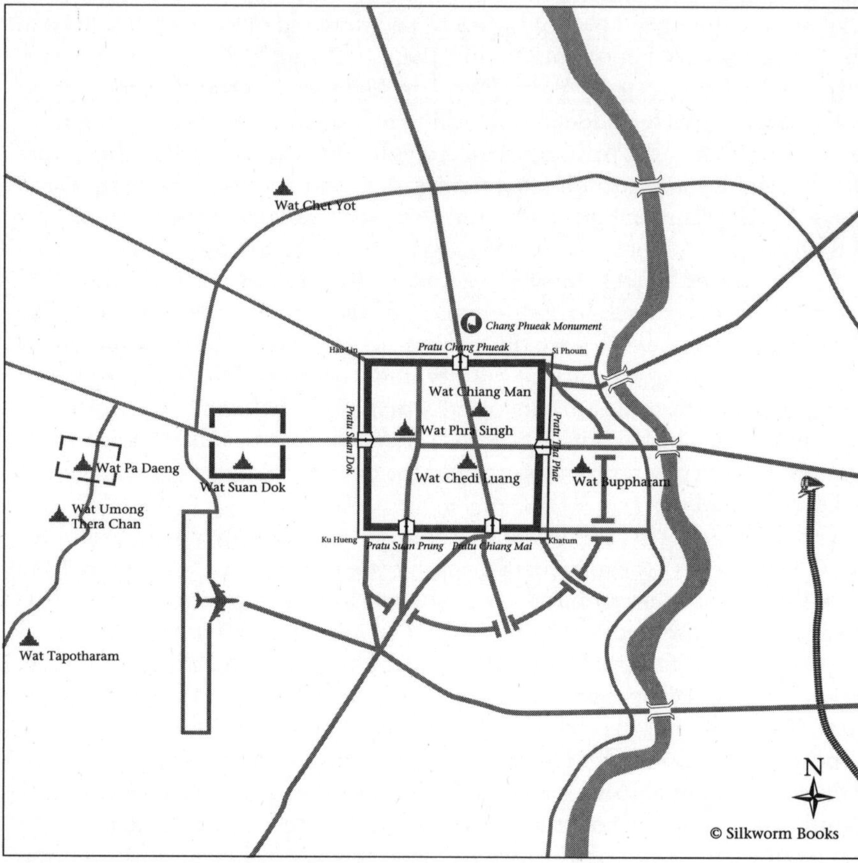

(Drawn after Hans Penth, *Jinakalamali Index*, p. xx)

27. Pa Daeng Temple at the foothill of Doi Suthep, a forest temple of Chiang Mai. (NAT, c. 1902–1927)

administration building, Chiang Mai district court, Yupharat School, the Chiang Mai Tobacco Office (once Chao Burirat's residence), and the Hua Khuang Temple.

In the past, the Khuang Luang, or royal plaza, was used for a variety of city activities, and particularly for important ceremonies such as coronations.[36] In wartime, it was probably used for mustering troops. A part of it was the site for the Chiang Mai market. The market covered the area on both sides of the road in front of Phra Singh Temple to the Klang Wiang intersection and continued north to include the stupa containing Mangrai's ashes, now located behind shophouses. Mangrai died at this market, according to the chronicles.

The people of Lan Na knew how to preserve the environment through traditional practices. For example, cremation, which was believed to be inauspicious, probably due to concerns around the density of the population, was forbidden inside the city walls. The dead had to be taken outside Hai Ya Gate for cremation. There was also a custom forbidding cremation within temple grounds or near sources of water, because it was considered offensive and could cause pollution.

Cutting down trees, particularly large trees near water, was also forbidden, because it was believed that this could destroy water sources. The people believed that a lack of water could cause the city's destruction. If the roar of

28. Chiang Mai, with Doi Suthep in the background west of town. The photograph shows the Ping River and the town full of trees. (PUA, c. 1927)

29. An elephant leading the procession of King Rama VII as it enters Chiang Mai at the Hua Wiang Gate (now Chang Phueak or White Elephant Gate). (PUA, 1926)

30. *Ho trai* (library) at Phra Singh Temple showing Lan Na architecture during the era of prosperity. The stupa in front has been demolished. (PUA, c. 1926)

31. Consecrated assembly hall at Phra Singh Temple (right) and Lai Kham Buddhist assembly hall (left). (PUA, c. 1926)

Pha Lat Noi Waterfall did not reach the city at night, the city would decline, residents believed. They also believed that if the water at Nong Bua dried up the city would be doomed.

RULERS IN THE FORMATIVE PERIOD (1296–1355)

The initial building of Lan Na into a stable kingdom happened during the reigns of five kings, from Mangrai to Phayu.

Phaya Mangrai (1261–1311). Mangrai, who founded Chiang Mai in 1296, laid the foundation for Lan Na by joining the Yon and Ping domains. Later, he expanded the territory further by taking Khelang (Lampang). During his reign, the core of the Lan Na kingdom comprised Chiang Mai, Lamphun, Lampang, and Chiang Rai. Mangrai also established wider political networks by sending his son, Khun Khrua, to rule Mueang Nai in the Tai Yai (Shan) region.[37] He also expanded into Chiang Tung. The Chiang Tung Chronicle mentions that Mangrai conquered the Lua, the indigenous people, built Chiang Tung, and sent Thao (King or Prince) Namthuam to rule it.[39] Mangrai ruled from Chiang Mai throughout his reign. It was followed in political importance by Chiang Rai, which was ruled by his son, Khun Khram. At this time Lan Na was divided into the northern region (the Yon domain) centered around Chiang Rai as its center, and the southern region centered around Chiang Mai. Several successive kings followed this administrative pattern. Outlying *mueang* were ruled by princes, relatives of the king, or trusted nobles. Mangrai and successive members of his dynasty ruled with a code of law called the Mangraisat, which may have been influenced by the legal code of the Mon of Hariphunchai.[39] Mangrai was also influenced by the Buddhism of Hariphunchai. He built Kanthom (Chang Kham) Temple, stupas, and Buddha images, and he donated lands and slaves to temples.[40]

After founding Chiang Mai, Mangrai continued to support efforts to push the Mongols out of the wider region. In 1299 he probably sent troops to help the Shan at Mueang Chokse fight the king of Pagan, who was close to the invaders.[41] The Mongols retaliated by sending a large army out in 1301, but it failed to make headway. Mangrai's troops then joined with an army from Chiang Rung to attack the enemy as far as Yunnan. The war continued until 1311 when the parties agreed to cease hostilities. The following year Chiang Mai and Chiang Rung began to send tribute to China.[42] Mangrai died around 1311.

Phaya Chaisongkhram (1311–1325). Mangrai's son Chaisongkhram resided in Chiang Mai for only four months before moving to Chiang Rai and appointing a son, Thao Saenphu, to rule the capital.[43] Despite the king's absence, Chiang Mai continued to be the seat of rightful power in Lan Na. Any fight over the throne meant a fight to control Chiang Mai. For example, Prince Khrua, Chaisongkhram's younger brother, sent troops from Mueang Nai to seize Chiang Mai[44] in an attempt to take absolute power. Khrua managed to take the city but he was later eliminated by another of

Chaisongkhram's sons, Prince Namthuam, who was then made ruler of the city. Still later, however, Chaisongkhram suspected Namthuam's loyalty and sent him to rule Chiang Tung. Saenphu was appointed *uparat* for the second time.[45] Chaisongkhram died in Chiang Rai.

Phaya Saenphu (1325–1334). Saenphu succeeded his father to the throne as the third king of the Mangrai dynasty. He lived in Chiang Rai and appointed his son, Khamfu, to rule Chiang Mai. In around 1327 Saenphu built Chiang Saen in the area of Ngoen Yang,[46] to defend against enemies in the north, and he resided there for the remainder of his life. Chiang Saen was built as a fortress, 700 *wa* wide by 1,500 *wa* long, and it had eight watchtowers. It served as a control center for *mueang* in the northern region such as Chiang Rai, Mueang Fang, Mueang Sat, Chiang Tung, Chiang Rung, and Chiang Khong.[47]

Phaya Khamfu (1334–1336). This son of Saenphu also resided in Chiang Saen for strategic reasons, and appointed Prince Phayu to rule Chiang Mai. Khamfu expanded towards the east, an indication that Lan Na was powerful at this time. He began by conquering Phayao. A bid to expand into Phrae was unsuccessful.[48] Khamfu died at Mueang Chiang Kham.

Phaya Phayu (1336–1355). The coronation of Phayu was arranged by nobles. Unlike his predecessors, he lived in Chiang Mai. This was probably because the northern area had been stabilized and Chiang Saen was by then an effective defense post against the Ho. Phayu worked to incorporate Phayao into Lan Na. He established lineage relations with Chiang Khong by marrying Chitrathewi, the daughter of its ruler.[49]

Phayu patronized Buddhism and ruled his kingdom "with the ten virtues of a king and with devotion to Buddhism . . ."[50] [The virtues are charity, morality, sacrifice, honesty, courtesy, perseverance, equanimity, justice, fortitude, and correct behavior.] He built the important Lichiangphra (Phra Singh) Temple in Chiang Mai. He invited monk Maha Akkhayachula Thera from Hariphunchai to become supreme patriarch and reside at Lichiangphra Temple.[51] Phaya Phayu's support of Buddhism laid the foundation for the spread of the religion in the region.

THE PERIOD OF LAN NA PROSPERITY (1355–1225)

The Lan Na kingdom prospered from the reign of Phaya Kuena (1355–1385) to the reign of Phaya Kaeo (1495–1525). It enjoyed a golden age during the reign of King Tilokarat (1441–1487).

KINGS

Phaya Kuena (1355–1385). The sixth king of Lan Na and a devoted Buddhist introduced the Langkawong (Sri Lankan) order to the kingdom from Sukhothai and was described as skilled in the arts. During his reign, the

32. Sukhothai-style stupa at Suan Dok Temple. The religious connection between Lan Na and Sukhothai began when Lan Na invited Sumana Thera from Sukhothai. The old Sukhothai style was lost when the stupa was restored in 1932. (NAT, c. 1926–1931)

kingdom was peaceful and productive.[52] The Langkawong order was considered a purer form of Buddhism than the earlier versions of the religion from Hariphunchai, Pegu, and Ava that were combined with indigenous beliefs.[53]

Kuena invited a leading Sukhothai monk, Sumana Thera, to Lan Na, in 1369, and the monk came with holy relics and spent the rainy season retreat in Phra Yuen Temple in Hariphunchai.[54] The king also invited 8,400 monks from an earlier sect that dated from the time of Queen Chamathewi to be reordained in the Langkawong order.[55]

In 1371, Kuena constructed the Buppharam,[56] or the Suan Dok Temple, in the Phayom Flower Garden for Sumana Thera, and the monk began to spend rainy season retreats there. In around 1373 Kuena built Wiang Suan Dok as a Wiang Phrathat, or town of holy relics.[57] Relics brought by Sumana Thera were deposited at Phrathat Doi Suthep and Buppharam temples. Sumana Thera died in 1389.[58]

Bupharam Temple became the center of Langkawong Buddhism, also known as the Raman (Mon) school, in the region. The name "Raman School" was a reference to Sumana Thera's being ordained and studying at Maha Sawami Uthumphon School in Martaban in the Mon kingdom. Kuena supported monks from other *mueang* such as Chiang Saen and Chiang Tung to study at Buppharam Temple.[59] There was an effort to make Chiang Mai instead of Hariphunchai the center of religion in the region.[60]

Lan Na was powerful during Kuena's reign. A chronicle mentions that when his son, Saenmueangma, was born, many foreign rulers sent tribute to him. This is why Phraya Kuena named his son Chao Pho Thao Saenmueangma, "one hundred thousand *mueang* came."[61] Kuena refused to send tribute to the Ho in Yunnan, which had been the practice since the early Mangrai dynasty. In 1365, Phaya Ho Lumfa, the Ho ruler, demanded, in vain, that "9,000 khan [540,000 kg.] of rice, 20 hap [1200 kg.] of elephant tusks, 400 ram [800 yds.] of white cloth, 1,000 dishes of chaesak ceramics, 500 with designs, 200 green, and 300 white, be sent as tribute for Chao Lumfa."[62] Succeeding rulers also refused to send tribute to the Ho.

Phaya Saenmueangma (1385–1401). Saenmueangma succeeded to the throne upon his father's death, and immediately faced a challenge. Thao Mahaphrom, younger brother of Kuena and ruler of Chiang Rai, tried and failed to seize Chiang Mai, and then looked for support from King Boromaracha I, king of Ayutthaya.

In 1386, Ayutthaya attempted to plunder Lampang, but failed and retreated.[63] Mahaphrom later broke with the king of Ayutthaya, and Saenmueangma sent him back to rule Chiang Rai.

Saenmueangma began to expand southward whenever he saw an opportunity. Sukhothai, for example, asked his help to fight Ayutthaya. But Sukhothai later turned on the Lan Na troops, in around 1387 or 1388, which suffered heavy losses.[64] Saenmueangma then turned away from war and

33. Phrathat Doi Suthep Temple, Chiang Mai. (NAT, c. 1947)

34. Chedi Luang. This stupa was first built during the reign of Phaya Saenmueangma in 1391 and later enlarged by King Tilokarat. The stupa collapsed in 1545 from an earthquake. The picture was taken before its restoration in 1990–1992. (NAT)

towards religion. He began the construction of Chedi Luang in 1391.[65] He also gilded the stupa in Hariphunchai Temple with gold weighing 252 kilograms.[66] Such projects indicate that the kingdom was prosperous during his reign.

Phaya Samfangkaen (or *Samphrayafangkaen)* (1402–1441). The eighth king of Lan Na and the son of Saenmueangma succeeded to the throne in 1402[67] at the age of thirteen with the support of his uncle.[68] Samfangkaen rewarded his sponsor by appointing him *chao simoen*, ruler of Phayao. Samfangkaen's elder brother and the ruler of Chiang Rai, Thao Yikumkam, tried to depose him with help from Sukhothai but was defeated.[69] Samfangkaen then faced the threat of invasion from the Ho, who were angry over Lan Na's refusal to send tribute. In 1404 and 1405, the Ho surrounded Chiang Saen. Samfangkaen drafted troops from Chiang Mai, Chiang Saen, Fang, Chiang Rai, Chiang Khong, and Phayao. The Ho were eventually defeated and were pursued as far as Sipsong Panna. Mueang Yong Huai was founded as a dependency of Chiang Mai, and it served as a forward defensive bastion against the Ho.[70]

Peace was then restored to Lan Na. The king was praised as an able and brave ruler.[71] He appointed his eldest son as *uparat*, or successor. The *uparat* stayed in Chiang Mai, indicating a decrease in Chiang Rai's status as it was no longer the residence of the *uparat*, or "second king."[72]

King Tilokarat (1441–1487). The ninth king of Lan Na was the sixth of Samfangkaen's ten sons. Originally called Thao Lok, (Prince Six), he once ruled Mueang Phrao. After committing a crime, he was punished by being sent to rule south Mueang Yuam (Mae Sariang). In 1441, he seized the throne from his father with the assistance of Nai Samdekyoi, a Chiang Mai noble. Samfangkaen agreed to ceremonially hand over the *mueang*. But a younger brother, Thao Choi, challenged Tilokarat.[73] In 1442 he asked King Boromaracha II, the king of Ayutthaya, for troops to attack Chiang Mai. They were defeated.[74]

King Tilokarat spent about ten years (1441–1451) reestablishing the stability and security of Lan Na. He seized Nan and Phrae, which made Lan Na even more powerful. He waged war with Ayutthaya again during the reign of King Boromatrailokanat, for about twenty-four years. The war began in 1451 when Phraya Yuthisathian, the ruler of Phitsanulok, pledged allegiance to Tilokarat, and they joined to attack Pak Yom (southern Phichit).[75] In 1460 the ruler of Chaliang in the vicinity of Sukhothai province also swore allegiance to Tilokarat,[76] and a year later Phaya Chaliang and Tilokarat unsuccessfully attacked Phitsanulok and Kamphaeng Phet.[77]

Boromatrailokanat tried to halt Tilokarat's advance by going up to rule Phitsanulok personally, in 1463. He also tried to build a kind of friendship with Tilokarat. When he was ordained as a monk in 1465, he asked Tilokarat for the eight requisite items used by a Buddhist monk [a robe, a folded cloth worn over the shoulder for ceremonies that also serves as a blanket, a cloth worn as a sarong under the robe and also used for bathing, a waist cloth that serves as a belt, a razor, an alms bowl, needle and thread, and a water strainer.] Tilokarat did not oblige. Boromatrailokanat also tried to weaken Chiang Mai by sending a sorcerer to destroy an auspicious banyan tree located at Siphum Corner and telling King Tilokarat to build his palace on the site. People at that time believed a great deal in sorcery.[78]

In 1474 Boromatrailokanat took back Chaliang and the following year, Ayutthaya and Lan Na ended their protracted war.[79]

King Tilokarat's seizure of Nan and Phrae helped Lan Xang (Luang Prabang) which was seized by the Dai Viet empire based in Hanoi in 1480. The Lao king and two of his sons lost their lives. Tilokarat helped the youngest son, Phaya Saikhao, to safety. An enraged Emperor Le Thanh-Ton raised troops from Luang Prabang to attack Lan Na, via Nan. The Lan Na troops fought back successfully, forcing the Dai Viet to withdraw. Phaya Saikhao became the new king of Laos and pledged allegiance to Tilokarat. The emperor of China also sent gifts to honor Tilokarat,[80] whose power and influence had grown significantly.

35. Stupa at Chet Yot Temple, from the golden age of Lan Na. (NAT, c. 1897–1902)

36. Stupa of King Tilokarat, Chet Yot Temple. (NAT, c. 1897–1902)

To the west, Lan Na expanded into the Shan States, taking over Mueang Laikha, Mueang Nai, Sipho, Mueang Yong Huai, and other areas. Tilokarat swept the countryside of Greater Tai families and resettled 12,328 people in Lan Na.[81] In the north, Tilokarat attacked and seized Chiang Rung and Mueang Yong. The Chiang Mai Chronicle mentions the capture of Lue people from Ban Pung, Mueang Yong, and their resettlement in Lamphun.[82]

Tilokarat came to be considered a god-king, equal in status to the king of Ayutthaya.[83] The Chiang Mai Chronicle bestows more praise on him than on any other ruler, calling him "Phrachao" [king, lord, god] Tilokarat. Normally, the term *phrachao* was used for Buddha images, such as Phrachao Kaotue and Phrachao Lan Thong.

Buddhism flourished during the Tilokarat's reign. He supported monks of the new Langkawong, or Sihon school.[84] He invited Maha Methangkon, a Sihon monk from Lamphun, to spend the rains retreat at Ratchamonthian Temple and gave him the title of Phra Maha Sawami. The king himself was temporarily ordained at Pa Daeng Temple.[85] There was a large increase in ordinations into the Sihon school. The ordinary people were said to have been very devout during this period. The Sihon school emphasized the study of Pali and proper conduct, according to Buddhist rules. The Raman monks began to increase their study of scripture also. Tilokarat had high praise for monks who were well versed in the Tipitaka. Several, including Dhamma-thin, Ñanakitti Thera, and Sirimangkhala, were well known for their knowledge. The Eighth World Tipitaka Council met in Wat Maha Bodharama (in Thai, Wat Maha Photharam, also known as Wat Chet Yot) for one year, in 1477. This assembly of highly learned monks from the region worked to eliminate discrepancies in different versions of the Tipitaka. The Tipitaka revised by this council was used by the monks of several schools in Lan Na thereafter.[86]

Tilokarat constructed many temples, including Chet Yot, Ratchamonthian, Pa Tan, and Pa Daeng temples. He brought the Emerald Buddha, a revered image and palladium of the kingdom, from Phrathat Lampang Luang Temple to an enlarged Chedi Luang.[87] During this time, beliefs around the power of *phrathat*, sites containing holy relics believed to have great power, became important. Buddhism became an increasingly important cultural glue linking the people of the region. The writing of chronicles helped encourage mutual awareness between Chiang Mai and other *mueang* in the kingdom.

King Tilokarat died in 1487. Over the forty-six years of his rule, Lan Na had prospered in every respect.

Phaya Yot Chiang Rai (1487–1495). The tenth king of Lan Na, also known as Thao Yotmueang, was the son of Thao Bunrueang, the only son of King Tilokarat. Yot Chiang Rai ruled the kingdom for eight years but didn't make a name for himself. The Jinakalamali, which provides more information than other sources, mentions him in connection with arrangements for the cremation of King Tilokarat at Maha Photharam Temple, after which he had a big stupa built as the depository for the ashes. In 1492, he built Tapotharam

Temple and marked his territorial boundaries at Don Thaen Island, Chiang Saen. He handed the throne over to his son.[88]

Phaya Kaeo (1495–1525). The son of Yot Chiang Rai and Nang Pongnoi was called Chao Rat Ratchabut, the crown prince, by the Chiang Mai Chronicle. He was also called Phaya Kaeo Phutta Thipati Racha Chao, shortened to Phaya Kaeo.[89] The Yonok Chronicle calls him Phra Mueangkaeo. The Jinakalamali called him Tilokpanatdathirat,[90] and praised him as highly as King Tilokarat, saying he was a ruler who possessed kingly virtues and helped Buddhism flourish.[91]

Kaeo had designs on Ayutthaya. He began in 1507 by attacking Sukhothai, unsuccessfully. A series of battles ensued. On occasion Lan Na control extended as far as Kamphaeng Phet and Chaliang. In 1515, King Ramathibodi II (1491–1529) of Ayutthaya captured Lampang but could not keep it.[92] He hastily swept the area of people and took them away. Kaeo then gave up on war with Ayutthaya and turned towards developing his kingdom. Ayutthaya also refrained from attacking Lan Na.[93]

He made a number of infrastructural improvements. In 1516, he ordered the construction of a wall of brick around Lamphun in response to Ayutthaya's attack the previous year.[94] He later constructed Chiang Mai's rectangular inner wall of brick. In the process, he ordered the dismantling of King Tilokarat's palace over the city moat at Siphum Corner. In 1517, he ordered the construction of a large bridge across the Ping River at Sathan Luang Pier.[95] In 1520–1521, he rebuilt the capital's administrative office.

37. A Chiang Mai rampart, possibly the one located at Hua Lin Corner. (NAT, c. 1906)

Kaeo also supported Buddhism. The Jinakalamali mentions his religious activities in detail. Steles record that he constructed and restored temples and donated land and slaves to temples throughout the kingdom. He built Buppharam (Meng) Temple in 1496[96] and Sisuphan Temple in 1500;[97] gave donations to Hariphunchai Temple every year;[98] had Phrachao Kaotue, a large Buddha image, cast in 1516; built the consecrated assembly hall and the library for Buddhist scriptures at Chet Yot Temple; and restored Pa Daeng Temple to its former grandeur. Chet Yot and Pa Daeng temples received the most patronage.[99] Kaeo appointed a Sihon monk as supreme patriarch and sponsored royal candidates for ordination in the Sihon school.[100] Monks received support for the study of Pali and the Tipitaka. A number of monks produced impressive collections of Buddhist literature in Pali, and their fame spread as far as Lan Xang and Burma.[101]

The monk Bodhirangsi, for example, wrote *Camadevivamsa*, Queen Chamathewi's biography, and the *Sihingabuddharupanidana*, a history of the Sihing Buddha image. Ratanapañña Thera wrote the important *Jinakalamali*. Sirimangkhala wrote *Vessantara-dipani*, explaining the Vessantara-jataka scriptures; *Cakkavala-dipani*, a book on the universe and various things in the universe; *Sankhyapakasaka-tika*, a handbook explaining the Sankhyapaka scriptures; and *Mangala-dipani*, a book explaining the content of the Mangala-sutta.[102] Buddhañana Chao and Buddhabukama wrote the Mulasasana Chronicle, which emphasized the history of the Raman sect of the Suan Dok Temple.[103] Ñanavilasa Thera wrote *Sankhyapakasaka*, a book explaining the counting and calculating of time, the systems of weights and distances, the seasons, minted currency in Buddha's time, etc.

The *Paññasa-jataka*, a collection of fifty *jataka* tales written by unknown authors, was also probably written in Kaeo's reign. The *Paññasa-jataka* was the origin of many later works of Thai literature, including the *Samuddaghosa-jataka* (Samuthakhot Khamchan) and *Sudhana-jakata* (Manora). The Panyasachadok became very well known; it spread to Burma and was translated into Burmese during the reign of King Phothaphraya (Burmese: Badawpaya or Padon Min, r. 1782–1819). The Burmese called it "Zinme Paññasa-jataka," (Chiang Mai's Paññasa-jataka).[104]

The last two years of Kaeo's reign (1523–1525), saw a great loss of life among nobles and commoners and a great weakening of the Lan Na kingdom. In 1523, Kaeo sent twenty thousand troops to attack Keng Tung. They were soundly defeated and suffered great losses. Many high-ranking nobles and governors of *mueang* lost their lives, including Chaonakhon Khun Luang, Moen Si of Mueang Soeng, Moen Khampha of Chiang Rai, Moen Khwa of Chiang Rai, and Khamyotfa, the ruler of Mueang Nai. A great number of commoners also lost their lives.[105] Kaeo was furious and ordered the execution of the commander-in-chief, Saen Yiphingchai. The kingdom could ill afford such losses. It had already lost at least ten high-ranking nobles and a large number of commoners in the war with Ayutthaya.[106] The second-to-last year of Kaeo's reign brought a further blow in the form of a large flood that cost a large number of lives.[107] The loss of so many people in a short time affected the stability and security of the kingdom. Kaeo died in 1525, at the age of forty-four.[108]

GOVERNMENT

The Monarchy. Lan Na society was centered on the monarchy. The kings of the Mangrai dynasty were the supreme rulers. A distinctive characteristic of the monarchy was its institutional simplicity. Lan Na kings did not generally cultivate pretensions towards the status of *devarajas* or god-kings, as was the practice among the kings of Ayutthaya. They did not take the names of Hindu deities such as Vishnu or Indra. Rather, their names were characteristic of the local area, such as Kuena (one hundred million rice fields), Kaeo (precious gem), and Ket (head). The Lan Na monarchy did not create a royal language in the manner of the Siamese kings. They simply used a polite language that demonstrated their difference from commoners. This simplicity was probably due to their being the leaders of what were quite small communities, and ones that had not come under Khmer influence. Lao Chong, the legendary early ruler in the region, had the status of a community leader. The chronicles called him Puchao, or Royal Grandfather, and his wife was called Yachao, or Royal Grandmother. Commoners referred to rulers in kinship terms, showing that there was no great divide between them. Leaders were perhaps simply seen as fulfilling a useful function—someone had to take charge to establish an orderly society. The Singhanawatikuman Chronicle reflects this idea. It reports that after Wiang Yon turned into a swamp, the surviving population consulted with each other to choose a leader. They concluded that the appointment should be "given to a village chief from Buem village named Khun Lang, and he was placed over the people."[109] Thereafter, Khun Lang directed the people to build a new town, and he named it Wiang Phrueksa, or the town of consultation. This type of local leader was traditional in Thai Yuan society.[110]

The institution of the monarchy developed gradually, and out of traditional local customs. In early society, the term used for the supreme ruler was *lao*, "lord" or "powerful personality." Later, this was replaced with a new term, *khun*, and still later, kings were known as *thao*. Mangrai and his descendants were *phaya*. The exception, Tilokarat, assumed the title *phrachao*, or god-king, to give himself equal stature with the kings of Ayutthaya. The development of the different terms for the rulers reflected the rising power of the monarchy and the great expansion of the state. In the latter period of the Mangrai dynasty, the kings promoted a link between Buddhism and royalty and began to regard themselves as *devaraja*s, that is, kings known for their charismatic greatness. The idea of the *dhammaraja*, or righteous king, was also developed. The king supported Buddhism, considering himself its greatest patron, and promoted its spread. The most important temples in Chiang

Mai were all built by kings. Saenmueangma, Tilokarat, and Maeku were ordained as monks. The Tipitaka Council meeting in Tilokarat's reign earned the king great merit and was seen as a reflection of his moral authority and political power. It is clear that there was a strong belief in the *dhammaraja* concept from the time of Kuena (1353–1385), who was praised as *phaya thammikkarat* or righteous king. It was believed that the prosperity of the kingdom depended upon the proper conduct of the king. If the king lacked the ten kingly virtues, the nobles could cite his lack of proper conduct as a reason to eliminate him. Besides belief in the *dhammaraja*, there were also less clear beliefs in the great emperor. This idea emphasized the greatness of a king who ruled over other territories as a sort of world conqueror. This concept existed as an ideal of kingship. Some kings were seen to embody the principle. Mangrai, for example, brought many *mueang* under his control, built Lan Na to be great, and took the title "Phrachao Sirithamchakrapat-tilokarachathirat," Great Righteous Emperor of the World, King of Kings. In reality, the power and size of his kingdom were limited.

The legitimacy of the king was based on royal descent, which could be traced through either the paternal or maternal lines. The principle of royal descent was an ancient tradition that was seen as going back to Lao Chong of the Lao dynasty, of which Mangrai was said to be the twenty-fifth king. Nobles, no matter how capable or powerful, could not become king, and it was unthinkable for commoners to do so.

The coronation ceremony was considered essential to becoming a fully recognized king. It was understood that a coronated king held the throne until death. During the coronation ceremony, the king would circumambulate the city on foot before entering through Hua Wiang Gate. At the head of the procession were Lua people, with a dog. When inside the city, the king had to "bathe and wash his hair"; that is, there was a ceremony of purification and consecration in which water was poured over his head. After the coronation, the king was provided with the royal regalia, which were understood to have been handed down from the time of Lao Chong.

The Nobility. The nobles had an important status, and a vital role in assisting the king to govern. There were two groups. Those of royal blood controlled large *mueang*. Nobles without royal blood but who were descendants of aristocratic families could also hold prominent positions, including the *singmueang*, four high-ranking posts titled *phraya saenphingchai* (or *saenluang*), *phraya samlan*, *phraya chaban*, and *phraya dekchai*.

Over time, limitations in the system of royal succession resulted in the nobles gaining increased power. In practice, old Tai states, including Siam, did not clearly specify who should succeed to the throne. Lan Na had no clear system for succession.

From the reigns of Mangrai to Khamfu, the king would appoint a capable and appropriate son, not necessarily the eldest, as *uparat*, or second king. Mangrai appointed Chaisongkhram as ruler of Chiang Rai because he was a good soldier.

The tradition was to elevate sons who possessed "brains and merit."[111]

The nobles' power grew after the death of Khamfu. Nobles put Phayu on the throne, and the trend continued. Kuena was made king with support from the nobles. The role of the nobles increased even more during the reigns of Saenmueangma and Samfangkaen, who became king at fourteen and thirteen years old, respectively. The young Saenmueangma was elevated by the high-ranking noble Saen Phanong. The kings had to reward the nobles well for their support. Samfangkaen, on ascending the throne, rewarded his uncle by making him the ruler of Phayao. Tilokarat managed to control the rise of the nobles, but only temporarily. By the reign of Ketchetarat, the nobles were both powerful and divided. Different factions tried to ensure that their favored royal would gain the throne. The resulting political conflict helped lead to Lan Na's weakness and decline.

ADMINISTRATION

Lan Na was made up of an inner zone, an outer zone, and peripheral tributary states. The capital area, comprising Chiang Mai and its satellite Lamphun, was under the direct control of the king. The chronicles usually mention these two *mueang* together. For example, "Because Phraya and the people were meritorious, Mueang Hariphunchai and Mueang Chiang Mai were very happy."[112] Generally, the king sent high-ranking nobles to rule Lamphun. Sometimes he would rule it himself.

The capital zone was highly productive for rice agriculture. It was in a position to trade easily with *mueang* in the south and was the wealthiest area in the region.

Generally, though not without exception, nobles of royal blood ruled areas close to the capital zone. Chiang Rai was usually ruled by a king's son. More distant relatives ruled less important *mueang*, which enjoyed close to absolute administrative power over their own areas. One result of this was that in wartime the king had no power to raise troops from the farther *mueang*. Also, relationships between the capital and other *mueang* were usually on a personal basis, so when a throne changed hands, the relationships also changed and instability could be the result. Outlying *mueang* ruled by royal nobles could challenge the power of the capital.

Tributary states were on the periphery of the kingdom. The king would have lords "of different nationalities and tongues" rule their own *mueang* according to local custom, and succession could pass down through their family lines. The rulers had to accept the suzerainty of the capital by sending tribute,[113] and by swearing loyalty in the ceremonial act of drinking the "waters of allegiance."[114] This decentralized system evolved out of the old custom of "building villages and *mueang*."[115]

The tributary states comprised a number of groups. There were ten Shan or Tai Yai *mueang*, of which Mueang Nai was the most important.[116] Most of the people of this area belonged to the Shan ethnic group. The Chiang Tung group had a population of Khoen, a Tai people. The Sipsong Panna group had a Tai Lue population, and comprised Mueang Long, Mueang Phong, and Mueang Tun (during the reign of Tilokarat).[117] Mueang Yong was Tai Lue. The Chiang Mai Chronicle says that King Tilokarat took his armies to fight the Lue of Ban Pung and Mueang Yong, and defeated them.[118] The status of the tributary states depended on the policies and strength of the individual king. For example, under King Tilokarat Phrae and Nan were made tributary states. However, Kaeo (1495–1525) who had a policy of tight control over the two *mueang*, sent high-ranking nobles to rule in place of the existing ruling lords.[119] The tributary states were only under the control of the center when Chiang Mai was powerful. When the center was weak, the tributary states could become independent or side with other more powerful states, such as China, Burma, and Lan Xang. For example, Mueang Nai sent troops to loot Chiang Mai in the mid-1500s, during the reign of Queen Chiraphrapha.[120]

The kings also tried to consolidate political power by building up the lineage system. Mangrai, who taught that one way for a king to expand his power was through marriage, married Nang Paikho, the daughter of the ruler of Pegu. Mangrai also said that a king should have seven wives. "To be a great Phraya, he should have close relations with the rulers of the nearby areas, who could bestow seven of their daughters to serve the purpose."[121] The early Lan Na region had two prominent lineage groups, the Chiang Rai–Chiang Saen group in the Kok River valley and the Chiang Mai–Lamphun group in the upper Ping River valley. Mangrai combined the two, but only loosely. After his death there was instability. Chiang Mai was also not yet the center of the kingdom in all respects. Three successive kings, Chaisongkhram, Saenphu, and Khamfu, moved their residence to Chiang Rai or Chiang Saen, indicating that the northern *mueang* were quite important.

Rulers of tributary states were appointed by the king to govern the *mueang*, literally "to eat the *mueang*"; they were unpaid but had power over people and land. Trusted nobles were appointed to various administrative positions. When Saenphu ruled Chiang Saen, he appointed nobles to hear legal cases, supervise the rice granaries, and maintain the palace.[122] Chaisongkhram established the post of *chaban* and *dapruan* to supervise affairs in Chiang Dao. The local ruler also possessed the power to appoint *panna* administrators. A *panna*, literally a thousand rice fields, was an administrative district. Evidence from Tilokarat's reign indicates that the king only had the power to appoint nobles in charge of *panna* within the Chiang Mai zone, although this was a period when the kingdom was highly centralized.[123] The aim of the *panna* system was the distribution of land to commoners or *phrai*, people who were subject to corvée labor and/or payments in kind to the king and lords. The system was designed to make the best use of land, and to achieve an appropriate match between the people and land. The size of a *mueang* depended on the number of *panna* it had. A large *mueang* like Phayao had thirty-six *panna*. Chiang Rai had thirty-two. Fang had just five. The *panna* administrator was titled *moen*. In Chiang Mai Moen Kumkam controlled or "ate" Panna Kumkam; Moen Thawon controlled Panna Thawon; in Phayao Chao Moen Donplaen controlled Panna Donplaen.[124] Within each *panna*, nobles held different administrative positions, including Moen Na, Lam Na, Panna Lang, and Saen Na. Panna were subdivided into *pakna* (literally one hundred rice fields), each of which included a cluster of villages that formed a subdistrict. Villages were governed by a *kaeban*, or village elder. The Chiang Mai Chronicle says that Phaya Ngammueang established friendly relations with Mangrai by giving him one *pakna*, which consisted of five hundred families.[125] The administrator of a *pakna* was a *phan*, and he controlled nobles with the rank of *pak*, such as Pak Mongkhon, Pak Koeng, and Pak Thep.[126]

The *panna* had two obligations to the *mueang*. First it had to send tribute, such as forest products and wild animals, as well as rice for the royal granaries to be kept for wartime provisions. According to the Chiang Mai Chronicle, Mangrai's son set up many granaries in Chiang Dao, "every one of them filled with rice, as food reserves for his troops, retainers, and brave warriors."[127] Second, the *panna* supplied corvée labor. In peacetime, labor could be drafted for the construction of public works. Labor was even more important in wartime. "Once Chao Khun Khram heard his father's order, he hastily called for troops from every mueang. Chao Khun Khram raised 518,000 troops, while Chiang Rai added another 204,000 men from its *panna*."[128]

The ruling lord of the *mueang* controlled the commoners; "those who lived in any *mueang*, whether slaves or lowborn *phrai*, belonged to their particular ruler."[129] Rulers lived in the *mueang* they ruled. Rulers had the right to donate land and people to temples within their jurisdiction without asking permission from the king. During Tilokarat's reign, the ruler of Lampang donated four families to the Phrathat Lampang Luang Temple.[130] The ruler of Wang Nuea donated twenty families and land capable of producing three hundred *thang* (roughly two hundred bushels) of rice per year (probably about ten *rai* or four acres) to Chantara Aram Temple.[131] The Mangraisat specified that a commoner who wanted to donate land to a temple had to ask permission from the ruler. "If vacant lands unclaimed by private persons or the government were cleared of forest by someone and readied for domestic use, and then that person wanted to donate that piece of land to a temple, he had to ask the ruler of the *mueang* before making the donation."[132]

It was believed that labor was power. According to the Mangraisat, "Any *mueang* with a large number of commoners cannot be harmed by foreign enemies. No one will look down on a *mueang* full of people, which could be compared to a bundle of sticks that cannot be broken, whereas a single stick can be broken at any time."[133]

The Mangraisat stipulated that commoners had to work for the state for ten days and could work for themselves for the next ten days.[134] Thus commoners worked for the state and themselves equally, during the Mangrai dynasty. During the Chao Chet Ton dynasty, commoners were conscripted for one to four months per year. In peacetime, they worked on constructing palaces, digging moats, and building royal granaries and temples. In wartime, they became troops. It is estimated that large numbers ran away during wartime, despite heavy legal penalties, including execution.[135] It is possible that commoners were conscripted for the entire duration of any given war. This was a heavy burden because they then had no time to earn a living.

Rulers were very concerned to prevent people from running away. Commoners had no right to resettle elsewhere. The laws of the king of Nan, or the Lakkham kingdom, clearly forbade commoners to move. "As for those *mueang* in the outlying areas, the people of Mueang Len, Mueang Chiang Khaeng, Mueang Luang, Mueang Phu Kha, Mueang Chiang Lap, or Mueang La, were the people of that locality. If they wanted to move to other areas to earn a living or move into town, they were forbidden to do so. In whatever *mueang* they lived, they were bestowed on that *mueang*."[136]

One way for rulers to keep commoners was to desist from oppressing them too much and by helping them earn decent livelihoods.

Rulers sought to gain income from trade, and marketplaces were constructed in towns for this purpose. The rulers earned cash from marketplace rentals as well as from taxes. They appointed nobles to trade with merchants from other *mueang*.[137] However the majority of the rulers' income came from monopolies or "forbidden goods." Anyone concealing or possessing these goods would be punished.[138]

Monopolies included various kinds of lacquer, honey, elephant tusks, rhinoceros horns, catechu (a plant material used for tanning and brown dyes), sappanwood (which yields a red dye), and the horns and hides of deer and some other animals. The rulers would sell these goods, mostly received as tribute in kind from commoners, mainly to Ayutthaya.[139] The commoners who paid tribute in kind mainly lived quite far from towns or in communities where it wasn't convenient to have them serve the government six months a year.[140] Many were from ethnic groups living in distant forests and mountains. Their products were highly prized by the rulers.

There were regulations regarding payments. "As for those skilled with gold and silver, and drum smiths, they were to present [the fruits of their labors] to whoever ruled the domain."[141] *Mueang* that could collect large quantities of tribute became wealthy, because tribute in forest products yielded very high profits. Evidence suggests that the individual *mueang* had a large amount of freedom in relation to trade. Chiang Mai requested only that the rulers trade according to the rates stipulated by the kingdom, without forcing down prices or using counterfeit money.[142] Sometimes, however, the capital tried to extract economic wealth from the *mueang* to the center, often without much success. Sources suggest that the rulers sent tribute to the capital only sometimes, and depending upon the power of the central king. At the beginning of his reign, for example, King Tilokarat was not very secure. Moen Loknakhon asked for four blessings, the last being a request for the rulers to be exempt from sending tribute. The king had to accede to this.[143] By the end of his reign, Tilokarat was powerful enough to order rulers to send "a lot of tribute for the royal caskets."[144]

THE CAPITAL AND ITS CONTROL OVER THE *MUEANG*

The great political independence of the *mueang* was dangerous to the stability and security of the capital, which had to continuously work to force or encourage them to accept the center's superiority.

One way of doing this was in the appointment and transfer of rulers, which was in the absolute power of the king. Naturally, he appointed people he trusted to the positions. When a king distrusted or wished to punish a ruler, he could send him to rule a a distant *mueang*. Chaisongkhram sent his son Thao Namthuam, who had previously ruled Chiang Mai, to Chiang Tung, as punishment for dishonesty. Samfangkaen sent Thao Lok, who had previously ruled Mueang Phrao, to South Mueang Yuam.

However, the transfer strategy did not always work. Thao Lok later seized Chiang Mai from Samfangkaen. The king could also execute rulers for serious crimes. Tilokarat executed Moen Soengsamkhaihan, the ruler of Mueang Soeng, for sending information to the king's enemies.

Another method of control was through the dissemination of traditional beliefs and teachings through literature and other means. Such teachings emphasized traditional beliefs around justice and compassion and included ideas such as taking care of the people, not abusing commoners, and not oppressing the people during planting and harvesting seasons. "The *khun* who rule the *mueang* should not oppress the people when they work in the rice fields. Allow them to work the fields."[145] Rulers were also enjoined to judge lawsuits with prudence and fairness."The ruler who passes judgment against the law commits a great sin. He has to be calm and not in conflict with his people or he will be fined."[146] Such teachings were intended to encourage the rulers to establish tranquility and happiness. However, they also underscored the fact that the administration of each *mueang* was the absolute right of its ruler.

Traditional teachings were also aimed at encouraging the people to accept their birth status. In the words of Mangrai, "If you are not a royal, do not expect to be king. If you are not a noble, do not expect to be a government official."[147] A clear demonstration of this idea emerges during Saen Khan's seizure of the throne from Tilokarat. As Saen Khan awaited his coronation in the royal residence, Moen Loknakhon tried to pursuade him to leave, saying, "You are not royal. . . You cannot stay here—you shouldn't."[148] Buddhist principles were also used to establish cohesiveness and control. This trend began with Phaya Kuena, who built Chiang Mai as a center of Raman Buddhism. Saenmueangma built the Chedi Luang Temple to be the largest stupa in the kingdom, reflecting the capital's superiority.

It is believed that the king began to play a religious role in the outer *mueang* in the reign of Samfangkaen, who donated a large piece of land to the Suwan Maha Wihan Temple in Phayao, probably to affirm his political rights.[149] Tilokarat frequently listened to sermons and donated to temples in other *mueang*. Such practices built closer relations between the king and the lesser rulers and also facilitated inspections of the *mueang*.

Kaeo followed the trend by traveling frequently to other *mueang* to make merit. He also stipulated that rulers could donate people to temples only after receiving permission from the king.[150] In the past, this permission had not been necessary. Kaeo donated labor, land, and benefits to many temples throughout the kingdom. This helped to demonstrate his righteousness, and to reduce the power of the rulers.

Depending on how powerful it was at the time, the capital also asserted its influence over the *mueang* by requiring them to send tribute and to conscript people in wartime . . . Only kings with great political power were able to mobilize manpower throughout the kingdom. When Mangrai was at war with Phaya Yiba and Phaya Boek, he was able to draft troops from Chiang Rai, Fang, Mueang Soeng, and Mueang Chiang Khong. When Samfangkaen was at war with the Ho, he conscripted troops from Chiang Saen, Fang, Chiang Rai, Chiang Khong, and Phayao. But during the reign of Queen Chiraprapha, Chiang Mai was completely unable to draft troops from neighboring *mueang*. The main reason for this was the failure of the capital to build a kingdom-wide bureaucracy in place of the system of nobles.[151] Of all the old Thai states, only Ayutthaya managed to do this.[152]

THE LAN NA ECONOMY

Lan Na's economy, which was based on agriculture, expanded gradually, especially during the period of prosperity starting in Kuena's reign. Trade networks were extensive. The Chiang Mai Chronicle says that the Chiang Mai merchants went as far as Pagan to trade.[153] The economy prospered under Tilokarat, who swept up large numbers of people and settled them in the kingdom. Extensive dependencies and tributaries were acquired. The construction of numerous and elaborate temples was a sign of growth and wealth.

Rice production was strong in the Chiang Mai–Lamphun and Chiang Rai basins. Lampang, Phrae, and Nan were sometimes unable to produce sufficient rice to feed their populations. However, Lan Na as a whole often had surpluses.

There is evidence of a river port for unmilled rice in the Chiang Saen area. There is also evidence that Lan Na once sent tribute of 9,000 *khan* or 540,000 kilograms of rice to the Ho. Still, rice production was far inferior to that in Ayutthaya, which had more expansive plains. Lan Na basically had a self-sufficient economy. Most people were farmers, who lived in scattered village communities. Production was for household consumption, not the market. Farmers grew rice, wove cloth, made tools and utensils, and gathered edible plants and forest products. Villages would help in the construction of irrigation canals. Every household that used the communal irrigation system was responsible for working on it. The impact of the state was minimal at village level. It was responsible for the very few large-scale irrigation systems that were built. It had the duty to pass laws to provide for the general peace of society. But local leaders played a more important role. They were the first to reap benefits from commoners. In theory, the king controlled the basic necessities of the economy, land, and labor under the *sakdina* system, which granted control of land and labor proportionate to one's status. In theory, the king owned all the land in the kingdom. In practice, it was impossible for the king to use all the land himself. Therefore, he donated some land to monasteries and some to nobles, which was called *nakhum kan mueang*, property granted according to one's political standing. The king possibly collected a rental fee or a share of the crop. Nobles were forbidden to retain *nakhum kan mueang* land for themselves, or to donate it to the temples or divide it and bequeath it to their relatives. When a noble died, the land had to be returned to the king.[154] If a noble had received *nakhum kan mueang* land but did not use it or allow other people to do so, it reverted to the state.

The king held land for himself, called the "king's private land," until the period of the Chao Chet Ton dynasty. The usually fertile and extensive royal fields were worked by conscripted commoners.[156] The *panna* system allocated appropriate numbers of commoners to land areas. Large *panna* would have a large population, to ensure appropriate benefits were reaped from the land. The Phayao Chronicle, Si Bunrueang Temple version, says that during Khun Chomtham's reign Phayao had a population of 180,000 and was divided into thirty-six *panna*. Five people were considered equivalent to one *na*, or ricefield. Individuals who worked the fields would receive 2.5 *thang* of rice seed (1 *thang* = about 20 liters or about 2.5 pecks).

> The ruler ordered a count of all the people of Mueang Pukamyao, and the nobles sent messengers with orders to list all the people in every village. Altogether there was a total of 180,000 people.
>
> Afterwards, the ruler divided the land into 36 *panna*, and every five persons was entitled to one *na* and each individual who worked the ricefield got ample rice.[156]

The king had the right to take land back at any time. He could punish a person by "removing the fields" from him. The poem "Phaya Kuena's Laws"

38. Rice threshing. (PUA, c. 1882–1927)

39. Rice is poured from containers onto a mat to separate the good grain from the bad with bamboo fans. (PUA, c. 1882–1927)

40. Rice is separated from the straw and stored in barns. (PUA, c. 1882–1927)

41. Children husking and winnowing rice. (PUA, c. 1882–1927)

42. Children helping to husk rice. (PUA, c. 1882–1927)

describes an astrologer's being punished by having all his land confiscated.[157] The Mangraisat prescribed the execution of troops who deserted and "the seizure of their families and their entire properties."[158] Land would also be seized if it had been abandoned or hadn't been put to use. The state wanted land to be utilized to its fullest, in order to collect tribute from the products. Sometimes the king seized land on the sole grounds that all lands belonged to him.[159] The Samuttarat law text reflected the king's desire to collect tribute and warned commoners not to be lax but to be diligent in working the rice fields.

> The king said, "The land where you plant rice is mine. You should work the field for me with a will. The tribute from that ricefield should be divided into five parts; three parts are the fee for my exhausting work of governing the kingdom."[160]

Although commoners lacked ownership rights to land, custom guaranteed certain rights. Lan Na laws stipulated that land could be passed on to descendants.[161] Commoners who cleared the forest for farming would be free from paying tribute for three years "in order to help commoners who make an effort to build the *mueang* be content. They are good citizens (the dust of the *mueang*)."[162] During the planting season, the nobles were told to free them to work the fields without delay. "Nobles who rule the *mueang* should not oppress the commoners. When it is the time for planting, they should allow commoners to work their fields without holding them back."[163]

Manpower, as stated, was indispensable. Wars were waged to "empty the families," that is, to capture more labor. Lan Na had a small labor force, judging from the various conscription rates for wars during the Mangrai dynasty. According to the Chiang Mai Chronicle, there were 725,000 troops at the time of Mangrai[164] while during the reign of Samfangkaen, who raised troops to fight the Ho in a large war, there were 350,000.[165] The figures suggest that the population during the kingdom era was at most one million people. The king wished to have accurate figures in order to be able to assess the strength of the kingdom. A census was required. The Samuttarat law text mentions that the king ordered Lua villages to report the number of deaths within each village every four years, which they couldn't recall. Thereafter, the Lua used the method of putting a wooden marker over individual graves.[166] The commoners' limited numbers made them highly valuable. In the Apparihaniya-dham Chet (the seven Dhamma on conditions of welfare), a set of guidelines for the administration of the kingdom, item number three states that the collection of tribute, fees, and excises and the exaction of penalties has to be fair. It was forbidden to collect tribute, fees, and excises that had not traditionally been collected, because that would cause trouble for the people.[167] If commoners committed crimes, it was appropriate to allow some leniency by stipulating that the first infraction should be treated as a lesson; the second should exact a price; and the third should still be treated with leniency. "If the fine was ten thousand, it should be lowered to one thousand; if it was one thousand, the fine should be lowered to one hundred."[168]

The Mangraisat recognized the high value of commoners. Originally, it stipulated that deserters should be executed. Later, the law was amended to tattoo the deserter's foreheads and release them.[169] There were no known peasant revolts in Lan Na during the Mangrai dynasty.

Slaves were used in household work and for agriculture.[170] They were also traded. Rich men with more slaves than they needed sometimes allowed their slaves to hire out and keep a share of the income. Figures indicate that the king owned approximately 1,500 slaves; the *uparat*, 1000; and Chao Ubonwana, 800.[171] The system of *phrai* and slaves produced no significant economic or handicraft innovations or technological development.

Trade between states supplemented the subsistence economy and was the main source of wealth. Chiang Mai depended on the Ping River as a trade

43. Chao Ubonwanna, the daughter of King Kawilorot. She played a very important role in trade. (NAT, c. 1882)

44. Right. A beautifully glazed jar from Wiang Ka Long kiln, an example of Lan Na art during Lan Na's golden age, located at Si Khomkham Temple. Lan Na pottery was of high quality and in great demand. Phaya Kuena was ordered to send pottery as tribute to the Ho in the fourteenth century. High-quality pottery was probably produced in the fourteenth century, not during the reign of King Tilokarat as originally believed. (SS, 1986)

Left. Glazed jar from Phayao kiln. In response to local demand, kilns sprung up in several locations in Lan Na. (SS, 1986)

45. Watermills in the Ping River, with scorpion-tail boats. (NAT, c. 1914)

46. Lan Na *phrai*s resting on a journey. (NAT, 1926)

47. Venders in front of Phra Singh Temple. The foreground of Phra Singh Temple or Lichiangphra Temple (*li* means market; *chiangphra* is the name of the community) used to be a marketplace that extended along the roadside to Klang Wiang, the center of town. (PUA, c. 1926–1932)

route to southern *mueang*. The poem "Mangthra Fought Chiang Mai" describes Mueang Hot on the Ping as a busy entrepot, visited by traders from Ayutthaya. There was also an important overland trade route from Martaban in the south, via Chiang Mai, to as far north as Dali in Yunnan.

Chiang Saen was on the route connecting Chiang Mai with *mueang* in the far north, including the Shan *mueang*, Chiang Tung, Sipsong Panna, Yunnan, Nan, and Luang Prabang. Customs posts were set up to check travelers and traders on this route. The Chiang Mai Chronicle mentions that Khamfu had a conflict with Phaya Nan, and he closed all markets so that the people "were unable to buy or sell food."[172]

Chiang Mai was the key trading center. Traders of different ethnic groups, such as Burmese, Shan, and Ho, conducted business at "the city of twelve languages." The poem "Phaya Kuena's Laws" says Chiang Mai had three markets, the Hua Wiang Market at Hua Wiang Gate, the Klang Wiang Market, a big market within the city walls, and the Chiang Ruak Market. These sold agricultural products from surrounding villages, such as rice, chilies, betel leaves, betelnut, cotton, and basketry.[173] Goods from ports in the south were fabrics and mirrors.[174] Weaving existed side by side with the purchase of woven material.[175] Skilled artisans living in urban society included goldsmiths, tanners, makers of gold leaf, tailors,[176] and launderers.[177] Pottery was a note-worthy local craft, produced in large quantities in locations such as the Wiang Kalong and Phan kilns in Chiang Rai; the San Kamphaeng and San Sai kilns in Chiang Mai; the Wang Nuea kilns in Lampang; and the Huay Mae Tam kilns in Phayao. Although some locations, such as Wiang Kalong, produced high quality products, it appears that they were used only locally. Transportation limitations were probably an important obstacle to exports.

The artisans who produced handicrafts and small industry products were privileged because of their special skills and limited numbers. Talented artisans were patronized by the nobles. They were linked with the *phrai* system and were not free laborers. Demand for their products was limited because local people had little purchasing power. Thus they lacked opportunities to develop their skills.

The king's interest in valuable forest products also played a part in the local trade system. In theory, the king was the sole owner of the natural resources and products of the forest. In practice, however, the rulers of the different *mueang*, who were "royal servants," (*kha luang*) also collected tribute of forest products. There is abundant evidence for the punishment of people who stole forest products.[178]

No evidence has been found for a government organization in charge of Lan Na's forest products. (Ayutthaya had the royal warehouse for this purpose). However, there is evidence for a noble who supervised the honey tribute, entitled "Saen Namphueng" [literally, 100,000 honey]. Honey was an important export item to Ayutthaya. Other goods were also probably under the supervision of nobles. Sources describe nobles with titles such as Moen

Lam, Moen Luang, and Moen Khaek. They served as inspectors and granted permission to traders from other *mueang* to buy goods (such as elephants, horses, slaves, cattle, buffalo, boats, and gold). Sellers had to bring goods in for inspection as well as to determine a fair price for the goods.[179] It is possible that commissioners were sent to deal with the sale of forest products for the state. The poem "Mangthra Fought Chiang Mai" tells of Saen Namphueng, the honey official, making a journey to Ayutthaya, possibly to negotiate trade.[180] Lan Na's inland location meant its main trade role was sending forest products to Ayutthaya and to provincial towns of the Mon. The Lan Na products did not need any sophisticated processing, nor did they need investment. There were few business risks attached to them because the market was not a free one. The nobles in charge of the trade were not true business people.

RELATIONS WITH NEIGHBORING STATES

The Tai states located north of Lan Na proper were mainly mountainous communities that practiced subsistence agriculture. Their locations and the topography limited opportunities for development. Important *mueang* included Chiang Tung, Mueang Nai, and Mueang Yong, now in Burma; Chiang Rung in Sipsong Panna in China; and Luang Prabang in Laos. There were numerous other small *mueang* squeezed into various valleys. To the south of Lan Na were the Sukhothai and Ayutthaya kingdoms.

RELATIONS WITH TAI STATES TO THE NORTH

The Tai states in the northern region were in the peripheral area of three larger states, Burma, China, and Lan Na. They were constantly at the mercy of their expansionist neighbors.

Relationships between the more powerful Lan Na and the northern Tai states were generally good. There were lineage ties with Chiang Tung, Mueang Nai, Chiang Rung, and Luang Prabang. There were shared religious beliefs and shared traditions of arts and culture. The people of the northern Tai states included the Tai Lue, who lived as far north as Sipsong Panna, the Shan, and Tai Lao (in Luang Prabang). All these groups shared a similar culture, with variations only in detail. The Tai Lue culture was the closest to that of the Thai Yuan in the areas of art, language, handicrafts, livelihood, and beliefs. When Lan Na was short of manpower, it often set out to forcibly relocate Tai Lue families to Lan Na.

Relations with the Tai states predated the founding of Lan Na. The folk hero Phaya Chuang, for example, was revered as a heroic king by the people of Ngoen Yang, Phayao, Lan Xang, and Sipsong Panna. Phaya Chuang reputedly built extensive ties between these areas. After his death they split further apart.

Relations with Chiang Rung. Chiang Rung and Ngoen Yang Chiang Saen were both located on the banks of the Mekong River, which helped build links between them, as well as with Luang Prabang and Vientiane. It is believed that these *mueang* arose around the eleventh to twelfth centuries. Chiang Tung and Mueng Yong located further inland on tributaries of the Mekong were founded in the late thirteenth century.

Chiang Rung was located close to China, which made it vulnerable to invasion. The Yuan (Mongol) dynasty seized Nanchao in 1253 and Chiang Rung in the late thirteenth century. Mangrai was engaged in prolonged wars with Mongol troops until the end of his reign.[181]

After Mangrai's death Lan Na began to send tribute to China. Gradually, there was a decline in the close relationship between Chiang Mai and Chiang Rung. However, the lineage tie continued. The Tilokachuthathewi says that Saenmueangma's wife was a Sipsong Panna noble. She gave birth to Samfangkaen while returning to Panna Fangkaen from Sipsong Panna (hence the "*fangkaen*" in his name).[182] Chiang Mai spread both the Raman and Sihon Buddhist sects to Chiang Rung. The Lue people there called the two schools Phai Pa and Phai Suan, or the Pa (forest) school and the Suan (garden) school.[184] Buddhist literature like Panyasachadok stories also spread. Tai Lue script developed from Lan Na Tham script.

Relations with Keng Tung. Mangrai founded Chiang Tung in 1267.[184] It was built as a northern fortress and was important because of the Mongol threat in the region. It was also on an important trade route between Yunnan and Lan Na and had been a Lua community. Mangrai "seized Mueang Thammila as his own."[185] He then appointed Namthuam, his nephew, as ruler. The descendants of the Mangrai dynasty continued to rule Chiang Tung until the aristocratic system was ended by the military government of Burma in the mid to late twentieth century. As a tributary state, Chiang Tung had self-government. The chronicles called this type of *mueang* "*lukban hang mueang*," or "people far from the state." Relations between Chiang Tung and Chiang Mai during the Mangrai dynasty can be divided into two periods. In the first period, the relationship was very close because the rulers were often direct descendants of the Chiang Mai kings. Chaisongkhram sent his son Chao Namnan to rule the territory and Phayu sent his son Chao Chetphantu. The relations between Chiang Tung and Chiang Mai in each period depended a great deal upon personalities and personal ties. For example, Chao Namnan cooperated with Khun Toengyokkhamsaen, the ruler of Mueang Nai, to attack Chiang Mai during the reign of Saenphu. Chao Namnan was later executed for this. In the reign of Phayu, the king presented his son Chao Chetphantu with a lot of possessions, slaves, courtiers, etc., and monks in order to establish stability in the area. This approach was successful and his descendants continued to rule Chiang Tung.

The second period covered from the reigns of Kuena to Kaeo, when the Raman and Sihon sects spread to Chiang Tung. During King Tilokarat's reign temples built in Chiang Tung included the Pa Daeng Keng Tung Temple, which adopted the Buddhist teachings of Pa Daeng Temple in Chiang Mai; and Yang Kuang Temple, or the Yang Kuang school, which followed the teachings of Suan Dok Temple. Conflict between monks of the Raman and Sihon sects in Chiang Mai also affected the monks in Chiang Tung. The Lan Na Tham script also spread to Chiang Tung, along with the similar Buddhist Tai Khoen script. Lan Na literature was propagated widely in Chiang Tung.

Relations with Mueang Yong. Mueang Yong is the easternmost of the Shan States, 157 kilometers northeast of Mae Sai district, next to Chiang Tung.[186] Travel to both areas started at Mae Sai and carried on to Mueang Ko, Mueang Len, and Mueang Phayak, where the route forks. One route led to Chiang Tung, Mueang La, Talua, and Chiang Rung. The other led to Mueang Yong, Mueang Yu, Mueang Luai, Mueang Luang, and then Chiang Rung. Mueang Yong is situated in a valley surrounded by mountains. To the north is Pangnao Mountain, 8,329 feet high, the highest peak in Chiang Tung province.[187] The Yong River valley is relatively wide. The area has always had a largely self-sufficient subsistence economy.

The history of the Yong area begins with the Lua, the indigenous people. The Yong Chronicle describes scattered settlements of Lua people around the plain. Seven Lua villages formed a community with Thao Wiru as its leader.[189]

The Yong Chronicle says that Chao Sunantha, a Thai Lue prince from Chiang Rung, suppressed the Lua and installed himself as ruler. There is no evidence to date the founding of the territory, but it was possibly contemporaneous with Chiang Tung in the late thirteenth century, because the chronicle discusses the Lua leader, Thao Wiru, waging war on Chiang Tung. Chao Sunantha invited the rulers of Chiang Tung, Chiang Rung, and Chiang Saen to attend his coronation ceremony. It is noteworthy that descriptions of the early history of the area in the Yong Chronicle do not mention Chiang Mai. Relations with Chiang Rai began during the reigns of King Samfangkaen and King Tilokarat.

Chao Sunantha is described as having killed the Lua leader and a large number of his *phrai*. Some of the defeated Lua fled to Lan Xang, others adopted Tai Lue culture, and some fled to the mountains. Today Lua and other hilltribe people regularly come to trade with the townspeople. They still barter and practice other aspects of their ancient culture. (On a visit to Mueang Yong, the author met Lua people who had adopted the Tai Lue style of dress. The Yong people themselves were wearing fashionable clothing and floral print tube skirts of factory-made fabric.)

Chao Sunantha ruled Mueang Yong independently, while keeping close contact with Chiang Rung through lineage relations, politics, ethnicity, culture, and Buddhism. According to the Yong Chronicle, "Our Lord Buddha Gotama came to help the world and went on alms rounds for food, walking from Mueang Witheharat to Mueang Mahiyangkha."[189]

The chronicle says that Chao Sunantha and his five descendants ruled

48. Phrathat Chomyong, the center of the Yong people's faith. (Phrathat Chomyong Temple publication, c. 1989)

49. Present-day Mueang Yong, at the main road approaching Hua Khuang Temple. (SO, 1993)

until the family line came to an end after a number of members entered the monkhood. Mueang Yong did not have a real ruler for sixty-five or sixty-seven years,[190] probably as a result of political turmoil. Mueang Yong was small, hemmed in, and on an invasion route for Ho forces traveling south from Yunnan.

King Samfangkaen and King Tilokarat made Yong and Chiang Rung into dependencies of Lan Na.[191] The Yong Chronicle describes events over a period of over a hundred years, during which "King Asoka" defeated the Ho, Kaeo, and Yong. This period coincides with King Tilokarat's expansions, described in great detail in the Chiang Mai Chronicle. "King Asoka" undoubtedly refers to King Tilokarat. After seizing the area, Tilokarat supported Buddhism in Yong and it flourished. Phrathat Chom Yong, the center of devotion for the Yong people, was restored and its wihan, the Buddha image hall, was constructed. The *mueang* and its people were donated to the temple. Donated people were exempt from payment of tribute or taxes. Even today, some Kom village people continue to be "servants of the Phrathat" and carry water up the mountain as an offering to the Phrathat, showing the continued survival of old beliefs.

King Tilokarat allowed self-government in Yong, but the rulers had to pay homage to the king once a year by sending dancers to perform in a ceremony of veneration. The Yong Chronicle says that the area had four rulers under Chiang Mai, including Thao Ma and from Phraya Anurut until Phra Inthawichai.[192]

From about the mid-sixteenth century, Yong was mainly under Burma. But when Burma was weak, others would step in. Thus Yong was ruled briefly, at various times, by Chiang Rung, Chiang Khaeng, and Chiang Mai. It was much troubled by wars, particularly in the mid-eighteenth century.

When King Kawila revived Chiang Mai, he swept up the people from Yong and nearby areas and forcibly resettled them in Lamphun, which he rebuilt in 1805. There were very few people left in Mueang Yong. This made Chao Mahakhanan, a descendant of the Chiang Tung ruling family, and Chao Phutthawongsa of Yong, very dissatisfied. The two nobles turned toward Burma. Chao Phutthawongsa gathered 150 households to rebuild Yong.

Relations with Mueang Nai. There has been little study thus far of Mueang Nai and the Shan (Tai Yai) people by Thai academics, due to the difficulties in visiting the area, lack of sources in the Tai language, political difficulties between Thailand and Burma, and lack of effort. Mueang Nai is located on the west bank of the Salween River. There are a number of other small *mueang* in this area, such as Mueang Pan, Mueang Chiang Thong, and Mueang Yong Huai. Mueang Nai was founded for strategic reasons and as part of an expansionist policy to build new settlements. Mangrai sent his son Khrua to rule the area. The Shan people regarded Khrua as their lord or *nai* and named the new town Mueang Nai.[193] When Lan Na was powerful, it was able to assert its influence over the area. For example, Tilokarat sent troops to recapture Muang Nai and then other small *mueang*. He forcibly took and resettled 12,328 men and women and ordered the ruler, Ngoenpongfa, to send him tribute. During Kaeo's reign, the ruler of Chiang Tung, Phaya Kai, and the ruler of Mueang Nai swore allegiance to Chiang Mai and presented Kaeo with a total of 23,220 Shan people, 38 elephants, and 250 horses to serve him. Mueang Nai was beyond traditional Lan Na territory and it was normally allowed its freedom, as long as it did not pose a threat. The possibility of a threat was real. Khrua, for example, attacked Chiang Mai with troops from Mueang Nai. Later, Khrua's son, Khun Toeng-yokkhamsaen, and Chao Namnan agreed to jointly attack Chiang Mai on two fronts. Toeng-yokkhamsaen successfully attacked Fang and failed to take Chiang Rai,[194] while Namnan attacked Mueang Phayao, Mueang Rai, and Chiang Saen. Later still, when Chiang Mai was weak during the reign of Queen Chiraprapha, Mueang Nai and Mueang Yong Huai besieged the city for a month and fifteen days, but were unable to take it.[195]

Relations with Luang Prabang. Luang Prabang, the center of the Lan Xang kingdom, had many other names in the past, including Nakhon Chiangdong-chiangthong, Chiang Tong, Mueang Chawa, Mueang Sao, and Sisatana-khanahu. The Nan Chronicle indicates that Luang Prabang and Mueang Nan were once closely linked and also shared relations with Sukhothai.

50. River transport between Chiang Mai and Bangkok. (NAT, c. 1901–1913)

Relations between Chiang Mai and Luang Prabang grew after Nan was incorporated into the Lan Na kingdom. Lan Na helped support Luang Prabang during the reign of Tilokarat, when the Lao kingdom was threatened by the Vietnamese. Dai Viet troops destroyed Luang Prabang in 1480, causing the death of the king and two of his sons. Phaya Saikhao, the surviving son, sought protection from Tilokarat, who sent troops to take him to safety in Chiang Khan. The Dai Viet then attacked Lan Na, but they were repulsed and destroyed. Tilokarat then appointed Saikhao as Phaya Lan Xang. Close relations between the two territories continued through the reign of Sethathirat. During the reign of King Phothisalarat of Lan Xang (1520–1548), relations further developed when the king's daughter married Ketchettharat, the king of Lan Na. Lan Na sent the Tipitaka and a group of monks from Chiang Mai to the Lan Xang kingdom, resulting in the similarity of literature in both kingdoms.[196] The Khosarat legal code of Lan Xang was written during the reign of Phothisarat and was also used in Lan Na.

At one point Sethathirat, the son of Phothisarat, governed both kingdoms. He was king of Lan Na in 1546–1547 and king of Lan Xang in 1548–1571, after the death of his father. During his reign very close cultural relations developed between the two kingdoms. Sethathirat was able to keep Lan Xang independent after Lan Na fell to the Burmese. He led an alliance of Lan Na rulers against the invaders.

RELATIONS WITH THE SOUTHERN THAI STATES

The three Thai states, Lan Na, Sukhothai, and Ayutthaya, were all established in the late thirteenth or early fourteenth century. Lan Na had a relatively competitive relationship with its southern neighbors.

Sukhothai grew quickly during the reign of King Ramkhamhaeng, but, sandwiched between Lan Na and Ayutthaya, was soon vulnerable.

Relations between Lan Na and Sukhothai began smoothly. Mangrai and Ramkhamhaeng were friends. After their deaths, the relations became more problematic.

Ayutthaya's first expansion into Sukhothai began when King Ramathibodi I (U-thong, 1350–1369), seized the Sukhothai capital, Phitsanulok. The Sukhothai king, Phaya Thammaracha I, or Phaya Lithai (1368–1374), sent tribute to the Ayutthaya leader and simply asked for the return of the seized town. Lithai tried to survive by building stability in the region, especially through the support of Buddhism. In 1369 the leading Sukhothai monk, Sumana Thera, was invited by the Lan Na king to help spread the Raman school of Buddhism. Phaya Lithai was seen as a great *dhammaraja*, or righteous king, throughout the region. Lithai also cultivated lineage relations by bestowing his daughter on the king of Ayutthaya.

Sukhothai's relations with Lan Na were amicable in the early reign of Saenmueangma (1385–1401) of Lan Na. In 1378 Ayutthaya attacked

Kamphaeng Phet in Sukhothai and in 1386 it attacked Lampang in Lan Na. Initially, Saenmueangma helped Sukhothai to drive out the attackers, but eventually the two allies fell out. Sukhothai was increasingly pushed towards tributary status during the reign of Ayutthaya's King Intharacha I (1409–1424). After the death of King Mahathammaracha IV, Sukhothai was entirely incorporated into Ayutthaya.

King Tilokarat (1441–1487) made war on Ayutthaya over a long period, for two reasons. To close off opportunities for Ayutthaya to expand north, he took Phrae and Nan, formerly under Sukhothai's sphere of influence. Tilokarat was motivated too by a pledge of support in 1451 from the former ruler of Phitsanulok, who was unhappy with Ayutthaya. And in 1460, the ruler of Chaliang also pledged support to the Lan Na leader. Tilokarat took the opportunity to attack Phitsanulok and Kamphaeng Phet.This caused such turmoil for Ayutthaya that King Boromatrailokanat himself had to come to Phitsanulok. A long war between the two kingdoms lasted for twenty-five years, ending in 1475, a year after King Boromatrailokanat regained Chaliang. Both sides had been much weakened and battered.

During Kaeo's reign, between 1510 and 1515, Lan Na troops made another series of attacks on the southerners, sweeping the countryside of a number of people from Sukhothai, Chaliang, and Kamphaeng Phet. Ayutthaya retaliated and captured Lampang. Lan Na was on the defensive from this point onwards.

THE DECLINE AND FALL OF THE LAN NA KINGDOM

The decline of the old Lan Na kingdom began after Phaya Kaeo died in 1525 and culminated when the kingdom fell to the Burmese in 1558. Kings during this period ruled only briefly, with each reign ending in execution, removal, or abdication. Both internal and external factors had contributed to the decline. Lan Na had its own economic and political problems, and its expansionist neighbors were keen to move in.

Phaya Ketchettharat (1525–1538) was also called Phaya Ket or Phaya Mueangketklao or Phaya Ai. After the death of Kaeo, the nobles invited Ket to rule Lan Na. Ket had previously ruled Mueang Noi and had no real political base in Chiang Mai, which made him vulnerable. A fire in the palace in 1530 was believed to have been caused by arson. In 1535, nobles headed by Moen Soisamlan, the ruler of Lampang, revolted. Moen Soisamlan was then captured and executed. In 1538, nobles removed the king and sent him back to Mueang Noi. They invited his son, Thao Chai, to rule (1538–1543) in his place, but he was assassinated. The nobles invited Ket to return to rule for a second time (1543–1545), and after just two years he too was assassinated.

The nobles in Chiang Mai and other *mueang* again scrambled for influence. Saen Khrao, the leader of the Chiang Mai faction, approached the ruler of

Chiang Tung and invited him to rule, but the offer was refused. He next invited the ruler of Mueang Nai, but Saen Khrao was assassinated before he arrived. Another group of nobles from *mueang* such as Lampang, Chiang Rai, Chiang Saen, and Mueang Phan wanted to invite Sethathirat from Lan Xang to be king. Queen Chiraprapha was invited to rule in the interim (1545–1546) before Sethathirat's arrival.

Phra Sethathirat (1546–1547), or Phaya Upayo, was the son of King Phothisan of Lan Xang (1520–1547) and Queen Yotkhamthip, the daughter of Ket. When he became king he promoted those nobles who had supported him, yet he had no real power base of his own. The nobles were able to take increased control. Sethathirat ruled for two years, returning to Lan Xang after the death of his father. Lan Na was then without a king between 1548 and 1551, during which time a civil war broke out. According to the Chiang Mai Chronicle, there was great chaos.[197]

Thao Maeku (1551–1564), or Phaya Mekuti or Chao Khanan Maeku, was the seventeenth king of Lan Na and the last king of the Mangrai dynasty. The former ruler of Mueang Nai, he was invited to rule in Chiang Mai by nobles. He sought to remedy the lack of a power base by bringing a group of nobles close to him from Mueang Nai, but this made the Chiang Mai power brokers unhappy. Conflict among the nobles caused a steep decline.[198] Lan Na fell to Burma.

THE NOBLES

The increasing power of the nobles had created severe problems. First, they were so powerful that they were able to appoint kings, and even to remove or assassinate them. The monarchy had fallen very low. Although the nobles could dictate who the kings were to be, they dared not take the throne themselves because they lacked the legitimacy of royal descent. They preferred to have figurehead kings. Second, the nobles were divided into two groups: those in the capital were in conflict with those in the outlying areas. The political problems had serious negative effects on the region's economic situation. The collection of tribute for the capital was dramatically reduced. A *sa* paper manuscript that concentrates on history and ancient laws belonging to the Pa Lan Temple in Chiang Mai contains the following passage in relation to the economic turmoil of the time:

> There are three important things that the nobles should not destroy . . . Do not debase the monies. If the monies are worth less than a hundred, do not make it one hundred. These things are inauspicious and will destroy the people and destroy the kingdom. For example, Phra Mueangkaeo raised the value of money worth 98 cowrie units to 100; Thao Ai Klao, from 80 to 100; Thao Chai, from 70 to 100; Thao Upayo, from 60 to 100; Phra Maeku, from 58 to 100. These things will destroy the kingdom. Consequently, if the value is less

> than ten thousand, do not raise it to ten thousand; and if it less than 1,000, do not raise it to 1,000; and if it is less than 100, do not raise it to 100 because it will bring total destruction.[199]

This passage points to the gradual decline in the economic situation caused by inflation and the debasement of money. This problem arose during Kaeo's reign and worsened until the economy collapsed in the reign of Thao Maeku. Invasions by the neighboring states of Ayutthaya, the Shan states, and Burma caused an already weakened Lan Na to decline very fast. Ayutthaya besieged Chiang Mai twice during the reign of Queen Chiraprapha in 1545. On the first occasion, Queen Chiraprapha decided to pay Ayutthaya homage. She arranged for the nobles to present him with tribute.[200] This resulted in the withdrawal of the Ayutthaya troops. The second time, Ayutthaya captured Lamphun and again besieged Chiang Mai, which this time refused to negotiate. Heavy fighting ensued and Ayutthaya withdrew, torching the surrounding area and suffering heavy losses itself.

The Shan area, composed of many small *mueang*, plundered Chiang Mai in 1545, right after the first withdrawal of Ayutthaya troops. The troops from Mueang Nai and Mueang Yong Huai tried unsuccessfully to fill the moats to enter the city. They then decided to burn out the troops at Wiang Suan Dok before turning back home.

The threat from Burma arose in Maeku's reign. He had earlier assisted the Shan *mueang* against the Burmese, and Burma wanted to destroy that kind of support. Lan Na, already in decline, fell in 1558. It took Burmese troops only three days to take Chiang Mai.

CHAPTER 4

LAN NA UNDER BURMESE RULE (1558–1774)

RETURN TO THE HISTORY OF DOMAINS

The more than two hundred years of Burmese rule was Lan Na's weakest era. The period lasted, with short interruptions, from the reign of Burmese King Bayinnaung in 1558 until 1774, when Lan Na swore allegiance to King Taksin of Siam.

SOURCES ON THE PERIOD OF BURMESE RULE

There is a scarcity of sources on the period of Burmese rule. For example, the Chiang Mai Chronicle contains only a short section about the period. The political upheaval of the time may have made it difficult to keep records. Even important events were not noted, such as a major flood at Wiang Kumkam that caused the town to be deserted.

Virtually no serious research has been done on the palm-leaf manuscripts covering this period. Sources for the period are mainly found in the Social Research Institute, Chiang Mai University, and the National Library. These include the Chiang Rai and Chiang Saen Chronicle, Methangkrawat Temple version, Tambon Nai Wiang, Mueang district, Phrae province, comprising eighty-two pages. It covers the history of Chiang Rai and Chiang Saen from the Lawachangkarat period to the period of Burmese rule. It describes Burmese administrative policies, the collection of tribute, and the division of spoils between Burmese and local nobility in Chiang Saen. Certain sections are similar to two works, the Chiang Rai Chronicle, and *Chotmaihet Lanna: Bantheuk hetkan prawatsat po so 2271–2397* (The Lan Na Gazette: Record of History 1728–1854). It is believed that they originated from the same source.

The Nan Chronicle, Phra Koet version, Tambon Wiang Nuea, Mueang district, Nan province, comprises 182 pages. It describes the history of Nan from the founding of the Phukha dynasty until the end of the Nan monarchy in 1825. It lists the rulers of Nan from 1564 to 1630 and describes the area's political status, which fluctuated according to circumstances. Sometimes Nan consented to Burmese rule; at other times it opposed it. The chronicle hints that it was Burmese policy to accept local Nan customs, for instance to support the Phrathat Chae Haeng Temple. The significance of this chronicle lies in its broad perspective on Burmese rule over medium-sized *mueang* that were of little benefit to Burma, unlike Chiang Mai or Chiang Saen.

The Chiang Saen Chronicle, number 9/*yo*, located at the National Library, discusses the history of the Lawachangkarat and Mangrai dynasties up to the time of Burmese rule. It describes the Burmese policy of using Chiang Saen as a secure base to recruit troops, and refers to the sharing of spoils between Burmese and local nobles. Burma also solidified its position by supporting Buddhism and appointing a Buddhist supreme patriarch. The Chiang Rai Chronicle, number 11/*ngo*, located at the National Library, discusses the chronology of events in Chiang Rai from its founding to the time of Burmese rule.

Burmese language sources have thus far been little studied by Thai researchers. However, some Burmese materials have been translated into English. The best known is the *Hmannan Yazawin Dawgyi* or Glass Palace Chronicle (Thai: Ho Kaeo Chronicle), translated by Phra Phraisonsalarak (Thien Suphinthu), published in *The Journal of the Siam Society*. It was compiled in 1829 during the Konbaung dynasty and has been an important source in the study of Burmese history ever since. The section relating to Lan Na during Burmese rule mentions important events in the region, Bayinnaung's policies towards the area, and local opposition to the Burmese. Another important work, written by Than Tun, is *The Royal Orders of Burma, A.D. 1598–1885*, parts 1–3. The book is in Burmese but contains an English abstract. It describes proclamations by Burmese kings regarding Lan Na.

THE DISINTEGRATION OF LAN NA FROM KINGDOM TO CITY-STATES

Lan Na's fall to Burma in 1558 represented the end of the area's independence. The kingdom disintegrated. Political traditions based on the lineage system of the old Mangrai dynasty were destroyed. The various Lan Na *mueang* began to separate from the center and become more or less independent. A multitude of independent localities of different sizes took shape, similar to the kind of city-states that had characterized the region prior to the establishment of the Lan Na kingdom. The individual city-states—including Nan, Phrae, Khelang, and Phayao—had maintained many of their former characteristics. They had been incorporated into Lan Na for only about two and a half centuries. Burma's inability to assert tight control spelt an opportunity for them. Burma's hands were full. It often did not have the time or resources to deal with the Lan Na city-states. When Burma did experience a reduction in internal strife, it tried to reassert its control.

Mueang that declared their independence from Burma included Nan in 1595, Chiang Rai in 1600, Lampang in 1614, and Chiang Khong in 1624. For the most part, each city-state acted on its own initiative—there was no mutual cooperation and no intention of reestablishing a wider kingdom in the area. Lan Na reached the nadir of its power as city-states fought the Burmese and sometimes each other.

Yet the rulers of the city-states struggled with a perceived lack of legitimacy. Lan Na society had always stressed royal accession via lineage lines, and no group had acquired more legitimacy than the Mangrai dynasty. After its disintegration, it was difficult to establish acceptable new rulers.

LAN NA AND THE FIRST PERIOD OF BURMESE RULE (1558–1664)

Burma's policies in Lan Na fluctuated according to its own internal situation and local political conditions. Burmese administrative rule can be divided into two periods. The first lasted from 1558 to 1664, or for approximately one hundred years. Lan Na was considered a semi-autonomous region. Local nobles and courtiers were permitted to participate in its administration. The Burmese tended to divide territories into provinces and to name them according the ethnicity of the population. Thus Burma called Lan Na "Yuan," the Tai Yai "Shan," and the Mon "Taleng."

The second period covered 1664–1774, or the last one hundred and ten years. During this time, Lan Na became an integral part of Burma. Nobles were sent from the Burmese court to govern the area directly. Local nobles played only a minor role. Chiang Saen was split off and governed separately as a key territory and control base. Resistance to Burma nonetheless continued. Burma lost control of Chiang Mai a number of times. In 1763, it smashed the city and deported the entire population. The year 1774, when Phraya Chaban of Chiang Mai and King Kawila decided to swear allegiance to Siam, was a turning point. Thai and Lan Na troops joined to expel Burma from Chiang Mai and then the rest of Lan Na.

BAYINNAUNG'S EXPANSION INTO LAN NA (1558–1581)

King Bayinnuang of the Tounggu dynasty expanded into Lan Na with the intention of setting an example for later Burmese kings. Bayinnaung's ambitions were fuelled by the belief in a universal ruler.[1] Similar beliefs existed in Lan Na, but less overtly than in Burma.

Bayinnaung began by overcoming outlying Mon *mueang*. He went on to conquer northern Burma. He was determined to cut off Chiang Mai's support for the Shan states and defeated them in 1557.[2]

Mueang Nai had always been connected to the Mangrai dynasty through lineage relations. Thao Maeku, the last king of the Mangrai dynasty and one-time ruler of Mueang Nai, had assisted the territory in its fight against Burma.[3] As a result, Bayinnaung pushed far into Lan Na. He took Mueang Fang and Chiang Mai in 1558, and it took him only three days and three nights to defeat Chiang Mai. This easy victory showed how Lan Na had weakened. The disunited kingdom had been ready to collapse at any moment. Bayinnaung then conquered other Lan Na *mueang* such as Chiang Saen, Thoeng, Nan, Phrae, Lampang, and Lamphun.[4] Bayinnaung's conquests were a great coup for the Burmese kingdom. From Chiang Mai it could control the Shan states, including Chiang Tung and Chiang Rung. Bayinnaung now also had a line of attack into Ayutthaya.[5]

BAYINNAUNG'S POLICIES

Acceptance of Local Customs. Lan Na's distance from the Burmese capital and its separate ethnicity and language meant that it was given semi-autonomy. The Singhanawatikuman Chronicle, published in *Prachum phongsawadan*, part 61, states that Bayinnaung asked about the customs of the land early on.

Then he called for elderly people and asked about the customs of the land. An old man named Simueang brought out a local manuscript that King Saenphu had composed and presented it to Prince Mangthra [Bayinnaung]. After Prince Mangthra listened to the details of the manuscript, he said, "Regarding territory that the great kings who ruled in the past have bestowed on anyone, I who am the king would act according to the custom of those kings. Territory belonging to any noble will remain with that ruler according to royal customs." Prince Mangthra made these stipulations.[6]

The old rulers were generally allowed to continue to rule their *mueang*, on condition that they accepted Bayinnaung's suzerainty. Thao Maeku was allowed to continue to rule Chiang Mai as regional *uparat*, on condition that he send tribute of elephants, horses, and cloth annually.[7] If Burma so required, Chiang Mai had to assist in its wars by drafting troops and providing transportation and provisions. In Chiang Saen, the ruler Phaya Kamphon fled to the Lao city-state of Mueang U. Bayinnaung ordered Phaya Chiang Khaeng, together with the rulers of Mueang Yong and Chiang Lap, to fetch Kamphon back, so he could continue to rule.[8] Phaya Thepluchai, the ruler of Nan, also fled to Lan Xang in 1558. In 1560, Bayinnaung appointed Phaya Nokhamsathianchaisongkhram to rule Nan.[9] The Burmese policy of following local customs was to its own advantage, notably in the collection of benefit from commoners. The *Ratchawongsa Phuen Mueang Chiang Mai* refers to this.

> In the year 931 (1569), the eleventh month, the tenth day of the waxing moon, Saturday . . . [Bayinnaung] ruled Mueang Phing and had Mangraesuai pay respect to him. The Burmese did not destroy the old customs of the Lan Na people and allowed its previous rulers to govern. The Thai commoners did not suffer difficulties, distress, or poverty; they had only happiness. [Mangraesuai] received the king's orders. If he followed the orders, Buddhism would prosper for a long time and the people would have an opportunity to make merit, keep the precepts, meditate, and extend loving kindness. High-ranking nobles like Mangraesuai would be happy and prosperous.[10]

The collection of tribute for the royal granary was a very old custom. It was stipulated that tribute was to be in the form of locally produced goods only, so that people would not have to suffer by having to buy items elsewhere.

> First, the Royal Treasurer collected the tribute and divided it according to custom. There was an inquiry with regard to the method and the collection of the tribute as well as a warning to plant rice, sesame, and other plants. The collection of tribute had to follow old customs. Those items that were bought from other places were not tribute.[11]

Burmese authorities, like the Mangrai dynasty before them, encouraged commoners to clear land for planting. Burma followed laws from the Mangraisat that stipulated that rice fields deserted for ten years could be cleared, and that anyone who cleared them would receive the right to plant rice for three years without paying tribute. After that period, they would have to pay the regular tribute.[12] The Burmese authorities also encouraged commoners to continue trading, without interference from the state. The stipulation of weights of goods also followed old customs. Burma wanted the old sources of state income to continue uninterrupted.[13]

CHIANG MAI AS THE CENTER OF BURMESE POWER IN LAN NA

The Tounggu dynasty's success in Lan Na rested on how effectively it could replace the Mangrai dynasty. The Burmese were few in number and had to rely a great deal on the cooperation of local leaders for ease of governance. It made sense to maintain the existing Lan Na administrative framework and to keep Chiang Mai as the center of political power. The rulers of Chiang Mai were to be either descendants of the Mangrai dynasty, (Thao Maeku and Queen Wisutthithewi, for example), or sons of Bayinnaung. In other Lan Na *mueang*, the power of appointment, transfer, and dismissal was in the hands of the Burmese king.

This manner of rule encouraged disunity among the Lan Na *mueang*. The rulers each controlled their own areas, where there were often internal power struggles. The *mueang* were also separated by the topography of the land.

Resistance to Burma was difficult.[14] Bayinnaung ordered a commander and troops to be stationed in Chiang Mai. Burmese sources say that the contingent included one hundred elephants, ten thousand horses, and fifty thousand men.[15] This coincides with the Chiang Mai Chronicle, which says that Prince Mangthra appointed Surayotha, ruling Mueang Mong Yi, as a public official; Phaya Pukkawut, ruling Mueang Sangyiap, as deputy; and *khun moen* [leader of ten thousand], *khun phan* [leader of one thousand], and another ten thousand men to serve King Maeku.[16] Troops were stationed in Chiang Mai from at least 1558 to 1565, according to an inscription at the base of the Buddha image at Chaiphrakiat Temple. Bayinnaung appointed Thao Maeku to share in the government and administration of Chiang Mai. The king reiterated that in order to maintain cordial relations, the Burmese commissioner in Chiang Mai had to respect Maeku as a descendant of the Mangrai dynasty. When he heard that this order had not been followed, he sent his royal seal to reemphasize the command and to enforce a show of respect toward the Chiang Mai royal.[17] In 1565, during the reign of Queen Wisutthithewi, Bayinnaung appointed Chaban Sankram as commander of the troops.[18] Other high-ranking Lan Na nobles retained their positions. The positions of *phraya saenluang*, *phraya samlan*, and *phraya chaban*, for example, were continued. In 1581, the Burmese king decreed that these were the three high-ranking nobles.[19] Nobles loyal to Burma were rewarded with promotions. In 1565, Bayinnaung promoted a noble with the rank of *phraya luang samlan* to *phraya saenluang*. Middle and lower-ranking noble positions, including *moen nangsue*, *moen tumtam*, *phan tumtam*, *phan pratu*, *phuak dapruan*, and *phuak lam*,[20] also continued.

Burma had insufficient soldiers and officials to effectively oversee outlying *mueang*. If the rulers there did not accept Burmese control they could be punished in a variety of ways, including by dismissal. Phaya Thepchai of Nan who fled to Lan Xang was dismissed. Rebellion was punishable by execution. Chao Chetthabut, another ruler of Nan, was executed for rebellion. Rulers who pleased Burma would be promoted. Chaophraya Phonsoeksaichai-songkhram, the ruler of Nan who assisted Burma untiringly to recapture control of Chiang Mai in 1614, was promoted to govern the city.

Control of Manpower and the Payment of Tribute. The Burmese relied on the long-standing method of controlling manpower, the *nai sip*, or leader of ten system, outlined in the Mangraisat. Manpower was especially important to the Burmese for the purposes of warfare. Clear orders regarding conscription were sent out and there was a careful check on commoners to prevent their running away.

> First, those who leave home and hide themselves will have their names written down and reported to the government office . . . Thus is the order.[21]

Lists of those who fled were sent to Prince Mangthra in Chiang Mai in order that they could be followed and brought back for punishment. The lists contained both the number of runaway commoners and descriptions of the context.

> When the government has work to do, the people will find a way to avoid this work. Collect the people and present them to the lord; that is all you have to do. If they come back, allow them to remain there. If they refuse and play tricks, use power to control them.[22]

When a particular work duty was finished, the people were forbidden to change their residence, for fear that they would not be found thereafter. Commoners could move from one house to another if it was due to necessity and not to avoid work.[23] But otherwise they would be punished.

> If there is some work to be done for the lord, send the sons to work. If the parents send them away and hide them in the forest in order to avoid work, capture both women and men.[24]

This regulation was probably most used in time of war, when the Burmese wanted fast and total mobilization. Those who escaped to the forests would be executed, along with their parents. Any nobles and local lords who failed to follow orders would receive heavy penalties. Troops who fled the army would receive severe punishment, and it was forbidden to assist runaway soldiers.[25] The Burmese particularly wanted troops for wars against Ayutthaya and Laos. On the two occasions when Burma took Ayutthaya, it had used Lan Na as a base for the collection of manpower and provisions. It is estimated that in the first defeat of Ayutthaya in 1569, Bayinnaung's troops had first captured and deported nine hundred thousand people from Lan Na and Laos to assist the troops and fight. His army was considered the largest force Southeast Asia had ever seen. It included more than a thousand Portuguese mercenaries armed with flintlock guns and artillery.[26] Chiang Mai also had to send tribute to Burma. Local sources say that a collection of items presented to Bayinnaung "was composed of gold trees, silver trees, white cloth, and money."[27] The Glass Palace Chronicle says the tribute comprised such items as 10 elephants, 10 horses, 100 baht weight [1.5 kilograms] of silver, silk with silver thread, satins, embroideries, amber, musk, and other goods.[28] These items were considered easy to obtain. They had to be sent annually at a specific time. Failure to do so would be regarded as rebellion.[29] Bayinnaung also brought a number of "good commoner" families to Pegu to serve at the Burmese court. The Glass Palace Chronicle says that skilled craftsmen of every kind were taken from many *mueang*, including painters, sculptors, goldsmiths, silversmiths, blacksmiths, lacquerware makers, embroiderers, dyers, and perfume distillers. Chiang Mai also sent expert elephant and horse trainers to help improve the Burmese forces.[30]

Establishing a Lineage System in Lan Na. Bayinnaung worked to create a power network based on the old lineage system. He placed consorts under his control in important positions in several *mueang*. Among the consorts were Queen Wisutthithewi from Chiang Mai and at least two princesses from Ayutthaya, Princess Thepkasattri and Princess Suphankalayani. Queen Wisutthithewi ruled Chiang Mai from 1564 to 1578 (after Thao Maeku was removed to Pegu). After her death, the son of the queen and King Bayinnaung, Nawrahtaminsaw, succeeded to the throne. Nawrahtaminsaw sent his sons to rule Mueang Fang, Lampang, and Nan.[31] Bayinnaung's strategy helped to end political unrest in Chiang Mai for a time. But the lineage system also had weaknesses. It depended overmuch on personal relationships. When Bayinnaung died in 1581, such personal relations changed. His successor Nandabayin, who reigned from 1581 to 1599, faced the problem of breakaway *mueang*, including Chiang Mai.

Beliefs and Buddhism. Bayinnaung associated himself with the theory of the world conqueror as well as the theory of the *dhammaraja*, or the king who supports religion and leads people to prosperity. Yet there are far fewer stone inscriptions that record support of Buddhism during Burmese rule than there are during the Mangrai dynasty.

The Burmese followed local customs in relation to the donation of slaves to temples. There is evidence of donation of slaves to Chiang Man (1581) and Ketkaram (1578) temples, during Bayinnaung's rule.[32] Such slaves could not be called on to engage in public works. When temple slaves were included in those who were captured and deported to Burma during the reign of King Tharlun (or Suthothammaracha), the king immediately ordered that they be separated from the group.[33] Sources from Nawrahtaminsaw's reign indicate that he inquired about the Mahathatchao Doi Tung Chronicle and the scriptures donated by King Tilokarat to Phrathat Doi Tung. The purpose of such inquiries was to gain knowledge about old customs and to follow them.[34]

Lan Na beliefs included the idea that *mueang* had guardian spirits. Such beliefs were permitted under the Burmese, especially when a *mueang* suffered a run of bad luck. There is evidence that a ceremony to worship the Mueang Nan guardian spirits was held according to old customs in 1624. Prince Mueangfong, a Burmese noble, sponsored the event with funds from the Royal Treasury.[35] Buddha images continued to be built in the Lan Na style, for example, Phrachao Munthong at Prasat Temple in 1590,[36] the Buddha image at Chaiphrakiat Temple in 1565,[37] and Prachao Lanthong Mangkhalasapaek built by the *myowun* of Chiang Saen in 1726.[38] Stone inscriptions mention the construction of stupas in Chiang Man and Ketkaram temples. There are no traces of stupas built in the Burmese style. (Temples in Chiang Mai and Lampang in the Burmese style were constructed during the reign of King Rama V by Burmese teak dealers). It does not appear that the Burmese had any great artistic influence over Lan Na. The organization of the *sangha* also remained unchanged.

51. Left. "Phraphuttha Mueangrai Chao," bronze image, Lan Na style, at Chai Phrakiat Temple. The Burmese comissioner, Chaban Sankram, built it in 1565, casting it from a collection of broken Buddha images. Its name honors Phaya Mangrai. At the base of the image is an inscription in Burmese giving the date and purpose of the casting. (HP, c. 1970–1971)

Right. Phrachao Munthong, Prasat Temple. An inscription in Northern Thai script at its base gives the date of its casting as 1590. (HP, c. 1970–1971)

LOCALITIES CONSPIRED AGAINST BAYINNAUNG

Bayinnaung was well aware of opposition from local leaders. Rulers of *mueang* who refused to submit to him were stripped of their positions and replaced by other locals who would be loyal. In reality, Burmese power was secure only in Chiang Mai (and later in Chiang Saen); in other *mueang*, such as Nan, Phrae, Chiang Khong, and Lampang, it was quite limited.

Unrest and opposition occurred immediately after the arrival of the Burmese. The rulers of Chiang Saen and Nan, for example, fled. After taking Chiang Mai, Bayinnaung stayed in the city for only one month and twelve days before hastily returning to Pegu to put down rebellions by the Tai Yai [Shan] and Siamese, who, with a force of ten thousand men, had burned down the palace.[39] Bayinnaung was in Pegu for two or three months when he learned that his troops in Chiang Mai had been attacked. He faced continual unrest from many directions.

52. The royal seals, from the reign of Queen Wisutthithewi (1567), made from silver, with her personal emblem. She gave them to the Ban Pae community for the care of Ban Pae or Ratwisuttharam Temple, which she had built, thus exempting the people from corveé labor. King Sutthothamaracha also continued this exemption. This photo was taken at Ban Pae, Chom Thong during the offering ceremony in 1990. The ceremony is performed every three years. (SO, 1990)

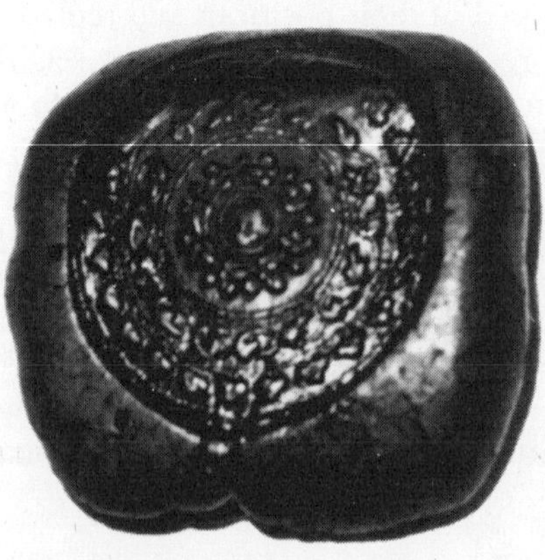

53. The royal seal, with lotus design on the front and Somdet Chao Ratchawisut (Queen Wisutthithewi) on the back. The seal was made of dark brown lac, five centimeters in diameter. The seal was once attached to a silver sheet. (SO, 1990)

Various groups in Lan Na initially cooperated against the Burmese, including the rulers of Phrae, Nan, Lampang, Chiang Rai, and Chiang Khong. Sethathirat (or Chaiyachettha), the king of Lan Xang, led the anti-Burmese opposition. In 1558, a joint army attacked the Burmese garrison in Chiang Mai, besieging the city with a force that was probably quite large. Bayinnaung responded by sending the ruler of Ava with 6,000 cavalrymen, 500 elephants, and 140,000 foot soldiers.[40] This was enough to defend the city. The opposition rulers fled to Lan Xang and Bayinnaung appointed new rulers.[41] Major unrest occurred again in 1564 when Bayinnaung attacked Ayutthaya. Thao Maeku refused an order to bring troops to join the Burmese forces in a flotilla, joining instead with the rulers of Chiang Saen, Chiang Rai, Nan, and Lampang, who were supported by King Sethathirat of Lan Xang. When the war with Ayutthaya was over, Burma again subjugated Lan Na. The opposing rulers again fled to Lan Xang, except for Thao Maeku, who decided to swear loyalty to Burma.[42] As punishment for his part in the anti-Burma effort, he was taken to Pegu and Queen Wisutthithewi, his consort, was made ruler of Chiang Mai. She was the last true member of the Mangrai dynasty to rule in Chiang Mai.

Political unrest continued, often because the Lan Na states were required to collect revenue and manpower for Burma. The Chiang Mai Chronicle states that in 1581, money collected in Lan Na had to be sent to the Burmese Court. The rulers were forbidden to hold back tribute for personal use or to keep it in Lan Na. Whoever followed orders would be allowed to continue to rule.

> When the order of the lord arrives, the ruler of that *mueang* has to collect and divide the money as previously agreed upon. Do not be dishonest. The royal tribute, which contains gold and silver trees, white cloth, and money, has to be delivered to the lord without delay or withholding. Local nobles who take control of the *mueang* and who follow orders will be appointed to rule the *mueang*.[43]

The local rulers had formerly reaped the benefits from tribute themselves. As a result, Burma faced constant opposition.

EXPANSION DURING THE REIGNS OF ANAUKHPETLUN AND THARLUN (1605–1648)

Burma by now considered Chiang Mai a part of the Burmese kingdom. Lists of outlying foreign *mueang* under royal command in Burmese documents usually include Chiang Mai.[44] Yet Burmese power was weak during the reign of Nandabayin (1581–1599), when Nawrahtaminsaw was ruler of Chiang Mai (1578–1607). Various localities broke away, including a group led by

Phraya Ramdecho, the ruler of Chiang Saen (c. 1596–1601), who had been appointed by Ayutthaya. Lan Na became divided into two spheres; the northern sphere centered in Chiang Saen under Phraya Ramdecho's influence, and the southern sphere centered in Chiang Mai under Nawrahtaminsaw's influence. Both rulers were under the authority of King Naresuan, who tried to mediate between the two. However, after 1608 Ayutthaya's power declined. Following the death of Nawrahtaminsaw, Chiang Mai plunged into turmoil. Between 1607 and 1614 competing groups supported different candidates for the position of king. Nawrahtaminsaw had three sons. Thulong, the eldest, was supported with troops from Ayutthaya. But he died and in 1608 Ayutthaya ended its role in Chiang Mai. In the same year the youngest son, Phra Choi or Sadokyo, was supported to the throne by a group of Chiang Mai nobles.[45] But another group of nobles, including Phaya Han, removed him and installed Phra Chaithip, the middle son, in his stead. Chaithip's rule ran counter to the interests of some high-ranking nobles. He was executed and Phra Choi was installed for a second time. Then in 1614 the Burmese king Anaukhpetlun (1605–1628), a grandson of Bayinnuang, intervened and seized the city. The subsequent herding of captives from Chiang Mai was detailed in the poem "Mangthra Fought Chiang Mai."

Anaukhpetalun (King Nongphakwan or Mahathammaracha) and his brother Tharlun (1629–1648) wanted to rebuild the Burmese empire to its former glory. Anaukhpetlun was determined to resolve the problem of breakaway *mueang*. He seized *mueang* in the Shan states and Sipsong Panna.

> After capturing Chiang Rung, they returned to their base at Sikongman in Chiang Saen. Mangraecho was located at Tung Yang Ngam and fought against King Suttho. The situation was chaotic for a day and a night. Once things returned to normal, Phaya Nokham was appointed as Phaya Chiang Saen . . .[46]
>
> . . . Fa Suttho subjugated the area as far as the Chian and Thae rivers, and the ruler of Mueang Chiang Rung was defeated. Chao Khamchaek and his brother fled to Mueang Luang. King Suttho gave Mueang Luang to Chao Khamchaek to rule while Chao Mueang Phaeng, the younger brother, was taken to Mueang Fang and was appointed to rule Chiang Rai. King Suttho appointed Ratchasurin to rule Mueang Yong.[47]

He then took Fang, Chiang Saen, and Chiang Rai before moving in to southern Lan Na.

Anaukhpetlun wanted to have loyal rulers in place in the various *mueang*. Phaya Phonsoeksai, the ruler of Nan as well as the adopted son of Nawrahtaminsaw, had supported Anaukhpetlun's recapture of Chiang Mai, and he was rewarded by being appointed ruler there (1615–1631). Anaukhpetlun also considered Chiang Saen very important and gave its ruler the title Prince Kaphuak, bestowed royal regalia on him, and ordered that from then on, all official business had to be submitted first to the King of Ava.[48] The ruler of Chiang Saen was directly under the Burmese king and served as his eyes and ears.

However, there was still always unrest among local rulers. Phonsoeksai took up arms to oppose the jailing of Chao Muakkham, ruler of Chiang Saen, and Chaofa Luang Thiphanet, his father, and the appointment there instead of Phaya Sisongmueang, ruler of Lampang.

Phonsoeksai's plan to take full control of Chiang Mai failed as King Tharlun seized it back in 1631. The Chiang Mai Chronicle states,

> Three years later, in the *luang met* year, s. 993 (1631/32), Prince Phawa Min Taya Suddhodhammaraja [Mangthra Sutho Thammaracha] again took Chiang Mai, capturing the king of Chiang Mai to imprison in Pegu, and appointed Phraya Thipphanet, the father of Phraya [Phaya] Chiang Saen, to eat [take over] the three million rice-fields of Chiang Mai, and appointed Phraya [Phaya] Chiang Saen to rule Chiang Saen as before.[49]

It took Tharlun three years to gain control of Chiang Mai and Fang. Chiang Saen was then the center of Burmese power in the region. The Burmese bestowed insignia of rank on large *mueang* such as Chiang Mai, Nan, Chiang Saen, Chiang Rai, Chiang Khong, Thoeng, Lo, and Lampang.

Political unrest began to drop away. Tharlun's policy was to send those who opposed him into exile. Phonsoekai and his family were sent to Ava. Phaya Sisongmueang, the ruler of Chiang Saen, was removed. Those who supported Burma were rewarded. Chao Luang Thipphanet was appointed ruler of Chiang Mai. Chao Muakkham returned to take his post as the ruler of Chiang Saen.[50] More outsiders were installed into key positions. The Burmese prince of Mueang Fong was sent to rule Nan in 1624, and the ruler of Mueang Maen, who was Lue, was sent to rule Chiang Rai, where four locals were made *mueang* officials.

Thalun tried to centralize the administration. In particular, he reformed the army so it would be in a state of readiness. He ended the old post of *uparat* and replaced it with the post of commissioner. The Hlutdaw Council replaced the Privy Council and the High Court.[51] The council was also responsible for the appointment of commissioners to govern the *mueang*. The royal court had an increasingly reduced role. The army was divided into groups, in order to be ready for war. It was forbidden for elephants and horses to be stationed outside army premises. Men over sixty years of age were not conscripted.[52] In 1637, *mueang* were ordered to register soldiers in preparation for war: one thousand men from each individual *mueang*. In 1638, new registration lists were prepared for thirteen communities, including Chiang Mai. Between 1638 and 1642, the elephant corps was greatly improved with assistance from Chiang Mai; that is, wild elephants were caught and herded to Burma, and experts were sent to train and look after them. The cavalry was also improved.[53]

Commoners were forbidden to move. Anyone wishing to make a journey had to have a proper document. He had to provide a detailed explanation to the village head of where he was going, why he was going, and when he would return.[54] Such reforms meant that the Burmese empire in the late Tounggu dynasty was relatively stable. Its power penetrated increasingly deeply into Lan Na, thus allowing for somewhat different administrative policies in the following period, 1664–1774.

LAN NA AND THE LATTER PERIOD OF BURMESE RULE (1664–1774)

During this period Lan Na changed from being a relatively free province of a "foreign country" to an integral part of the Burmese kingdom. Burmese nobles held important and influential positions. There were two important results of these changes.

First, they strengthened the Burmese empire and became the foundation for later Burmese expansion. In 1656, during the reign of Pindale (1648–1661), local sources mention that the king of Mueang Maen, who also ruled Chiang Rai, asked King Pindale to appoint five brothers of the Maen ethnic group to rule Phayao, Mueang Phan, Mueang Thoeng, Mueang Salao, and Mueang Lo.[55] Second, they protected Lan Na from infiltration by Ayutthaya. At one point Chinese troops attacked various points north of Lan Na and the Chiang Mai leader Phraya Saenluang had sought support and troops from Ayutthaya.[56] By 1660, when King Narai sent the troops, the situation had improved. Fearing repercussions from Burma, Chiang Mai turned on the Ayutthaya troops and they in turn attacked Lan Na areas such as Mueang Thoen, Lampang, Mueang Long, Mueang Phromkhiri, and Mueang Inthakhiri.[57]

ADMINISTRATION BY THE BURMESE NOBILITY

The Burmese court created a variety of positions for its nobles in Lan Na. The post of *myowun*, was the supreme power in Chiang Saen and Chiang Mai and was reserved for Burmese.

> At that time (1741), the King of Ava appointed Palanaraksa the *myowun* of Chiang Saen and appointed Phra Ngam, the son of the late Prince Yodngammueang, the ruler of Chiang Saen and gave him the title Prince Ngam according to custom . . .[58]

Phraya Hanwangtun gathered the families and presented them to the King of Ava. The king was very pleased and appointed Phraya Hanwangtun, a noble from the ruling family of Mueang Phong, the ruler of Chiang Saen, controlling the area east of the Mekong River. Palachapaek was the *myowun*.[59]

The *chakkai*, or *sitke*, served as the *myowun*'s assistants in military affairs. Two of these officials were stationed in each Lan Na *mueang*. Both Burmese and Lan Na people held these posts. One source mentioned that "Mueang Nan had a Thai *chakkai* . . . the Yom area had a Burmese *chakkai*."[60] Each *mueang* had two positions for the collection of rice tribute, the *na sai* [left fields] and the *na khwa* [right fields]. "The seven left *panna* paid their customary tribute to the Chao Na Sai while the eight right *panna* paid the Chao Na Khwa."[61] In addition, each *mueang* had two positions of *nakham* as well as various positions for *chare*, investigators and inspectors who were under the direct jurisdiction of the Burmese court.

An increased number of nobles were sent to Lan Na during the reign of King Mangra of the Konbaung dynasty. In 1763 a *po*, a military commander, was sent instead of a *myowun*. After Po Akiakhamuni captured Chiang Mai, King Mangra appointed him to rule Chiang Mai.[62] There were two kinds of rulers in *mueang* other than Chiang Mai and Chiang Saen. The first type was a local person who was appointed by the Burmese king and received Burmese insignia of rank. The second type was an outsider, either Burmese or Shan. For example, Burma sent commissioners to rule Nan: Prince Myongkhongmakin in 1707, Prince Muaicha in 1716, and Chao Luang Tunmahawongsa in 1726.[63] In Chiang Mai, the rulers were probably princes from the Shan States, because they were called by the royal title *fa* or *chaofa*, for example, Chaofa Chiang Thong, Fa Withura, Fa Mueang Phaen.[64] *Mueang* rulers were transferred frequently for fear that they would accumulate too much personal power.

THE ESTABLISHMENT OF CHIANG SAEN AS THE NORTHERN CENTER OF BURMESE RULE (1701)

Burmese kings had long seen the importance of Chiang Saen. It was incorporated as a province of Burma in 1701. Lan Na was split into two regions, Chiang Saen and Chiang Mai. The elevation of Chiang Saen was a means of cleaving the strength of Chiang Mai.

> In the year 1063 (1701/02), Chiang Mai killed Moi No Chai of Chiang Saen at Nong Phainong Chom, and news of the incident reached the king of Burma. As No Chai was innocent, the king ordered the separation of Chiang Saen from Chiang Mai, the separation of the whole administration, including the sending of tribute and gold and silver trees. Chiang Saen should send these directly to the king. Chao Mangchatukamani Mangnemoi, a high-ranking noble, informed them . . . [but] Chiang Mai refused to submit and was not honest to the king. Hereafter, Chiang Mai will no longer be above the other *mueang*. Every *mueang* will be equal. If there is administrative work and delivery of tribute and gold and silver trees, Chiang Mai will no longer receive them.[65]

This did not stop challenges to Burma; there is evidence that Chiang Mai troops attacked Chiang Saen but were defeated.

> In the year 1090 (1728), on the fifth waning day of the fifth month (February 18 1729), seven enemy troop units from Chiang Mai invaded Chiang Saen, which entered into combat with the enemy. Chiang Mai was defeated and [Chiang Saen] captured three elephants, five cannons, and thirty guns. Two days later, the troops of Phra Tiam of Chiang Mai reached Tha Khao Pluak. [Chiang Saen] came out to fight and killed a large number of enemy forces, confiscating three cannons and seventy guns.[66]

The Burmese king decided to cut the strength of Chiang Mai again in 1733 by ordering Phrae, Nan, Lampang, Mueang Fang, Mueang Sat, Chiang Khong, and Mueang Thoeng to report directly to Chiang Saen.[67]

ECONOMIC BENEFITS

Burma's collection of tribute greatly increased during this later period. The people of Lan Na had to shoulder the burden of providing for the Burmese nobles and their entourages. Local sources describe the resulting distress caused by this burden.

> In the year 1063 (1701/02), Mahatham of Ava appointed Rayachesung as *myowun* and Aephon-ae as *chakkai* of Chiang Saen with three subordinates. All the nobles, without any alternative, had to join together and collect rice and give it to the *myowun* every month, rice worth 100,000 *bia* [cowrie shell money], food, chilies, salt worth 250,000 *bia*, and betel ingredients that would last for one month. There were men to supply labor, two men to collect fodder for the *myowun's* horses while the *chakkai* had two men, one for collecting firewood, the other for collecting fodder for his horses. The firewood cutter was selected from the Lua at Ban Thonnung and the other Lua from Ban Yoem Ban Chang.
>
> Ever since Engche became Mahatham of Ava, we Lan Na Thai have suffered increasingly because we had to collect money to feed the Burmese.[68]

In Chiang Rai, the burden of welcoming the *chakkai*, who changed position every three years, fell on the local people.

> One *chakkai* of Chiang Rai had two subordinates. Each month, he was taken care of with rice worth 90,000 *bia* and 18,000 *bia* in money, while the two subordinates received 50 *bia*, one mat, one mosquito net, one pillow, and houses were built for them and people worked for them.[69]

THE DIVISION OF SPOILS IN CHIANG SAEN

The benefits reaped from the people were divided into three portions, two portions for the *myowun* and the *chakkai* and the remaining portion for local nobles. One document notes:

> In the past, Chiang Saen had thirty-two *khun mueang* [local dignitaries]. These nobles received their income from the fields, water fees, service fees, court fees, elephant tusks [and other forest products], slaves, elephants and horses, and the payment of customs fees. These had been collected from old times. The amount received would be divided into three portions, two portions for the *myowun* and *chakkai* and one portion for the thirty-two local nobles. The seven left *panna* customarily paid the *chao na sai*; the eight right *panna* paid the *chao na khwa*; and the nine *mueang panna* paid the ruler. These thirty-two nobles had no possessions and provisions like the ruler.[70]

Moreover, the local nobles, *khun sanam*, also collected tribute in the form of silver and gold and sent it to the Burmese court. "All tribute would be brought to the Government Office of Mueang Chiang Saen. The collection of tribute according to the list was composed of gold and silver. The *myowun*, the *chakkai*, and the twelve *khun sanam* sent gold and silver tribute to the king.[71] An order from the Burmese king specified that local nobles had to send charcoal, iron, silk thread, rubber, and other goods according to the requirements of the Burmese court.[72]

Labor conscription continued to be of great importance. According to one source from Nan, in peacetime Burma used the manpower of Lan Na commoners to work on several projects, such as sending them off to different *mueang* to find a kind of grass to make paper for books.[73] Conscription in wartime was much more important. Ballads from the records of the Ayutthaya-Burmese War in 1779 show the suffering incurred. The Burmese deported people from the various *mueang* along the route from the Shan states of Saenwi, Chiang Khaeng, Sat, Yong, Nai, and Chiang Tung. It was stipulated that there must be fifteen hundred men from each *mueang*. Any *mueang* that was slow to respond would be punished. The forces would meet up at Chiang Saen. The Burmese managed their forces according to the system of ten. "Ten people would have one *achap* to lead them; ten *achap* would appoint one *nai roi* [leader of one hundred] as their head."[74] Provisions and carts for the troops were also confiscated. A total of eleven hundred oxen were used to transport rice. The Burmese collected arms such as spears, curved-blade pikes, and swords, as well as provisions. The Burmese "kept on taking things," causing great suffering among the population. "Every *mueang* was enlisted to help, north and south. The northern Thai suffered greatly."[75]

In Chiang Saen, the *myowun* had set up several villages and appointed heads to assist in *mueang* affairs. "Organized villages" were set up in order to mobilize manpower. In case of urgent need, these village reserves could be mobilized at any time.[76]

POLITICAL UNREST AMONG LOCAL POLITICAL GROUPS

During the last 110 years of Burmese rule, opposition groups grew more diverse. They can be divided into three groups—monks, commoners, and rulers.

Groups of monks, *tonbun*, or persons of merit, began to take a role in the mid-eighteenth century, a period of great disorder. The people were suffering, and the monks tried to help solve their problems. A number of *tonbun* played prominent roles.

In 1732, Tonbun Nayang, a monk at Nayang Temple in Lampang and a practitioner of magic, drew an increasing number of supporters when Lampang had no ruler. Tonbun Nayang and his immediate assistants disrobed and died fighting Thao Mahayot from Lamphun, who was mistreating the people and collecting taxes from them.

During the unrest in Lampang, monks at Chomphu Temple spearheaded opposition to the mistreatment in Lamphun. They arranged for a local called Nan Thipchang to fight.

In 1761 Chao Pat overthrew his brother Chao Chan, who controlled Chiang Mai at the time, and invited Chao Khihut, a monk from Duangdi Temple in Chiang Mai, to disrobe, take charge as ruler, and fight the Burmese.

Commoners also formed several groups, as armed bandits or guerrillas. The Chiang Saen Chronicle says that the *mueang* abounded with banditry and fighting. "Ever since King Makso ruled Ava and Prince Ngam ruled Chiang Saen, there was fighting and banditry."[77] Some groups ambushed Burmese troops. For example, a commoner called Saen Khwan Rongchang plundered Burmese valuables in Chiang Saen. According to the Chiang Mai Chronicle, the Prime Minister's Office version, Saen Khwan Rongchang brought his men and ambushed the Burmese as they guarded three piles of gold.[78] Afterwards, he attempted to plunder Burmese troops in Chiang Mai, but failed and was captured. Sometimes groups under village leaders combined to fight the Burmese. The leader of Chom village tried to protect the community but was defeated by the Burmese.[79] Other groups tried to seize *mueang*. In 1737 Ai Lun led eight hundred men to fight with Mueang Fang.[80] And in 1777, "Lakhon guerrillas smashed Mueang Fang."[81]

In 1727, Thepsing from Mueang Yuam (Mae Sariang district) captured Chiang Mai from Mangraenra, pursuing and killing groups of Burmese and Mon. The Burmese then supported Ong Kham (also known as Ong Nok), a descendant of royalty in Lan Xang, who then took Chiang Mai. Burmese troops were then made to flee to Phayao, and then to Chiang Saen. Ong Kham appointed Lua temple-slaves to the positions of *phraya phran* and *phraya wat* to take care of the Phrachao Thong-iang Temple (Phrachao Tonluang Temple in Phayao) as before.[82] Ong Kham enjoyed good relations with the Mon—his daughter, Nang Ong Thip, was the consort of Chao Kuaihongsa (Samingthokuai). When Mon territory fell under Burmese rule, Chao Kuai fled to Chiang Mai. Ong Kham and his descendants ruled Chiang Mai independently for thirty-six years, from 1727 to 1763.

Several other city-states also became independent. In 1765, Phra Mueangchai of Lamphun conspired against the Burmese Po Akiakhamuni. The Burmese king fought back. The king went to fight with Lamphun with the help of 99,990 men. Phra Mueangchai could not bear to stay; he gathered his family and cooks as best he could and tried to break out all night until Mueang Lamphun was lost."[83]

Phaya Meng of Chiang Rai conspired with Phayao unsuccessfully against the Burmese in 1780; he then fled to Lampang to ask assistance from King Kawila.[84] The *phaya* of Phrae and Prince Kong of Mueang Yong jointly attacked Burmese troops in Chiang Saen until the city was taken and they deported many families.

The unrest in this later period was very diverse in character. Burma's increased control of important positions such as *myowun*, *chao mueang* [ruler], *chakkai*, *na sai*, and *na khwa* had made concerted opposition more difficult. The opposition then filtered down to the lower levels of society.

SUPPRESSION OF LAN NA DURING THE REIGN OF MANGRA OF THE KONBAUNG DYNASTY

King Hsinbyushin, or Mangra, of the Konbaung dynasty reigned from 1763 to 1776. He commanded the troops that captured Chiang Mai for the third time, in 1763. The chronicles state that he deported the entire population. After taking control again of all Lan Na, the Burmese destroyed Ayutthaya in 1767.

The Konbaung dynasty ruled Chiang Mai for only eleven years (1763–1774). During this brief period, Chiang Mai was ruled by a *po*, or military commander. The *po* governed through force, squeezing high profits for themselves, oppressing the people, and causing great distress. According to the Chiang Mai Chronicle,

> At that time, the [Burmese] commander [Po Chiak] who had gone to the Lao domain returned and rested his army at Lampang Luang. . . . [Afterwards] the Burmese . . . executed [the men], ten or twenty per day. They took their wives and children to be slaves, to be servants, to be wives and children, as they wished.[85]

Monks also suffered. The Chiang Mai Chronicle states that the Burmese "oppressed the country with fines and extortion. Townsmen and villagers everywhere were troubled, and even the princely class and the monks were distressed."[86] Moreover, some *po* did not tend to government affairs but only searched greedily for wealth. One particular Burmese *po* became the *myowun* of Chiang Saen, but he did not work except to order his men to search for wealth. The people called him Po Phiwin [monster].[87]

The oppression of the local people led King Mangra to order the *po* to be less abusive, but to no avail.[88] At this time Burma faced the serious problem of a Chinese invasion. It had to throw its full force into that war in upper Burma.

The oppression led to conflict between the *po* and local nobles, who were used as instruments, for example, to help conscript commoners for war and to collect taxes for the personal benefit of the *po*. Conflict between the *po* and the local nobles resulted in clashes. In 1769 Noiphrom, a *chakkai*, fought with Po Huakhao in Chiang Mai and was killed. In 1771, the *phraya chaban* fought with Po Huakhao but was defeated. Po Huakhao's oppressive rule led Lan Na leaders to decide to switch allegiance to Siam.

CHAPTER 5

A TRIBUTARY STATE OF THE SIAMESE KINGDOM (1774–1899)

THE RESTORATION OF LAN NA

In 1774, local leaders in Lan Na swore allegiance to the Siam king, Taksin of Thonburi. Initially, the various Lan Na *mueang* maintained their own local governments, in accordance with old customs. Cultural differences between the two areas meant that the Siamese considered Lan Na a foreign land. Siam appointed Lan Na rulers to the position known as *chao prathetsarat*, or ruler of a tributary state, but the people of Lan Na regarded them as *chao luang* or *phraya luang*, king. For example, the Phra Boromathat Chom Thong inscription refers to *phraya luang wachiraprakan* (*phraya chaban*), the ruler of Chiang Mai, as the "king of Chiang Mai."[1]

Lan Na was severely weakened under Burmese rule. It was sandwiched between two more powerful states. There seemed no option but to choose sides. Its leaders hoped that joining with Siam would provide better opportunities. The region entered a new era as a tributary of Siam.

REBELLION AGAINST BURMA AND ALLEGIANCE TO SIAM

The people of Lan Na had revolted repeatedly over the more than two hundred years (1558–1774) of Burmese rule, particularly during the eighteenth century. The rebellions had two distinct characteristics: a lack of unity and support from Thonburi.

Lan Na leaders generally failed to cooperate against Burma; they fought amongst each other. Their relations with Burma varied greatly. In some cases, local leaders cooperated with the Burmese, for example, in the case of Phochao Thipchang (or Phraya Sulawaluchai), the founder, ironically, of the Chao Chet Ton dynasty who would later turn towards Siam. Thipchang was originally a hunter who helped the people of Lampang to fight off troops from Lamphun. During his twenty-seven years in power in Lampang (1732–1759), Thipchang relied on Burmese support to fend off the old ruling group. He sent tribute to the Burmese king and was rewarded with the title *phraya chaisongkhram* [Victorious in War].[2] Burma appointed his son, Prince Chaikaeo, as Chaofa Singharachathani.

Lan Na rulers intent on opposing Burma usually had to depend on assistance from Thonburi. By the late eighteenth century Burmese nobles had oppressed local nobles and commoners to the breaking point. Local opposition had increased, particularly under Po Huakhao, who followed extremely oppressive policies. An open conflict between the *phraya chaban* and Po Huakhao resulted in fighting in the center of Chiang Mai in 1771. According to the Chiang Mai Chronicle, the *phraya* "had a force of 300 to fight the Burmese without even guns or swords, using only clubs and cudgels, and he himself only bore a long sword to engage the Burmese force."[3] The *phraya chaban* was defeated, and his younger brother died in the battle.[4] The *phraya chaban* had discovered that acting alone meant failure. He and Kawila decided, for the first time, to side with Siam. They were also motivated by the fact that Siam had unsuccessfully attacked Chiang Mai in 1770.

The *phraya chaban* traveled to Thonburi to request support. King Taksin sent troops, who took just seventeen days to reach Thoen.[5] There, Thoen's Burmese commissioner was executed, as arranged with Chao Kawila.[6] Kawila volunteered to be in the vanguard in an attack on Chiang Mai and succeeded in taking the city in 1774. Taksin awarded the *phraya chaban* the title of Luang Wachiraprakan Kamphaengphet,[7] and named him ruler of Chiang Mai. Kawila was named ruler of Lampang, where he ruled with the assistance of his six younger brothers; Chaofa Singharachathani was appointed the *uparat*, or second king, and Chao Bunma was made *ratchawong*, a title given vassal princes.[8] The Chao Chet Ton [the seven brothers] provided a strong defense for Lampang when Chiang Mai again fell to the Burmese. Lampang served as a strong base for the Thai side.

On his way home to Thonburi, Taksin was presented with King Kawila's niece as his consort. This helped build good relations and increased the power of the Chao Chet Ton line. Around the same time, Kawila's younger sister, Chao Si-anocha (Chao Rotcha), became a consort of Chaophraya Surasi (Bunma), the younger brother of the future first king of the Chakri dynasty.[9] Chao Si-anocha earned herself special favor by assisting Phraya Suriya-aphai in the suppression of Phraya San of Cambodia during unrest at the end of the Thonburi era.

Chao Si-anocha probably helped to increase Siam's trust in the Chao Chet Ton. After receiving news of King Rama I's coronation, Phraya Kawila and his brothers went down to have an audience with the king, who promoted Kawila to be *phraya wachiraprakan*, king of Chiang Mai, replacing the *phraya chaban*, who had died. He also appointed Chao Khamsom, the second brother, as the ruler of Lampang; Chao Thammalangka, the third brother, as the *uparat* of Chiang Mai; Chao Duangthip, the fourth brother, as the *uparat* of Lampang; Chao Mula, the fifth brother, as *phraya ratchawong* of Lampang; and Chao Khamfan, the sixth brother, as *phraya burirat* of Chiang Mai.[10] Siam by this time was using Lampang as a secure base from which to fight

Burma. Kawila worked to persuade other Lan Na rulers to pledge allegiance to Siam. Chao Nai Noi Withun, the son of the Nan ruler, accepted Siam's rule.[11] After Chiang Mai became stable, the Chao Chet Ton brothers continued to try to convince the leaders of other *mueang* such as Phrao, Fang, Yong, and Chiang Tung, to revolt against the Burmese and swear allegiance to Siam.[12]

During the reign of King Rama I, 1782–1809, the remaining Lan Na leaders decided to swear wholehearted allegiance to Siam. Nan, for example, which had previously wavered, submitted to Siam in 1788.

CHIANG MAI'S SITUATION UNDER *PHRAYA LUANG WACHIRAPRAKAN* (PHRAYA CHABAN BUNMA)

King Taksin appointed Phraya Chaban Bunma as the "king of Chiang Mai," now a tributary state, in a ceremony at Phrathat Hariphunchai temple.

Chiang Mai faced severe manpower shortages, due to the continued long warfare. The Chiang Mai Chronicle says that there were only nineteen hundred men, not enough to defend the city. Po Huakhao was defeated and fled, but he returned after two months to besiege the city for eight months until the people were starving, "with nothing to eat, [not] even chameleons, skinks, crickets, and grasshoppers."[13] Finally, after troops from the south drove off the Burmese, in 1776 Bunma abandoned the city and its people dispersed. "During that time, the people were starving so they fled, some to the north, and some to the south."[14]

Bunma took his family to reside in Lampang and asked for assistance from the Chao Chet Ton group. However, in 1777, he then moved back to the border area of Chiang Mai and Lamphun, where the Burmese had little influence. Later, he moved from Lampang to Tha Wangphrao, to Wiang Nonglong and to Wang sakaeng Sopli. Around 1779 the king of Thonburi sent him to prison charged with executing the Uparat Konkaeo. Bunma died in Thonburi, ending for a time the hope of reestablishing Chiang Mai, which was deserted for about twenty years.

THE CHAO CHET TON AND THE RESTORATION OF LAN NA

King Kawila was appointed ruler of Chiang Mai in 1782 while the city was still deserted. Reviving the city was going to be difficult, due to the great scarcity of people and Burma's continued control over other Lan Na *mueang*. Kawila gathered people slowly. He first asked for three hundred commoners from Lampang, together with another seven hundred commoners who used to be under Bunma in Wang Sakaeng.[15] With these he built the temporary settlement of Wiang Pa Sang in 1782. The author's field research suggests that Wiang Pa Sang was located on the banks of the Tha River and was one thousand meters in length. It appears to have been strongly fortified, as there are traces of four surrounding walls. There were two reasons for choosing Wiang Pa Sang. First, the area was fertile, sitting on a low-lying plain at the meeting of three rivers, the Ping, Kuang, and Tha. Second, the Burmese had less influence south of Chiang Mai. If a threat arose, Kawila could easily ask for assistance from nearby Lampang. Wiang Pa Sang became a place for "collecting people" from between 1782 and 1796. Historians refer to Kawila's reign as the time of "collecting vegetables for baskets and collecting people for *mueang*."[16] The gathering of people to populate the *mueang* can be divided into three periods.[17] During the first period, Kawila tried to persuade people who had fled to the forests to return. This had some results but was too slow for his purposes. He began to forcibly round up people from *mueang* in the north and resettle them in Lan Na.

Kawila had few men at this time, and Burmese power in the Chiang Saen area was still strong, so he moved gradually. The first raids were in small *mueang* along the west bank of the Salween River. The Chiang Mai Chronicle says the Chao Chet Ton group would sometimes first try persuasion by sending nobles with gifts of clothes and fine porcelain. But mostly they used small

54. Royal stupas located in the foreground of Suan Dok Temple containing the ashes of the rulers and their Na Chiang Mai descendants. Phrarachaya Chao Dararatsami collected the ashes of her relatives that used to be interred near the Ping River and relocated them in the stupas at Suan Dok Temple in 1909. (NAT, c. 1926–1932)

military forces to attack and round up small numbers of people. For example, Chao Chantharacha and Chao Noi Kawila commanded 100 men, crossed the Salween River, and attacked Ban Omchuak; Chao Chantharacha and Thao Sitthi and 150 men attacked Ban Satoi, Ban Wanglung, and Wangkat; Chao Ratanahuamueangkaeo and 500 men swept up families at Mueang Pan and Mueang Tongkai.[18] They then incited *mueang* north of Chiang Mai, including Chiang Tung, Mueang Yong, Mueang Fang, Mueang Sat, Mueang Phrao, and Mueang Chiang Rai, to revolt against the Burmese. Burma was able to suppress the revolts, but people escaped to the Chao Chet Ton in Lampang for protection.

The second period (1796–1806) continued in similar fashion. The years 1798–1801 were characterized by the repeated carrying off of families in the Salween River area. There were attacks on Mueang Pu, Ban Ngualai, Ban Satoi, Soirai, Thachang, Ban Na, and other locations. In 1802, there were successful attacks on Mueang Sat and Chiang Tung, cutting off the Burmese troops besieging Chiang Mai. In 1804, following an unsuccessful effort the year before, troops from Chiang Mai, Lampang, Vientiane, and Bangkok succeeded in taking Chiang Saen, and some of the Thai Yuan people there were then taken to Ban Hom in Chiang Mai.

The Chiang Saen victory facilitated the herding of more families from *mueang* in the north. From 1805 onwards, the people of Mueang Yong, Mueang Yu, Mueang Luai, Chiang Tung, Mueang Chiang Khang, Mueang Wa, Mueang Luang, and other places were forcibly relocated on a large scale, mainly to Chiang Mai. Kawila needed to repopulate the capital, and to depopulate other areas to prevent them from being used as bases by the Burmese. Large numbers were taken again from Mueang Yong in 1805 and again in 1809.

By the third period (1807–1813), the manpower situation was no longer critical, and Lan Na was increasingly stable. By now *mueang* in the north were almost deserted. The depopulation was so extreme that those remaining could no longer protect themselves, so they deserted. The huge forcible removals of populations remained in the memory of the people for many years as the "Wars of Persuasion."

People were taken in the years 1808–1810 from Chiang Tung, Mueang Yong, and *mueang* in the area of the Salween River.[19] Kawila's last such operation was a little later in Yong in 1813.[20] The forced migrations continued after Kawila's reign, but were fewer. A *pap sa* manuscript in Lan Na Tham script of Pasa Temple, Tambon Sansi, Saraphi district, Chiang Mai province, states that Phraya Chiang Mai Changphueak sent troops to capture people.

> The *phraya uparat* became the king of Chiang Mai. He ordered Phraya Phrankhonkhao and Thao Siri to take charge of about one hundred or so men in the attack on Ban Chiangkoe located on the west bank of the Salween River. They met with success and rounded up families, seized their weapons,

> and brought them down to offer to the king along with the *mueang*. Phrachao Chiang Mai Changphueak ordered Nai Khammun and Nai Kaeomueang to take charge of two hundred men to capture the Burmese at Tha Soppu. They captured three or four Burmese and brought them back before Nai Khammun returned and crossed the Salween River and attacked Ban Tongkai but could take only a few families and crossed back at Tha Phadaeng. He also captured a Burmese and presented him to the king. Phraya Chiang Mai Changphueak ordered Nai Noi Kawila and Nai Phrom to take charge of over one hundred men in the attack on the Suai people, and they presented them to the king, who ordered them to remain in Chiang Mai.[21]

Forced resettlement continued until the time of Phraya Chiang Mai Khamfan and Phraya Phutthawong. Phraya Phuttawong carried off families from Mueang Pu, Mueang Sat, and Mueang Tuan and brought them to Chiang Mai.[22] In the later periods, other factors were involved in the movement of people to the area. Some people followed their relatives to the resettlement sites because it was easier to earn a living there or because of political unrest.

Forced resettlements also happened in Nan and Phrae. Nan, in particular, tried to compete with Chiang Mai in building manpower. The Nan dynasty, the Wong Chao Luang Tun, was not connected to the Chao Chet Ton. Nan swore allegiance to Siam after the Chao Chet Ton group, but it dedicated itself to the war to drive out the Burmese from Chiang Saen in 1804. It also gained favor through the resettlement of Lue people from Sipsong Panna. This resulted in Nan's flourishing again in the early Ratanakosin period.

THE REESTABLISHMENT OF CHIANG MAI IN 1796

It was important for Kawila to establish his command in Chiang Mai, which had been the center of Lan Na for five hundred years. Kawila wanted to establish a Chao Chet Ton presence that would be comparable with that of the Mangrai dynasty.

He began with the resumption of old coronation customs, entering the city for his own ceremony in the same way that the Mangrai kings had entered before him. He claimed possession of royal regalia from the Mangrai dynasty, such as the Sikanchai dagger, to demonstrate his power against his enemies.[23] He lived in the auspicious center of Chiang Mai. Sacred places and objects were rebuilt, for example, the statues of two white elephants at the "head" of the city to the north, the figures of lions in the Khuang Singh area, the figures of the ogre Kumphan and the hermit Suthep at Chedi Luang Temple. Stupas, monks' residences, Buddha image halls, and ordination halls were restored. There was support for Buddhist studies, which resulted in the revival of the writing of chronicles on palm-leaf manuscripts, as well as appointments of monks. The city walls and fortifications were restored and moats and other

55. Chang Phueak Monument originally was built during the reign of Phaya Saenmueangma in approximately 1400. The two white elephants were located on both sides of the road, facing each other. Phaya Saenmueangma erected the monument in remembrance of Ai Ob and Ai Yira who took turns carrying him while fleeing the Sukhothai troops back to Chiang Mai. Originally the Chang Phueak Gate was called Hua Wiang Gate. After the erection of the white elephants, the gate was renamed the Chang Phueak Gate or the White Elephant Gate. During King Kawila's restoration of Chiang Mai, the old Chang Phueak Monument was probably in deteriorating condition, and he rebuilt it as it appears today. (NAT, c. 1900–1903)

56. The two lions at Hua Wiang, located at Khuang Singh, were considered an auspicious symbol of Chiang Mai. This location was used for gathering the troops for war during King Kawila's time, also known as the period of "collecting vegetables for the basket and people for the *mueang*." (NAT, c. 1926)

water channels dug out. Such projects helped revive city life. The leaders felt the changes represented an important historical development, and they gave the city a formal new name, Mueang Ratanatingsa Aphinawaburi Chiang Mai, "A Great New City Full of Thirty Precious Things."[24] In short, the Chao Chet Ton was set on replacing the Mangrai dynasty and carrying on local customs.

The great forced resettlements led to various ethnic groups settling in different places around Chiang Mai and Lamphun. The most important sites, used for the residences of nobles and their entourages, were within the city's rectangular inner wall. Only the Thai Yuan were allowed to reside in the inner city, a practice that had probably been in effect since the Mangrai dynasty. Relocated commoners were classified. Artisans and high-ranking commoners were settled within the city, such as the Khoen lacquerware experts from Chiang Tung, who resided at Haiya, between the southern inner and outer walls. The Yuan people from Ban Hom resided between the eastern inner and outer walls and were experts in making paper flowers, preparing food, and trading.[25] The Tai Yai, or Shan, were traders, and they settled in the business areas of Chang Phueak and Chang Moi. Unskilled commoners were relocated to outlying areas to work as farmers, such as the Khoen in San Sai and Doi Saket and the Yong in Lamphun.

The resettled people often named their new villages after the places they had been forced to leave; thus there were new localities called Ban Mueang Luang, Mueang Wa, Mueang Len, Mueang Khon, Mueang Kai, Mueang Sat, Ban Yu, Ban Luai, and Phayak. Other localities were named for local characteristics. For example, Ban Mueang Kung was settled by a group from Mueang Pu. Some villages of Khoen people can now no longer trace their origins in Chiang Tung because their ancestors gave their relocation village a new name. Such communities include Ban Chang Kradat in San Pa Thong district, Ban Palang in Hang Dong district, Ban San Klang in San Kamphaeng district, and Ban Padu in Doi Saket district.

The resettlements involved all social levels, from nobles to commoners. Resettled nobles were allowed to continue to govern their own people, under the supervision of Lan Na leaders. There is clear evidence that entire resettled *mueang* kept their old cultural systems. The Lue from Mueang La, Sipsong Panna, resettled at Ban Nong Bua, Nan province, continued to perform the ceremony of giving food to the spirit of the founding ruler of Mueang La once every three years. Information on the Mueang Yong group, resettled in 1805, indicates that the Yong ruler swore allegiance to Lan Na, was favorably treated, and ordered to resettle his people in Lamphun. With his relatives, he established a community at Wiang Yong on the east bank of the Kuang River. Villages of Yong commoners were established in the vicinity to serve them. Ban Tong was for builders; Ban Luai for weavers; and Ban Yu for poets.[26] Probably the Yong commoners had to pay rice and other tribute to their

57. Lue woman from Nan. The Lue were herded to Nan during the period of "collecting vegetables for the basket and people for the *mueang*." (NAT, n.d.)

lords. The evidence suggests that Chao Chet Ton clan were respectful in the manner in which they treated groups such as the Yong. Evidence exists that there were discussions among the rulers of Chiang Mai, Lamphun, Mueang Yong, and Chiang Tung as well as with other nobles, their descendants, and courtiers before proclaiming laws.

> The year 1193 (1831), the year of the rabbit, the fourth month, the eighth day of the waning moon, the fourth day, two kings, the *chao luang* and Chao Maha Uparat Narathibodisisuwan, were the leaders. The *chao ratchawong*, the king of Chiang Tung, Chao Suriyawong of Mueang Yong, *chao ratchabut*, Chao Chaiyawong, nobles, high-ranking courtiers, and all officials who took charge of government offices consulted with each other in 1193 that in the future there would be a law stipulating that there would be only four courts in a city, and they must not be duplicated.[27]

Moreover, there was an order in 1811 concerning the descendants of the Chao Chet Ton family of Mueang Yong, Chiang Tung, Mueang Kai, and Mueang Wa. It was decreed that they should be united as though they were one *mueang*. If charges were made, they had to present the case to the *khun sanam* first. If the parties were not satisfied, they could present their case to the ruler of Mueang Yong and finally appeal to the king.[28] However, the "migrant noble groups" gradually lost their roles, probably in the late nineteenth century before the administrative reforms, through integration with the local people.

During the Chao Chet Ton restoration of Lan Na, the seven brothers ruled separately in Chiang Mai, Lamphun, and Lampang. (One brother, Phraya Uparat Mula, died before having an opportunity to take office.) Phraya Khamsom ruled Lampang from 1782 to 1794. Kawila and Khamsom assisted each other. There is evidence that Kawila left Wiang Pa Sang in 1784 to assist Lampang against the Burmese, and they successfully held the city until Siamese forces arrived and drove the Burmese off.[29] In 1788, Khamsom helped Kawila in a failed attack on Chiang Saen. When Khamsom died in 1794, King Rama I appointed another brother, Phraya Uparat Duangthip as the ruler of Lampang and Phraya Ratchawong Mula as *phraya uparat*. Nai Khanan Chaiwong, the son of Phraya Khamsom, became *phraya ratchawong*. Chiang Mai and Lampang continued to be closely linked.

Lamphun was reestablished in 1805 and was ruled by Phraya Burirat Khamfan from Chiang Mai. It was next in importance after Chiang Mai and Lampang. Chao Bunma, the youngest of the Chao Chet Ton, was *phraya uparat*.

THE SEVEN BROTHERS OF THE CHAO CHET TON DYNASTY

Ruler	Ruler of Chiang Mai	Ruler of Lampang	Ruler of Lamphun	Source
1. King Kawila	(1782–1816)*	1774–1782	–	Chiang Mai Chronicle
2. Phraya Kamsom	–	1782–1794	–	"
3. Phraya Thammalangka	1816–1822	–	–	"
4. King Duangthip	–	1794–1825	–	Yonok Chronicle
5. Phraya Uparat Mula	–	–	–	
6. Phraya Khamfan	1823–1825		1805	Yonok Chronicle, Rama II Chronicle
7. King Bunma	–	–	1815–1827	Yonok Annals

*Although named king of Chiang Mai by Rama I in 1782, King Kawila was unable to reestablish Chiang Mai until 1796.

THE CONTROL OF CHIANG MAI

There were nine Chao Chet Ton rulers with the following reigns.

1. King Kawila ([1782–1796] [1796–1813), originally called Chao Khanan Kawila, was born in Lampang in 1742. He was the first son of Chaofa Chaikaeo, the ruler of Lampang, and was reportedly an able assistant to his father as a youth. In 1774, he joined with the *phraya chaban* from Chiang Mai to oppose the Burmese by swearing allegiance to King Taksin of Thonburi. After the Burmese were driven off, Taksin appointed Kawila ruler of Lampang. He ruled there from 1774 until 1782, fighting the Burmese with determination and saving Lampang as a base for the Thai. After King Rama I took the throne in 1782, Kawila was promoted to *phraya wachiraprakan*, the ruler of Chiang Mai, at the age of forty, though Chiang Mai had yet to be seized back from the Burmese. He first established a base at Wiang Pa Sang, and in 1796 here established Chiang Mai. He later extended his territory to Chiang Tung, Chiang Rung, and Sipsong Panna. He restored important temples and established the Buddhist ecclesiastical hierarchy according to old customs. In 1802, he was promoted to the position of king. Two years later, he drove the Burmese out of Chiang Saen. From then until his death in 1813 he worked to develop a stable and secure Chiang Mai.

2. Phraya Thammalangka (1815–1821), originally named Chao Noi Thammalangka, was the third son of Chaofa Chaikaeo. In 1774, he was *phraya ratchawong* of Lampang. In 1782, he became the *uparat* of Chiang Mai. Thammalangka was a prominent commander and worked vigorously to assist his elder brother, Kawila, in the resettlement wars. His important achievements as *uparat* were an attack on Mueang Sat in 1802 and the seizure of its ruler, Racha Chomhong, who had sided with the Burmese and was sent to Bangkok; and action in the war of 1804 to drive the Burmese out of Chiang Saen. His abilities were widely recognized, so that after Kawila's death he was made king.

After presenting a white elephant to King Rama II, Thammalangka was promoted to the title of Phraya Chiang Mai Changphueak [White Elephant]. The people addressed him as "Chao Changphueak," or Lord White Elephant. Chiang Mai was peaceful and orderly during his reign. Prominent temples such as Phra Singh and Phra That Si Chom Thong temples were restored. Improvements to the city included the construction of an outer moat from Ku Huang Corner to Haiya Gate[30] and the construction of an outer wall from Siphum Corner on to the southern side.[31] Water channels were constructed inside the city from Hua lin Corner to Siphum Corner and on to Khatam Corner.[32]

3. Phraya Khamfan (1823–1825) was the sixth son of Prince Chaikaeo, and the people called him "Chao Luang Setthi," or Rich Lord. In 1782, he was Phraya Burirat of Chiang Mai and was a strong military leader in the subjugation of other *mueang*. In 1805, he became ruler of Lamphun. He was subsequently promoted to *phraya uparat* of Chiang Mai (1815–1821). Phraya

Khamfan traveled to Bangkok in 1823 to accept the appointment as ruler of Chiang Mai.

He ruled for only three years. There was chaos during his reign as a result of power struggles between himself and Phraya Ratchawong Suwannakhammun, according to the Chiang Mai Chronicle.[33]

4. *Phraya Phuttawong* (1826–1846) was titled Phraya Kakawanna Thiparacha Wachiraprakan, but the people of Chiang Mai called him "Chao Luang Phaendin Yen," or Lord of the Peaceable Kingdom. He was the son of Nai Phoruan, the younger brother of Prince Chaikaeo. He had assisted in the forced resettlement programs of Kawila's reign. In 1823, he was *phraya uparat* of Chiang Mai. After Phraya Khamfan's death, he succeeded as ruler and had the longest reign in this dynasty. During his reign, Chiang Mai was peaceful, as the old enemy Burma was at war with England. The village area around the city was greatly expanded. It appears to have been a time of prosperity. Dr. David Richardson, a British military doctor and explorer, came to Chiang Mai in 1829 to buy elephants as well as cattle and buffalo to feed British military forces in Lower Burma and made several similar trips afterwards. British and British subjects began to trade in the area and to engage in logging.

5. *King Mahotaraphrathet* (Phraya Mahawong, 1847–1854), originally called Chao Khanan Mahawong, was the son of Thammalangka. In 1826, he held the post of *phraya uparat* of Chiang Mai. He was an able administrator, whose role was especially important at the end of Phuttawong's reign when the king was quite old. In 1847, he was appointed Phraya Mahawong, the fifth king of the Chao Chet Ton line. Important events during his reign included the three Chiang Tung Wars, the first in 1849–1850 in the reign of King Rama III, the second in 1852, and the third in 1854 during the reign of King Rama IV, who promoted him to the title of King Mahotaraprathet in order to encourage him in the third Chiang Tung War. The forest industry expanded greatly during his reign.

6. *King Kawilorot Suriyawong* (1856–1870) was originally named Chao Nan Suriyawong. He was a son of King Kawila. He was also called "Chao Chiwit Ao," or Lord Taker of Life, because he would order people to be beheaded by uttering the word "*ao*" [take]. In 1826, he became *phraya burirat* and in 1856 he was promoted to rule Chiang Mai. His reign saw improvements in the laws and the courts. He renovated temples and other important sites. The British and their subjects came to trade and many went into logging, which eventually led to litigation involving the forests.

In 1866, the American Presbyterian missionary, Daniel McGilvary, wrote that Kawilorot was a very powerful ruler who was greatly feared by the people.

> Within his own realm, Kawilorot was really "Lord of Life." He was absolute head both of church and of state. He brooked no rival and no contradiction in either . . . The highest positions in the religious hierarchy were bestowed or

58. Chao Chiwit Ao or King Kawilorot Suriyawong, the absolute ruler. (NAT, c. 1864)

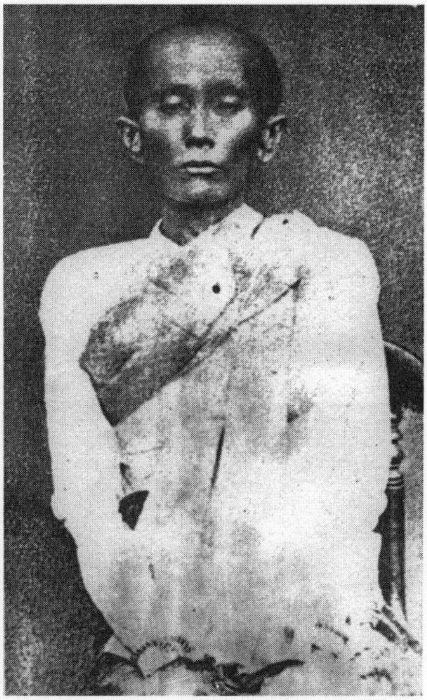

59. Chao Usa, the queen of King Kawilorot Suriyawong. (NAT, c. 1864)

> withdrawn at his pleasure. His own brothers-in-law languished in exile in Siam, because it was not thought safe for them to return and be within his reach. At home he had vanquished or terrified into submission all possible rivals. Even the court of Siam seemed inspired with a wholesome fear of meddling with him . . .
>
> . . . He was a tender father. He could be a warm, though a fickle and inconstant friend. In many respects he was a good ruler. He was absolute and tyrannical, but there was no petty thieving in his realm.[34]

Kawilorot died at the age of seventy-one. He had ruled Chiang Mai for thirteen years. He had two daughters, Chao Thepkraison and Chao Ubonwanna.[35]

7. *King Inthawichayanon* (1873–1896), originally named Chao Inthanon, was called "Chao Ta Khao," or Lord White Eyes, by the people. He was the son of Phraya Rachawong Mahaphrom Khamkhong, and the grandson of Phraya Khamfan. He was also the son-in-law of King Kawilorot, through his marriage to Chao Thepkraison. In 1856 he was *phraya burirat* and in 1869 he was promoted to the post of *phraya uparat inthanon*. In 1870, he became the

60. Chao Inthanon or King Inthawichayanon. (NAT, c. 1892–1897)

61. Chao Thepkaison, the queen of King Inthawichayanon. (NAT, c. 1864)

acting ruler of Chiang Mai, and he was appointed ruler three years later. In 1882, he was made King Inthawichayanon. His queen, Chao Thepkraison, was an intelligent and knowledgeable assistant, who acted in effect as an able regent for her weak husband until her death in 1884.

During his reign, the central government proceeded with a policy of merging the tributary *mueang* of Lan Na with Thailand. In 1874, the government sent a commissioner to be stationed in Chiang Mai for the first time. It subsequently introduced a new form of local government for Lan Na, which was renamed Monthon Phayap. King Inthawichayanon was the last king of the Lan Na tributary state.

8.Chao Inthawarorot Suriyawong (1901–1909), originally called Chao Noi Suriya, was born in 1859. He was the son of King Inthawichayanon and Chao Rinkham, the daughter of Chao Chailangkaphisankhun. He became *chao ratchabut*, the equivalent of crown prince, in 1889, and in 1901 he became Chao Inthawarorot Suriyawong. As king of Chiang Mai, he received annual money and benefits worth not less than 200,000 baht. During his reign, he had no power in the government because all affairs were under the power of Chiang Mai's commissioner. He died in 1909.[36]

9. Major General Chao Kaeonawarat (1911–1939) was the ninth Chao Chet Ton ruler and the last king of Chiang Mai. He was the son of King Inthawichayanon, and like his predecessor had no direct control over administration, but the central government honored him as the titular head of Chiang Mai.

CHIANG MAI'S INTERNAL POLITICS

The Chao Chet Ton were a powerful clan. They were able to establish a strong regional government and for a time enjoyed considerable independence from Siam. At the beginning, the position of ruler of Chiang Mai was handed down from elder to younger brother, and undoubtedly the clan had the support of other high-ranking nobles in the region. Following Lan Na tradition, it was customary to consider the suitability of candidates before choosing a ruler, although seniority played a part in the rise to power of the first three brothers.

The entire land was bestowed on the ruler of Chiang Mai in a traditional coronation ceremony.[37] It appears that initially, news of a new king would be dispatched to Bangkok, and the new ruler would go down to Bangkok to receive his commission and the insignia of rank. He would then be crowned for a second time in Chiang Mai. Such ceremonies were certainly held in the case of Phraya Thammalangka (1815–1821), Phraya Khamfan (1823–1825), and Phraya Phutthawong (1826–1846). The appointment and coronation system indicates that Chiang Mai had a great deal of political freedom at the time.

There is no evidence of strife among the seven brothers during Kawila's reign. In times of war, Chiang Mai, Lampang, and Lamphun assisted each other. Lan Na was surrounded by enemies, so cooperation was necessary. Kawila, the strong-willed eldest brother, lived long and was a stabilizing force. Power struggles began during the reign of Phraya Khamfan (1823–1825) who was in conflict with his cousin Phraya Ratchawong Suwannakhammun, the son of Nai Phoruan. The Chiang Mai Chronicle says the dispute took the form of religious competition. Khamfan made many donations to temples and Ratchawong Suwannakhammun followed suit. In the past, no one dared equal the amount of donations given by a king. A threat of civil war was averted when the king's brothers made a show of force in Chiang Mai.[38] King Duangthip of Lampang brought two thousand men, and King Bunma of Lamphun another one thousand men. Khamfan entered the monkhood at Buppharam Temple (Suan Dok Temple) for a short period before returning to rule until his death.[39] It is believed that Ratchawong Suwannakhammun had received support from his brothers, Phraya Uparat Phutthawong and Phraya Burirat Noi Kawila. The three held high-ranking positions, *chao khanhabai* [five minister positions: *phraya mueang* (king), *phraya uparat*, *phraya ratchawong*, *phraya ratchabut*, and *phraya burirat*] which put them in line for the throne. Khamfan's son, Chao Pimphisan, was appointed crown prince, but he lacked the charisma of Nai Phoruan. Both Phutthawong and Ratchawong Suwannakhammun had important positions. They appear to have been second only to the king and Phraya Uparat Thammalangka.

During the reign of Thammalangka, the two brothers had roles that were not inferior to that of Phraya Uparat Khamfan and were possibly even more important. They had escorted the white elephant to Bangkok to present to King Rama II and they helped in wars along the border.[40] During Khamfan's reign, the largest quota of the highest-ranking positions of the *chao khanhabai* went to Nai Phoruan's family. As their influence increased, the conflicts grew between Ratchawong Suwannakhammun and Khamfan.

No information about the disputes appears in Bangkok sources, possibly because they did not grow big enough to be widely known and there was felt to be no need to inform Bangkok. Possibly there was an understanding that after Khamfan's reign Phutthawong, the senior and most influential among the sons of Nai Phoruan, would come to power.

Immediately after Khamfan's death, King Duangthip of Lampang led almost one thousand men to Chiang Mai, and King Bunma of Lamphun, or Nong La [the youngest], brought six hundred men. "They hurriedly picked up the families of the dead king, and a collection of valuables. Chao Phimphisan, or the *chao ratchabut*, crown prince, could not withstand them. He paid his respects to the body of his father and, taking Chao Thammakitti Suriyamakkanarin, his younger brother, fled by boat and sought protection from the Bangkok king."[41] Chao Phimphisan returned to Chiang Mai at some point before 1842. Khamfan was succeeded by Phutthawong, making Nai Phoruan's family line the most powerful for a brief period. After Phutthawong's reign, power was returned to descendants of the Chao Chet Ton. Other powerful members of Nai Phoruan's family line had died. Ratchawong Suwannakhammun died in 1825 shortly after the deaths of Khamfan and Duangthip, and Phraya Burirat Noi Kawila died in 1827.[42] There is no evidence either in Lan Na or Bangkok of power struggles during Phutthawong's reign, perhaps due to his charismatic power and respect for his clan. Chiang Mai was peaceful so the people gave him the epithet Lord of the Peaceful Kingdom. In 1846, the monarchy of Chiang Mai devolved back to descendants of the Chao Chet Ton.

More problems surfaced in the reign of King Mahotaraprathet, the fifth king of the restored Chiang Mai (1847–1854). An open rift appeared during the Chiang Tung War (1849–1850), when the king's son, Phraya Ratchabut Noi Mahaphron, and Phraya Uparat Phimphisan set out to attack Chiang Tung. The *ratchabut*'s troops reached Chiang Tung first and attacked the city without waiting for the other contingent, possibly because the *ratchabut* was trying to gain his father's favor. Then when he failed to capture Chiang Tung, he asked for support from the *phraya uparat*, who deliberately delayed and refused to help. The attack on Chiang Tung failed primarily because of the antagonism between the two leaders.[43] King Mahotaraprathet complained to Bangkok that the *phraya uparat* had not assisted his son. The antagonism between the two men may have originated in their rankings in the *chao khanhabai*. Any member of this group of five, under the supreme leader, was eligible to become ruler, but the post of *uparat*, or second king, was closest in line to the throne. Thus Phraya Uparat Phimphisan seems to have been senior to the *chao ratchabut* and the other sons of King Mahotaraphrathet. However, the king felt that the succession should follow his bloodline.

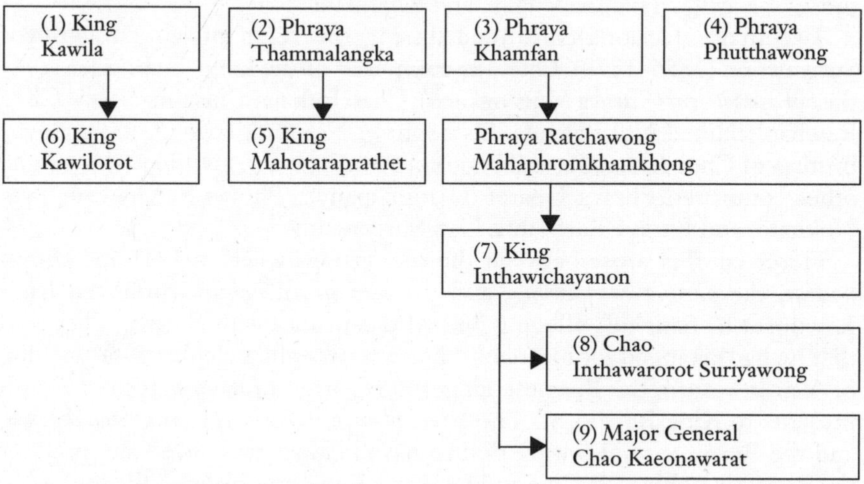

When the king died, King Rama IV ordered two commissioners, Chao Phraya Mukhamontri (Ket) and Luang Wisutsombat (Phrom) to attend his funeral and end the conflict in Chiang Mai. The commissioners brought "Phraya Mueangkaeo Nan Suriyawong, the son of King Kawila, Nai Noi Mahaphrom, Nai Nansuriyawong, who was the son of King Mahotaraprathet, the *phraya* of Lamphun, and the *phraya uparat* of Lampang"[44] to Bangkok in 1856 for consultations about who should become the next ruler. For the first time the central government was participating in the selection of the ruler. King Rama IV then appointed Phraya Uparat Phimphisan as *chao mueang changwang*, Phraya Mueangkaeo Nan Suriyawong as the ruler of Chiang Mai, and Phraya Rachabut Noi Mahaphrom as *uparat*. But while consultations were continuing Phraya Uparat Phimphisan, who was ill in Chiang Mai and had been unable to journey down to Bangkok, passed away, so the arrangements had to be changed. Furthermore, the rulers of Lampang and

Lamphun proposed that Phraya Ratchabut Noi Mahaphrom be detained in Bangkok because of his "insubordinate attitude and unwillingness to follow orders of his superiors."[45] Phraya Ratchabut Noi Mahaphrom was appointed Phraya Utarakankoson, but he remained in exile in Bangkok until his death.

Phraya Mueangkaeo Nan Suriyawong, the son of King Kawila, became King Kawilorot Suriyawong of Chiang Mai; Nai Nan Thamma Panyo, the son of Phraya Khamfan, became *phraya uparat*; Nai Nan Suriyawong, the son of King Mahotaraprathet and grandson of Phraya Thammalangka, became *phraya ratchabut*; Nai Inthanon, the son of Phraya Ratchawong Mahaphrom Khamkhong, became *phraya burirat*.[46] The appointments continued the system of apportioning quotas for the three prominent Chao Chet Ton family lines, those of Kawila, Thammalangka, and Khamfan.

Two major factions continued during the reign of King Kawilorot Suriyawong (1856–1870). One was composed of the king's close relatives—the *phraya burirat* (Phraya Mueangkaeo); Chao Inthanon, his son-in-law; Chao Ratchaphakhinai Noi Phaenfa, his nephew; Nai Bunthawong, the younger brother of Chao Inthanon; and Nai Noi Phutthawong, his adopted son. The other comprised Phraya Uparat Thammapanyo, Phraya Ratchawong Noi Nokham, and Phraya Ratchabut Nan Suriyawong.

Fierce conflict arose between the two groups when in 1855 the *phraya uparat*, the *phraya ratchawong*, and the *phraya ratchabut* denounced King Kawilorot to Bangkok, alleging he had taken sides with Burma. They said that he had arranged for his men to present two white elephants to the king of Ava. In return, the Burmese king was reported to have sent nobles with presents to King Kawilorot. The king, *phraya burirat*, *chao ratchaphakhinai*, and the Burmese nobles were said to have held secret conversations. After the Burmese nobles left Chiang Mai, King Kawilorot ordered the execution of the Burmese interpreter, who lived in Chiang Mai.[47] In addition, the three Chiang Mai nobles were said to have decided "if Bangkok ordered them to have an audience with the king, they would not go; and if Bangkok pressed them, they would fight back. The king of Chiang Mai, the *chao burirat*, and the *chao ratchaphakhinai* said that to die fat was better than to die thin."[48]

The central government called King Kawilorot and all the nobles involved in the case to Bangkok in 1866. Kawilorot testified that the ruler of Mueang Nai had originally planned to buy the two white elephants, but that Kawilorot felt that to take a little money for them would be a loss of honor, so he decided to present the elephants as a gift instead. Later the Mueang Nai ruler presented the animals to the king of Ava, who in turn ordered that valuable presents be given to King Kawilorot to repay the favor. During Kawilorot's audience with King Rama IV, he presented the gifts from Ava to the Bangkok king, who replied, "The king of Ava gave these presents to the king of Chiang Mai. Let him keep them, but I will keep just one ruby ring so as not to disappoint King Kawilorot."[49] Ministers assigned to judge the case concluded that King

62. Phraya Uparat Bunthawong, the younger brother of King Inthawichayanon, was a powerful person because he could dismiss King Inthawichayanon's orders. He was considered the second king while he was *uparat*. (NAT, c. 1873–1882)

63. A missionary's overland journey with elephants. (PUA, c. 1882–1927)

Kawilorot had acquitted himself well. "King Kawilorot Suriyawong is found not guilty of any of the charges."[50] He returned to Chiang Mai to rule while his accusers, the *chao ratchawong*, the *chao ratchabut*, Nai Noi Mahawong (the son of the *chao uparat*), Nai Nan Mahathep, and Nai Noi Thepawong were ordered to remain in Bangkok. An exception was made for the *chao uparat*, who returned to Chiang Mai and died in 1867. Two years later, Phraya Burirat Inthanon was appointed *phraya uparat*.

King Kawilorot died in 1870, and was succeeded by Phraya Uparat Inthanon in 1873, on the condition that he fully accept the power of Siam and act according to the provisions of the Treaty of Chiang Mai of 1873. King Kawilorot had refused to accept the Bowring Treaty, which gave the British and their subjects certain rights in the area. Kawilorot had granted teak concessions to British subjects but friction over these led to the first Treaty of Chiang Mai, which clarified elements of the Bowring Treaty. The central government wished to avoid further problems, so in 1873 it drew up the "Agreement concerning the King of Chiang Mai, who will keep the country in order."[51] The important details of this document were similar to the first Treaty of Chiang Mai. Inthanon accepted all its conditions. Foreign sources describe the king as "kind-hearted but weak."[52] Administration during his reign was effectively in the hands of Chao Uparat Bunthawong and Chao Thepkraison, the queen. The *uparat* died in 1882 and the queen in 1884.

Siam was now taking an increasingly important role in the matter of who would rule in Chiang Mai, partly due to the internal power struggles among the Chao Chet Ton descendants.

64. Kao Sanam Luang Office, Nakhon Lampang. (NAT, c. 1902)

INTERNAL RULE IN CHIANG MAI

The central government in Bangkok was well aware of Lan Na's former independence and the area was initially allowed to continue much as it always had. Initially, the various Lan Na *mueang* maintained their own local governments, in accordance with old customs. The Lan Na rulers that Siam appointed were regarded by the people as kings. Lan Na continued to use the Mangraisat legal system handed down from the Mangrai dynasty, but it was adapted as needed. Rulers of individual *mueang* could promulgate their own laws. For example, the ruler of Mueang Nan promulgated laws called *Anachaklakkham*, or rules of the kingdom.[53] The ruler of Mueang Chiang Mai promulgated his own *lakkham*, with sections for fines, tribute, etc. Individual rulers retained their power over the courts, acting as the highest court.

Relations among the *mueang* in Lan Na were based largely on mutual assistance and cooperation, and the central government did not interfere. There is evidence that Mueang Nan, Chiang Mai, Lampang, and Lamphun promulgated laws together in 1844 to solve mutual problems, for example, commoners fleeing, assaults, itinerant trade, etc.[54] The economy and its benefits were still in the hands of the locality and its ruler. The local government commanded a share of labor, rice, and other tribute in kind for the royal granary and for distribution among the nobles and ministers. Trade conducted by the nobles was carried out without reference to the central government. The monetary system and coinage within the *mueang* were regulated by the individual ruler. In short, the *mueang* treasury and the management of income and expenditures fell entirely into the hands of the local governments. However, the central government received economic benefits in the form of tribute in kind, the royal tribute, and periodic levies in kind.

One reason that the central government allowed a certain freedom to local governments was the great difficulty of communication with Bangkok. The journey to Chiang Mai was via the Ping River, which had many rapids. In 1867, it took the missionary Daniel McGilvary three months to travel from Bangkok to Chiang Mai by boat.[55]

In general, individual *mueang* rulers held the five top-ranking positions known as the *chao khanhabai*. In theory these appointments were in the hands of Bangkok, but in practice, they were decided in Lan Na and only rubber-stamped by Siam. There was also a head administrative office or *kao sanamluang*, a body that could be traced back to the Mangrai dynasty. This body was composed of thirty-two committee members of high-ranking nobles. They were hierarchically divided into two *phraya kao sanam*, ten first-class *phraya sanam*, ten second-class *phraya sanam*, and ten third-class *phraya sanam*.[56] The *kao sanamluang* acted as an advisory body to the ruler and assisted in administrative duties such as deciding lawsuits. Local administration was divided into villages and *tambon*, or subdistricts of a cluster of villages. A *kamnan* (*khwaen*) administered a *tambon* and a *phuyaiban (kaeban)* administered a village. Their responsibilities included general day-to-day supervision while real power was in the hands of the *kao sanam luang*. *Khwaen* and *kaeban* held the ranks of *saeng*, *thao*, or *phraya*. It is believed that the localities close to the city of Chiang Mai were directly responsible to the ruler. The administration of *mueang* outside Chiang Mai was divided into inner and outer *mueang*, and peripheral *mueang* on the borders. The inner *mueang* such as Chiang Dao, Phrao, Hang Dong, and Chom Thong, were directly responsible to Chiang Mai. The ruler of Chiang Mai likely appointed trusted people to rule these *mueang* and to collect rice tribute and other kinds of tribute. The outer *mueang* included Chiang Rai, Chiang Saen, Mueang Fang, Mueang Ngai, Mueang Pai, Mueang Mae Hong Son, Mueang Khun Yuam, and Mueang Yuam; and they did not send rice tribute.[57] The author believes that the ruler of Chiang Mai stipulated the delivery of rare forest products in lieu. The outlying *mueang* on the border felt Chiang Mai's influence only occasionally.

THE ADMINISTRATION OF CHIANG MAI AS A TRIBUTARY STATE OF THAILAND

The central government in both the Thonburi and early Ratanakosin periods supported the use of Chiang Mai as a buffer to defend against invasion from the Burmese. In the early Ratanakosin period the central government used several methods to strengthen Chiang Mai. Bangkok dispatched troops in 1797, to help King Kawila in the early years after the city had been reestablished. According to the Chiang Mai Chronicle, Kawila would not have been able to protect Chiang Mai alone. King Rama I appointed his younger brother Kromphraratchawang Bawon Maha Surasinghanat (Bunma) or *wang na* (colloquial), the King of the Front Palace [also known as the second king or deputy king and often next in line of succession] to assist until the Burmese were defeated. In 1802, King Rama I ordered Chiang Mai and Lampang to attack Chiang Saen, then a stronghold of Burma, and he provided guns and ammunition.[58] The effort to strengthen Chiang Mai had achieved results by the end of King Rama I's reign. By 1804, with the assistance of troops from Bangkok, Chiang Mai was able to expel the Burmese from Chiang Saen. Troops from Chiang Mai and other Lan Na *mueang* joined to attack other oulying *mueang* under Burmese control. In 1805, they were able to extend their influence to Chiang Tung, Chiang Rung, Mueang Lue, and Sipsong Panna. Bangkok also returned a number of the families that Chiang Mai had captured and then presented to Siam. Kawila had directed that families taken from attacks on Mueang Sat, Mueang Pan, and Mueang Pu be presented to King Rama I. The king returned them to Chiang Mai and also gave money and clothes to the military officers as rewards for their meritorious service.[59] Such returns continued through the reign of King Rama III.[60] The central government helped with the reestablishment of Lamphun, Chiang Rai, Phayao, and Mueang Ngao.[61] The reestablishment of Lamphun occurred in 1805, when Chiang Mai was relatively stable. Chiang Rai, Phayao, and Mueang Ngao were reestablished during the reign of King Rama III. The rulers of Chiang Mai, Lampang, and Lamphun asked permission to reestablish these cities at the same time, in 1843. King Mahotaraprathet sent a descendant of the Chao Chet Ton family with troops to reestablish Chiang Rai, and the ruler of Lampang sent members of his clan to reestablish Phayao and Mueang Ngao. As a result, the Chao Chet Ton family controlled many *mueang*. During the reign of King Rama III, many *mueang* were being ruled by nobles who were more senior than the Chao Chet Ton descendants. King Rama III gave the Chiang Mai ruler the right to admonish and punish them. He also gave him the right to propose the names of suitable people for the posts of ruler and *uparat* of Lamphun.[62] However, in an official letter to the rulers of Chiang Mai, Lampang, and Lamphun, the king stressed the need for the three *mueang* to assist each other.

The central government allowed Chiang Mai a high degree of autonomy in internal affairs. Nevertheless, it utilized several direct and indirect strategies of control. One important method was the appointment of the *chao khanhabai*, the highest-ranking political posts, which were bestowed by the king of Siam.[63] The new appointees had to travel to Bangkok for the presentation of their letters of appointment and their insignia of rank. All insignia had to be returned to Bangkok after death. There is evidence that the insignia of rank returned after the death of King Phutthawong of Chiang Mai (1826–1836) were short by five items, but Bangkok did not press for their return.[64] The rulers of the tributary states had to hold ceremonies showing their loyalty to the king in Bangkok. For example, with a change of reign in Siam, the rulers and their descendants had to be present at the funerary rites and have an audience with the new king. The ceremonial drinking of the water of allegiance was conducted twice a year at an important temple, with the *chao khanhabai* and other nobles and their relatives required to participate. Those who did not participate would be suspect. Both King Rama III and King Rama IV stressed the importance of this ceremony.[65]

There were also very direct displays of Siamese power. Local rulers could be summoned for interrogation. King Taksin summoned Phraya Chaban and King Kawila over the execution of the Uparat Konkaeo, for example. Taksin punished Kawila by clipping his ear lobes and punished Chaban with imprisonment. In another case, King Rama IV summoned Kawilorot to Bangkok over the rumors of his pro-Burma attitude. If the central government was uncertain about a person's loyalty, he could be given a position in Bangkok. Phraya Phrae Mangchai, for example, had been captured by the Burmese and remained with them for ten years (1775–1785). He later assisted Thai forces attacking Chiang Saen and brought its former ruler to Bangkok. But King Rama I continued to have doubts and ordered Phraya Phrae Mangchai to take a position in Bangkok.[66]

Chiang Mai had two obligations as a tributary state, the sending of tribute—the royal tribute, the annual tribute, and special assessments—and the defense of the country.

The royal tribute had to be sent once every three years. Failure to do so would be considered rebellion. Important items of tribute included a pair of gold and silver trees of equal size. During the reign of King Rama IV, the royal tribute comprised seven-tiered gold and silver trees about a meter and a half high and 300 teak logs.[67] In some years 150 or 300 tubes of liquid black lacquer from varnish trees would be sent in place of teak logs. The gold and silver trees were not very valuable compared to other items.

The annual tribute had to be sent each year at a specific time. Important tribute from Chiang Mai was teak logs. During the reign of King Rama III, Chiang Mai sent five hundred teak logs, Nan four hundred, Lampang four hundred, Phrae two hundred, and Lamphun two hundred.[68] Sometimes the tribute fell short of requirements and was then considered to be an unpaid debt. However, there is no evidence of demands for full payment from Chiang Mai or urgency in sending the amounts owed. But when Phrae did not send the full tribute of teak logs required, the central government demanded the shortfall be made up at once. The ruler of Nan asked permission not to send teak logs for three years, but King Rama IV refused and admonished him.[69] Apart from teak logs, Chiang Mai also sent 200 bolts of white cloth per year and 537 coconut shell measures (about a liter each) of liquid lacquer from Black Varnish (*melanhorrea usitata*) trees.[70]

The central government also made special levies for royal ceremonies, such as funerals. For King Rama I's funerary rite in 1809, Chiang Mai was ordered to send 20,000 bound papers, Lampang 15,000, Lamphun 5,000, Phrae 20,000 plus 5 piculs of flax (1 picul = about 60 kg), Nan 3,000 plus 5 piculs of flax.[71] When the central government was constructing palaces and temples, it would make a special levy of teak logs.[72] For example, when King Rama IV was constructing a palace at Lop Buri, Lampang had to deliver 1,000 teak logs, but the amount demanded from Chiang Mai is unknown.

In return for tribute, the central government would bestow presents on the tributary states by giving them to the commanders of the tribute processions. The presents were usually items hard to find in the locality or things requested, but they were not specific either in kind or quantity. For example, in 1802 King Rama I gave the following presents to Chiang Mai:

2 guns with a 2-inch bore
3 small cannon with a 3-inch bore

2,500 cannon balls for 3-, 4-, and 5-inch cannon
300 kg of tin
180 kg of gunpowder
2,000 small cymbals
7 iron pans
5,000 sheets of gold leaf
300 kg of heavy mirrors[73]

In 1847, King Rama III gave iron plows, which could be collected from the iron tax officials at Mueang Chai Nat. The *chao uparat* was the head of Chiang Mai's tribute procession at that time with thirty-four people in his entourage. The king gave them food and goods, including 34 *thang* or buckets of rice (1 *thang* = 20 liters), 500 pieces of firewood, 42 mats, and 130 liters of coconut oil.[74]

After the ruler of Nan had presented the royal tribute to King Rama IV, the king gave him the following items: gold weighing 10 baht (1 baht = 15.2 gm, the weight of a baht coin) worth 300 baht, good carpets worth 64 baht, 12 lengths of good wool worth 156 baht, a good double-barreled shotgun worth 200 baht, 8 bolts of white linen worth 120 baht, and one curtain of good quality worth 40 baht.[75] Probably the central government did not give every item requested by the tributary states. During the reign of King Rama V, Mueang Nan sent the royal tribute and requested large quantities of goods. "Nan asked for 100 guns, 500 rounds of ammunition, 3 piculs (180 kg) of gunpowder, 2 piculs (120 kg) of tin, 10,000 flints, 8,000 baht in money, medicine made up of nine ingredients, as well as nutmeg, mace, cardamom, cloves, and pepper."[76]

King Rama V did not meet every request, as his memoir indicates:

> Everything requested has been met, but 100 flintlocks were too many and I gave Nan a reasonable amount. Money should not be freely given unless there is silver in exchange. If one would like to borrow, it has to be formally recorded as a loan, not an item in return for the royal tribute.[77]

The presents depended entirely on the generosity of the Thai king. The aim was to keep good relations between the two sides. Official documents always showed the Thai king's concern for the well-being of the Lan Na nobility. In case of sickness, the Thai king would send medicine or the royal physicians.

The tributary states were also obligated to assist in the defense of the country. In wartime, troops had to be conscripted and sent off to help quickly to avoid suspicion of rebellion. Chiang Mai troops were conscripted many times, such as during the Chao Anuwong revolt by the ruler of Vientiane in 1826. The tributary states had to be prepared to defend the country at any time. In return, Bangkok acted as protector to Lan Na. If Chiang Mai,

Lamphun, or Lampang faced the threat of war and informed Bangkok, troops would be dispatched to assist them and prevent the loss of any of the country's territory.[78] Siam's control of its tributary states relied on leniency and mutual assistance, which contributed to smooth relations before the period of administrative reforms.

CHAPTER 6

BURMESE INVASIONS, SIAM'S EXPANSION OF POWER, AND THE CHIANG TUNG WARS

BURMESE INVASIONS

Burma continued to pose grave problems for Lan Na leaders in the late eighteenth century. Kawila had driven the Burmese out of Chiang Mai in 1775, but as early as the following year, Burma was raising troops for a new attack with a large and powerful force. Phraya Wachiraprakan Bunma, the ruler of Chiang Mai, had insufficient manpower to defend the city, so he abandoned it and took refuge in Mueang Sawankhalok. Burma considered the region a strategic necessity because of its close lineage ties with, and assistance to, the Shan States. Access to the manpower, provisions, and weapons of Lan Na was also important to Burma in its wars with Ayuthaya. Twice, Burma defeated Ayuthaya by first invading Lan Na and seizing Ayuthaya's northern *mueang*. The Burmese were also keen on the economic benefits to be reaped in Lan Na during peacetime.

Siam could not afford to allow Lan Na to fall once more into the hands of its old adversary. It was determined to drive the Burmese out.

King Rama I was faced with a major challenge in 1785 when King Padung of Burma sent nine army divisions along four routes to attack the Thai simultaneously from all sides. Chiang Mai was still deserted and the Burmese directed their efforts towards Lampang, where they encountered strong resistance from Kawila, assisted by troops from Bangkok. Eventually the Burmese forces broke and fled to Chiang Saen.[1] In 1787, Burma seized Fang and was planning another attack on Lampang.[2] King Rama I was aware of the dangers of Chiang Mai being deserted. He appointed his brother, the Wang Na, to help reestablish Chiang Mai in 1791.

Kawila reestablished Chiang Mai in 1796. In the following year, Burma sent another large force to besiege the city. Kawila asked for military assistance from Bangkok and the Burmese were dispersed. By the end of 1797 there was some stability in the area and it began to revive.

Burma continued to attempt to reassert its influence. In 1797, it threatened Siam in a note hung at a border checkpoint in Kanchanaburi. The note demanded the return of Lan Na, and claimed that Britain would assist Burma in making war against Siam. "Phraya Cheng, Phraya Tavoy, Phraya Chiang Mai, Mueang Vientiane, Mueang Luang Prabang are all our people of old. If you do not send these people to us, the bold British soldiers are ready to attack Ayutthaya."[3] However, the Thai decided that the threat was a meaningless attempt to sow confusion.

Burma tried, perhaps repeatedly, to persuade Kawila to switch sides. In 1802, Racha Chomhong, ruler of Mueang Sat, volunteered to try to persuade Kawila to change allegiance. For his efforts, Racha Chomhong was appointed "Chao Maha Suwannahangsa Chakkawatirat." He was said to have controlled fifty-seven Lan Na *mueang*. He sent an envoy with a letter offering to negotiate with Kawila, who not only refused to comply but ordered Phraya Uparat Thammalangka and Phraya Burirat Khamfan to attack Mueang Sat. According to the Chiang Mai Chronicle, Racha Chomhong was captured, and Kawila presented him to King Rama I in Bangkok. Kawila was then rewarded with the title of king.[4]

Thai troops under the leadership of Kromluang Thepharirak and Lan Na troops from Chiang Mai, Lampang, and Nan embarked on a war in 1804 to expel the Burmese from Chiang Saen. The troops besieged Chiang Saen for more than a month when many of the soldiers became ill. The central Thai troops withdrew, leaving the others to fight alone. The people of Chiang Saen were starving and decided to pledge allegiance to Bangkok. Lan Na forces then defeated the Burmese. Lan Na went on to capture and resettle more than 23,000 people from the area.[5]

Chiang Mai was later able to expand its political influence to Sipsong Panna. King Rama I considered the Lue *mueang* of Sipsong Panna dependencies, and they presented him with gold and silver trees as tribute. "Despite their allegiance, Bangkok cannot protect them due to their proximity to Burma and China. If war arises, Bangkok would not be able to send its troops in time."[6]

Burmese influence in the area ended after its troops were driven out of Chiang Saen. Yet Burma continued to try to meddle in the region. In 1808, Kawila ordered Phaya Phimphisan to persuade the people in various *mueang* of Sipsong Panna who had fled when Chiang Mai attacked the region in 1805, to return to their *mueang* in order to repopulate them. It appeared that the ruler of Saenwi had been so persuaded and was about to send tribute to Chiang Mai as a sign of acquiescing to its control, when Burmese troops arrived. The ruler of Saenwi, caught red-handed between the two powers, tried to resolve his dilemma by saying that the tribute belonged to Kawila, who was preparing to send it to Ava. He asked Phraya Phimphisan to support his ruse, promising that Ava would reward him, and Phimphisan agreed. The Burmese prepared a big reception for Phraya Phimphisan. But when they found out that Kawila knew nothing about the tribute, they decided to try a trick of their own by sowing distrust between Siam and Lan Na. At the fifth

Thai-Burmese parley of that year Phraya Inthachak, Akapanyi, Phaya Phimphisan, and fourteen commoners brought a letter from a high-ranking official of Ava to Bangkok, as well as gold plate and eleven boxes of other valuables.[7] They informed the Thai that the items had been sent as tribute from the ruler of Chiang Mai to King Badowpaya (King Padung, in Thai) to show his intention of becoming a Burmese vassal. But Badowpaya, they said, wished to have friendly relations with Siam and so had refused to accept the tribute.[8] Phimphisan was sent with the letter, and tribute, along the Kanchanaburi route back to Bangkok. Siam sent Phraya Thainam to investigate the matter halfway at Ratchaburi. Phraya Phimphisan and his followers had to explain the whole story in front of the Burmese commissioner. In the end, the Siam investigation confirmed that Kawila had had no knowledge of the situation.[9]

SIAM'S EXPANSION AND THE CHIANG TUNG WARS

Throughout the early Ratanakosin period the Thai tried to strengthen Lan Na as their northern line of defense. The policy was so successful that by the reign of King Rama III Lan Na was on the offensive and ready to invade Chiang Tung, which was then under the Burmese sphere of influence.[10] Chiang Tung's fate was always allied to its three neighboring powers—Burma, China, and Lan Na—and it swore allegiance at any given time to whichever of the three was most powerful. Mangrai had founded Chiang Tung for the forward northern defense of Lan Na, and appointed his relatives to rule there. In the period between the reigns of Tilokarat and Kaeo, links with Chiang Mai flourished again, especially in the areas of Buddhism and literature. Then all Lan Na became a dependency of Burma. Chiang Tung was persuaded to pay allegiance to Lan Na once more in 1804 when its ruler, Chao Maha Sirichaisaram Phraya (Sirichaichotisaram Phraya), submitted to King Kawila. Later, Phraya Uparat Thammalangka persuaded the Chiang Tung ruler to abandon the *mueang* and evacuate its people to Chiang Mai. The evacuation of the Khoen to Ban Haiya included the royal family, nobles, monks, and commoners. The ruler and his family were given honors and helped to govern their people in the new location. Such large resettlements helped Chiang Mai to develop rapidly, but Chiang Tung was left deserted and defenseless. This was in order to prevent the Burmese from using it as a base for amassing manpower and provisions.

A number of Chiang Tung nobles refused to cooperate. however. Chao Maha Khanan, the younger brother of Chao Maha Sirichaisaram Phraya, fled with his people to Mueang Yang and entrenched himself there,[11] then to Mueang Kang, and finally to Mueang Long. From there, he asked Chiang Mai to attack the Burmese at Mueang Yang.

65. The road to Keng Tung, a city located on a high, mountainous plateau and very difficult to reach. (NAT, 1942)

Lan Na forces failed in a bid to seize Yang and Chao Maha Khanan decided to throw his lot in with Burma, which appointed him ruler of Chiang Tung in 1813.[12] This prompted the Thai to work to strengthen Lan Na, which ultimately led to the reestablishment of Chiang Rai, Phayao, and Ngao in 1843.[13]

The Thai were intent on targeting Chiang Tung. Their first step was to try to persuade Chao Maha Khanan to submit, but this failed. Three Chiang Tung wars followed.

THE FIRST CHIANG TUNG WAR (1849–1850)

The Thai wanted to attack Chiang Tung in order to reduce the threat from Burma. Chaophraya Chakri sent a message to this effect to Chiang Mai in 1844.

> Furthermore, if Chiang Tung remains, our Chiang Rai will not feel secure and must waste the time of its people in protecting the country each year. If Burma is no longer at war [with the British], it will think about quickly seizing

> Chiang Tung, either in the Year of the Snake [1845] or the Year of the Horse [1846]. If Chiang Mai is slow to act and the Burmese regain firm control of Chiang Tung, it will be difficult. The Burmese might get the idea of giving the *mueang* to the English so that it will be a dependency of two sides. The Burmese think we have good relations with England, and our actions in Chiang Tung will interfere with this. Let's take Chiang Tung quickly and forestall any such thoughts of the Burmese. Let the *phraya* of Chiang Mai, the *phraya uparat*, Nai Phimsan, the *phraya* of Lakhon, the *phraya* of Lamphun, the *phraya ratchawong*, Phraya Ratanamueangkaeo, the *phraya ratchabut*, and relatives of all the *saenthao phraya lao* old and new of the three *mueang* consult each other. The preparations for the capture of Chiang Tung can be preceded by the use of persuasive measures to win over the nobles and commoners of Chiang Tung in order to uproot the entire population. Control through peaceful means is preferable because it does not waste troops. Chiang Tung is apprehensive because we have established Chiang Rai. If persuasion does not work, it will be necessary to send troops. Investigate their attitude to be sure, then send troops to attack and carry off the entire population of Chiang Tung to prevent the *mueang* from becoming the base of the enemy. Once we take Chiang Tung, Chiang Rai will be peaceful and contented, and we can think about expanding our territory more extensively.[14]

A second justification for war was that nobles in Chiang Rung had requested assistance. Chiang Rung was in the middle of internal power struggles. Around 1843 its ruler, Chao Mahawang, passed away, and his uncle Chao Maha Khanan Punoi succeeded to the throne. But Mahawang's son, Chao Ratchabut Sarawan and his brother-in-law, Mom Maha Chai, conspired to execute the new ruler and link the area with China. The son of the executed man, Chao Mom Nokham, fled to Chiang Tung. There, Chao Maha Khanan asked for assistance from Burma to establish him on the throne of Chiang Rung. The Burmese king agreed, on condition that Chao Mom Nokham pay a certain amount of money. Burma had been defeated in the First Anglo-Burmese War, and needed cash to pay the huge indemnity demanded by the British.

The Burmese king then ordered the *chakkai luang* to attack Chiang Rung with troops from Mueang Mok Mai and Mueang Nai. However, the *chakkai luang* was bribed by Chao Sarawan. They agreed to a ruse whereby the *chakkai luang* would pretend to make Chao Mom Nokham ruler, but three days later Chao Sarawan would seize power again. The plot was successful, and Chao Mom Nokham took refuge again in Chiang Tung. Thereafter a larger force defeated Chiang Rung, and Chao Mom Nokham was installed as ruler. Chao Sarawan fled to China. The *chao uparat* was sent to Ava.

Chao Mom Nokham ruled Chiang Rung for a period before there was another power struggle. Chao Sarawan and the *chao uparat* offered the king of Burma 1,220 *chang* [1 *chang* = 80 baht] in exchange for the throne of Chiang

66. Phrachao Luang Temple in Chiang Tung, built in approximately 1925. (NAT, 1942)

67. The conscription of commoners for the Chiang Tung Wars showing the transportation of provisions in the Chiang Tung War of 1942, one of the latter wars. Travel here must have been as difficult as during the reigns of Kings Rama III and IV. (NAT, 1942)

Rung. The Burmese king accepted.[15] When he returned in 1849, Chao Sarawan collected money to send to Burma, causing great distress among the people in Sipsong Panna, which led to a revolt. Chao Sarawan was defeated and fled to Burma. The *chao uparat* and his family took refuge in Luang Prabang and asked for assistance from Bangkok. King Rama III's view was "If we can subdue Chiang Tung, Chiang Rung will be ours."[16] He ordered conscription in Chiang Mai for an attack on Chiang Tung.

Chiang Mai complied by conscripting 5,000 men, Lampang 1,000, and Lamphun 1,500, for a total of 7,500 men in eight divisions, organized into two forces, which planned simultaneous attacks on Chiang Tung. The first force led by Phraya Ratchabut Noi Maha Phrom overran Mueang Sat and quickly moved on to attack Chiang Tung. The *ratchabut* had not waited for the additional forces that were due to assist him, and he had to withdraw. The second force headed by Phraya Uparat Phimphisan attacked Mueang Yong. They took their time and were slow to offer assistance to the *ratchabut*. The failure of the two leaders to work together helped ensure that the attack on Chiang Tung was unsuccessful. It is understood that the *ratchabut* hastened to the attack in hopes of a reward. The failure of the attack may also have been the result of hilly and difficult terrain, and insufficient provisions and ammunition.

THE SECOND CHIANG TUNG WAR (1852)

King Rama IV wanted to retake Chiang Tung, for similar reasons. There had been another request for assistance from the ruler of Chiang Rung. Chao Sarawan, now ruler, swore allegiance to Siam and asked for the return of the *chao uparat* and his mother. King Rama IV considered it inappropriate to refuse the request. The ministers also advised him to assist.

> The king's prestige will extend to other countries. Besides, the soldiers and officials will gain experience in war. If we plan to assist Mueang Lue, we must first attack Chiang Tung . . . If we can cut down Chiang Tung, the Burmese will find it difficult to harm Chiang Rung due to its distance and the difficulty of sending provisions. If we do this, we will be able to keep Chiang Rung.[17]

Other reasons included the fact that Burma was weakened by losses during the Second Anglo-Burmese War, there was turmoil in Sipsong Panna, and Siam desired to maintain its prestige. King Rama IV sent royal instructions to his younger brother, Kromluang Wongsathiratsanit, who was appointed commander of the troops:

> In fact, the situation we have to deal with in Chiang Tung is temporary because this year there is fighting in Burma as well as a revolt by the Chinese of Mueang Yuwannongsae in the Ho territory and in Sipsong Panna, none of which can

> be settled this year. However, the Lao, both commoners and nobles, think they understand the situation of this distant territory and foolishly accept that Burma is powerful and probably will quickly chase off the English and protect Chiang Tung . . . With regard to our side, there is war between Burma and England and our wish to be victorious over Chiang Tung. There is a narrow window of opportunity this year. What shall we do? King Rama III once ordered Chiang Mai to deal with Chiang Tung, but his reign ended and we succeeded to the throne. If we remain inactive without making a success of it, we will lose prestige. Countries that know about past events will think that we are cowardly, have little power, and cannot make war. If Burma cannot reach a settlement with England or even if Burma is defeated, she will not be completely destroyed. When the Thai fight with Chiang Tung, they will ask Burma to send troops to help, and it will be more difficult. Therefore, we must act with determination to maintain our prestige.[18]

Kromluang Wongsathiratsanit first went to Nan. He appointed Chaophraya Yomarat to lead troops from Bangkok and to conscript people from Saraburi, Chai Nat, Kamphaeng Phet, Tak, Sawankhalok, and Thoen which would join with troops conscripted in Lan Na. This was war on a grand scale. There were altogether about thirty thousand men, including central Thai troops, Lan Na troops, and troops from Luang Prabang.

The troops planned to meet at Chiang Saen before separating and traveling

68. Kromluang Wongsathiratsanit, the younger brother of King Rama IV and the commander in the Chiang Tung Wars. (NAT, n.d.)

on different routes to attack Chiang Tung simultaneously. The troops from Chiang Mai and those under Chaophraya Yomarat besieged Chiang Tung first, but they were coming from a disadvantageous, low position and lacked provisions. When the central Thai troops arrived, they received news that Burma was gathering reinforcements, so they ordered the Thai army to withdraw.[19] The commanding heights of Chiang Tung, its distance, and the Thai's poor cannon had played a part in the failure. Provisions were extremely low due to the bad harvest in Lan Na that year, which had resulted in a reluctance in Chiang Mai to support the war.

Kromluang Wongsathiratsanit stayed in Nan with his troops and sent a letter informing King Rama IV about the difficulties. A successful attack would require an additional 30,000 to 40,000 troops with modern arms and sufficient provisions, he said.[20] King Rama IV was of the opinion that the war should continue. He wrote:

> The work at Chiang Rung and Chiang Tung is not over. To take them, we must be quick to be successful. We want you to make up for your loss by making a success of it. There is still opportunity as Burma remains at war with England. If we do not take Chiang Tung, its people will disparage the ability of the Thai and will so inform Burma.[21]

THE THIRD CHIANG TUNG WAR (1854)

King Rama IV ordered Chaophraya Sisuriyawong, who was in charge of the military, to take more soldiers and modern arms to Kromluang Wongsathiratsanit. However, there were many new problems. It took a longer time to conscript the larger numbers of people. Many conscripts fled. By the time everything was ready, the rainy season had arrived. Heavy rain prevented the troops from transporting provisions, and soldiers fell ill.[22] Due to the size of the force, movement was slow, and they were attacked by Burmese troops along the route. When Kromluang Wongsathiratsanit's men arrived at Chiang Tung, they discovered that it was being protected by a large number of Burmese troops camped outside. They fought for twenty-four days until their ammunition and provisions were depleted and they had to withdraw.[23] Chaophraya Yomarat's troops had traveled only halfway to the area when they heard the news that the other forces were retreating, and they decided to return to Chiang Mai.[24] After all the troops had returned, the two leaders sent a message to the king, asking to return to Bangkok. King Rama IV decided to end the Chiang Tung Wars. He gave the following reasons:

> The route to Chiang Tung is extremely barren. It crosses over high mountains and through crucial narrow passes. It is difficult to transport provisions and ammunition. It will be hard to keep the troops for years, and the only action possible is to attack like guerrillas. Now the Burmese know the situation and

> can arrange troops to protect the town. Our troops attacked the town twice but failed. If we continue, we would have troops exhausted and battered for two dry seasons already.[25]

There were several causes for the failure of the Third Chiang Tung War. Heavy rain made the movement of troops and the transportation of provisions difficult, and oxen could not carry their burdens across swollen streams.[26] The troops did not reach the full strength of 10,500 men expected from the north; only 6,150 men were conscripted from Chiang Mai, Lampang, and Lamphun.[27] Provisions did not meet the targets either, due to the bad harvest in Lan Na. There was also a lack of coordination between the generals from Bangkok and the nobles from Chiang Mai. Finally, there was the reluctance of the rulers of Chiang Mai, Lampang, and Lamphun to join the war. When the central Thai forces were preparing to depart, the three rulers asked for a postponement until the following year, citing the lack of provisions. Their request was denied, and they were told to move quickly. Chiang Mai troops was reluctant. A report sent by Chaophraya Surenratchasena to Chaophraya Sisuriyawong said:

> In this war, the son of the Chiang Mai ruler did not join the main force, but he went by way of Mueang Pu and Mueang Sat. Only the son-in-law and some distant relatives joined the troops. We lacked a full contingent. When we went to the ruler, he lied to our face but behind our backs he was pleased and did as he wanted. They had troops march out in the daytime, but at night they returned to their homes. The use of troops from Chiang Mai, Mueang Lakhon, and Lamphun to attack Chiang Tung absolutely will not work.[28]

Probably local rulers were reluctant due to the lack of provisions and because there had already been two wars with Chiang Tung. The conscription of troops and the levies of provisions for several successive years had created great distress among the Lan Na people. Lan Na also did not see the need to get involved in a war with a related *mueang*.

Taking Chiang Tung continued to be an ambition of Siam, however. King Rama V sent his brother, Krommoen Phichitprichakon, to Lan Na in 1884 to reform its administration, but the official also hoped to expand the northern boundaries to include the Shan *mueang* and Chiang Tung, by taking advantage of Burma's conflict with England. But the Thai were not prepared to use force, particularly in an area where Britain was by then involved.[29] Britain completed the conquest of Burma in 1885. Soon, border disputes were followed by the demarcation of boundaries between Siam and Burma. In a set of decisions that were unfavorable to Siam, Chiang Tung, Yong, and the Shan States became a part of Burma.

Hopes to retake Chiang Tung revived during World War II under

69. The use of oxcarts as a means of transportation in the Chiang Tung War of 1942. (NAT, 1942)

70. The royal residence of Chaofa Konkaeo Inthalaeng, built in the British style. The royal residence was eighty-four years old when it was demolished by the Burmese government at the end of 1991, thus destroying the symbol of Chiang Tung royalty. (NAT, 1942)

Phibunsongkhram, the Thai military dictator who collaborated with Japan. Phibun had irredentist dreams of a greater Thailand that would include all the former Thai states. In 1942, Thai troops captured Mueang Ko, Mueang Len, Mueang Phayak, Mueang Yong, and Chiang Tung. Siam appointed Chaofa Phromlue and Chao Mae Thiphawan to rule Chiang Tung. It was under the Thai for three years. When the tides of war turned in Asia, the Thai forces were withdrawn.[30]

CHAPTER 7

THE IMPACT OF WESTERN IMPERIALISM

Western imperialism began to impact on Siam at the end of the reign of King Rama II (r. 1809–1824). Scientific and industrial revolutions had dramatically changed economic, political, and social conditions in Europe. Trade liberalization stimulated a boom in business and industry. The middle classes and industrial capitalists were taking an increased political role. A rise in nationalism accompanied a desire to build national prestige and expand abroad. It was considered the "white man's burden" to uplift people in countries whose economic, political, and social development lagged behind that of Europe. Such lands provided sources of raw materials and markets for European products and increased the European states' economic security, political strength, and prestige.[1] Britain and France became major political threats to Siam. Britain was on Siam's western borders. France was immediately to the east. Lan Na was threatened by both.

The arrival of Western imperialism brought about the decline of the old Siam and Lan Na. Lan Na history can be roughly divided into traditional and modern periods, with imperial aggression and King Rama V's administrative reforms as the dividing line. The old Lan Na was characterized by local traditions that had been handed down for many centuries. Modern Lan Na experienced change in all areas.

Lan Na was first drawn into closer relations with the colonial British government of Burma in the early nineteenth century. Siam's lenient policy towards her tributary state allowed it the freedom to trade with the British and with British subjects in neighboring Mon territory. An important overland trading network passed from Moulmein to Rahaeng, Lamphun, and Chiang Mai, and on to Chiang Rai, Chiang Saen, and Chiang Tung, ending at Dali in Yunnan. This route had long been more significant than the route from Chiang Mai to Bangkok. To facilitate trade, rupees from British-controlled India began to be used in Lan Na, which had insufficient local coinage. Rupees were used until the second half of King Rama V's reign, when a policy to use Thai baht was introduced.

THE ARRIVAL OF THE BRITISH AND BRITISH SUBJECTS IN LAN NA

After the First Anglo-Burmese War in 1826, Britain took the Mon state adjoining Lan Na. Dr. David Richardson came to Chiang Mai in 1829 to buy elephants, cattle, and buffalo from people in Chiang Mai, Lamphun, and Lampang, after an epidemic in the Mon territory killed a large number of cattle and buffalo there. The people of Lan Na sold so many elephants, cattle, and buffalo that the numbers were depleted, and the ruler of Chiang Mai eventually forbade the sale of the animals.[2] A number of people who had already received payment refused to deliver animals to the buyers. Dr. Richardson sent a petition to the central government in Bangkok. He had not understood that Lan Na was actually a separate, though tributary, state at the time.

Siam replied that it was forbidden to trade the animals outside the country because they were needed for internal use. In times of war, elephants and cattle were used as beasts of burden for provisions, while buffalo were used in the rice fields. Bangkok said that the northern nobles would arrange for the return of money to the buyers, or, failing that, arrange for the sellers to deliver the animals. Dr. Richardson accepted this arrangement. King Rama III sent Phraya Surenratchasena to Lan Na to explain the situation to the Lan Na nobles.[3] Trade with the British expanded quickly, particularly after the signing of the Bowring Treaty in 1855. Siam opened the country for free trade, ended state monopolies, and allowed extraterritoriality to Westerners and their subjects.

British subjects began to engage in logging in Lan Na around 1840. During the reign of King Rama III, a number of Mon and Burmese from Moulmein began to cut trees in the forests of Tak, Chiang Mai, and Lamphun. They later gave five hundred rupees as payment to Phraya Thanuchak, the patrol official assigned to investigate the activities of the Burmese and British, to be given to the central government. However, the government ordered Phraya Thanuchak to return the money. It considered that the forests were for the benefit of the tributary states, and that trade and logging rights were the perogative of their rulers. An official letter informed Lan Na of the policy of non-interference in its internal affairs.[4]

After the Second Anglo-Burmese War, Mon and Shan British subjects traveled to Lan Na to engage in small-scale logging.[5] The Lan Na administration allowed the newcomers easy access.

PROBLEMS WITH LOGGING

The British Borneo Company and the Bombay Burmah Company of England began logging in the Mon territory of Burma after 1824, processing teak in Moulmein sawmills for export abroad. The large logging companies were very politically influential—the Third Anglo-Burmese War erupted after a dispute between logging firms and the Burmese court. The companies expanded into Lan Na through Mon and Burmese British subcontractors. Logs were sent down the Salween River to Moulmein. At first there were few problems, as the business was limited and the contractors were respectful of the Lan Na nobles, who were making money from the arrangements.

Lan Na forests were considered the property of the rulers and the nobles. The permission to log a concession was inscribed on palm leaves.

Concessionaires paid a fee for every tree they cut.[6] Officials collected the fees and sent the money to the ruler, who would divide it into three portions—one portion for the owner of the forests, another for the official who collected the fees, and the last for the ruler himself.[7]

At first, fees were not fixed. Traditionally, forests had not been seen as a commercially valuable resource but were used for local needs. The owners normally distributed forest land among their kin, permitting them to enlist commoners to cut down about one hundred to two hundred trees a year to sell, without royalty payments.[8] As the forests acquired more value, fees were collected. A typical early fee was one rupee per tree.[9] During the reign of King Mahotaraprathet, (1847–1854), when the logging business expanded greatly, the fees were revised and divided into three categories. A tree of 8 to 10 hands' breadth (1 hand's breadth = about 8 inches) paid one rupee; 11 to 13 hands, two rupees; and 14 to 16 hands, three rupees. By 1896 when the Department of Forestry was established, the fee was twelve rupees per tree.

Problems arose when competition grew for concessions. There were issues over overlapping concessions or multiple concessions for the same forest area.[10] This wasn't solely the result of greed. There was sometimes confusion or misunderstanding over the ownership of tracts of forest. Boundaries were often not clearly demarcated, so the areas of concession were unclear and overlapped. Sometimes when a concession expired, the concessionaire might not contact the owner, so a new concession would be granted to another person. In some cases a new concession was granted before the existing one had expired.

Prior to the Bowring Treaty, the Mon and Burmese were subject to the arbitrary authority of the Lan Na nobles and were forced to accept the outcome of lawsuits based on local practices. In 1854 Mong Suainit, a Mon, paid the *chao ratchabu*t (Noi Mahaphrom) 500 rupees for a logging concession at Mueang Yuam for three years. Later, the *chao ratchabut* confiscated the 350 logs, worth about 4,231 rupees, his workers, and his elephants. When Suainit brought the case to the Chiang Mai court, King Kawilorot stalled the case. The *chao ratchabut* defended himself by accusing Suainit of buying elephants from thieves, and therefore claimed that he himself was justified in confiscating the logs.[11] In 1859, Mong Suaikan brought suit against King Kawilorot of Chiang Mai. Suaikan failed to pay the *chao ratchabut* regularly for a logging concession at Mueang Yuam. After that, Karen people attacked Mueang Yuam and the forest surrounding the area. Mong Suaikan fled to Moulmein and left the logging business. Three years later Suaikan returned to Chiang Mai to renew the concession, extending it for another ten years. But King Kawilorot had already claimed his right, as ruler, to grant the concession to a British Eurasian, Linan. Mong Suaikan then filed a lawsuit with the British consulate in Bangkok. Sir Robert Schombourg, the consul, and Sir Thomas Knox, the vice consul, considered the case several times in different forms. Eventually Mong Suaikan lost on the grounds that he had violated the terms of the concession by not logging it for three years.[12]

Mong Suaikan's case provides an example of some of the problems associated with the logging business. Fees were often paid irregularly. Terms of the concessions were often imprecise. At times Karen people in the border areas robbed and attacked loggers.

71. Piles of teakwood logs ready to be transported out of the forest by cargo train (NAT, c. 1912–1932)

Logging cases tended to pile up for long periods before action was taken. In 1873, there were forty-two forestry-related cases in Chiang Mai. The court dismissed thirty-one, but eleven cases had strong evidence of wrongdoing on the part of the accused, King Inthawichayanon, (r. 1873–1896). He was fined 466,015 rupees, too much for him to pay in full, and the central government had to advance him the money, to be paid back in installments within seven years.[13] The central government, fearing Britain's ire, hastened to solve the problem of long cases. Siam also wanted to be conciliatory towards the ruler of Chiang Mai. After losing the lawsuits, the Chiang Mai ruler continued to have the right to grant forest concessions, and many more new cases arose.[14] Finally the central government decided to take control of all the forests.

French and Danish logging firms also moved into Lan Na. Teak logs brought in fantastic profits to foreign investors, but only a meager return to local leaders and nothing at all to the local commoners who lived on the forests.

TURMOIL IN THE BORDER REGIONS OF LAN NA

The precise outline of the Lan Na state had never been clear and there had been no definite borders between it and its neighbors. This had not been a problem until Western countries demanded clear demarcation lines. The eastern side of the Salween River was considered a peripheral area of Lan Na. It was known as the five Shan *mueang*: Mueang Hang, Mueang Sat, Mueang Tuan, Mueang Tha, and Mueang Chuat (Chawat). The people were Shan (Greater Tai). Mueang Nai, on the west bank, had been founded by Mangrai and ruled by his son.

This territory was continually contested by Burma and Lan Na. In 1809, King Kawila and Fa Pho, the ruler of Mueang Yang Daeng, an independent Karenni (Red Karen) state on the west bank of the Salween, agreed that the river would be the demarcation line between the two areas.[15] It stipulated that Lan Na's sphere of influence extended to the east bank of the Salween while Fa Pho of Mueang Yang Daeng held sway over the west bank. The agreement was made following traditional practice.

> A water buffalo was felled for the feast, then one of its horns was divided into two parts; one part was kept at Mueang Yang Daeng and the other at Chiang Mai. Both pledged that the middle of the Salween River was the demarcation line. Everything to the east of this river was for the benefit of Chiang Mai whereas all to the west belonged to Yang Daeng. Anything in the middle of the river would be equally divided. "So long as the waters of the Salween River do not go dry, the horns of the buffalo do not straighten, and the White Elephant Cave does not collapse, Chiang Mai and Mueang Yang Daeng will not sever their bonds of friendship."[16]

72. Khun Lu, a Shan nobleman and son of Phraya Phithak, governor of Mae Hong Son. (NAT, c .1901–1910)

This custom-based agreement created obligations that were understood by all parties. No need was seen for more strict dividing lines. Westerners introduced an entirely new way of thinking about such matters, and lack of understandings on all sides led to disputes and controversy.[17]

The ruler of Chiang Mai did not have tight control of the *mueang* in this area. They were ruled as autonomous states, only nominally under Chiang Mai's control.[18] The situation became increasingly confused, particularly when Britain began to govern Burma. The border *mueang* began to claim independence, which led to frequent battles. Some *mueang* began to enter the five Shan territories to conscript people. Mueang Pan conscripted people, and requisitioned arms and provisions from Mueang Hang, Mueang Sat, Mueang Tuan, and Mueang Chuat (Chawat) to fight Mueang Mok Mai. The situation was chaotic. Brigands were active and British subjects were frequently robbed and murdered. In 1881, British subjects and traders, Mong Tathuai, Mong Unong, and their hired servants, were killed.[19]

A report written by a Captain James Brown, during his visit to Lan Na between March 27 and May 30, 1871, informed the British consul in Bangkok that hundreds of Karen along the Salween were crossing into Lan Na to plunder areas in which British subjects lived. Britain demanded that the Thai government send troops to protect her subjects in Lan Na. Britain further demanded that the ruler of Chiang Mai pay an indemnity for losses, particularly to loggers who had to stop their business. The British had suffered a large loss of taxes on logs being prevented from traveling down the Salween to Moulmein. The Thai government felt that it was vital to solve the problems. If it did not, the British would have an excuse to intervene in Siam.

LOSS OF TERRITORY IN 1892

The five Shan *mueang* and the eastern Karenni *mueang*, a total of thirteen *mueang*, were rich in teak. King Rama V understood this well, as can be seen from a passage in his letter to Krommoen Damrong Rachanuphap, the minister of the interior. "I see only England's desire for profit, and if she is given the forests she wants, she will not be much interested in sharing, not even a pile of stones."[20]

In the Chiang Mai treaties of 1873 and 1883, Britain had accepted that the Thai boundary extended to the eastern bank of the Salween. Britain later changed its mind about the issue, citing the absence of written documentation. Britain claimed further that the Siamese government had no legal power to rule over the area, as the people were Burmese and Shan. In 1884 when Krommoen Phichitprichakon came to Chiang Mai, he claimed the right over these *mueang* and sent troops to protect them, but the Siamese government did not press the case.[21] In 1885, after Britain won the Third Anglo-Burmese War, it claimed the right over the thirteen *mueang*, claiming they were formerly part of Burma. Siam claimed that the area had been under Lan Na's control for hundreds of years, citing passages from the chronicles that mentioned that Chiang Mai troops had subjugated the areas. Siam also cited the agreement between King Kawila of Chiang Mai and the ruler of Mueang Yang Daeng. The two sides each had half a water buffalo's horn as evidence.

Kromluang Thewawongwarophrakan, the Siamese foreign minister, was informed in 1888 that "the queen's government wanted to have these five territories under British control and therefore had already declared this to be the case."[22] Finally the Siamese government decided to end the controversy. In 1892 it relinquished its interest in the Shan and Karenni territories. An announcement from the minister of the interior stated:

> His Majesty said that territory connected to Burma that is under Britain was previously in dispute. Now we have conferred and compromised with the British Crown, and Britain has agreed to relinquish Mueang Chiang Khaeng and the territory west of Chiang Saen to us in exchange for the Shan and Karen *mueang*, Yang Daeng or the areas called Mueang Chae, Mueang Mai, Mueang Tha, Mueang Chuat, Mueang Hang, Mueang Tuan, Mueang Sat, Mueang Yuam, Mueang Tum, Mueang Kwan, Mueang Hai, Ban Hongluk, and Mueang Ko to Britain.[23]

MAP 11. MAP OF THIRTEEN TOWNS IN SOUTHERN SHAN STATE, SEIZED BY ENGLAND IN 1892

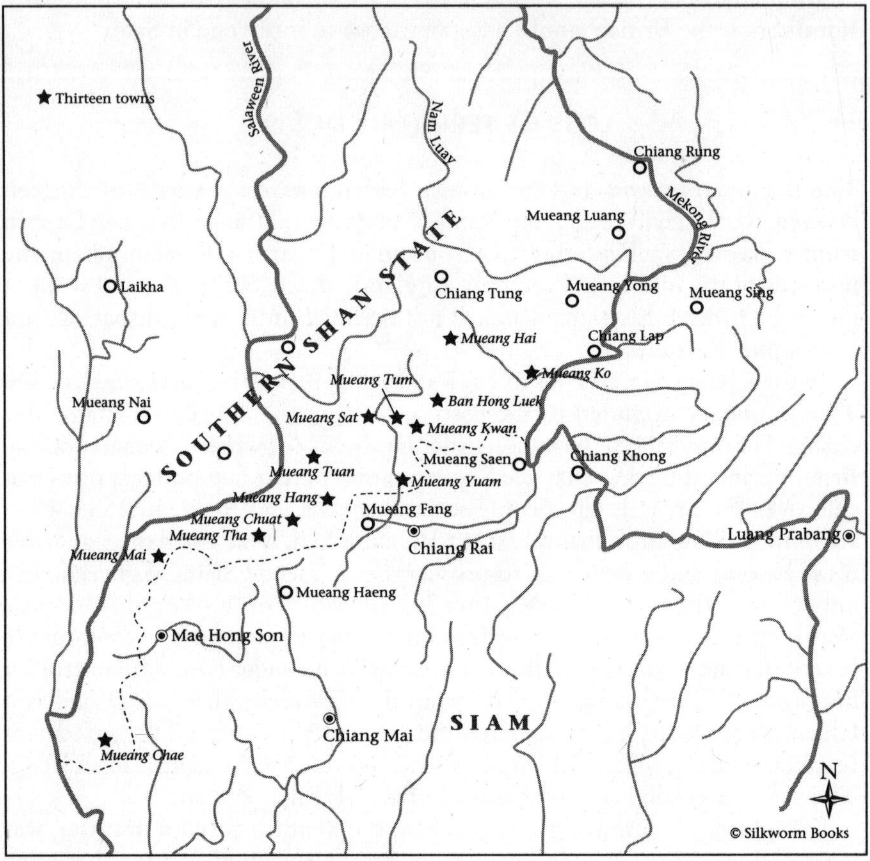

(Drawn after Sarassawadee Ongsakul, *Prawatsat Lan Na*, p. 342

BRITISH POLICY IN LAN NA

In the 1880s, King Rama V began the reorganization of the administration of Siam, grouping provinces into *monthon*, or circles, controlled by commissioners, who were often his brothers. Lan Na became Monthon Phayap. The loss of the thirteen *mueang* eliminated the old natural boundary between Lan Na and Burma, the Salween River. British policy was not to invade across the Salween. It wanted to avoid sharing a boundary with France, which was penetrating the eastern part of Lan Na. It suited Britain to have a buffer zone between it and France. This may be the chief reason why Britain stayed out of Chiang Mai, despite its being a highly economically productive area. There were other reasons. Britain had only relatively recently gained control of the entire Indian subcontinent. The British government of India was opposed to further expansion. And the Bowring Treaty meant that England could do business in Lan Na without actually having to control the areas.

Siam's problem with France escalated after the Paknam crisis of 1893, in which two French gunboats forced their way up the Chao Phraya River to Bangkok and were fired upon by the Thai. The French then imposed a naval blockade. Ultimately Siam was forced to accept a French ultimatum to cede all territories east of the Mekong River and to pay a large indemnity. French territory then bordered Nan. France also controlled Mueang Sing (Chiang Khaeng), which Britain had relinquished to Siam in exchange for the thirteen *mueang*. Britain was very displeased about Mueang Sing falling to France and attacked the area on March 21, 1894. However, both imperial powers realized that confrontation was hardly worthwhile. After discussions they reached an accord signed on January 15, 1896, which left Mueang Sing with the French and guaranteed the independence of Siam.

The accord, however, contrary to Thai belief, did not guarantee Thai sovereignty over all its lands, in particular the peripheral areas. Such regions were divided into British and French spheres of influence. Later on, both imperial powers tried to intrude into Thai territory, claiming it was in their sphere of influence.

The British and French governments agreed that neither side would send troops to the Thai seashore from Mueang Bang Saphan to Mueang Klaeng, or in the north from the Ping, Wang, Yom, and Nan river basins to the Ing River. It is notable that this accord did not mention the Northeast (Isan), the East, the South, or the twenty-five kilometers east of the Mekong River. Thus it provided an opportunity for France to invade the northeast of Monthon Phayap, particularly around Nan.

MAP 12. MAP OF THE EAST BANK OF THE MEKONG RIVER, SEIZED BY THE FRENCH IN 1903

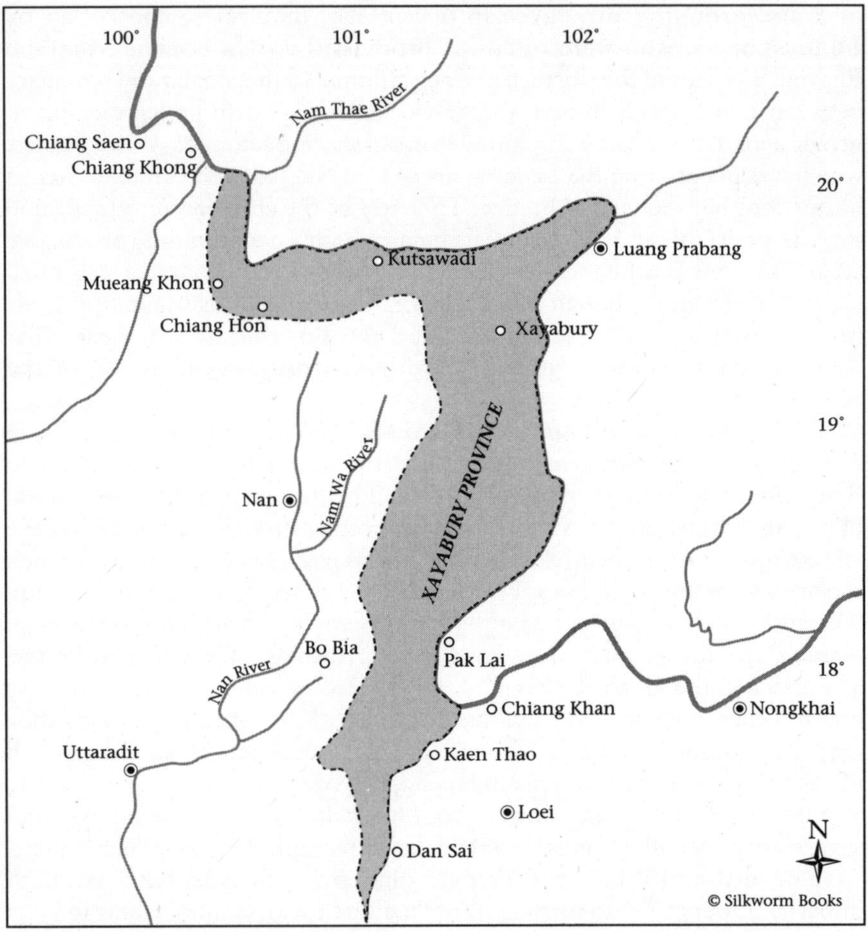

(Drawn after Sarassawadee Ongsakul, *Prawatsat Lan Na*, p. 350)

THE LOSS OF THE WEST BANK OF THE MEKONG RIVER IN NAN TO FRANCE IN 1903

The immediate area on the west or right bank of the Mekong River was in Lan Na's sphere of influence. In 1872 when a British trader was murdered at Mueang Ngoen on the right side of the Mekong, the ruler of Nan paid compensation.[24]

The peripheral *mueang* on the right bank comprised Mueang Ngoen, Mueang Khop, Mueang Chiang Lom, and Mueang Chiang Hon. Nan had close supervision of these areas but problems arose after the treaty was signed with France on October 3, 1893. Articles 3 and 4 referred to the twenty-five kilometers on the west bank of the Mekong River. Article 3 stated that the government of Siam could not construct patrol posts or military camps in Battambang or Siem Reap (areas considerably to the southeast of Lan Na and now part of Cambodia) or in other provinces located within twenty-five kilometers of the west bank of the Mekong River. Article 4 specified that patrol units would be comprised of civilians, and they would carry out their duties according to local traditional practices. There must not be any regular or conscripted troops or military camps in those areas.[25]

As a result, the Siamese government was deterred from protecting the area against invasion by the Lao of Luang Prabang, backed by the French. The Siamese government interpreted Article 4 to mean that Siam could send civilians into the area. France later claimed that even civilian officials were forbidden. It expelled Thai officials and sent its own people from Luang Prabang to govern the region.

There was also competition for control over local salt wells, whose products yielded taxes, particularly near the headwaters of the Nan River. Mueang Ngoen (Mueang Kutsawadi) had a large number of such wells. This fertile area on the Ngoen River was home to at least five thousand inhabitants, mostly Lue people who had been resettled from Mueang Phong, a dependency of Mueang Sing.

The majority of the Lue were loyal to the ruler of Nan, who administered the region and collected taxes.[26] Other *mueang* within twenty-five kilometers of the Mekong, including Mueang Khop, Mueang Chiang Lom, and Mueang Chiang Hon, faced similar predicaments. Luang Prabang moved into the area. In Nan, a French consul put pressure on the local ruler over the issue. From 1895, Monsieur Harduvin, the French deputy consul in Mueang Nan, put the case for the Luang Prabang ruler's actions to the Nan commissioner, Phra Phromsurin. Harduvin cited the fact that Luang Prabang had formerly held sway over this area,[27] (even though the French had accepted that this was Thai territory in the accord of October 3, 1893.) The Thai refused to concede the point.

The ruler of Luang Prabang sent Phraya Mueang Phaen with troops and civilian officials to Mueang Ngoen.

Thai civilian officials were forbidden to enter the territory, which the French had declared a no man's land.[28] The Luang Prabang group tried to persuade people in the area to resettle on the east bank of the river and to become French subjects.[29] Whoever resisted would be arrested and forced out.[30] Luang Prabang also sent officials to rule Mueang Khop.[31] At Tambon Bochao, French soldiers seized a salt well.[32]

Siam did not respond assertively. Rather, it tried to use diplomacy, knowing that it would be at a disadvantage in the event of armed confrontation. The Thai also ordered the governors of the *mueang* within twenty-five kilometers of the Mekong to maintain the rights and sovereignty of the Thai over the area. The order allowed the governors of individual *mueang* to conscript local troops for defense.

Meanwhile, the Nan commissioner tried to reiterate to officials and residents that the land belonged to Siam. He wanted them to unite to defend the land and to refuse to pay anything to Luang Prabang.[33]

His efforts were in vain, in the face of French determination. King Rama V commented to Kromluang Damrong Rachanuphap. "I do not see any way to prevent Luang Prabang from invading our territory as they wish."[34]

Kromluang Damrong Rachanuphap, the minister of the interior, had been telling the king since 1895 that the only solution was to cede the west bank to the French.[35] After successive failures to solve the problem, the Thai government decided to accept his advice. Siam relinquished the territory to France in a treaty on February 13, 1903.[36]

Siam's loss of territory to the imperial powers meant that it had lost its old natural boundaries with Burma and Laos: the Salween and Mekong rivers. The new boundary lines were unclear, cutting through forests and mountains. They made it difficult to defend the country. The impact of this loss of territory continues today.

CHAPTER 8

UNIFICATION WITH BANGKOK UNDER THE ABSOLUTE MONARCHY

Lan Na changed dramatically in all aspects after it was brought under the authority of Bangkok. Local customs dating back hundreds of years came to an end. Lan Na was no longer able to direct its own destiny.

FACTORS THAT CONTRIBUTED TO ADMINISTRATIVE REFORMS

External factors, notably Western imperialism and pressure from the capitalist sector, were important catalysts for change in Thai society during the reign of King Rama V. Internal factors were also a major influence. Professor Nidhi Eoseewong has pointed to economic and social forces, as well as the changing worldview of the Siamese ruling class in the early Ratanakosin era, as the basis for a growing "open door policy."[1]

Siam had been made up of a relatively loose linkage of tributary states populated by different ethnic groups with different languages. Local rulers had the status of king in their own locality. This structure was based on the concept of *rachathirat*, a system in which the Great King at the center controlled local vassal kings. The system meant there was no unified government and power was limited to the center.[2]

The Siamese ruling class was ready for new ideas, partly after the emergence of a rapidly growing export economy in the early Ratanakosin era. Accumulating wealth became as much a priority for the elite, who controlled the buying from and selling to foreign markets,[3] as their former control over commoners. They were keen to replace the old political system with a new, centralized structure under an absolute monarchy.

It was seen as necessary to learn Western ways. Western culture and technology gained wider attention during the reign of King Rama III, when an increasing number of foreigners came to the region. The ruling class began to keep abreast of changes in the outside world. Gradually an Eastern worldview began a subtle shift westwards, in the direction of science and technology.[4] Western-oriented learning gained ground during the reign of King Rama IV, whose innovations became the basis for the far-reaching administrative reforms of King Rama V.

THE COMMISSIONER OF THE THREE REGIONS (1873)

Logging-related conflicts and other turbulence had affected British subjects in the outlying areas of Lan Na and the British colonial government in India demanded that Siam take action. The Treaty between the Government of Siam and the Government of India to Promote Commerce between British Burma and the Territories of Chiang Mai, Lampang, and Lamphun, was signed in Calcutta on January 14, 1873. It prioritized a number of issues.

The first issue was to provide protection for people along the Lan Na and Burmese border: "As Chiang Mai, Lampang, and Lamphun belong to Siam, and the boundary of the British colony adjoins Chiang Mai, traders who travel back and forth are disturbed by bandits and other factors. It is necessary to stop the malefactors to allow traders on both sides to trade conveniently."[5] The treaty stipulated that Siam establish patrol checkpoints and send police to inspect the area east of the Salween River in the border area of Chiang Mai. Both sides would cooperate to capture criminals and return them to their own jurisdictions. It was stipulated that British subjects from Burma had to carry passports when traveling to Chiang Mai, Lampang, and Lamphun. Those with passports could enjoy unrestricted passage. Those without a passport would not be permitted to enter, but would also not be harmed.

The second matter focused on clearing up the backlog of lawsuits between British subjects and Siamese subjects. Britain agreed that its Asian subjects could, if they wished, pursue civil suits in a court in Chiang Mai. If they did not so wish, they could send their suit to the British consul in Bangkok or to British officials at Yongsalin in Burma. This was the first time that Britain consented to a Thai court having the power to try British subjects. The treaty also stipulated that Siamese judges be appointed to supervise and improve logging agreements.

Siam then appointed Phra Narinthararatchaseni (Phum Sichaiyan), the deputy of accounts in the Ministry of Defense (Kromphra Kalahom), to the position of commissioner of the three regions, (Chiang Mai, Lampang and Lamphun), stationed in Chiang Mai.[6] Luang Seniphithak from the Ministry of the Interior was appointed his second-in-command. Around seventy soldiers, clerks, lawyers, interpreters, and commoners were also sent to Chiang Mai. Each official received a yearly allowance; altogether the bill totaled 162 *chang* [12,960 baht], 12 *tamlung* [48 baht].[7] The government was aware that the arrival of Bangkok officials would bother the local nobility; to reduce local resentment the salaries were paid from Bangkok.

The commissioner was charged with "supervising and assisting" the local rulers. Concerned to mollify the Chiang Mai ruler, the government was keen to act slowly and carefully. This concern is evident in a letter from King Rama V to Phraya Rachasamparakon (Luan Suranan), the commissioner of the three regions from 1883 to 1884.

73. A Siamese commissioner on a litter surrounded by his followers. (NAT, c. 1892–1910)

74. Commissioners sent by the central government to Chiang Mai, in front of their residence near the Ping River. (NAT, c. 1902–1917)

> As the commissioner of the three regions, you must consider it your responsibility to foster power and tend to the orders from Bangkok in every respect. You must also understand the intentions of Bangkok and say we believe Mueang Chiang Mai continues to be a tributary state and not part of our territory. It will still be a tributary state as long as we don't think to eliminate its royalty. But we wish to hold real power . . . in short, to make it like a machine that we can control or guide forward or back as we please . . . However, it is necessary to use intelligence more than force; we must not make them feel oppressed, and must point out the advantages of change and the disadvantages of the current situation as the basis.[8]

At the beginning, therefore, the commissioner focused on the urgent problem of lawsuits involving foreigners. He had an additional title, the foreign court commissioner, and he was mandated to carry out the duties specified in the Treaty of Chiang Mai. The new Act for the Commissioner in Trying Lawsuits was drawn up.

The commissioner was responsible for civil lawsuits involving less than five thousand rupees between British and Siamese subjects or between British subjects. The cases were to be tried according to Thai law. British subjects had the right to appeal, in which case the court commissioner at Chiang Mai had to settle the case with the judge at the British court at Yongsalin. If they could not agree, the case could be sent to the consular court in Bangkok.

In the case of civil suits involving five thousand rupees or more, the court commissioner had to inform the consular court in Bangkok, which could either decide it or refer it back to Chiang Mai. In criminal cases, the commissioner had the power to arrest and investigate suspects who were British subjects. The case would then be considered by the British consular court in Bangkok. If it decided the defendant was guilty, the commissioner could decide the verdict but he would be penalized in Bangkok.

If British subjects filed lawsuits against the ruler of Chiang Mai or other high-ranking nobles, the defendants had the right to appoint lawyers to argue in their stead. They had to promise to accept the verdict. Commoners had no right to appoint lawyers to act in their place. If indigenous people brought suit against each other, the *kao sanam* or the ruling officials would decide the case, according to local custom, unless the dispute was linked to government affairs or war. The commissioner and the ruler of Chiang Mai had to report court verdicts to Bangkok once a month.

The act also contained prohibitions for the commissioner and other Bangkok officials. They were forbidden to take bribes. They could not use their positions to seek profit in trade or business. They could not smoke opium, drink alcohol, or gamble. They could not take local wives, even if people presented women to them willingly. They could not conscript people for their personal use. If labor was needed, it should be hired. Very importantly, they were forbidden to demand or request anything of a personal nature from the ruler, his children, or his nobles.[9] For their part, besides their duties in the act, the local rulers had to arrange for commoners to patrol and protect the commissioner's residence and the foreign court, as well as appoint local officials to carry out court orders.

However, litigation involving logging and border disputes continued. The commissioner's limited powers meant that most lawsuits ended up in Bangkok. In 1882 Mr. James F. McCarthy, the first director of cartography, investigated the Foreign Court in Chiang Mai and found it strange that it had not completed a single case.[10] Central government was also slack about dealing with urgent logging disputes, probably in order to avoid antagonizing the rulers, whose profits were threatened.

The Bangkok representatives in Lan Na had a challenging task. Some of the early commissioners in the early period were not of royal blood, which meant Lan Na nobles and even commoners looked down on them.[11] Some misused their power. Yet any commissioner who quarreled with the rulers and nobles was recalled to Bangkok. Phraya Ratchasena, commissioner from 1880 to 1883, became embroiled in disputes with the *uparat* of Chiang Mai, the ruler of Lampang, and Phraya Chaisongkhram. Officials under him used force to loot and kill, and he refused to listen to a petition from victims. This caused hatred and division between "the Thai and the Lao." He was also faulted for not sending regular reports to Bangkok, and was eventually recalled by King Rama V.[12] The man who succeeded him, Phraya Ratchasampharakon (Luan Suranan) was reminded to prioritize good relationships with the local rulers.

The Siamese and British governments negotiated a second Treaty of Chiang Mai in 1883. It stipulated that British subjects must first go to the foreign court for both civil and criminal cases. But the British consul had the right to withdraw a case from the foreign court and try it at the consular court whenever it deemed appropriate. The British were permitted to establish a consulate in Chiang Mai.

ADMINISTRATIVE REFORM IN LAN NA

During negotiations on the second treaty, various outlying dependencies of Burma had attacked Lan Na's border *mueang*. The turmoil was more than Chiang Mai, which had internal difficulties, could handle. This provided an opportunity for the central government to step in with reforms, as part of new moves to establish an absolute monarchy in Siam.

The process of reform can be divided into two periods—the period prior to the *thesaphiban* system of *monthon* administration (1884–1899) and the period of the *thesaphiban* system.

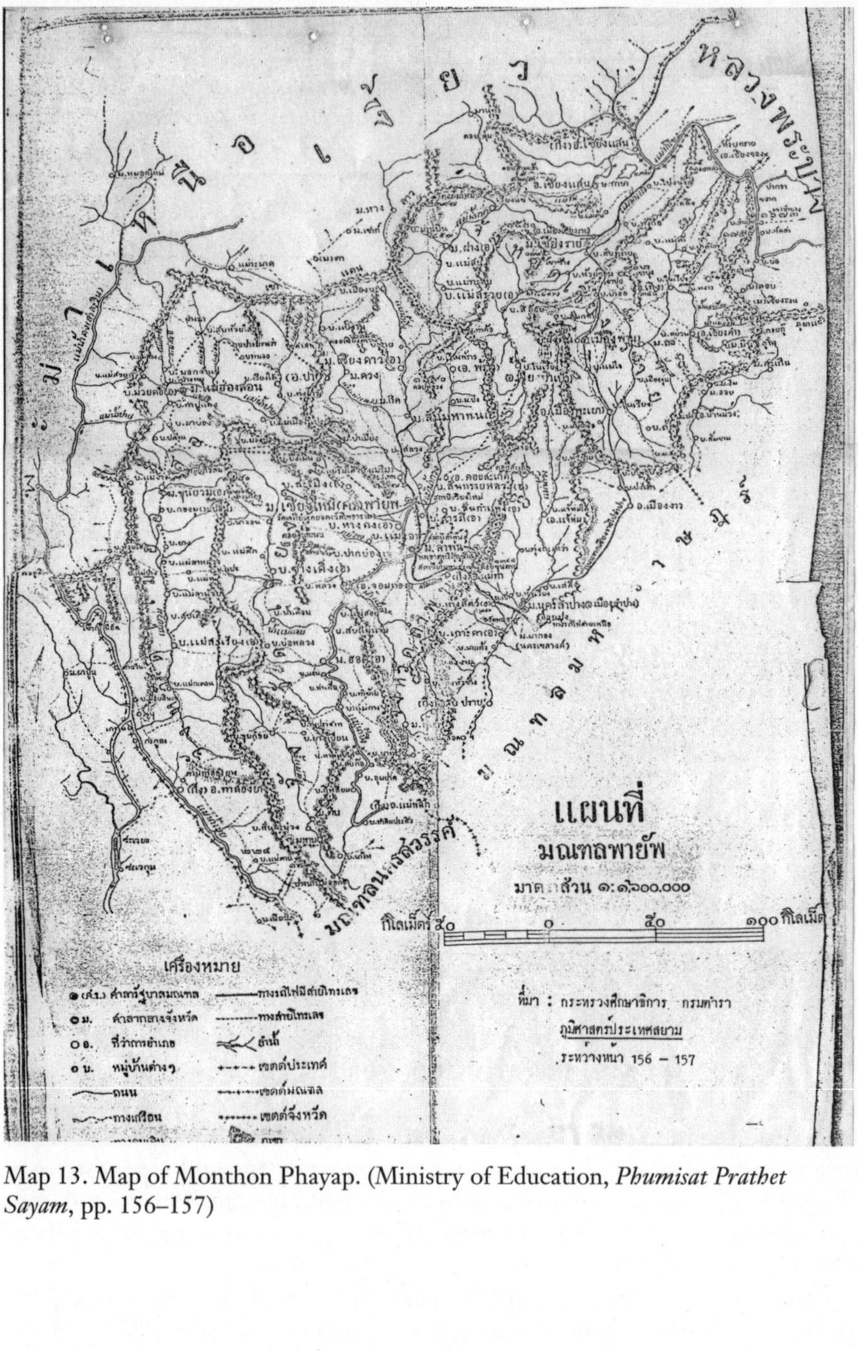

Map 13. Map of Monthon Phayap. (Ministry of Education, *Phumisat Prathet Sayam*, pp. 156–157)

The second step was the integration of "*khon mueang*," the local people, and the many ethnic groups in Lan Na, such as the Lua, Karen, Lue, and Shan. The goal was that they would all feel themselves to be Thai and would be perceived as Thai. Old categories would have to change. For example, the Siamese called the *khon mueang* the "Black-Bellied Lao." The Chiang Mai ruler and his relatives were called "Lao nobles" because the languages of the central Thai and the northern people were mutually incomprehensible, to the point that commissioners from Bangkok, particularly those who dealt with court litigation, had to use translators. The different languages and sentiments meant there was a lack of unity of feeling and spirit. Bangkok embarked on a process of educational reform. In Lan Na, a new system of Thai schools with Thai books replaced traditional learning in the temples. Pupils were required to study in the Central Thai language, or standard Thai, instead of the Thai Yuan language.[13]

THE PERIOD PRIOR TO THE *THESAPHIBAN* SYSTEM OF *MONTHON* ADMINISTRATION (1884–1899)

The Reform of Monthon Lao Chiang (1884–1892). The introduction of Monthon Phayap (or Monthon Lao Chiang) meant a great loss of power for Lan Na nobility. Bangkok therefore proceeded with great caution. The Lan Na leaders still believed they were the ruling "Lords of Life." The Bangkok appointees were mainly high-ranking nobles of royal lineage, who, it was hoped, the Lan Na nobles would accept and respect. King Rama V appointed his brother, Krommoen Phichitprichakon, as special commissioner in 1884. According to a passage in a letter from the king to the chief official in charge of civil affairs:

> It will take a long time to organize the Lao *mueang* and we should find someone who can clear the way. If we choose someone who is not familiar with the bureaucracy or is not respected, the Lao might raise objections . . . Krommoen Phichitprichakon has a wide knowledge of the bureaucracy, intelligence, strategic planning, and shrewdness in dealing with lawsuits, both Thai cases and cases with British subjects. He should be trusted with the job. He can preserve customs and traditions as he deems appropriate and influence the direction of things sufficiently in the beginning. The Lao would respect him more than lower-ranking noble officials and he would smooth the way.[14]

The Lan Na nobles respected Prince Phichitprichakon, and because his role was initially to solve very specific problems, they were obliged to conceal their strong opposition to him. However, they were not above resorting to asking spirit mediums to contact a spirit lord to demand the repeal of taxes, excises, and reforms.[15] Phichitprichakon eventually suppressed the spirit mediums.

Map 14. Map of Monthon Maharat. (Ministry of Education, *Phumisat Prathet Sayam*, pp. 148–149)

Krommoen Phichitprichakon laid the foundation for reform in many areas. He also built relationships between north and south by asking that Chao Dararatsami, the daughter of the Chiang Mai ruler King Inthawichayanon, become a consort of King Rama V. She was later promoted to the position of Phraratchachaya (the Princess Consort). Chao Dararatsami was the only relative of a tributary ruler to receive such an honor.

Solving the Problem of Border Intrusions. In 1886 Prince Phichitprichakon announced to the rulers of the border *mueang* that Siam was custodian of the area northwest of Chiang Mai extending to the Salween River. A passage from the announcement reads:

> The area in the northwest that reaches the middle of the Salween River and continues northward to the high ground of Khun Maetuan, as well as the area in the vicinity of the Hang River and Mueang Tuan, Mueang Hang, all these *mueang* are territories of Bangkok . . . Hence, no nobles of either side should send forces to intrude . . . If any noble does not listen and intrudes with his troops or sends his men to oppress the people, our side must consider that they oppress us . . . We will have to retaliate.[16]

This announcement confirmed the Salween River as the natural border between Burma and Siam. Both treaties of Chiang Mai had accepted that the area east of the Salween belonged to Siam.

75. The Karen or Yang procession during King Rama VII's reception ceremony. The procession is passing near the road along the city moat. A remnant of the city wall appears in the background. (NAT, 1926)

Prince Phichitprichakon united the five Shan *mueang*—Mueang Tuan, Mueang Hang, Mueang Chuat, Mueang Tha, and Mueang Maesakun—into one *mueang* called Wiang Chaipricha.[17] It was to be a frontier bastion against Burma. He appointed Chao Mahawong to rule the area, build fortifications, dig moats, and prepare thousands of fighting men. Other border *mueang* were also aided with arms and men.[18]

The commissioner planned to take control as far as Chiang Tung by taking advantage of the political turmoil in Burma. He commented:

> It's a shame about Chiang Tung. It is nearer to us than to the Burmese and has abundant rice and water. The distance is the same as to Mueang Tak. Now is a very good time because Burma will probably not be in a position to help anyone. If we can control Chiang Tung, it will be as if we were to get four or five *mueang* later . . . Chiang Tung is worth 100,000 rupees per year or about one thousand–plus *chang*. The *mueang* is there on its own for the taking, and it should be easy. It would be a shame to let it go without doing anything. We should claim it. Whether we are successful or not doesn't matter. We have nothing to lose.[19]

However, King Rama V did not intend to use force to hold the *mueang*.[20] The moves to control the area proceeded only spasmodically, as Britain was signaling its own designs on the region.

Administration. Lan Na was considered a special region, with special local characteristics that needed to be accommodated, at least initially, so the early reform process often yielded to expediency. The old positions of *chao khanhabai* and *kao sanamluang* were continued, but their importance declined as new positions were established. The key new posts were those of the six *sena*, or heads of the departments of Interior, Military, Finance, Justice, Royal Household, and Land. Local nobles were given the positions of *sena*, while Bangkok officials were appointed to the posts of deputy, or *phraya phuchuai thai* (Thai assistant). In reality, since the nobles did not understand the new system, the assistants were in control. Nobles were also appointed to assistant positions, such as *phraya* (*phraya rong lao*, or Lao deputy), which were relatively unimportant but helped keep the goodwill of the local people.

The Department of the Interior took charge of administration; census lists; and the construction, repair, and maintenance of public works, such as fortifications, city moats, embankments, canals, and roads. The Department of Defense was charged with protecting the peripheral area, preparing conscripted troops for war, and arranging for arms. The Department of Finance had responsibility for the area's financial assets. It dealt with taxes and excises, and prepared accounts of revenue and expenditures to be sent to Bangkok annually. The Department of Justice controlled the police and the courts, sitting in on the foreign court and explaining Lan Na customary practices to it. The Department of the Royal Household administered affairs within the ruler's household, such as receiving official visitors, arranging traditional Lan Na ceremonies, and taking responsibility for the list of foreign travelers entering the region. The Department of Land supervised forests and fields and maintained provisions for wartime use.[21]

The department heads were selected by the *kao sanamluang*, the provincial administrator, who submitted the list to the ruler, who officially appointed them and had the right to transfer or dismiss them. Therefore, the Chiang Mai ruler had some control over the six department heads and tried to keep them from acting too independently.

Prince Phichitprichakon gradually extended his program to western Lan Na—Lamphun, Lampang, Mueang Yuam, Mueang Khun Yuam, and Mueang Mae Hong Son. Administrative reforms began in Mueang Phrae and Mueang Nan in around 1893.

Tax Collection. Central government policy was that the expenses of the reform process should be covered by local taxes. Any regional budget surpluses had to be sent to Bangkok. This process began with Commissioner Phraya Thepprachun (Phum Sichaiyan), who came to an agreement with the ruler of Chiang Mai to collect more taxes, such as on pigs and gambling dens, in cash. The income was to be divided into three parts: one part for the commissioner and his men for their monthly salaries and two parts for the ruler. Thus the government gradually pushed the burden of shouldering the costs of the commissioner and his men onto the local area.

The tax system in Lan Na had been compatible with its subsistence economy; tribute was collected according to levels of agricultural production. For example, for each *sat* (twenty liters) of rice seed planted, an equal measure of rice had to be sent to the royal granary after harvest. (King Kawilorot Suriyawong doubled the rice levy to two *sat* (forty liters) per *sat* planted.) Other agricultural products, such as betel, coconuts, and chili, were taxed at the rate of 20 percent. There was also a household tax: five *thaep*, a northern coin equivalent to a rupee, from the households of married couples and two *thaep* from households headed by widows or divorcées.

Phichitprichakon spearheaded a number of tax reforms. First, he set up a monopoly system on some goods and opened up a bidding process for the post of tax collectors, also known as tax farmers. The state lacked the personnel to do the job itself. To start, there were five kinds of taxes on goods that were already subject to taxes—alcohol, pigs, rice fields, *lac*, and tree products.[22] He also changed the system from payment in kind to payment in cash at a time when the cash economy was not yet widespread. The new system brought the North in line with other parts of Siam and meant that income could be easily diverted to Bangkok. Finally, new taxes were introduced under nine categories:

1. Natural resources, including forest land, minerals, precious stones, coal, and tar. People who dealt with these types of businesses had to ask permission from the *Mueang* Council and pay fixed taxes upfront.

2. Forest products, such as latex, wicker, and bamboo. A yearly permit cost 2 *thaep* per person; people who produced charcoal paid 3 *thaep* per person.

3. Land. Land larger than twenty *wa* [40 meters] in width and length paid half a *thaep* annually.

4. Garden and orchard crops. Betel palms were taxed at half a *win* (1 win = 12.5 *satang*; 100 *satang* = 1 baht) per tree; jackfruit trees, 1 *win* each; four coconut trees taxed at 1 *win*; two marian plum trees or two mango trees taxed at 1 *win*.

5. Prohibited goods. There was a tax on such items as saltpeter, sulfur, guns, lead, poison, narcotics, and opium, and these goods required special permits.

6. Trade within Lan Na. Taxes were collected directly from buyers or sellers, such as on granulated sugar, brown sugar, and pepper.

7. Construction costs. For example, a person who built gambling instruments paid a 40 percent tax; shipbuilders paid a 20 percent tax; gold and silver furnace owners paid 6 *thaep* per furnace per year while cement, brick, and tile furnace owners paid 5 *thaep* per furnace per year.

8. Exports. Those people who took goods from Monthon Phayap for sale elsewhere had to pay duties according to fixed rates, such as elephant tusks, 60 baht per picul (60 kilograms); gamboge (a gum resin for dyeing) 6 baht per picul; rhinoceros horns, 50 baht per picul; cardamom, 14 baht per picul; and bastard cardamon, 6 baht per picul.

9. Imports. People who brought goods to sell in Monthon Phayap had to pay duties according to fixed rates. Goods on which duty had already been paid in Bangkok could enter Monthon Phayap without paying additional duties.[23]

This new system imposed dramatic changes to the Lan Na economy and resulted in hardship for ordinary people.

Forestry was the most pressing problem. The central government promulgated two acts dealing with the issue. The first act was for rulers entering into agreements with foreigners; now they were required to receive prior permission from Bangkok. The second act dealt with taxes on teak and other timber trees. The two acts were basically aimed at solving the problem of overlapping logging concessions.[24]

The 1883 Chiang Mai Treaty required British subjects to obtain permission for concessions from the central government, and it forbade the owners of forests to issue more than one concession for the same area of forest.[25]

Phichitprichakon announced that the owners of forests had to register with officials. Forest land that was not registered would be considered the property of the government. Taking timber from non-registered forest would be regarded as theft of government property.

Forest registration was followed by the collection and recording of information. Maps demarcated concession boundaries. There were details on the contents of the forests, the amount of timber, and the names of those holding logging concessions and for how long.[26] Even the manner of logging was recorded. Permits were systemized under the office of the commissioner of five regions, to those seeking to log within Chiang Mai, Lamphun, Lamphang, Phrae, and Nan.[27] The new system boosted logging fees and government income.[28]

Krommoen Phichitprichakorn returned to Bangkok after only a year, having made significant inroads into the reform process. The next appointee, Phraya Montrisuriyawong (Chun Bunnag), the commissioner of the five regions (1885–1887), was not of royal blood, and the rulers of Lamphun and Lampang refused to follow his orders. When he requested six elephants for transportation, he received only four. The rulers also delayed sending government funds collected in their *mueang* to the Chiang Mai treasury.[29] However, Montrisuriyawong got support from King Inthawichayanon, who arranged for the official's residence to be close to his own, and who cooperated in maintaining strict order, including forbidding the carrying of arms at night.

Krommoen Phichitprichakon's reforms became vulnerable, however, when Phraya Phetcharaphichai took over as commissioner in 1888 and sided with King Inthawichayanon in abandoning various earlier policies. The king issued a proclamation demanding that the central government terminate the *sena* system and return to the old tax system of taking 20 percent, to be sent to the *kao sanam*. The king claimed that the deities who protected the country were displeased with Phichitprichakon's changes and had not allowed the rain to fall according to the seasons, so that grain yields were less bountiful than in the past.[30] The king was using traditional beliefs to make his own demands.

King Rama V refused to change any of the measures, but after a few months, his representative in the north, Phraya Phetcharaphichai, allowed the local king to terminate the Bangkok tax system. Phetcharaphichai was on the take. He embezzled 16,377 rupees from the royal treasury[31] and allowed the reopening of gambling dens, which had earlier been prohibited.[32]

Such serious misconduct resulted in his immediate recall to Bangkok. Administration in Chiang Mai came to a standstill as conflict raged among the Siamese officials in the area, some of whom were trying to protect the interests of the central government. The ruler of Chiang Mai took the opportunity to demand the return of his power and perquisites.

The central government then appointed Prince Sonabanthit as special commissioner and Phraya Mahathep as commissioner of the five regions. However, in the immediate aftermath of the appointments, the local political conflicts became increasingly serious. Meanwhile, there was no relief of the distress of the heavily taxed ordinary people. Tax collectors were charging more than the people could bear, and the commoners revolted.

The Phraya Prapsongkhram Revolt began in 1889 in Tambon Nong Chom, San Sai district, Chiang Mai. It is an interesting story and has been the subject of a variety of research, though findings are thus far inconclusive.[33] The author interviewed elderly people in the locality about the matter and also conducted research in the National Archives.

Phraya Prapsongkhram was a local administrator and a capable commander of Chiang Mai troops. He was also a tax collector in an area east of the Ping River that included Nong Chom, Khu (Mae Khu), and Kok subdistricts.[34] An official source clearly indicates that Prapsongkhram was a *khwaen* (subdistrict head). An excerpt from a report from Chaophraya Phonlathep to King Rama V states, "He was the head of lower-ranking officials,"[35] equivalent to a district officer (*nai amphoe*) today. Local people interviewed said that Prapsongkhram was a well-known and respected local leader, versed in magic and warfare.

The cause of the revolt was the tax monopolies on items such as betel nut, betel leaves, and coconut trees. Prince Sonabanthit introduced an annual tax on such products. The tax was collected before the goods had actually been sold. People were unable to pay.

One tax collector, Noi Wong, had paid a high price to get the tax monopolies on coconuts and betel leaf; 41,000 rupees annually,[36] 16,000 rupees higher than previously. He was therefore keen to get the best return for his money. In August 1889 he began to collect at higher rates than before; one *win* for two betel palms and one *win* per coconut tree. Two areas under Phraya Prapsongkhram's jurisdiction, Khwaeng Chom and Khwaeng Kok, grew betel trees in such abundance that the growers had to count them by taking bundles of one hundred bamboo strips and binding individual strips at the foot of each tree; the odd number of trees left were calculated from the remaining bamboo strips.[37] Individual households were charged taxes of between eighty and two hundred rupees, a very high rate when compared to earlier charges.[38] Phraya Prapsongkhram had collected five rupees per household.

When the tax collectors came to collect in Khwaeng Chom, a number of people who were unable to pay in cash, offered to pay in kind instead. The tax collectors responded by tying people up and putting them into stocks. Locals became angry and joined together under Prapsongkhram, who announced a ban on tax collectors in Tambon Nong Chom. Increasing numbers joined the group, to the point that there was a plan to attack Chiang Mai and to kill Bangkok officials and Chinese tax collectors,[39] but the group was put down. Prapsongkhram escaped, gathered some forces, and captured Mueang Fang with the assistance of the ruler of Chiang Tung. But in the end he was suppressed.[40]

Previous academic studies of the revolt have focused on the involvement of the Chiang Mai nobles. Yet the administrative reforms that resulted in local officials, such as the subdistrict and village heads, losing some of their benefits under the old tax system may have been more significant. The local officials were very put out over their losses. There is clear evidence that they were among those who instigated the revolt; individuals included Phraya Khatiya (Khwaen Me Khu), Thao Yawichai (Kaeban Pabong), Phraya Ratanakhuha (Kaeban Tham), Phraya Chinchai (Khwaen Chom), Phraya

76. Khun Klin, *nai khwaeng* of Mueang Hot. He was a Siamese and is posing here with some nobles, *khon mueang*, and Chinese. (NAT, c. 1900–1917)

Chomphu (Kae Huafai), Thao Khuankham (Khwaen Kok), and Thao Khat, Thao Chai, Thao Khuankhaeo, Thao Rat, Thao Khankham, and Saen Thepsurin.[41]

The author believes that Phraya Prapsongkhram led the revolt primarily because he had lost his tax collector role. Support from the Chiang Mai nobles may also have been a motivation, as well as genuine anger over the suffering of the people. He was said to have been a good and just man.[42]

The central government took a lenient stance towards the northern nobles after the revolt. King Inthawichayanon was allowed to abolish the positions of the *sena* as he had requested. Chao Phrommaphiphongthada, the ruler of Lampang, seized the opportunity to end the tobacco tax and to return, without permission, to collecting the rice field tax in kind for the royal granary.

King Rama V realized that the administrative reforms could not possibly all be achieved at once. He wrote:

> Dealing with the region cannot be done quickly within a month or two. I think that to put the Lao territory in order, it will be necessary to do it two or three times . . . Find somebody to clear a path in the beginning. If nothing comes of it, we will learn details about the Lao country to consider in future policy.[43]

77. Phraya Prachakitkorachak (Chaem Bunnag), when he was Luang Prachakadikit. As commissioner, he took charge of the survey of the five Ngiao regions (1889–1892) and published his research on Lan Na in *Tamnan Yonok* or the Yonok Chronicle, around 1907. The work has been continuously reprinted up through the present. The Yonok Chronicle is of great value in the study of Lan Na history. (NAT, n.d.)

ADMINISTRATIVE REFORM OF MONTHON LAO CHIANG (1893–1899)

The need for administrative reform gathered momentum again after the Thai government ceded the five Shan *mueang* and Karen *mueang* to England in 1892, and the east side of the Mekong River to France in the following year. Phraya Songsuradet (An Bunnag) was the high commissioner of Monthon Lao Chiang from 1893 to 1899. He established the Monthon Lao Chiang Division and his reforms encompassed several fields.

Administration. Phraya Songsuradet was high commissioner and supreme authority. Deputy commissioners headed the Interior, Justice, Treasury, and Forestry ministries.

Mueang Chiang Mai. Songsuradet appointed six Thai assistant *sena*, reestablishing the positions that had been abolished by the Chiang Mai ruler in 1890. He used a method called "a trick to seduce the Lao,"[44] to persuade the ruler of Chiang Mai to make the appointments. He put officials from the *Monthon* Division into important posts, such as assistant *sena* of treasury and assistant *sena* of land, and had them work at the Lao Chiang *Monthon* Office. This was actually equivalent to taking over the posts and the administration at the *mueang* level. The nobles were unhappy, fearing the rapid loss of their traditional power. They were afraid that the government would relocate all administrative posts to the *Monthon* Office and they petitioned King Rama V over the matter.

Mueang Lamphun. Songsuradet administered Lamphun with Chiang Mai. Former rulers were transferred to *mueang* on the western border, including Mae Hong Son, Mueang Pai, Mueang Khun Yuam, and Mueang Yuam. There was conflict between the *chao uparat* and *chao ratchabut*. Songsuradet thought that the *chao uparat* was loyal, and supported him as interim ruler. Once his work showed clear results, he would be officially appointed the ruler of Lamphun.

Mueang Lampang. The nobles were divided into two factions. One was under the elderly Chao Phrommaphiphongthada, who had been appointed *chao changwang*. The other comprised Chao Norananthachaichawalit and his supporters. The *chao changwang* appointed the *chao ratchawong* to take charge of the *mueang*, without the permission of Bangkok.[45] Since the *ratchawong* had earlier been punished for wrongdoing, Bangkok was annoyed. Songsuradet persuaded the *chao changwang* to return the seal of office to Chao Norananthachaichawalit, and he was given a yearly allowance of 3,000–5,000 rupees in return.[46]

Mueang Phrae. Phrae had been entirely in the hands of Phraya Phiriyawichai, the local ruler. The appointment of six *sena* in Phrae in 1894 distributed his power to officials from Bangkok and other nobles. Phiriyawichai tried to resist the process, and Songsuradet was uncertain about how to deal with

78. Monthon Lao Chiang office building, located near the Ping River. The picture shows lines of officials seeing off the people in the boat. (NAT, c. 1894–1910)

him. In conversation with Kromphraya Damrong Rachanuphap, the minister of the interior, Songsuradet said, "Because the ruler of Phrae is knowledgeable, he is probably afraid that the benefits of his *mueang* will fall into the hands of other people, and he wants to keep them all himself."[47] Songsuradet suggested that if Phiriyawichai could keep the *mueang* in order under the six *sena*, he would propose that Bangkok officially install him as ruler. Phiriyawichai had little choice but to agree.[48] Administrative reforms then proceeded rapidly.

Mueang Nan. The importance of Nan increased rapidly after the Paknam crisis of 1893. Nan now bordered Mueang Luang Prabang of France. As a result, the central government wanted to have firm control of the area. Previously, it had been relatively independent.

The changes began in earnest in 1896 when Phraya Sunthonnurak, the second commissioner stationed in Mueang Nan, the Nan ruler, and other nobles, joined together to establish the positions of the six *sena*. At that time, it was merely a notional move because the *mueang* lacked officials from Bangkok and locals had insufficient knowledge of the government system. However, Songsuradet had earlier founded a training school in Central Thai script in order to train northern nobles and other local people for office, which eventually helped lessen the personnel shortage.[49] In time, the new administrative arrangements proceeded relatively smoothly in Nan. The Nan ruler managed to maintain firm control while also showing loyalty to the central government.

79. Chao Inthayotyongchot, the ninth ruler of Lamphun (1895–1911). (NAT, n.d.)

80. Ho Kham or the royal residence of the Nan ruler. Now it is the National Museum of Nan. (PUA, 1882–1927)

The Courts. Songsuradet combined the area's scattered courts under the Department of Justice, with the *chao burirat* as the minister of justice. Judicial reform began at the *monthon* level with the introduction of laws and judicial procedures of the central government, using lawyers sent from Bangkok. The Monthon Phayap Court was established in 1884 and was an appellate court for cases sent from other courts in the region. It did not try cases beyond the scope of *mueang* courts, according to the Phrathamanun Court Act of 1895.

People preferred the *monthon* court to the *mueang* courts, which were still under the power of local nobles. But the *monthon* court did not set a sufficient standard of fairness, and King Rama V was informed about problems. For example, in the case of Nai Noi Miu, Chao Ratchaphatikawong used the customary punishment of flogging to force him to admit guilt. After the trial, King Rama V forbade flogging.[50]

The central government tried to be tolerant. It did not abruptly eliminate the power of the nobles, but allowed them to continue to have a judicial role for a time. Songsuradet did not consider the courts as urgent as other matters.[51]

Treasury and Taxation. Songsuradet combined the Chiang Mai treasury and the *monthon* treasury. He had absolute power over expenditures and taxation in Chiang Mai, Lamphun, and Lampang, particularly expenses connected with the nobles. Their salaries (excluding fees from logging and other extra income) were itemized. The Chiang Mai ruler would receive 80,000 rupees per annum; the Lampang ruler 30,000 rupees per annum; and the Lamphun ruler 5,000 rupees per annum.[52] If the ruler was in need of a large amount of money, he could borrow not more than 10,000 rupees at a time from the *mueang* treasury. Anything exceeding that amount required prior permission from the Ministry of the Treasury. The nobles felt the loss of control over their finances deeply. King Inthawichayanon said, "Mueang Chiang Mai was left with the bones; they took all the meat to eat."[53]

When King Inthawichayanon passed away Songsuradet took the opportunity to cut the ruler's annual income from 80,000 to 30,000 rupees; he also cut the monthly salaries of the nobles and their relatives who were officials. He transferred or discharged some local officials and replaced them with Siamese on higher salaries.

Taxation was still a major problem. Earlier, the central government had allowed the Chinese to monopolize the collection of taxes. But there were many complaints.[54]

Songsuradet introduced state-paid tax officials, who first collected on rice fields and tobacco. The first of these collectors were the nobles who held the positions of treasury *sena* and land *sena*, with the exception of the rice fields of the ruler and nobles. The ruler had a tax exemption for 1,000 *rai* (1 *rai* = 1,600 square meters or .4 acre); the *chao uparat* had 500 *rai* exempt; 200 *rai* was exempt each for the *chao ratchawong*, *chao ratchabut*, and *chao burirat*; other

81. *Mueang* office building during the *thesaphiban* system. (NAT, c. 1897–1917)

lower-ranking nobles had exemptions according to their rank.[55] However, they quit after one year because of the difficulty of the job and the decline in tax revenue. The central government had to send officials from Bangkok to replace them. Meanwhile, the Chinese continued to monopolize the collection of other kinds of taxes. The high commissioner decided which individuals would get the jobs. The ruler had no power in this matter.[56]

82. Judges together in front of Lampang's tribunal during the *monthon thesaphiban* system. The sign is written in both Central Thai and Lan Na Tham scripts. (NAT, c. 1893–1910)

Forestry. The Forestry Department was established in Chiang Mai in 1896 and was directly responsible to the minister of the interior. Mr. H. Slade, a forestry expert, was appointed the first director general of the Forestry Department. Successive directors were also Westerners until 1924, when the Siamese took over.

The Forestry Department improved matters in many respects. A major step was the transfer of the region's forests to the state. The government began by holding negotiations on the matter with the rulers of Phrae and Nan; and subsequently with the rulers of Lamphun, Lampang, and Chiang Mai. All except the ruler of Chiang Mai agreed to transfer their forests to the government. King Inthawichayanon tried to negotiate with the assistance of Phraratchaya Chao Dararatsami, his daughter, who was a consort of King Rama V. However, the king made it clear that there should be no special exception for Chiang Mai. The government provided a sweetener—it gave a half share of the "stump fees" to the rulers and nobles every year. It also permitted the nobles in Lampang, Nan, and Phrae who had previously been engaged in logging to lease concessions of stipulated limits.[57]

A second major change was restructuring the concessions and closing loopholes in matters such as permits, length of leases, the fee rate per tree, the size of the trees to be cut, and the length of time trees should be girdled. (Trees were typically girdled for three years before being cut, so they would dry out enough to be floated downriver.) The government also wanted to preserve and improve the forests. In 1897 an act was promulgated related to mapping and protecting the forests. In the following year another act dealt with false branding of logs. (Concessionaires had to brand logs which were floated downriver for months or even years before reaching sawmills near the sea.)

The new arrangements aroused such discontent among the nobles in Chiang Mai that a rift developed between them and the commissioner. It became so severe that it created a territorial division; the commissioner was in control of the area near the bank of the Ping River (the site of the Chiang Mai Municipal Office nowadays) while the nobles were inside the city walls. Chao Uparat Inthawarorot and the nobles sent a petition to the king asking for the removal of the high commissioner. King Rama V tried to solve the problem by recalling Songsuradet to Bangkok. However, his reforms had already cut the power of the nobles to a great extent and had prepared the region for the *thesaphiban* system of *monthon* administration.

THE PERIOD OF THE *THESAPHIBAN* SYSTEM OF *MONTHON* ADMINISTRATION (1899–1933)

Under the *thesaphiban* system of provincial administration introduced in 1899, Lan Na became Monthon Phayap. The *monthon* was subdivided into provinces, districts, subdistricts, and villages. The highest position was *thesaphiban* commissioner. Each province had a governor. Officials from the Ministry of the Interior in Bangkok were sent to administer the region. Only positions at the *tambon* [subdistrict] and village level remained under local people.

Monthon Phayap was governed under the *thesaphiban* system until 1933. The thirty-four year period can be divided into three sections—the period of establishing the system (1899–1902), the period of building consciousness of national unity under the absolute monarchy (1902–1925), and the abolition of the special region of Monthon Phayap.

Establishing the Thesaphiban System. The *thesaphiban* system was first established in areas near Bangkok in 1894 and had spread throughout Siam by 1906. For a time Lan Na was administered differently from other *monthon* due to its wish to be in accord with traditional administration, and due to its long-standing local customs. Change proceeded gradually through the promulgation of special regulations, including the Regulations with Regard to the Administration of Monthon Phayap of 1900 and the Act Related to Wages for Labor in Lieu of Conscription in Monthon Phayap of the same year. After 1917 there were gradual adjustments to conform to the general regulations used in other *monthon*.

A civil service system was put in place which served as the instrument of the modern Thai state. The civil servants replaced the old *chao* system of rulers. Civil service offices were built on city-center sites formerly reserved for nobles. This was symbolic of the new power system. The rulers and nobles had always lived in the center. According to traditional beliefs in Chiang Mai, the center of the city was equivalent to the center of the universe.

In 1900 Phraya Sisahathep surveyed potential locations for government offices and decided upon the residence of Chao Noi Laokaeo (in 2004 the site of the district court). He purchased it to be used for a temporary administrative office for the *kao sanamluang*, the *mueang* governor. The governor later moved to what became the site of the old provincial government offices.[58] Over time many nobles donated their residences to the government. King Ao's former residence became the site of the provincial government offices. The location of the current Chiang Mai women's prison, the district office, Chiang Mai Technical School, Handicraft School for Girls, and the Tobacco Company offices are all in what used to be the area of Wiang Kaeo, King Kawila's royal residence. King Inthawichayonon's residence was at the site of what is now Yupharat School.[69] Finally, the descendants of the old Chiang Mai ruling house moved out of the inner city, which has since been developed with no concern for its historical heritage. The ashes of Phaya Mangrai, the founder of Chiang Mai and its first king, are buried in a site currently concealed behind private shophouses.

After the *thesaphiban* commissioner and *kao sanamluang*, the next important officials were commissioners of justice, revenue, treasury, public works, and forestry.

The administrative structure was adjusted to existing local structures somewhat. The Administrative Council responsible for *mueang* administration consisted of the *kao sanamluang*, the ruler, the *mueang* commissioner, and the assistant commissioner. Phraya Udomphongphensawat (M.R. Prayun Isarasak) held the position of *mueang* commissioner in Chiang Mai; the *chao uparat* (Chao Inthawarorot Suriyawong) was interim ruler; and Khun Rathakit was the assistant commissioner. Most of the power at the *mueang* level was held by the *mueang* commissioner. To no avail, the *chao uparat*, the interim ruler of Chiang Mai, demanded that the local ruler's old powers be returned.[60]

Despite their unsuitability for the times, the positions of the six *sena*, or ministers, remained, in order to mollify the nobles. The government gradually tried to abolish the positions by appointing officials from Bangkok to posts such as assistant *mueang* commissioner, public prosecutor, district lieutenant governor, and conscription registrar.

Special Commissioner Phraya Sisahathep traveled to every *mueang* to implement the system, beginning with Phrae, then Nan, Lampang, Lamphun, and finally Chiang Mai.

Large *mueang* such as Chiang Mai, Nan, and Lampang were divided into

83. The Chiang Mai women's prison, built on the site of Khum Wiang Kaeo, which used to be the main royal residence of the Mangrai dynasty. (PUA, c. 1910)

84. Pha Lat and the road to Doi Suthep. (NAT, c. 1893)

inner and outer sections. The *kao sanamluang* was in charge of the inner *mueang*, and the distant outer *mueang* was under a commissioner. Chiang Mai was divided into the inner section where the streams emptied into the Ping River and the outer section north of Chiang Mai, that is, Mae Hong Son, Mueang Yuam, Mueang Khun Yuam, and Mueang Pai. In Nan, the outer areas located along the bank of the Mekong River to the north were called Northern Nan; Mueang Lampang grouped areas of Mueang Phayao and called it Northern Lampang. Afterwards these various areas became provinces.

In 1900 the names of administrative positions were changed into the local language in order to promote better understanding among the people.

> The *thesaphiban* commissioner was called the *khaluang yai* (high commissioner).
> The *mueang* commissioner was called the *kao sanamluang*.
> The district, or *amphoe*, head was called *nai khwaeng*.
> The subdistrict head or *kamnan* was called *khwaen*.
> The village head or *phuyaiban* was called *kaeban*.

The high commissioner decided on the government divisions from *mueang* to district (*amphoe* or *khwaeng*). Each district had a *khwaeng* committee made up of the *nai khwaeng*, the district head, one or two assistants, and an accountant. The committee had to maintain peace and order, check on the actions of the *nai khwaen* (the subdistrict heads) and the *kaeban* (the village heads), and collect taxes. In the beginning, due to shortages of qualified personnel, the districts were few in number and large in size, so they were difficult to administer. For example, the inner area of Chiang Mai was made up of only six districts—Khwaeng Nakhon Chiang Mai, Khwaeng Chom Thong, Khwaeng Ping Tai, Khwaeng Mae Tun, Khwaeng Khun Ping, and Khwaeng Mae Tang. Lamphun had only two districts—Khwaeng Nakhon Lamphun and Khwaeng Li. Each district head had to be a Siamese civil servant from Bangkok. The large number of nobles and their relatives were consoled with positions as assistant *khwaeng*.

Power and benefits were shifting increasingly to Bangkok. In Chiang Mai the local rulers could no longer collect taxes or hold state money. Other *mueang* had not yet implemented a similar changeover. During his official visits of inspection, Sisahathep ordered audits of the state funds held by the rulers. When he discovered that the ruler of Phrae had used state funds in his own logging business, Sisahathep detained him for almost twenty-four hours and ordered him to repay the money in full. That was seen locally as disrespectful to the local ruler and aroused opposition.

The rulers and their relations had earlier enjoyed three main kinds of economic benefits. They had once totally controlled logging fees, until the government gradually took this sector over. A second source of income was government salaries given to nobles who were civil servants, including the ruler and the *chao uparat*. A share of the labor tax in lieu of conscription provided a third source of income. This tax had replaced the rulers' old ability to conscript labor under the *phrai* system.

In addition, the rulers continued to receive special rights over four hundred commoners without payment of the conscription fee or other taxes.[61]

King Inthawarorot received a sizable annual income from these three sources, of about 240,277 baht. But this was not enough to cover his expenditures, as he was responsible for a large number of nobles, relatives, and retainers. His income fluctuated depending on stump fees from logging and labor taxes, and it appeared to decrease each year. Finally the king asked to receive compensation only in the form of a government salary. After calculating income from the three sources, the government paid him a monthly salary of 20,000 baht from 1908 onwards.[62]

The government eventually terminated the special rights of the nobles to be exempt from taxes for a certain amount of rice fields. This increased the government's income almost tenfold, as most land belonged to the nobles.

A new tax was introduced to replace the old system of conscription for public works and for the ruler. The nobles were compensated with a share of the tax. Under the new arrangements, males between the ages of eighteen and sixty had to pay four baht annually. Those who could not pay were required to work for twenty-four days on public works. But in practice, even those who had paid the tax were liable to be drafted, now for a small wage, to work on projects such as roads, bridges, irrigation canals, or catching outlaws. Commoners were unhappy—now they had to pay tax and work for just two *salung* (four *salung* = one baht) a day. The hardship caused resentment towards the new Bangkok officials, who didn't hesitate to conscript labor.

Both commoners and nobles had cause to be unhappy during the first year of the *thesaphiban* system. In August 1900 rumors of an uprising swirled in the area. A secret telegram from M.R. Udomphongphensawat to the interior minister read:

> There is strange news about, but I don't know if it is true or false, that the Lao and the Burmese, Ngiao, and Chinese in Chiang Mai along with the *uparat* and *ratchawong* among others will revolt and exterminate the Siamese. They say the Siamese increasingly control, and the Lao are increasingly pushed aside to the point that they have to fetch their own drinking water. There will be no slaves to use. The forests are gone . . . They say that the Lao are getting together in every *mueang* in this *monthon*. Perhaps they will start things soon . . . People say that they are collecting weapons. The one hundred and nine guns in Nakhon Lampang are out of the ordinary and perhaps fit in with this.[63]

The current of dissatisfaction exploded in the Shan Uprising of 1902. At that time the government lacked qualified civil servants at every level, particularly for the position of district officer, who was required to be Siamese. District officers were few, the districts were quite extensive, and communication was difficult. As a result, a *nai khwaeng* could not look after all of his area. In addition, some *nai khwaeng* had contempt for the local population and made oppressive demands for labor. Opposition grew, especially in Phrae.

The Shan were unhappy at the government's treatment of them. Under the terms of the Bowring Treaty, they were British subjects. The government prohibited British subjects from owning land, houses, or places of business and banned them from cutting trees to build a house or temple. British subjects who traded in Siam had to have proper passports. Shan who lacked proof that they were British subjects had to pay the labor tax of four baht per year. Traditionally, the Shan had had close ties with the people of Lan Na. Some had long been settled in Lan Na, and others traveled back and forth for trade as they pleased. But as Siam changed in the direction of becoming a modern state, there began to be a sharp division between those who were Siamese and those who were not.

The rebels in Phrae were Shan hoodlums, supported by local nobles. After the rebels seized the city of Phrae, more Shan and other commoners looted the city and executed the commissioner and other Siamese officials. More than twenty people died. Shan in other areas including Mueang Phayao, Chiang Rai, Chiang Saen, and Khwaeng Mae-on (Sankamphaeng district) also attacked government offices.[64] Eleven Shan looted the distillery at Ban Paphai, Tambon Chae Chang, and burned down the district office.[65]

In Chiang Mai, there was also opposition to labor conscription. Phraya Naritsararatchakit sent a telegram to Bangkok on March 1, 1901: "The people and *kaeban* of Khwang Mueang Chiang Mai complained that *kao sanamluang* had conscripted them to construct roads. They said they had already paid cash in lieu of labor conscription but continued to be conscripted."[66]

Violent protest and refusal to follow government orders erupted again on May 2, 1902 at the Khwaeng Mae Ngat office. About six hundred people equipped with knives, swords, and sticks came to the district office to protest, and a clash arose between them and the Khwaeng Committee and ten policemen. Six protesters died and two were wounded. Two committee members were also wounded. There were more protests in Lamphun and Lampang, where the people refused to construct roads.[67]

The Shan Uprising provided the government with an excuse to take full control in Monthon Phayap. It sent troops to destroy the rebellion, dismissed the ruler of Phrae and appointed Bangkok officials to all local positions. The intention was to demonstrate the futility of revolt to all other *mueang* in the region. Local nobles began to change their attitude, and to accept state control.

85. Chang Lo Road along the southern moat of Chiang Mai. (PUA, c. 1927)

86. A performance by the Shan people on the occasion of King Rama VII's reception ceremony, 1926. (NAT, 1926)

87. Postman in Mae Hong Son posing with a Shan family. (NAT, c. 1902–1922)

88. A Shan religious procession passing by the *khwaeng* office building in Chiang Mai. The sign is in both Central Thai and Lan Na scripts. (NAT, c. 1982–1910)

The Shan Uprising had revealed clear splits and lack of understanding between *khon mueang*, Lan Na people, and *khon Thai*, Thai people. The idea that everyone was part of one people, one nationality, under the absolute monarchy had a long way to go. After the uprising there were more reforms in education and religion, improvements in infrastructure in the areas of communication and public health, and the spread of Bangkok culture to the north. There were efforts to promote national unity and there was more regional development of Lan Na. Gradually the traditional character of Lan Na broke down in virtually every area, from politics, the economy, society, and education to religion, the arts, and culture.

Building Consciousness of National Unity. The extremely able Phraya Surasiwisitsak (Choei Kanlayanamit) was appointed *thesaphiban* commissioner in 1902. He began by selecting quality staff who could build good relations with the local nobles and commoners. He reduced labor conscription. He also put increased emphasis on district-level administration. He revised districts into more appropriate sizes, renovated dilapidated government offices, and built new ones. In some places officials had been working out of the home of the district officer. The high commissioner tried to find the budget to build two or three new *khwaeng* per year until the problem was solved.[68] He also upgraded certain areas to the status of *mueang*. A part of western Chiang Mai became Mueang Mae Hong Son; northern Chiang Mai became Mueang Chiang Rai. The administration proceeded relatively smoothly, due to the cooperation of the rulers.

The treasury was improved through strict audits of government funds. Tax income rose significantly. The labor tax which had created hardship was reduced to two baht in some areas.

In 1903, the government established an army division headquarters in Chiang Mai. Army units were also located in other *mueang*, under commanders from Bangkok. There was no conscription in the military (until 1914), but there was, from 1899, conscription in the police. Draftees kept running off, and there was a severe manpower shortage before the establishment of the army base. A family census was carried out. Soldiers were given incentives such as opportunities for promotion. There were strict penalties for runaways.

The government expanded the road system for better and faster communications. Construction of the northern rail line was also a priority. Health centers were constructed to provide care and prevent epidemics. Doctors were stationed at the *monthon*, *mueang*, and subdistrict levels. Cholera and smallpox were serious problems. There were too few doctors to vaccinate against smallpox. However, missionary hospitals helped ease the burden.

Education and religion were key elements in building awareness of the state. Lan Na had developed its own traditional knowledge in the fields of arts, linguistics, local lore, and culture over many hundreds of years. Temples were educational institutes, and the monks taught Dhamma (the teachings of the Buddha), Lan Na Tham script, inscription of palm-leaf texts, literature, astrology, traditional medicine, carpentry, etc. Some temples specialized: Nantharam Temple specialized in traditional medicine, and Mo Kham Tuang and Methang temples specialized in astrology.

Perennial manpower shortages in the region meant that only a limited number of men could afford to be monks. Many chose to be novices, which also meant they would get an education. It was socially acceptable to be ordained in order to study. After leaving the *sangha*, men's names had the prefix "Nan" if they had been monks and "Noi" if they had been novices.

There was also on-the-job training for family trades such as silversmith, goldsmith, lacquerware maker, and potter.

Education and *sangha* reforms proceeded simultaneously. Educational reform aimed at the building of a sense of unity between the Lao and the Thai. The new system emphasized training the younger generation to be conscious of being citizens of Siam. School-leavers in the new system would be eligible to gain entry to the new civil service system. The king commented:

> The desire is not only for knowledge in reading and writing but for teaching about the government and for understanding the benefits of being united with the Thai. To get along one must have thoughts and feeling for each other and desire the progress of the country in which we are joined together. Therefore, those in charge of education should not be haughty nor look down on the Lao people as inferior to the Thai in every respect. They must be intelligent in finding a way to teach and make the Lao people feel that the government officials and the ordinary people are one with the Thai. If the Lao are good, they will be rewarded like the Thai.[69]

Historically, the territory of Lan Na had its own history, culture, traditions, and language. The Lan Na people had closer ties with the Burmese, Shan, Lue, and Lao than with the Thai. They felt little in common with the Siamese, who felt likewise about their northern neighbors.

By 1903 it was government policy that Central Thai script be taught in schools throughout the kingdom. In the beginning, the study of local languages was also allowed. The government believed that a lenient approach would eventually lead to the disappearance of local languages, particularly given the rule that government officials had to know Central Thai. The use of Lan Na Tham script has continued to decline to the present day, together with knowledge of the old texts.

Phraya Surasiwisitsak encouraged the nobles, district committees, merchants, and common people to join in donating land, construction materials, and money to found Thai schools. They also had to find money to support the schools, since the national education budget was a tiny 3.2 percent of the whole budget, the vast majority of which was poured into defending the country.

89. Mahat Lek Luang School in Chiang Mai, founded during the reign of King Rama VI between 1915–1925. It was located in the foothills of Doi Suthep where a dairy farm is today. (BS, n.d.)

90. Tha Phae Road in front of Mahawan Temple. In the past, the road was lined with large trees. (PUA, c. 1932)

The local nobles regarded supporting education as a meritorious act and threw their support behind the changes. They donated private lands in the center of the cities for model school sites. Chao Bunyawat of Nakhon Lampang donated land for the construction of Bunyawat School; Chao Inthawarorotsuriyawong of Chiang Mai donated land for Yupharat School, regarded as the region's leading school; Chao Chakkhamkhachonsak of Lamphun donated land for Chakkhamkhanathon School; and Chao Suriyaphongphalitdet of Nan donated land for Suriyanukhro School. In the outlying districts, the district committees helped people construct public elementary schools. There were also missionary schools, including the Prince Royal's College, the Dara Academy, and the Kenneth McKenzie School. In the beginning, the missionary schools taught English and Thai Yuan, or Mueang, script. After the educational reforms, they changed to Central Thai and English.

Educational policy under King Rama VI emphasized the implanting of loyalty to the nation, religion, and king. Thai language teaching aimed at encouraging locals to read, write, and speak in Central Thai. Students were taught Thai geography and history. They were required to sing the royal anthem, and school walls were adorned with pictures of the king and with the country's flag, the symbols of the nation.[70]

Monks and novices were encouraged to study, speak, and preach in Central Thai. Males had to know Central Thai to become monks. The government paid particular attention to the *sangha*, the Buddhist clergy, because of its role in education—most elementary schools were located in village temples. Gradually, knowledge of the local scripts and the old Lan Na texts began to disappear.[71]

The Lan Na *sangha* had been under the *sangharaja*, the highest-ranking monk, who was appointed by the ruler. Bangkok wanted to create a national *sangha* administration. It was said that Lan Na monks did not observe strict discipline, and their practices varied overmuch.

In 1902, the national Sangha Administration Act was promulgated and independent traditional practices were abolished. The supreme body was now the Mahathera Samakhom, or the Ecclesiastical Council. It comprised eight high-ranking monks, three of whom were heads of regions—the lord abbot of the north, the lord abbot of the south, the lord abbot of the center—and the lord abbot of the Dhammayutika Sect, together with another four senior abbots. The Ecclesiastical Council made absolute decisions on the *dhamma vinaya* rules in decisions that were absolute.[72]

The *sangha* was organized hierarchically, paralling the structure of government. Ranking abbots (*chao khana*) headed up *monthon*, *mueang*, district, subdistrict, and village *sangha* organizations.

There was a certain amount of opposition in Lan Na to the reforms. Khruba Siwichai (1878–1937), a charismatic monk from Lamphun with a wide following, continued to ordain monks without authority from the *sangha* hierarchy and to follow local Thai Yuan practices. He proceeded independently until 1935, when he was summoned to Bangkok and detained for six months in Wat Benchamabophit (the Marble Temple), whose abbot was the lord abbot of the North. Khruba Siwichai finally agreed not to conduct any more ordinations and was allowed to return to the north—and the government also became a bit less strict about local practices. Khruba Siwichai symbolized the last wave of opposition to administrative reform in Lan Na.[73]

Phraya Surasiwisitsak worked to reform the administration of Lan Na until 1915, by which time the region was firmly under the control of Siam in all aspects, including government, economy, society, education, art, and culture.

In the period between 1915 and 1925, Monthon Phayap functioned like other areas under Bangkok. The arrival of the railway in 1921 resulted in a great rise of exports of rice and other crops, and a new influx of goods and influences from the central region into Lan Na.

The period between 1925 and 1933 was the final stage of the *thesaphiban* system. King Rama VII, who came to power in 1925, instigated various changes, in a period of economic depression, the now obsolete positions of the six *sena* were abolished. It was decreed that from 1926, while the local ruler would receive a salary for life, he would not be replaced after his death. Major General Chao Kaeonawarat, the last king of Chiang Mai, died in 1939.

A year after the People's Party coup in 1932, Thailand's *thesaphiban* system was abolished. The *monthon* system was replaced with provinces. Chiang Mai, formerly the center of the Lan Na kingdom, became a province of Siam.

CHAPTER 9

SOCIETY AND ECONOMY (1774–1933)

LAN NA SOCIETY UNDER THE CHAO CHET TON LINE

THE NOBILITY

Lan Na society divided people into two main classes, nobility (*munnai*) and commoners (*phrai*). At the top was the king or *chao luang*.[1] Just beneath him, in descending order of rank, were his close relatives in the positions of *chao uparat*, *chao ratchawong*, *chao ratchabut*, and *chao burirat*. Together they formed the group of five ruling nobles, or *chao khanhabai*.

Nobles enjoyed a decreasing variety of rights and benefits as the line extended from brothers and sisters to their children, grandchildren, and great grandchildren. There were two kinds of nobles: those born to the nobility and those appointed to special positions.[2]

Unlike in Bangkok, Lan Na nobles were not assigned a defined set of rights over land and commoners (*sakdina*) according to their rank. (In Bangkok, for example, the king's brother by the same mother was granted 20,000 *sakdina*; the king's son 15,000; the king's half brother by lesser wives 7,000; the king's daughter and granddaughter 6,000; the king's granddaughter lower in the hierarchy 4,000; *mom chao* 1,500; and *mom ratchawong* 500.)

Also unlike Bangkok, where nobles gradually lost rank through the generations and ended as commoners after the fifth generation, members of the Chao Chet Ton family never descended to commoner status. Thus the number of *chao* increased, until finally some of the lower-ranking of them were given administrative duties at the village level, as in the case of *chao mahawong*, who at one time administered San Sai village, Saraphi district in Chiang Mai.[3]

Nobles who were not well off could be called upon to perform official duties from time to time. Carl Bock, the Norwegian who surveyed Lan Na in 1881, mentions that two nobles guided him during a journey from Lampang to Chiang Mai. Such people did not consider it a loss of prestige to work for modest pay.[4]

"Nobility by position" referred to those people, who may or may not have been nobles by birth, who were appointed to positions of rank. The most important of these were the *phraya kao sanam* of the first rank, *phraya sanam* of the second rank, *phraya sanam* of the third rank, *phraya* of the Royal Household, and *phraya nai uparat*, down to *khwaen* (subdistrict head), and *kaeban* (village head).

From the beginning, the Chao Chet Ton clan was determined to restore Lan Na to its former glory. "The Chao Chet Ton cleared the forests and built the *mueang* like those kings who preceded them in fifty-seven Lan Na *mueang* . . .[5] and made the cities beautiful, and made Buddhism flourish as King Mangrai had done."[6]

The family built up its legitimacy as rulers by reviving and placing themselves at the center of traditional customs, such as the coronation ceremony and oath of allegiance ceremonies.

The coronation ceremony was the key signifier of the king's legitimate right to rule. Phraya Thammalangka (r. 1815–1821), Phraya Khamfan (r. 1823–1825), and Phraya Phutthawong (r. 1826–1846) each had two coronations, one each for the purposes of being legitimized by the Chao Chet Ton clan and the king of Siam. The rites followed traditional practices that dated back to the Mangrai dynasty. The coronation route of King Kawila of Chiang Mai was described as follows:

> In 1796, the king rode a beautiful elephant . . . in the early morning. He proceeded to Bupharam Temple following the traditional practice of the former kings. In order not to violate tradition the procession continued toward the south, then west, then in the direction of the Chiang Yun Temple to the north, where he paid respect to the Buddha image. In the late afternoon, he led his entourage and entered the city through the Chang Phueak Gate, or the north gate. The Lua who preceded the procession pulled a dog and entered the city first and stayed overnight across from Chiang Yun Temple. On the following morning, the king took a bath, washed his hair, adorned himself, and had his meal. At an auspicious time, he went to the auspicious site, which had been the site of the royal residence of the former kings.[7]

Oath of allegiance ceremonies also dated back to the Mangrai dynasty. In the tributary period, the *chao khanhabai* and other nobles would hold two such ceremonies a year honoring the Siamese king. During the events the nobles demonstrated their loyalty by drinking sacred water of allegiance. There were similar ceremonies demonstrating loyalty to the local rulers. The author has found evidence for the oath of allegiance taking place for local rulers in the reigns of King Kawilorot and King Inthawichayanon. It is likely that similar ceremonies took place in earlier periods, probably in important temples. "The *phraya ratchabut* and relatives of the king read the oath and vowed to be loyal and honest to the king of Chiang Mai and all received another round of the water of allegiance to drink."[8]

91. Wiang Kaeo, Chiang Mai. (NAT, n.d.)

92. Wooden *wihan* of Phan Tao Temple. Originally, it was the *ho kham* of King Mahotaraprathet, which was donated to the temple by his descendants. (SO, 1982)

The oath of allegiance ceremony honoring the local ruler normally lasted for seven consecutive days. It was performed in Chiang Mai and Lamphun when a ruler was newly installed. Outlying *mueang* held similar ceremonies, demonstrating loyalty to Chiang Mai. Nan performed a version of the ceremony every year,[9] and Lampang fined people who were required to attend its ceremony, but did not, the sum of 7.50 baht.[10]

As well as holding such ceremonies, the Mangrai dynasty had claimed its legitimacy to rule through its possession of sacred objects handed down from ancestors, including regalia such as the Chai sword, and the Sikanchai dagger.[11]

The powerful Chao Chet Ton family, though from a commoner background, probably also claimed ownership of the sacred Sikanchai dagger in the early period of their reign. Phaya Uparat Thammalangka reportedly used the sacred knife in the war to expel the Burmese from Chiang Saen in 1804.[12] Later, the family relied more on its possession of a variety of new sacred objects, "the insignia of rank." Kings were surrounded by these insignia. "The king reclined on his high pillow on the carpet in the middle of a large square seat, surrounded by his insignia of rank, such as the betel tray, spittoon, and another tray, each beautifully made of gold."[13] When King Inthawichayanon made a journey, even for a short distance, at least twelve people in his entourage were tasked with carrying his insignia of rank.[14] The king bestowed a variety of insignia on other nobles, which had to be returned after their death.

The Chao Chet Ton also took possession of sacred objects from other *mueang* and brought them to Chiang Mai. Phaya Uparat Thammalangka brought back a sacred Buddha figure, Phrachao Thongthip, after taking Chiang Khang.[15]

Later on, as Lan Na's tributary status ended, the oath of allegiance to local leaders was gradually discontinued. Prince Sonabanthit, special commissioner of Monthon Lao Chiang (approximately 1888–1890) introduced a policy that oaths of allegiance should only be made to Bangkok. Phraya Songsuradet, the high commissioner from 1893 to 1899, stipulated that the rulers, *phaya*, *thao*, *saen*, district head, *nai ban*, and tax collectors perform the ceremony of allegiance to Bangkok at a temple. Nobles in distant *mueang* had to perform similar ceremonies.[16] It is possible that such ceremonies were held in every *mueang* in Lan Na.

The ruler's way of life was designed to demonstrate his superiority over the people. The lifestyle was modeled on court life in Bangkok. Lan Na nobles had residences called *khum*, or palace, or the more luxurious *ho kham*, or gilded palace, located in the auspicious center of the city. King Kawila's residence was located in the area of Wiang Kaeo, former home to the kings of the Mangrai dynasty. King Inthawichayanon, and possibly King Kawilorot, had a residence called the Khum Luang Klang Wiang at the site of what is now the Chiang Mai court.[17]

Daniel McGilvary, a missionary who had an audience with King Kawilorot

(r. 1856–1870), reported that the residence had a large and spacious throne hall. "On reaching the grand reception hall at the palace, we encountered such an array of princely state as we had never before seen among the Lao. Every prince, princess, and officer who could come was already there."[18] The throne hall was similar to the one in Bangkok, but on a smaller scale.

The daily lives of the ruler and high-ranking nobles also demonstrated their power; for example, they had a large number of *phrai* servants, including the city's leading tailors and dressmakers, carvers, painters, dancers, and soldiers. The king's residence was the center of art and culture. King Inthawichayanon hired dancers from Bangkok to teach their counterparts at his residence and to perform at the Royal Theater.

The ruler's patronage of Buddhism also enhanced his status and legitimacy. Local kings built and restored temples, commissioned the casting of important Buddha images, and made larger donations than anyone else. (If the latter custom was broken there was trouble. Phraya Khamfan (r. 1823–1825) felt that Phraya Ratchawong Suwanakhammun's large religious donations were a challenge to his power).

The ruler also had the power to appoint the supreme patriarch and other Buddhist positions. King Kawilorot issued instructions that any monk who violated his code of proper conduct would be punished by the state.[19]

COMMONERS (*PHRAI*)

Those who were not nobles were either commoners (*phrai*) or slaves. The *phrai*, the largest population segment, were very important to the state. They had to be registered with the noble of the area in which they lived, and they had to serve the state for a period each year. They were called "*phrai* who performed government duties." If they wished to absent themselves from such duties, they had to pay compensation in cash or in kind. Labor conscription mostly involved males, but females could also be called upon. *Phrai* women, for example, accompanied high-ranking female nobles to Bangkok when they went to present tribute to the Siamese king.[20] In 1873, conscripted *phrai*, including females, constructed the ring road inside the city moat.[21]

The Mangraisat is very clear about the importance of *phrai*. "The rulers could rule the kingdom because of the *phrai*."[22] It was vital for individual *mueang* to have a sufficient number of *phrai*. Many *mueang* tried to get more by making wars of "resettlement," which involved capturing people and carrying them off. Towns were often left deserted after their population was entirely uprooted.

In 1782, when King Kawila first became king of Chiang Mai, the city was deserted and the king faced a serious shortage of manpower. He founded nearby Wiang Pa Sang by taking three hundred *phrai* from Lampang and

93. Business in the marketplace. (LA, c. 1902)

94. Female venders returning from the market. (LA, c. 1902)

seven hundred *phrai* belonging to the *phraya chaban*.[23] He then began a period of "collecting vegetables for the baskets, collecting people for the *mueang*." Using a mixture of persuasion and force, he took people from the Salween and Sipsong Panna regions to Chiang Mai as *phrai*. People from the *mueang* who refused to submit to him were taken as slaves. The *phrai* were allowed to resettle in their own ethnic communities, led by their own leaders, and Chiang Mai grew into a multi-ethnic society made up of locals as well as people of other ethnicities such as the Khoen, Lue, Shan, Kha, Lua, and Burmese. All the newcomers would eventually become *khon mueang*, as they adopted local culture in order to elevate their social standing or to receive privileges as "people of the state."

Registration of Lan Na *phrai* was probably done by family; their lord was called "lord of the family."[24] There is no clear evidence with regard to the details of registration, and it seems there were few detailed regulations on the matter. In the central region, the *phrai* system grouped children from the age of nine years old up; these would not be conscripted until they were registered and tattooed with numbers when their height was about fifty inches measured from feet to shoulders. They would be discharged only when they were seventy years old.[25]

The Lan Na *phrai* received identification papers, and were not tattooed.

> But for those *phrai* from Mueang Nan, Luang Prabang, Chiang Mai, Lakhon Lampang, and Lamphun who became the sons-in-law in these northern *mueang*, the Siamese king would appoint a commissioner to set up a department of tattooing. It did not actually tattoo the *phrai* but only called for lists to get their numbers . . . Luang Khunmun was appointed to check the lists of White-Bellied and Black-Bellied Lao in the tributary states to get the exact number of *phrai* of individual *mueang*. A person certified the numbers, then their wrists were tied with cord, which was sealed with *lac* and they were issued proper papers identifying their birth marks and a paper was given to each one of them.[26]

The author has discovered that though every *phrai* had to be registered under a lord, they were not necessarily registered under a government office.[27] Thus they were not in the same position as the official *phrai*, or *phrai luang*, of the central region. It can be said that all *phrai* in Lan Na belonged to their lords, including the ruler, as *phrai som*, or personal, non-official *phrai*.[28]

Those *phrai*, called *phrai suai*, who lived in remote areas and who had difficulty traveling could send money or goods instead of contributing labor. Such tribute was an important source of income for the state. Forest products suitable for export were particularly important. The lords were often more in need of tribute in kind than labor tribute.

Phrai could be transferred from one lord to another. When the local king died, the *phrai* under his control would be divided among the new ruler, the

95. The people of Lampang waiting in line during King Rama VII's visit to Monthon Phayap in 1926. (NAT, 1926)

96. The people of Lampang assembled for King Rama VII's visit. (NAT, 1926)

deceased's descendants, and other nobles.[29] King Rama IV insisted that *phrai* stay with the new lords voluntarily. Nobles were forbidden to grab people, or to "take low-ranking nobles like *saen* and *thao* or servants and *phrai*."[30] In the event of a noble being removed from office for political reasons, his *phrai* were divided out. When Nai Noi Mahaphrom, the son of King Mahotaraprathet, was kept in Bangkok, his *phrai* were reallocated. "Phraya Ula received eight new male and female *phrai* from Nai Noi Mahaphrom."[31]

It is understood that the king, as the supreme lord, had the largest number of *phrai*. He also possessed the power to order lower-ranking nobles to make their *phrai* work according to his wishes, either for war or for public works.[32] In the case of war, a victorious commander would present the vanquished people to the king.[33] It is likely that the ruler kept a portion of such groups of people and awarded the rest to the nobles who helped win the war.

It was the king's duty to prevent *phrai* from running away and to bring them back when they did. This implied an obligation to assist the nobles in preventing their manpower from being taken by other *mueang*.[34] One way to achieve the return of *phrai* was to report the matter to Bangkok. In 1784 King Kawila petitioned King Rama I for the return of *phrai* from Mueang Rahaeng, Ban Tak, Ban Chiang Ngoen, and Mueang Thoen[35] who had fled from the Burmese threat to Ayutthaya.[36] The king granted his request. In 1859, King Kawilorot asked King Rama IV for the return of twenty-eight Chiang Mai *phrai* who were in Mueang Tak,[37] and this was granted. Such requests were probably made only infrequently.

The Chao Chet Ton family early on tried to tackle the problem of runaways. Prince Chaikaeo called on the seven brothers to offer mutual assistance in the matter.

> Though you have the great good fortune to rule in various domains, you must consider them to be a single domain. Those evil ones who steal and flee, the elder seeking out the younger and the younger the elder, you should not harbor, but send back [from whence they came]. Don't consider such persons to be your siblings.[38]

Bangkok had similar problems with runaways. During the reign of King Rama III, a sealed document was sent from Chaophraya Chakri to Chiang Mai, Lampang, Lamphun, and Phrae, requesting the return of runaway *phrai*.

> Concerning those *phrai* who ran away from their lords and hid in another *mueang*, do not side with the wrong people or be concerned with such small individuals. If their lords come to look for them, return them, because we are all part of the same territory. Do not create differences but assist each other and help keep peace and happiness within the kingdom.[39]

Requesting the return of *phrai* was probably also seen as a way to discourage potential new runaways. Yet the main way to avoid the problem, as advocated by Bangkok, was seen as looking after the *phrai* properly and helping them to earn a living. The government ordered "the *chao ratchabut* to be kind to his relatives and look after his *phrai*, care for their fields and for their peaceful livelihood. Do not oppress them or other citizens. Do not violate tradition in ruling the kingdom."[40]

One reason why *phrai* ran away was poverty resulting from failed harvests. Lampang faced severe and repeated agricultural failures, including from 1848 to 1851 and from 1854 to 1855. Distressed *phrai* took their families to Chiang Mai and Lamphun to work in the fields there for a few years. The Lampang ruler ordered lower-ranking nobles to fetch them back, but the *phrai* refused to come.[41] In 1884, the *phrai* in Lampang faced hardships again, as noted by Phichitprichakon.

> Nowadays the price of rice in Mueang Nakhon is even higher. The people keep fleeing the *mueang*. There are thieves competing for rice. About forty or fifty people did not loot valuables or harm the owners, they only opened the granaries for rice. This has occurred very frequently until rice has become scarce, insufficient for consumption.[42]

The official announced that people who had nothing to eat should migrate to Chiang Saen, Mueang Ngai, or Mueang Pai, where they would receive rice and plots for rice fields.[43]

The rulers had the duty of keeping records of the *phrai* under their control. After the *chao ratchawong* was installed as ruler of Phrae in 1848, he made a census of the area, compiling a long list totaling 2,500 people.[44] King Kawilorot undertook a census after ascending the throne in 1856: Chiang Mai (excluding Chiang Rai) had 30,000 people; Lampang had 30,000; Lamphun 8,000; and Nan 10,000.[45]

The census was used for the conscription of *phrai* for public works. "Honghoen," a ballad composed around 1881, relates:

> Three thousand people, from near and far, are checked in haste, entered into lists. Come report now. Do not miss anyone.[46]

The Mangraisat stipulated that *phrai* work half the year for the state. The Chao Chet Ton reduced this to between one to four months a year.[47]

In peacetime, *phrai* were required to labor on various kinds of public works, such as constructing and repairing city walls,[48] temples, and royal residences; digging city moats; constructing irrigation canals;[49] cutting teak to be used for tribute;[50] and constructing a shed for the white elephant that was to be presented to the Siamese king.[51] They were also used as a police corps in

97. A religious procession to Phra Singh Temple. The picture shows the three-way intersection in front of the temple. (NAT, c. 1902–1917)

98. The people offering food to the monks at Phra Singh Temple. (NAT, 1926)

assisting the nobles to follow and capture outlaws,[52] or for work on frontier checkpoints in border *mueang*.[53]

Phrai worked on the rice fields of the rulers, who probably supervised such work carefully. "The *chao luang* (Lampang) was supervising the harvest and there was no one at his residence."[54] "The *chao luang* of Chiang Mai went out to check his rice fields."[55] "The ruler of Lamphun was not at his residence but was found at the rice fields several miles away from the town."[56] The ballad "*Ai Roikhod*" relates: "In the streams and ponds, canals and rivers, the *mueang* people everywhere all worked in the fields planting rice. Every member of Thai *phrai* families and the servants of the nobles were all busily working."[57]

In wartime, the *phrai* were taken as troops, and runaways were liable for the death penalty. The *phrai* could be held for the entire period of a war, making it very difficult for them to support their families.

Efforts to keep relations smooth between the lords and the *phrai* depended upon each being aware of their positions as well as their duties. The lords had to be kind and generous towards the *phrai*, while the *phrai* had to follow their lords' instructions, as well as accept their humble position. Literature and maxims reinforced such messages. The poem "*Chao Withun Son Lan*"[Chao Withun Teaches His Grandson] taught the lords to use polite words, to help the *phrai* when they were in distress, and to assist the *phrai* and repay them when the *phrai* brought presents to the lords. Another poem taught ladies how to use polite words and show kindness towards their *phrai*.

Phrai were taught to abstain from thinking about politics because it was not their concern; rather, they should give their attention to working their fields and orchards, and earning money, leaving government business to the nobles and other officials; their duty was to listen and follow instructions.[58]

SLAVES

Slaves, considered the personal assets of their lords, were at the bottom of the hierarchy. Wealthy lords possessed a very large number of slaves, with the ruler holding the most. A very few well-off *phrai* also had a number of slaves. If a lord had more slaves than he needed, he would hire them out to others for an annual fee,[59] for work such as climbing betel trees, selling liquor, and trading.[60]

The need for labor led to the widespread selling and buying of slaves. Proof of sale and of payment was made at the Mueang office. The *Anachak-lakkham*, Mueang Nan's law code, said, "Concerning the people of our four *mueang*, if any person sells elephants and people in any *mueang*, both the buyer and seller have to arrange the sale at that *mueang* office."[61] It was not uncommon for slaves to be kidnapped. There were laws against slaves running away and against sheltering runaways. The Chiang Mai nobles traded slaves with the Karen or exchanged cattle for slaves brought by Karen from the Shan States.[62]

Slaves were divided into three types—captive slaves, debt slaves, and temple servants. Captive slaves were those taken in war and then divided among high-ranking soldiers. They were regarded as property and could be inherited. If they could redeem themselves in cash, they could be freed.[63] The prices of slaves stipulated in the Act Regarding the Type of Slaves in the Northwest Monthon of 1900 were:

Nakhon Chiang Mai	Male 54 baht	Female 72 baht
Nakhon Nan	Male 62 baht	Female 62 baht
Nakhon Lampang	Male 45 baht	Female 60 baht
Nakhon Lamphun	Male 54 baht	Female 72 baht
Mueang Phrae	Male 48 baht	Female 48 baht
Mueang Thoen	Male 42 baht	Female 64 baht

The prices generally depended on the demand for labor. Busy Chiang Mai and Lamphun had a great need of workers and so prices there were high. Female slaves fetched a higher price than males because the women could bear children, who would also be slaves.

Debt slaves were those who sold themselves, or were sold into, slavery. These included slaves born during their parents' servitude. They could redeem themselves in cash. It is likely that the majority of slaves were debt slaves.[64]

Some slaves were donated to temples, especially those built by kings. Phra That Chom Thong Temple in Chiang Mai had seven hundred slaves who worked in shifts.[65]

Conditions for slaves were probably adequate. Slave owners presumably had an incentive not to oppress them, in order to prevent their running away. Slaves had rights: the right of inheritance from their parents, the right to receive medical care from their lord when sick, the right to life (the lord could not deliberately kill his slaves), the right to redeem their freedom. A slave also had the right to his wife. If the lord took a slave's wife without her consent, she would be free; if with her consent, then her husband would be free. If the lord allowed male slaves to enter the monkhood, they would be free after their ordination. If the lord tried to kill his slave, the slave would go free.

SOCIAL CHANGE AND THE ABOLITION OF THE NOBILITY, *PHRAI*, AND SLAVES

The administrative reforms of Monthon Phayap gradually stripped the rulers and their relatives of their old power. Change in the *phrai* system began when Krom Moen Phichitprichakon placed them under the jurisdiction of the Interior and Defense departments. The Interior Department had begun a regional census in about 1890 that gathered detailed information, including the names of village heads and subdistricts; the number of houses; the male and female population; the ages of people, such as young adults, young children, and babies; the number of elderly and the number of handicapped, both male and female; the quantity of guns, spears, swords, elephants, horses, cows, and buffalo. Since the majority of village and subdistrict heads were illiterate, the census proceeded slowly. Krommoen Phichitprichakon also ordered a survey of young adults, an important manpower group for the Department of Defense. The census and other reforms were paving the way to the end of the *phrai* system.

In 1900, the Act Regarding the Collection of Cash in Lieu of Labor Conscription in the Northwest Monthon was introduced. The aim was to allow *phrai* to become free citizens of Siam, under the absolute monarchy. The act was also a key moment in the integration of Lan Na into the Siamese kingdom. The act stipulated that adults between the ages of eighteen and sixty had to pay four baht annually in place of labor conscription and tribute payment. Those who refused to pay had to work for twenty days. The *phrai* system was now becoming a cash matter. Traditional tribute payments were ended. There was no more conscription of labor for between one and four months a year for the lords.

Slaves also had to pay four baht in lieu of public labor. A lord was responsible for paying the tax for those slaves who worked in his household; this was sometimes a heavy burden and was possibly designed to make slave ownership less attractive. Slaves who worked outside the lord's household had to pay themselves.[66]

On September 21, 1900, the Act Concerning Slavery in Northwest Monthon also went into effect. It divided slaves into captive slaves and debt slaves. The prices of slaves were decreased: males were valued at twenty-five baht and females at thirty-two baht. Captive slaves were entitled to redeem their freedom by paying the stipulated cost. All slaves who reached the age of sixty were freed. The children of slaves born on or after December 16, 1897 (the day King Rama V returned from Europe) were also freed.[67]

The act immediately reduced the number of slaves and within a decade slavery was no more. The practice was ended rather slowly partly in order to prevent the nobles from feeling overly put out by their losses. Official thinking can be seen in a case in which two slaves who belonged to the Lampang *chao ratchabut* ran away and joined the army. The lord decided to forego trying to get them back. When news of this reached King Rama V, he said:

> The Lao's voluntary sacrifice of his money to support the defense is not a good idea. With this kind of example, a large number of slaves will join the army. The owners can only sacrifice a hundred or two hundred rupees, but if it reaches a thousand rupees, the wealthy slave owners will be resentful and it will lead to widespread and heated discussion . . . In the future, it is forbidden to take slaves into the army.[68]

99. The provincial police corps, Chiang Rai. (NAT, c. 1899–1910)

By 1912 when a new Act Concerning Slavery was promulgated in Monthon Phayap there were very few slaves left.

Taxes. The new system of collecting the labor tax proceeded in stages. At first, income from the tax was divided into six portions—one portion for the ruler, one for the nobles and their descendants, two for administrative purposes, and two portions for the Ministry of Finance. Nobles were exempt from the tax, and the ruler could exempt up to four hundred servants. Others exempted included government officials, monks and novices, and handicapped people and paupers.

The act stayed in place in Monthon Phayap until 1917, when it was replaced by the Act of Cash Collection. This measure provided for collection of a cash tax called *kha ratchakan*, or the cost of government. It was collected from adults aged eighteen to sixty and was not to exceed six baht per person per year. Temporary exemptions were given on an annual basis to people who had donated money to the government that year exceeding the stipulated rate, or to those with special identification papers. A special exemption was given to monks, to people who had migrated and settled down for their first year, and to students who had just completed six years of schooling. Permanent exemptions were given to nobles, soldiers, government officials, subdistrict heads (*kamnan*) and their assistants, village heads (*kaeban*), handicapped people, people who had children and had already paid for three persons, and registered Chinese. The rulers were no longer entitled to receive four hundred papers of identification annually, so they had to pay the tax for their servants.[69]

Some people were unable to pay the increased cash and had to be conscripted for public works instead. Monthon Phayap had more people conscripted for public works than any other *monthon* in Siam. In 1922 1,289 people were compelled to work instead of paying cash, among whom were 1,247 Thai, 9 Shan, 1 Burmese, 17 Khamu, and 17 others.[70] Since the same rate was collected without regard to income, and only from commoners and not nobles, the tax was very regressive. It was abolished in 1938.[71]

Police and Army. Major changes in the police and army also heralded significant social change. Conscription of police, actually a form of military conscription, began around 1899. A great number of young adults were seized, and there were subsequently a great number of runaways. Not surprisingly, perhaps, the police gained a reputation for inefficiency. The Lampang provincial police were repeatedly unable to suppress Shan bandits at Ban Bo Kaeo, and the bandits captured Mueang Phrae in 1902. That led to the establishment of the Monthon Phayap military headquarters in 1903. It had a standing army of 1,600, among whom were 1,000 men from Nakhon Sawan and Phitsanulok and only 400 from the local area. Runaways remained a problem. For example, among 300 conscripted men, 160 ran away.

New censuses were undertaken. Mueang Phrae was the first to complete its census. Other *mueang* had complied by 1904. It is understood that the problem of runaways then decreased. Locals were persuaded to see the benefit of joining the army—among the inducements were the possibility of promotions and a lifetime exemption from the head tax for conscripts who served for two years.

In 1914, the Act Concerning Military Conscription of 1905 was introduced in Monthon Phayap. Former nobles and educated and wealthy people were exempt from conscription, as they were exempt from paying the head tax. Thai society continued to have two social classes, the privileged and those who shouldered the replacement of the old *phrai* system.[72]

THE LAN NA ECONOMY (1774–1933)

THE ECONOMIC SITUATION PRIOR TO THE REFORM OF MONTHON PHAYAP IN 1884

When King Kawila reestablished Lan Na in 1796, the local economic situation was very unstable and there was an acute shortage of manpower. Kawila's response was to introduce the policy of "collecting vegetables for the baskets, collecting people for the *mueang*." By the end of his rule, the economic problems had eased. Production surpluses suggest that the kingdom was economically secure as well as peaceful by the reign of King Phutthawong (1826–1846).[73] Trade with the British in Burma brought Lan Na into the cash economy. Rupees minted by the British in Madras became the medium of exchange. Still, the local economy continued to be based on the *phrai* system, not free labor, and the use of money was not widespread.

Prior to the late 1800s, trade was generally conducted through barter. Individual communities specialized in different crops, depending on the local geographical, soil, and water conditions.[74] The fertile plains of the Ping and Kok river valleys provided ample rice, which could be traded for other food crops or forest products. Highland communities such as Mae Taeng, Chiang Dao, and Samoeng districts produced *miang*, fermented tea leaves, Phrae produced tobacco, Lampang produced field crops, and Nan was the source of forest products.

Salt deposits in Nan led to the production of rock salt, which was sold as far away as Yunnan. The Lua village in the Bo Luang area of Chiang Mai had iron deposits, which led to smelting to make tools. In Chiang Rai, Chiang Mai and Lampang, there were communities with expertise in pottery.[75]

Lan Na's economic system was based mainly on production for household use. Carl C. Zimmermann, who surveyed the northern economy in 1930, described rice production in the region as on the level of "subsistence."[76]

Trade. Chiang Mai, the most important trading center, had daily morning markets. During the reign of King Rama V the main and oldest market, dating back to the Mangrai period, was the Klang Wiang Market, located from in front of the Phra Singh Temple to as far as the *bodhi* tree in the center of the city.[77] There was another market at Tha Phae Road. Female traders sold agricultural products including vegetables, rice, tobacco, wax, flowers, fruit,

100. Marketplace in Nan, with vendors spreading out their goods on the ground for sale. (NAT, c. 1892–1910)

101. Tha Phae Road, an important business district of Chiang Mai. (PUA, c. 1927–1932)

102. A caravan at rest, near the water. (NAT, 1942)

103. A caravan at rest. (NAT, 1942)

104. The road used by caravans in transporting goods. (NAT, 1942)

betel nut, lime, and dried fish, on the roadside.[78] The market traders were all female, with the exception of the male pork sellers. Behind the line of these local female traders squatting along the road were stalls belonging to Chinese and Burmese traders, who sold items such as umbrellas, vegetables, cotton, silk, muslin, brass trays, wood trays, and lacquerware.[79] Peddlers occasionally came to trade. The ballad "Kawila" mentions a lively trade in Chiang Mai.[80]

Internal trade within the region was relatively limited. Trade among villages in the same vicinity happened at occasional markets, probably once a week, rotating from village to village. People brought their own products, such as vegetables, beef, pork, chicken, fish, and fruit, to exchange for goods from outside such as fabrics, thread, crockery, and matches. Such markets were found throughout Yunnan, Sipsong Panna, and Lan Na.[81]

Caravan traders were often part-time farmers who went on the road in the dry season, from around November to May. A typical caravan comprised a number of traders and some fifty to sixty draft cattle and oxcarts. They bought and sold mainly local goods in the communities they passed. As trade increased between Lan Na and Burma, caravan traders increasingly sold manufactured goods such as clothes, thread, kerosene, and matches.[82]

The several trade routes included an important one between Chiang Mai, which was a source for betel nut, fabrics, salt and other goods, and Chiang Rai, which supplied mainly dried fish.

On the Chiang Mai-Lamphun-Lampang route, salt and iron tools from Kat Mek village in Lampang was traded for rice from Lamphun and Chiang Mai.[83] The Chiang Mai-Phayao-Mueang Pung route supplied *miang* from Chiang Mai in exchange for dried fish from Phayao and tobacco from Mueang Pung.[84]

The majority of the caravan traders traded within Lan Na. The obligations of the *phrai* system probably placed time limitations on the local traders, preventing them from expanding their business. Chinese and Shan traders mainly conducted the long-distance trade between Yunnan and Lan Na and Burma.

Long-distance trading required a big investment of draft animals, carts, and people. Shan traders used about one hundred draft cattle on trips bringing goods such as wax, honey, *miang*, hides, betel nut, dried chilies, and cotton from the Shan States.[85] Some traders then continued on to Moulmein in Burma. Chinese traders brought goods from Yunnan once a year, including honey, silk, wool, musk, opium, and kitchen utensils made of brass. On the return trip, they took products such as cotton, salt, and betel nut.[86] The important route from Chiang Mai to Dali was known as the "golden route" due to the quantity and value of the goods involved. A typical Chinese caravan might comprise twenty-three traders and assistants and forty-five horses.[87] In another caravan, there were ten to twelve men and sixty mules carrying goods worth about $12,000–15,000 in the currency of that day.[88]

There was also river trade with Bangkok, using the Ping, Wang, Yom, and Nan rivers. This trade expanded greatly after the signing of the Bowring treaty. The river journey from Bangkok to Chiang Mai and back took two to three months. Goods taken on this route included salt, dried fish, silk, and umbrellas.[89] Exports from Lan Na included forest products such as *lac*, hides, horns, and honey.[90] Bangkok would sell these on to other countries. Chiang Mai became a conduit for forest products from the Shan States and Yunnan as well as Lan Na.

In Lan Na, the ruler, nobles, and officials were the main beneficiaries of local trade. Their income sources were mainly in the form of tribute, such as agricultural and forest products; taxes and excises; and monopolies of certain goods, such as guns, forest products, opium, and slaves. Logging concessions became another important source of income.

The profit from these incomes was evidently divided into four equal portions. The first portion was for the ruler; the second portion was divided into thirds with the *chao uparat* receiving two-thirds and the *chao ratchawong* the remaining one-third. The third portion was for nobles and their relatives who had received commissions and were government officials; and the fourth portion was for the lower-ranking nobles such as *thao* and *phaya*, and for clerks.[91]

EXPANSION OF THE ECONOMY AND OF THE CAPITALIST SECTOR (1884–1921)

The entry of Westerners into Lan Na, particularly in the logging industry, began to change the subsistence economy. Trade expanded with Burma and Bangkok. The Chinese had an increasing role as tax collectors and moneylenders. The political, administrative, and social structure in Lan Na began to undergo profound changes. The nobles in particular were forced to adjust to the new economic situation.

The Timber Industry. Mon and Burmese British subjects began to receive logging concessions in the Chiang Mai, Lampang, and Lamphun areas around 1840. By 1885, when all of Burma became a British colony, British logging companies were increasingly looking to Lan Na, as Burma's teak forests were rapidly being depleted.[92] The British Borneo Company began logging in Lan Na in 1889, with Mr. Louis T. Leonowens (the son of the well-known royal tutor Anna) as its general manager. It was followed by the Bombay Burmah Trading Corporation in 1892, followed by the Siam Forest Company.[93] There were also French and Danish companies and a number of smaller Burmese, Shan, Thai, and Lan Na loggers.

In Chiang Mai, Lamphun, and Lampang, the logging companies leased forest areas or received concessions from the forest owners or from the rulers. In Phrae and Nan, which were logged later, the nobles first cut their own logs and sold them to the companies. Later, they also gave concessions to British companies.[94]

The logging companies had long had a great deal of political influence in the region. Conflict between the British logging companies and the Burmese court was a factor in the three Anglo-Burmese Wars, which ended with the British seizure of all of Burma. The arrival of the companies in Lan Na forced the Thai government to proceed carefully.

The highly capitalized Bombay Burmah Trading Corporation had the most political influence.[95]

Its ample coffers meant that it succeeded before others in obtaining logging leases from the Forestry Department. Many smaller players got into debt. Chao Bunyawatwongmanit, the ruler of Lampang, for instance, entered into a 300,000-baht contract to sell logs to the corporation. After fulfilling less than half the contract, he owed 145,143 baht. The corporation asked the government for assistance with the remainder due, but the Siamese government refused because it was a personal debt.[96] Apparently, the Lampang ruler finally had to relinquish his forest to the company. Eventually the majority of logging was in the hands of the British companies.[97]

The majority of logging workers were Khamu from Luang Prabang, who were regarded as hard and cohesive workers and were gathered into groups of between five and fifty men under the control of a *nairoi,* or group leader. They were paid sixty rupees per year while working in Chiang Mai, Lamphun, and Lampang[98]—a lower sum than was demanded by other groups such as the Shan and Karen. Local workers were tied to the *phrai* system and therefore were not free labor—they also may not have wanted the difficult and dangerous work.

The British companies were intent only on profit. They did not maintain the forests, tried to avoid paying stump fees, and illegally cut small or green trees. The cutting down of large numbers of immature trees resulted in serious damage to the forests, particularly in Chiang Mai and Lampang. From 1891 on, teak was hard to find in these areas, except in deep forests far from rivers, which was difficult for transportation.[99] The British companies made large profits from Thai natural resources at every step of the logging business,

105. The Khamu from Laos, an important labor force in logging. (PUA, c. 1892–1910)

106. The Khamu joining the procession at King Rama VII's reception ceremony in 1926. (NAT, 1926)

107. Teak logs in the Ping River in Chiang Mai on their way to foreign markets. (PUA, 1932)

108. Sichum Temple, a Burmese temple in Lampang. (NAT, c. 1926)

109. A scorpion-tail boat on the Ping River. (NAT, c. 1893)

from the logging concessions, to the building of sawmills, the sale of logs, and their transport by steamboat. By comparison, the Thai government and the Lan Na nobles received little.

Expansion of Trade (1884–1921). Trade had increased between Lan Na and Burma after the signing of the Bowring Treaty in 1855 and it rose again after the opening of the British consulate in Chiang Mai in 1884. Burmese, Shan, and Indian traders, now British subjects, settled in Lan Na and set up shops. Almost all shops on both sides of Tha Phae Road in Chiang Mai from the Upakut Temple intersection to Saen Fang Temple were run by people from Burma.[100] In Lampang, most traders in the market were Burmese, with others including Chinese, Sino-Thai, and Indians.

Burmese traders traveled from Moulmein to Chiang Mai with manufactured goods such as clothes, kerosene, and matches from factories in England.

Export goods from Lan Na remained mainly forest products, such as *lac* and elephant tusks. In 1909 palm sugar and tobacco were added, and in 1910 rice was exported to Burma for the first time. Gradually agricultural products replaced forest products.[101] Farmers began to plant two rice crops a year in areas such as Saraphi and Fang. Rice production had increased since the arrival of large companies, which purchased the crop for their workers. But rice for the market only really took off with the arrival of the railroad.

By around 1900, important trade had switched from the overland trade with Moulmein to river trade with Bangkok. At this time the Siamese government was making efforts to increase its ties with Lan Na. Around 70.5 percent of imports to Lan Na came by river, and the trade was mainly conducted by Chinese business people.

Most traders traveled as far as Paknampho in Nakhon Sawan, about halfway to Bangkok, to purchase goods. Those with more funds would travel on to Bangkok, in order to eliminate the middlemen. Annual river trade between Bangkok and Chiang Mai involved around one thousand sampans, each capable of carrying about two and a half tons of goods. Important exports from Chiang Mai were *lac*, hides, horns, and lard, while imports from Bangkok were clothes, fabrics, thread, kerosene, matches, soap, iron tools, and salt.[102] There was also trade via the Wang River between Bangkok and Lampang. Exports from Lampang were mostly forest products, while the important import was fabric.[103]

The balance of trade appears to have been unfavorable to Lan Na. In 1911 imports from Bangkok to Lampang totaled 380,700 baht, as against 75,700 baht of exports. Imports from Bangkok to Chiang Mai totaled 839,000 baht; exports from Chiang Mai to Bangkok were worth 286,750 baht.[104]

Another reason for the increased volume of trade between Bangkok and Chiang Mai was a change in the route for transporting teak, from the rough overland trails to the Salween River to the cheaper Chao Phraya River route.

110. Ket Temple located near the Ping River in the first Chinese settlement in Chiang Mai. (NAT, n.d.)

Over time, the overland trade with Burma gradually declined in importance.[105] Over time, too, local caravan traders gradually lost their role as they had little contact with the goods of foreign countries and had less capital than others. Chinese traders began to decline in number from 1908.[106] As roads were constructed to link up with the railroad, oxcart caravans were replaced by trucks. Chinese traders replaced the locals. The expansion of trade contributed to the increased use of money, and the increased introduction of cash taxes, including for rice fields, forest products, and garden crops,[107] using Chinese as tax collectors.

The Economic Role of the Chinese (1884– 1921). Trade between Lan Na and Bangkok expanded alongside an increase in the number of Chinese. In 1884, around two thousand Chinese people were living in Lan Na. By 1919, the number had increased to 3,626.[108] One reason for the increase was an outflow from the large number of successful Chinese immigrants in Bangkok; some decided to move north to areas such as Paknampho, Tak, and Chiang Mai, where there was less competition. The newcomers received assistance from those Chinese already settled in the north, and they benefited from being able to receive credit from their contacts with the community in Bangkok.

The first Chinese community was located in the area in front of Ket Temple. Today this community is in a state of decline, but old traces remain. The community gradually expanded to Laocho Lane, Ton Lamyai, and Warorot markets, and to Tha Phae Road, where Burmese and Shan traders were still active. In Lampang, the Chinese community was located near the Wang River. The "Chinese Market," as it was called, relied on the river for transporting goods. Goods were stored in the back of the shops.

The Chinese had a role in every aspect of business, including the river trade, tax collection, money-lending, and the retail trade. They relied on connections with powerful rulers in order to enter into businesses such as tax collection. A Chinese businessman named Teng (Teng Sophanodon), owner of the Kim Seng Lee Company, constructed a royal residence in Bangkok worth 50,000 rupees[109] for King Inthawichayanon and was rewarded with the post of tax collector for pigs, cattle, tobacco, opium, betel nut, betel leaves, and coconuts, worth some 53,100 rupees. Khun Phathong, whose residence was located in Ban Mae Kha near Tha Phae Road, monopolized gambling dens in Chiang Mai with the support of King Inthawichayanon.[110] Nobles and commissioners accepted bribes from Chinese competing for the tax collector positions. Sometimes the nobles accepted bribes but later appointed a competitor who had paid more, which led to litigation. A Chinese named Su accused Phraya Krikosa, the commissioner, of refusing to appoint him as collector of levies on pigs in Lamphun because the official had received a bribe worth 2,500 rupees from a competitor, Mongseng.[111] Sometimes nobles granted rights to collect taxes without written permission or without consulting the Siamese commissioner.

111. King Inthawichayanon's residence, built by the Chinese, Teng. Today, it is the Bangkok Noi Railway Station. (NAT, c. 1894)

112. Major General Chao Kaeonawarat leading a dancing procession of the northern nobility at King Rama VII's reception ceremony. (PUA, 1926)

The tax collectors wanted a good return for the money they had spent on bribes, so collection was strict. Sometimes they cheated farmers. Ieo Chai, a Lampang tax collector, reportedly used a short measuring stick to measure the rice fields, forcing the farmers to pay more tax. Farmers who usually paid fifteen *thaep* [roughly fifteen rupees] were forced to pay twenty-eight *thaep*, while those who usually paid seven *thaep* were forced to pay eleven *thaep*. Distressed farmers complained to the ruler.[112]

Ieo Chai became the tax collector for Nan after bidding thirty thousand rupees and eighteen thousand *thang* of rice. He also constructed a residence for the ruler and presented ten thousand rupees to the commissioner. Such large bribes reflected the large profits anticipated. Sometimes, after collecting the taxes, the collectors evaded payment to the treasury, insisting that they had been unable to collect the targets.

After acquiring wealth in a short time, rich tax collectors often invested in other businesses. Teng Sophanodon entered the logging business; others invested in trade or moneylending. The tax collector business created great hatred towards the Chinese among the local people. During the Phraya Prapsongkhram Revolt, locals planned to kill Chinese at Ket Temple. Wealthy Chinese became moneylenders, gave out mortgages, and got involved in pawnbroking. Moneylenders included the Shinawatra family (Mr. Chiang Shinawatra), the Chutima family (Luang Anusansunthon), the Nimmanhemin family (Mrs. Kimho Nimmanhemin), and the Wibunsanti family.[113] Small-scale Chinese traders who received loans had an advantage over caravan traders of other ethnic groups, who did not receive such credit. Chinese traders, therefore, gradually became dominant in every level of business in the cities and in outlying districts.

The nobles also borrowed from the moneylenders. Lampang nobles who overspent brought their valuables and land to Mrs. Daeng Phanitchaphan as collateral, eventually losing the lot. Similar situations occurred in Chiang Mai and resulted in the transfer of possessions and land from the nobles to Chinese moneylenders. Gradually the Chinese replaced the nobles' traditional dominant economic role.

Changes in the Economic Conditions of the Nobility. The centralization of power in the absolute monarchy resulted in the gradual political, economic, and social decline of the rulers and nobles. Since 1884, a portion of local taxes had to be sent to the government in Bangkok. The arrival of trade treaties with Westerners, and Western businesses, resulted in the termination of the monopolies formerly held by the nobles. Free trade opened opportunities for British subjects to control the bulk of local trade and the teak trade. Without political support, the nobles could not cope with the economic competition. The nobles lost out in all directions. They lost ownership and income from the forests. They lost control over the tribute and labor they had received from their *phrai*. They were intensely unhappy. Petitions sent to Bangkok produced no results. Finally, they supported the Phraya Prapsongkhram

Revolt and the Shan Uprising in Phrae, but these upheavals also got them nowhere. Realizing that they could not alter the direction of change, they increasingly began to look for new sources of income, such as logging, the construction of irrigation canals and dams, and trade.

Some nobles leased forest tracts, reckoning that this was a business with which they were already familiar. In a conversation with Kromphraya Damrong Rachanuphap, the *chao ratchawong* of Nan said, "Now that the nobles and myself are all impoverished because we have no way to earn our living, only logging is a possibility."[114] King Inthawarorot Suriyawong, the ruler of Chiang Mai, leased a teak forest in Tambon Huai Mae Chaem in Chiang Mai for six years and later extended the lease for another fifteen years. King Bunyawatwongmanit, the ruler of Lampang, leased a logging concession in Tambon Mueang Long in Lampang from 1900 to 1923, and the ruler of Nan and other nobles also leased forest land.[115] The nobles usually subleased their concessions to other parties. They were not very successful in the business.

The idea behind their clearing land and constructing irrigation dikes and canals was to create rice fields near the city that could be rented out, as well as to collect water fees. Some nobles used their remaining influence to conscript labor to clear uninhabited land, thus contributing to the extensive expansion of rice fields and to rice becoming a market product. The nobles laid claim to large tracts of land, and eventually their descendants were able to live off the rents.[116]

The fresh food markets had been under the control of a group of high-ranking

113. Warorot Market. (NAT, 1929)

nobles since the Mangrai dynasty, and still yielded income from the lease of spaces. Even after they were stripped of power, the Chiang Mai nobles constructed the Warorot Market, or the main market, on an old cremation ground. In Lampang nobles constructed Thipphawan Market (currently Boribun Market). These eventually became the property of Chinese traders, who acquired them as collateral for loans or through the buying of shares.[117] The nobles also dealt with other kinds of business. Chao Bunyawatwongmanit became involved in the weaving industry. Chao Suanbun, the wife of the Lamphun ruler, dealt in tobacco and experimented with temperate climate crops.[118] The nobles also tried to adjust by educating themselves for the civil service.

PRODUCTION FOR THE MARKET (1921–1933)

Dramatic economic change in the North came with the arrival of the railroad in Lampang in 1916 and Chiang Mai in 1921. Roads were constructed to connect to the railroad;[119] routes extended from Chiang Mai to Chiang Rai, Lampang to Phayao, and Phrae to Nan. New roads were also constructed within each province. Transporting goods between the North and Bangkok was now faster, cheaper, and could be done in large quantity.

Chinese immigrants began to replace the old Burmese, Indian, and Shan traders. In Lampang, Burmese traders had run a market selling goods such as clothes from Mae Sai, lacquerware, forest products, glass, lamps, and herbs from Burma. However, after the railroad arrived the Chinese gained control over almost the entire market. The Chinese had good contacts and access to credit from Bangkok. The Burmese, Shans, and Indians had no such access and were eventually almost all bought out. A similar situation occurred in Chiang Mai around 1932.[120]

Imports from Bangkok comprised foreign manufactured goods, mostly from England. Inexpensive goods from Germany and Japan were cheaper than English goods. Luxury goods included porcelain, glassware, cigarettes, perfume, wool, straw hats, bicycles, motorcycles, cars, trucks, and buses. Consumer and small business goods included kerosene, gasoline, machinery, tools, and sewing machines. Foods included items such as fish, salt, and sugar.[121]

The main export from the North after 1921 was rice and there was extensive expansion of rice land. Chiang Mai, Chiang Rai, and Fang exported rice in large volumes. In 1924, rice exported from the North by train was 650,000 *hap* (or *picul*), a dramatic increase; in 1910–1921 rice exports had been 5,000 to 20,000 *hap*. This increased amount was equivalent to 5 to 9 percent of the rice exported from the docks in Bangkok.[122] Rice prices went up. In 1920, the price of rice in villages near Chiang Mai was 70–80 baht per 100 *thang*; by 1922–1923 it had increased to 110 baht per 100 *thang*.[123]

Chinese traders had a role in every step of the rice trade, starting with the purchase from farmers. Caravan traders brought rice from fairly inaccessible

114. The Khun Tan tunnel in Lampang, during its construction. The tunnel was completed in 1914 and the railroad in 1918. (NAT, n.d.)

areas and sold it to traders in the cities. Chinese traders owned rice mills. In 1930, there were eleven, mainly small, mills in Chiang Mai, with a capacity for milling eight *hap* of rice per hour or about twenty to thirty tons per day. Rice mills in Bangkok could mill between a hundred and two hundred tons per day As a result, milled rice accounted for only 35 percent of the rice exports from the North. (By 1954, the number of rice mills in Chiang Mai had increased to 28 percent of total mills, or sixty-two rice mills in the upper northern region.[124]

The Chinese rice traders also gave loans to farmers at 15 to 24 percent interest per year,[125] to be paid in rice. Farmers unable to repay the loan had their rice fields confiscated. The Chinese traders also claimed land and constructed irrigation dikes and canals, like the nobles who had started this practice in around 1890. The acquisition of land by both nobles and Chinese traders resulted in a rise in landless farmers. In 1930, approximately 27 percent of farmers in Chiang Mai were landless and had to look for new land further north in such places as Fang, Phan, and Chiang Saen.[126]

Other, much less important export products included *lac*, pigs, and tobacco. A report by Carl C. Zimmermann in 1930 said that the production of beans, cabbages, shallots, garlic, and longans was insufficient for a market economy.[127] In that same year, the government encouraged soybean production. The production of other crops expanded rapidly after 1947.

115. The Chiang Mai Railway Station when it was first built. (BS, c. 1927)

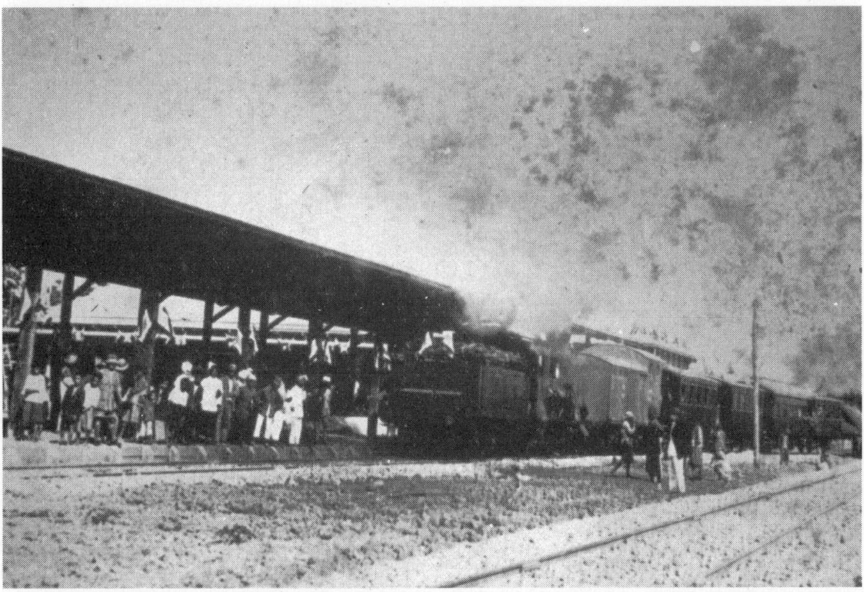

116. The Chiang Mai Railway Station. The northern railroad reached Chiang Mai in 1921 bringing great changes to the Lan Na economy that are still evident today. (NAT, c. 1932)

GLOSSARY

Apparihaniya-dham Chet	the seven Dhamma on conditions of welfare
chaiyaphum	auspicious location for the construction of a town and its important sites
chakkai	Burmese assistant to the *myowun* for military affairs
chai ban	"heart" of the village
chao khanhabai	five minister positions: *phraya mueang* (king), *phraya uparat*, *phraya ratchawong*, *phraya ratchabut*, and *phraya burirat*
chao luang, phraya luang	kings
devaraja	god-king
dhammaraja	righteous king
doi	mountain
ho kham	the royal residence
ho tham	(temple depositories)
ho trai	library
kaeban	village elder
kao sanam	the ruling officials
kao sanamluang	the provincial administrator
kha luang	royal servants
khon mueang	the local people
khuang luang	royal plaza
Kumphan Asura	the ogre that protected the city from anything inauspicious)
miang	fermented tea leaves
monthon	a Siamese administrative district comprising a number of *mueang*
mueang	city-state; autonomous or semiautonomous principalities that varied greatly in size and influence. The *mueang* was centered on a town or city and included surrounding rural areas. Some were little more than large villages, but others were powerful and exercised their power over other *mueang* that served as tributaries

naga	serpent-like creatures with supernatural power
oppatika	born by itself, without parents
pakna	an administrative division of a *phanna*; literally one hundred ricefields
pap sa, pap nang sa	manuscripts made of *sa* paper, folded accordion-style into a long, narrow book
phanna	an administrative division of a mueang; literally one thousand ricefields
phaya	title preceding the name of a king or chief
Phi Pu Sae and Ya Sae	Grandfather Spirit and the Grandmother Spirit
phrai	commoners tied to the land and owing service to a lord
phrathat	Buddhist relic; temple housing a Buddhist relic
phuen	history
sangha	the Buddhist clergy,
sangharaja	the highest-ranking monk,
sakdina	a system that granted control of land and labor proportionate to one's status
tambon	a subdistrict consisting of a group of villages
tamnan	chronicle
tonbun	persons of merit
tua mueang	the local script or Northern Thai script
tua tham	Northern Thai script, also called Lan Na Tham script, for religious texts
wiang phrathat	a town containing a sacred relic
yang tree	a tall, resinous, semi–hardwood tree found in Southeast Asia

MONEY, WEIGHTS, AND MEASUREMENTS

baht	15.2 grams, the weight of a one baht coin in the past Gold and silver were measured in baht weights
bia	cowrie shell money, 100 *bia* equal 1.5 satang
chang	monetary unit equal to 80 baht
hap	60 kilograms
khan	60 kilograms
picul	about 60 kilograms
rai	1,600 square meters or 0.4 acre
ram	2 yards
sat	about 20 liters
satang	smallest currency unit
thaep	a coin used in the North; a rupee or 80 satang at that time
thang	about 20 liters or 2.5 pecks

wa	2 meters
win	monetary unit equal to 12.5 satang or one-eighth of a baht

LAN NA OFFICIAL RANKS

chao	lord or noble
chaofa or *fa*	royal title
chaomoen	a leader of 10,000 commoners
chaophan	a leader of 1,000 commoners
chaosaen	a leader of 100,000 commoners
kaeban or *phuyaiban*	head of a village
kaosanam	the highest administrative official (*khao* or *kao* means head in northern Thai)
khwaen or *kamnan*	head of a tambon or a group of villages
moen	the rank of a *phanna* administrator
myowun	Burmese governor
nakhwa, *nasai*	officials appointed by the Burmese to collect rice tribute
nairoi	a leader of 100 commoners.
naisip	a leader of ten commoners.
po	Burmese military commander.
phraya	title before the honorific name conferred with the second highest rank of nobility

OFFICIAL SIAMESE NAMES FOR LAN NA

Monthon Lao Chiang	1884–1893
Monthon Phayap	1893–1899
Northwest Monthon	1900
Monthon Phayap	1901–1933

APPENDIX I

THE MANGRAI DYNASTY (1261–1578)

Lan Na King	Reign
Phaya Mangrai	(1261–1311)
Phaya Chaisongkhram	(1311–1325)
Phaya Saenphu	(1325–1334)
Phaya Khamfu	(1334–1336)
Phaya Phayu	(1336–1355)
Phaya Kuena	(1355–1385)
Phaya Saenmuangma	(1385–1401)
Phaya Samphrayafangkaen	(1402–1441)
Phraya Tilokarat	(1441–1487)
Phaya Yot Chiangrai	(1487–1495)
Phaya Kaeo	(1495–1525)
Phaya Ketchettharat	(1525–1538)
Thao Chai	(1538–1543)
Phaya Ketchettharat	(1543–1545) (second time)
Mahathewi Chiraprapha	(1545–1546)
Phra Chaiyachettha	(1546–1547)
— no ruler —	(1548 –1551)
Phraya Maeku	(1551–1564)
Wisuthithewi	(1564–1578)

Sources: The Jinakalamalipakaranum Chronicle, stone inscription (LP./9), and the Phuen Mueang Chiang Mai.

APPENDIX II

BURMESE RULERS OF CHIANG MAI (1578–1774)

Ruler	YC	CMC	MFCP
1. Nawrahtaminsaw	1579–1607	1578–1607	1578–1607
2. Phra Choi	1607–1609	1607–1608	1607–1608
3. Phra Chaithip (Mongkoito)	1609–1611	1607–1613	1608–1613
4. Phra Choi (second reign)	1611–1614	1613–1615	1613–1614
5. Nan Ruler	1614–1631	1615–1631	
6. Phraya Luang Thipphanet	1631–1650	1628–1655	
7. Phra Saenmueang	1650–1663	1655–1659	
8. Phrae Ruler	1633–1672	1659–1672	
9. Uparat Ungsae (Ava)	1672–1685	1672–1675	
10. Son of Chao Chekutra (Chephutrai)	1685–*	1675–*	
11. Mangraenra	1707–1727	1707–1727	
12. Thepsing	1727–1727	1727–1727	
13. Ong Kam	1727–1759	1727–*	
14. Chao Chan	1759–1761	*–1759	
15. Chao Khihut (former monk of Duangdi Temple)	1761–1763	1761–1763	
16. Po Aphaikhamini (Po Akiakhamuni)	1763–1769	1762–1768	
17. Po Mayu-nguan (Po Huakhao)	1769–1774	1768–1774	

Note: YC = The Yonok Chronicle
CMC = The Chiang Mai Chronicle
MFCP = "Mangthra Fought Chiang Mai" Poem
*unrecorded

APPENDIX III

CHAO CHET TON DYNASTY (1782–1939)
RULERS OF CHIANG MAI

Name	Reign	Sources
1. Kawila	1782–1816	Chiang Mai Chronicle
2. Thammalangka	1816–1822	Chiang Mai Chronicle; Yonok Chronicle
3. Khamfan	1823–1822	Chiang Mai Chronicle; Yonok Chronicle
4. Phutthawong	1825–1846	Yonok Chronicle
5. Mahotaraprathet	1847–1854	Yonok Chronicle
6. Kawilorot	1856–1870	NAT, *ro.* 5, *mo.* 58/191
7. Inthawichayanon	1873–1896	NAT, *ro.* 5, *mo.* 58/40
8. Inthawarorot	1901–1909	NAT, *ro.* 5, *mo.* 58/143
9. Kaeonawarat	1911–1939	NAT, *ro.* 6, *mo.* 27/3

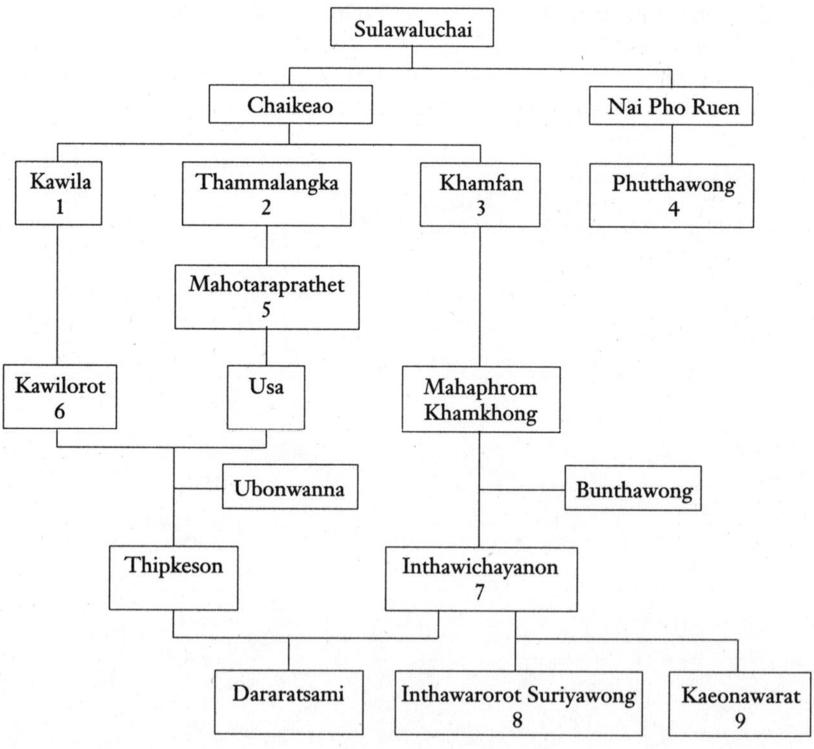

NOTES

CHAPTER 1: THE STATE OF LAN NA HISTORICAL STUDIES

1. *ประชุมศิลาจารึกภาคที่ 3,* คณะกรรมการจัดพิมพ์เอกสารทางประวัติศาสตร์ วัฒนธรรม และโบราณคดี สำนักนายกรัฐมนตรี 2508, หน้า 136.

2. คำอ่านศิลาจารึกกษัตริย์ราชวงศ์มังราย ลพ./9, *ศิลปากร* ปีที่ 24, เล่ม 2 (พฤษภาคม 2523), หน้า 46-47.

3. David K. Wyatt, Aroonrut Wichienkeeo, *The Chiang Mai Chronicle*, 2 nd ed. (Chiang Mai: Silkworm Books, 1998), p. 4.

4. เรื่องเดียวกัน, หน้า 3.

5. ดู สงวน โชติสุขรัตน์. "ตำนานราชวงศ์ปกรณ์," *ประชุมตำนานลานนาไทย* (พระนคร: สำนักพิมพ์โอเดียนสโตร์, 2515), หน้า 161-544.

6. Winai Pongsripian, "Traditional Thai Historiography and its Nineteenth Century Decline," (Ph.D. Thesis, University of Bristol, 1983), p. 61.

7. ตำนานพระพุทธรูป เช่น รัตนพิมพวงศ์ (ตำนานพระแก้วมรกต) ตำนานพระสิงห์ พุทธปฏิมาเจ้า ตำนานพระศิลา วัดเชียงมั่น ตำนานพระแก่นจันทน์

8. ตำนานวัด เช่น ตำนานวัดเจ็ดยอด ตำนานวัดเจดีย์หลวง ตำนานวัดบุปผารามสวนดอกไม้

9. ตำนานพระบาท เช่น ตำนานพระบาทดอนกลาง จอมทอง ตำนานพระบาทสี่รอย

10. ดู *ตำนานพระธาตุหริภุญชัย* (พิมพ์เป็นอนุสรณ์งานพระราชทานเพลิงศพ พระพิจิตรโอสถ (รอด สุตันตานนท์) 29 พฤษภาคม, 2505), หน้า 41.

11. ดู สงวน โชติสุขรัตน์, *ประชุมตำนานลานนาไทย,* หน้า 161-544.

12. สรัสวดี อ๋องสกุล ปริวรรต "จดหมายเหตุล้านนา: บันทึกเหตุการณ์ประวัติศาสตร์ พ.ศ. 2271-2397" หลักฐานประวัติศาสตร์ล้านนาจากเอกสารคัมภีร์ใบลานและพับหนังสา 2534, หน้า 12-37. (อัดสำเนา)

13. "จารึกลานทองสมเด็จพระมหาเถรจุฑามุณี พุทธศักราช 1919," *จารึกสมัยสุโขทัย* (กรุงเทพฯ:: กรมศิลปากร, 2527), หน้า 384-388.

14. ดู นิธิ เอียวศรีวงศ์ "ความฉงนของรอบ 700 ปี," *จารึกพ่อขุนรามคำแหงใครแต่งกันแน่?* สุจิตต์ วงษ์เทศ, บรรณาธิการ (กรุงเทพฯ: สำนักพิมพ์ศิลปวัฒนธรรม, 2513), หน้า 52-61.

15. เพ็ญพักตร์ ลิ้มสัมพันธ์, *อักษรธรรมอีสาน,* ภาควิชาภาษาตะวันออก คณะโบราณคดี มหาวิทยาลัยศิลปากร, 2532.

16. ประเสริฐ ณ นคร "ที่มาของอักษรไทยล้านนาและไทลื้อ," *งานจารึกและประวัติศาสตร์ของประเสริฐ ณ นคร,* หน้า 23.

17. เรื่องเดียวกัน, หน้า 25.

18. กรรณิการ์ วิมลเกษม, "อักษรฝักขามที่พบในศิลาจารึกภาคเหนือ," *ภาควิชาภาษาตะวันออก* คณะโบราณคดี มหาวิทยาลัยศิลปากร 2526, หน้า 1. (อัดสำเนา)

19. เรื่องเดียวกัน, หน้า 18.

20. ดูรายละเอียดหัวข้อที่มีการศึกษากันแล้วใน ม.ร.ว. รุจยา อาภากร, "พัฒนาการทางประวัติศาสตร์และสังคม: สถานภาพของการศึกษาประวัติศาสตร์และสังคม," เอกสารประกอบการสัมมนาเรื่อง "สถานภาพล้านนาคดีศึกษา" จัดโดยโครงการศูนย์ส่งเสริมศิลปวัฒนธรรม มหาวิทยาลัยเชียงใหม่ 22-24 สิงหาคม, 2529.

22. ตัวเลขนี้อาศัยบัญชีจารึกในคลังข้อมูลล้านนา ส่วนรายละเอียดเริ่มพิมพ์เผยแพร่บ้าง ดู *จุลสารคลังข้อมูลจารึกล้านนา* ฉบับที่ 5, สถาบันวิจัยสังคม มหาวิทยาลัยเชียงใหม่ (เชียงใหม่: บุญไชยการพิมพ์), หน้า 65.

23. ประเสริฐ ณ นคร "ประวัติศาสตร์ล้านนาจากจารึก," *งานจารึกและประวัติศาสตร์ของประเสริฐ ณ นคร* (พิมพ์เนื่องในโอกาสฉลองอายุ 6 รอบ ศ. ดร. ประเสริฐ ณ นคร 21 มีนาคม, 2534), หน้า 85.

24. เรื่องเดียวกัน

25. นิธิ เอียวศรีวงศ์ "ปัญหาการศึกษาและการประยุกต์ใช้ประวัติศาสตร์ไทย," เอกสารการสอนชุดวิชา *สังคมศึกษา 5* (ประวัติศาสตร์ไทยสำหรับครู) มหาวิทยาลัยสุโขทัยธรรมาธิราช, 2529 หน้า 1027.

CHAPTER 2
THE ERA OF DOMAINS AND CITY-STATES BEFORE THE BEGINNING OF THE LAN NA KINGDOM IN THE LATE THIRTEENTH CENTURY

1. นัยนา โปร่งธุระ, "อักษรธรรมล้านนา," *ภาควิชาภาษาตะวันออก* คณะโบราณคดี มหาวิทยาลัยศิลปากร, 2527, หน้า 100-101. (อัดสำเนา)

2. สมโชติ อ๋องสกุล, "ความเป็นมาของคำ 'ล้านนา-ลานนา' ในประวัติศาสตร์นิพนธ์ไทย," ใน *แถลงงานประวัติศาสตร์ เอกสารงานโบราณคดี* ปีที่ 20, เล่ม 2 (กรกฎาคม-ธันวาคม 2530), หน้า 1-19.

3. *พจนานุกรมล้านนา-ไทย* ฉบับแม่ฟ้าหลวง, จัดทำในวโรกาส "แม่ฟ้าหลวง" เจริญพระชนมายุครบรอบ 90 พรรษา, 2533, หน้า 86.

4. พระรัตนปัญญาเถระ, *ชินกาลมาลีปกรณ์,* แปลโดย ศ. ร.ต.ท. แสง มนวิทูร (พิมพ์เป็นอนุสรณ์งานพระราชทานเพลิงศพ ศ. ร.ต.ท. แสง มนวิทูร 20 เมษายน, 2517), หน้า 102.

5. พระพุทธพุกามและพระพุทธญาณเจ้า, *ตำนานมูลศาสนา,* สุด ศรีสมวงศ์ และ พรหม มาลา แปล, ประเสริฐ ณ นคร ตรวจสอบ (พิมพ์เป็นอนุสรณ์งานพระราชทานเพลิงศพ มล. เดช สนิทวงศ์ 17 ธันวาคม, 2518), หน้า 217-221.

6. พระยาประชากิจกรจักร์, *พงศาวดารโยนก,* (กรุงเทพฯ: สำนักพิมพ์คลังวิทยา, 2516), หน้า 319.

7. David K. Wyatt, Aroonrut Wichienkeeo, *The Chiang Mai Chronicle,* 2nd ed. (Chiang Mai: Silkworm Books, 1998), p. 1.

8. นวลศิริ วงศ์ทางสวัสดิ์, *"ภูมิศาสตร์กายภาพภาคเหนือของประเทศไทย,"* พิมพ์ครั้งที่ 3, ภาควิชาภูมิศาสตร์ คณะสังคมศาสตร์ มหาวิทยาลัยเชียงใหม่, 2534, หน้า 15. (อัดสำเนา)

9. ใน 4 เขตนี้ แต่ละแห่งมีพื้นที่มากพอสมควร จริงๆ แล้วยังมีที่ราบเล็กแทรกตัวอยู่ทั่วไป เช่นที่ราบแม่สะเรียง ที่ราบแม่แจ่ม ที่ราบปาย ที่ราบแม่ฮ่องสอน ที่ราบต่างๆ ที่เกิดเป็นเมืองเล็กเมืองน้อย

10. จิตร ภูมิศักดิ์, *ข้อเท็จจริงว่าด้วยชนชาติขอม* (กรุงเทพฯ: สำนักพิมพ์ไม้งาม, 2525), หน้า 23.

11. สงวน โชติสุขรัตน์, "ตำนานสุวรรณคำแดง" ใน *ประชุมตำนานลานนาไทย,* เล่ม 2 (พระนคร: สำนักพิมพ์โอเดียนสโตร์, 2515), หน้า 117-160.

12. จากการคำณวนตรวจสอบศักราชของ ศ. มานิต วัลลิโภดม ดู *ตำนานสิงหนวติกุมาร* ฉบับสอบค้น ของมานิต วัลลิโภดม (คณะกรรมการจัดพิมพ์เอกสารทางประวัติศาสตร์ สำนักนายกรัฐมนตรี, 2516), หน้า 32.

13. เรื่องเดียวกัน, หน้า 104.

14. *The Chiang Mai Chronicle,* p. 4-9.

15. จิตร ภูมิศักดิ์, *ข้อเท็จจริงว่าด้วยชนชาติขอม,* หน้า 23.

16. "ตำนานสุวรรณโคมคำ" ใน *ประชุมพงศาวดาร* ภาคที่ 72, เล่มที่ 45 (พระนคร: องค์การค้าของคุรุสภา, 2512), หน้า 173.

17. เรื่องเดียวกัน, หน้า 226.

18. "ตำนานสิงหนวติ" ใน *ประชุมพงศาวดาร* ภาคที่ 61 (พิมพ์เป็นอนุสรณ์ในงานพระราชทานเพลิงศพพลตรีเจ้าราชบุตร (วงษ์ตะวัน ณ เชียงใหม่) 12 มกราคม, 2516), หน้า 67.

19. จิตร ภูมิศักดิ์, *ข้อเท็จจริงว่าด้วยชนชาติขอม,* หน้า 27.

20. การตรวจสอบร่องรอยของเมืองสุวรรณโคมคำจากภาพถ่ายทางอากาศ ผู้เขียนได้รับคำอธิบายจาก ผศ. ดร. นวลศิริ วงษ์ทางสวัสดิ์ จึงขอบขอบพระคุณไว้ ณ ที่นี้ด้วย

21. ดี.จี.อี. ฮอล์ล, *ประวัติศาสตร์เอเชียตะวันออกเฉียงใต้* เล่ม 1, แปลโดย วรุณยุพา สนิทวงศ์ ณ อยุธยา และคณะ (กรุงเทพฯ: ไทยวัฒนาพานิช 2522), หน้า 127. และดู David K. Wyatt, *Thailand: A Short History* (Bangkok: Yale University and Thai Watana Panich Press, 1984), p. 18.

22. *ตำนานสิงหนวติกุมาร* ฉบับสอบค้น, หน้า 32.

23. เรื่องเดียวกันหน้า, หน้า 42.

24. ตำนานที่กล่าวถึงลัวะ-ไตมีความสัมพันธ์กัน เช่น ตำนานเชียงแสน ตำนานสุวรรณคำแดง ตำนานเมืองพะเยา ฉบับหอสมุดแห่งชาติ

25. นิธิ เอียวศรีวงศ์ "คนไทยมาจากโน่นด้วย และคนไทยอยู่ที่นี่ด้วย," *ศิลปวัฒนธรรม* ปีที่ 11, ฉบับที่ 12 (ตุลาคม 2533), หน้า 81.

26. *ชินกาลมาลีปกรณ์,* หน้า 101.

27. ไกรศรี นิมมานเหมินท์ "ความรู้พื้นฐานด้านล้านนาคดี: ด้านศาสนาและวัฒนธรรม," ใน *ลานนาปริทัศน์* (พิมพ์เนื่องในวาระครบรอบปีคล้ายวันมรณะ นางกิมฮ้อ นิมมานเหมินท์, 2525), หน้า 60.

28. *ตำนานสิงหนวติกุมาร* ฉบับสอบค้น, หน้า 52.

29. ศรีศักร วัลลิโภดม, "ขุนเจือง: ความสำนึกร่วมทางวัฒนธรรมของคนในลุ่มน้ำโขงตอนบน," *เมืองโบราณ* ปีที่ 20, ฉบับที่ 1 (มกราคม-มีนาคม 2537), หน้า 22.

30. ประคอง นิมมานเหมินท์ "มหากาพย์เรื่องท้าวบาเจือง: การศึกษาเชิงวิเคราะห์," (วิทยานิพนธ์ปริญญาดุษฎีบัณฑิต สาขาวิชาภาษาไทย บัณฑิตวิทยาลัย จุฬาลงกรณ์มหาวิทยาลัย, 2530), หน้า 111-113.

31. Georges Condominas, *From Lawa to Mon, from Saa to Thai,* translated by Stephanie Anderson, Maria Mogannon, and Gehan Wijeyewardene (Canberra: Department of Anthropology, Research School of Pacific Studies, Australian National University Press, 1990), p. 45.

32. *ตำนานสิงหนวติกุมาร* ฉบับสอบค้น, หน้า 104.

33. ฮันส์ เพนธ์, *ประวัติความเป็นมาของล้านนาไทย,* (เชียงใหม่: ทิพย์เนตรการพิมพ์, 2526), หน้า 15-16.

34. *ชินกาลมาลีปกรณ์,* หน้า 100.

35. *ตำนานสิงหนวติกุมาร* ฉบับสอบค้น, หน้า 52.

36. *ประวัติพระธาตุดอยตุง,* ฮันส์ เพนธ์, บรรณาธิการ, (กรุงเทพฯ: มูลนิธิแม่ฟ้าหลวงและธนาคารไทยพาณิชย์, 2536), หน้า 106-107.

37. สรัสวดี อ๋องสกุล, ปริวรรต, "พื้นเมืองเชียงราย," *หลักฐานประวัติศาสตร์ล้านนาจากเอกสารคัมภีร์ใบลานและพับหนังสา,* โครงการปริวรรตคัมภีร์ใบลานและพับหนังสาจากอักษรธรรมล้านนาเป็นอักษรไทยกลาง 2534, หน้า 34.

38. พระยาประชากิจกรจักร์, *พงศาวดารโยนก,* หน้า 91.

39. ดู สรัวสดี อ๋องสกุล, ปริวรรต, *พื้นเมืองน่าน* ฉบับวัดพระเกิด, หน้า 53.

40. หวัง จื้ หมิน "ความสัมพันธ์ระหว่างเมืองเชอหลี่กับเมืองปาไปซีฟู," (วิทยานิพนธ์ปริญญาอักษรศาสตร์มหาบัณฑิต สาขาวิชาประวัติศาสตร์ บัณฑิตวิทยาลัย จุฬาลงกรณ์มหาวิทยาลัย, 2531), หน้า 49.

41. อรุณรัตน์ วิเชียรเขียว และจินตนา มัธยมบุรุษ, ปริวรรต, "ตำนานเมืองพะเยาและค่าวซอเล่นคำเป็นแท้," (ศูนย์วัฒนธรรมจังหวัดเชียงใหม่, 2527), หน้า 18-21. (อัดสำเนา)

42. *The Chiang Mai Chronicle,* p. 14-15.

43. ประพฤทธิ์ ศุกลรัตนเมธี และวินัย พงศ์ศรีเพียร, 'ปอเล่อ' ใน "หมิงสือลู่กับการคลี่คลายของประวัติศาสตร์ไทย," *วารสารอักษรศาสตร์* ปีที่ 24, ฉบับที่ 1 (มกราคม-มิถุนายน 2535), หน้า 7-8.

44. ประเสริฐ ณ นคร, เรียบเรียง, *มังรายศาสตร์หรือกฎหมายพระเจ้ามังราย,* (กรุงเทพฯ: มหาวิทยาลัยศรีนครินทรวิโรฒ ประสานมิตร, 2521), หน้า 2.

45. เรื่องเดียวกัน, หน้า 5.

46. สรัสวดี อ๋องสกุล, ปริวรรต, "อาณาจักรหลักคำ," *หลักฐานประวัติศาสตร์ล้านนาจากเอกสารคัมภีร์ใบลานและพับหนังสา,* หน้า 80.

47. เมื่อลาวจงโอปปาติกะ ได้สถิตย์ใต้ร่มไม้พุทราซึ่งอยู่กลางหมู่ไม้ยาง ไม้ยางในบริเวณนี้อาจมีจำนวนมากก็ได้ เพราะตำนานเรียก "ป่ายาง" และมีชื่อหมู่บ้านว่า "บ้านยางเสี้ยว" ซึ่งต่อมาเป็นที่ตั้งของเมืองเงินยาง เหตุที่ได้ชื่อเงินยาง เพราะมีต้นศรีมหาโพธิ์มีสีขาวดั่งเงินต้นหนึ่ง แวดล้อมด้วยหมู่ต้นยาง

48. สรัสวดี อ๋องสกุล, ปริวรรต, "รวมเรื่องเมืองเชียงใหม่: หลักฐานประวัติศาสตร์," *หลักฐานประวัติศาสตร์ล้านนาจากคัมภีร์ใบลานและพับหนังสา,* หน้า 106.

49. นิธิ เอียวศรีวงศ์ "ความสำคัญด้านประวัติศาสตร์ ศาสนา และวัฒนธรรมของดอยสุเทพ-ปุย" *อุทยานแห่งชาติดอยสุเทพ-ปุย: การจัดการและการอนุรักษ์,"* เชียงใหม่: โครงการศูนย์ส่งเสริมศิลปวัฒนธรรม มหาวิทยาลัยเชียงใหม่ 2536, หน้า 10-14.

50. *ตำนานสิงหนวติกุมาร* ฉบับสอบค้น, หน้า 36-42. และ *จารึกล้านนา* ภาค 1, เล่ม 1 "จารึกจังหวัดเชียงราย น่าน พะเยา แพร่," มูลนิธิเจมส์ เอช ดับเบิ้ลยู ทอมป์สัน (จัดพิมพ์เนื่องในวโรกาสสมเด็จพระเทพรัตนราชสุดา สยามบรมราชกุมารี พระชนมายุครบ 3 รอบ, 2534), หน้า 14-16.

51. สันติ เล็กสุขุม, *ศิลปะเชียงแสน (ศิลปะล้านนา) และศิลปะสมัยสุโขทัย,* (นครปฐม: โรงพิมพ์มหาวิทยาลัยศิลปากร, 2534), หน้า 76-78.

52. ฮันส์ เพนธ์, *ประวัติความเป็นมาของล้านนาไทย,* หน้า 23.

53. ดู สรัสวดี อ๋องสกุล *เวียงกุมกาม: การศึกษาประวัติศาสตร์ชุมชนโบราณในล้านนา,* หน้า 48.

54. สันติ เล็กสุขุม "ประติมากรรมและสถาปัตยกรรมเมืองพะเยา," ใน *พะเยา: วิถีชีวิตและภูมิปัญญา,* หน้า 39.

55. ดู *จารึกล้านนา* ภาค 1, เล่ม 1 "จารึกจังหวัดเชียงราย น่าน พะเยา แพร่," หน้า 99-245.

56. ดูรายละเอียดเรื่องนี้ใน สรัสวดี อ๋องสกุล, "พญางำเมือง: บทวิเคราะห์ใหม่จากตำนานเมืองน่าน" *พะเยา: วิถีชีวิตและภูมิปัญญา* (กรุงเทพฯ: สำนักงานคณะกรรมการวัฒนธรรมแห่งชาติ 2537), หน้า 48-54.

57. นวลศิริ วงศ์ทางสวัสดิ์, *ภูมิศาสตร์กายภาพภาคเหนือในประเทศไทย,* หน้า 25.

58. *ตำนานเมืองพะเยา ฉบับหอสมุดแห่งชาติ,* หน้า 9.

59. เรื่องเดียวกัน, หน้า 10.

60. โปรดดู คัมภีร์ใบลานเรื่อง "พื้นเมืองพะเยา, จดหมายเหตุน้ำท่วมเมืองพะเยาและการกลับมาตั้งอยู่ใหม่," วัดศรีโคมคำ จังหวัดพะเยา รหัสไมโครฟิล์ม ศูนย์ส่งเสริมศิลปวัฒนธรรม มหาวิทยาลัยเชียงใหม่ พย 01 140 10 00, หน้าลานที่ 1 (คัมภีร์ผูกนี้มี 18 หน้าลาน).

61. วราวุธ ศรีโสภาค, "การศึกษาวิเคราะห์ความสัมพันธ์ของกลุ่มเมืองโบราณที่มีคู-คันดินล้อมรอบในบริเวณเมืองพะเยา," (สารนิพนธ์ปริญญาศิลปศาสตร์บัณฑิต (โบราณคดี) ภาควิชาโบราณคดี คณะโบราณคดี มหาวิทยาลัยศิลปากร, 2533), หน้า 246.

62. พระยาประชากิจกรจักร์, *พงศาวดารโยนก,* ตารางไม่ระบุหน้า

63. "พงศาวดารเมืองเงินยางเชียงแสน," ใน *ประชุมพงศาวดาร* ภาคที่ 61, หน้า 27.

64. *ตำนานสิบห้าราชวงศ์* เล่ม 1 (เชียงใหม่: สถาบันวิจัยสังคม มหาวิทยาลัยเชียงใหม่ 2524), หน้า 55.

65. ดู สรัสวดี อ๋องสกุล, ปริวรรต, *พื้นเมืองน่าน* ฉบับวัดพระเกิด, หน้า 42-44.

66. โปรดดูคัมภีร์ใบลานเรื่อง "ตำนานพะเยา," วัดศรีโคมคำ จังหวัดพะเยา รหัสไมโครฟิล์ม ศูนย์ส่งเสริมศิลปวัฒนธรรม มหาวิทยาลัยเชียงใหม่ พย 01 140 02 00, หน้าลานที่ 55 56 (คัมภีร์ผูกนี้มี 61 หน้าลาน).

67. *The Chiang Mai Chronicle,* p. 62.

68. เรื่องเดียวกัน, หน้า 86-87.

69. สงวน โชติสุขรัตน์, "ตำนานเจ้าสุวรรณคำแดง," ใน *ประชุมตำนานลานนาไทย,* หน้า 117-160.

70. สงวน โชติสุขรัตน์, *ประชุมตำนานลานนาไทย* เล่ม 2, หน้า 330, 418.

71. เรื่องเดียวกัน, หน้า 314-327.

72. โปรดดู คัมภีร์ใบลานเรื่อง "อวหาร 25 ประการ," วัดบ้านปิง อำเภอเมือง จังหวัดเชียงใหม่ รหัสไมโครฟิล์ม สถาบันวิจัยสังคม มหาวิทยาลัยเชียงใหม่ 78.021.03.033.033, หน้าลานที่ 1-4 (คัมภีร์ผูกนี้มี 67 หน้าลาน).

73. นิธิ เอียวศรีวงศ์, *ความสำคัญด้านประวัติศาสตร์...,* หน้า 10.

74. สรัสวดี อ๋องสกุล "รวมเรื่องเมืองเชียงใหม่...," หน้า 112.

75. *The Chiang Mai Chronicle,* p. 43.

76. เทิม มีเต็ม, ปริวรรต, "ตำนานนพบุรีเมืองพิงค์เชียงใหม่," คัมภีร์ใบลานอักษรธรรมล้านนา สยามสมาคม มัดที่ 50 เลขที่ 506 หน้าลานที่ 37 (คัมภีร์ผูกนี้มี 59 หน้าลาน) และดู *กำแพงเมืองเชียงใหม่,* หน้า 40.

77. *The Chiang Mai Chronicle,* p. 169.

78. เรื่องเดียวกัน, หน้า 19.

79. A. B. Griswold and Prasert Na Nagara, "An Inscription in Old Mon from Wiang Mano in Chiang Mai Province," *Journal of the Siam Society* 59, (January 1971): 153-156.

80. ต้วน ลี เชิง, "ประวัติศาสตร์ไทยสมัยก่อนกรุงศรีอยุธยา," ใน *พลิกต้นตระกูลไทย,* (กรุงเทพฯ: สำนักพิมพ์เคล็ดไทย 2529), หน้า 78.

81. ดูเรื่องละโว้ได้จาก สายชล วรรณรัตน์, "ละโว้สมัยก่อนอยุธยา," ใน *รวมบทความประวัติศาสตร์* ปีที่ 2, (มกราคม 2524): 84-127.

82. *ตำนานมูลศาสนา,* หน้า 165.

83. เรื่องเดียวกัน, หน้า 166.

84. *ชินกาลมาลีปกรณ์,* หน้า 98.

85. *จารึกในประเทศไทย* เล่ม 2, (กรุงเทพฯ: หอสมุดแห่งชาติ กรมศิลปากร 2529), หน้า 119-126. และ "ลพ. 1," ใน *ศิลาจารึกในพิพิธภัณฑ์สถานแห่งชาติหริภุญไชย* (กรุงเทพฯ: กรมศิลปากร, 2522), หน้า 8-11.

86. *จารึกในประเทศไทย* เล่ม 2, หน้า 119-216.

87. เรื่องเดียวกัน และ "ลพ. 2," *ศิลาจารึกในพิพิธภัณฑ์สถานแห่งชาติหริภุญไชย* (กรุงเทพฯ: กรมศิลปากร, 2522), หน้า 14.

88. *ชินกาลมาลีปกรณ์,* หน้า 99. และ ประเสริฐ ณ นคร "สมัยไทยก่อนสมัยสุโขทัย," ใน *สารัตถคดีประเสริฐ ณ นคร,* หน้า 61.

89. ดู พิริยะ ไกรฤกษ์, *พิพิธภัณฑสถานแห่งชาติหริภุญไชย,* (กรุงเทพฯ: กรมศิลปากร จัดพิมพ์, 2522), หน้า 4-55.

90. *ตำนานมูลศาสนา,* หน้า 220.

91. เรื่องเดียวกัน, หน้า 165.

92. ผาสุข อินทราวุธ "ผลการขุดค้นเมืองโบราณสมัยทวาราวดีที่จังหวัดสิงห์บุรีและนครปฐม," *เมืองโบราณ* ปีที่ 10, (ตุลาคม-ธันวาคม 2527): 28-42.

93. ผ่องศรี วนาสิน และทิวา ศุภจรรยา, *เมืองโบราณบริเวณชายฝั่งทะเลเดิมของที่ราบภาคกลางประเทศไทย: การศึกษาตำแหน่งที่ตั้งและภูมิศาสตร์สัมพันธ์* (กรุงเทพฯ: โครงการเผยแพร่ผลงานวิจัย ฝ่ายวิจัย จุฬาลงกรณ์มหาวิทยาลัย, 2524), หน้า 106-118.

94. *ตำนานมูลศาสนา,* หน้า 146.

95. *ชินกาลมาลีปกรณ์,* หน้า 88-89.

96. ศรีศักร วัลลิโภดม "เวียงมโน," ใน *วารสารเมืองโบราณ* ปีที่ 4, (มกราคม-มีนาคม 2521): 67-75

97. *จารึกในประเทศไทย* เล่ม 2, หน้า 108.

98. Gordon H. Luce, *Old Burma-Early Pagan,* Vol. I (Locust Valley, N.Y.: J.J. Augustin, 1969).

99. ในสมัยหริภุญไชย ไม่มีการแบ่งหน่วยการปกครองเป็น "พันนา" ระบบพันนาใช้ในล้านนาสมัยราชวงศ์มังราย การที่ตำนานพื้นเมืองเชียงใหม่เรียกบริเวณนั้นว่าพันนาทวนพันนาปูคา ก็เพราะตำนานเขียนขึ้นในสมัยราชวงศ์มังราย เมื่อบ้านเมืองใช้ระบบพันนาไปแล้ว

100. *The Chiang Mai Chronicle,* p. 30.

101. *ตำนานมูลศาสนา,* หน้า 168. ดอยอ่างสรง หรือบางครั้งเรียกดอยอ่างสลุง

102. ดู สิงฆะ วรรณสัย, ปริวรรต, "พุทธตำนานพระเจ้าเลียบโลก," ผูกที่ 9 (ลานที่ 10), หน้า 117. (พิมพ์ดีด)

103. George **Cœdès**, *The Indianization States of Southeast Asia,* translated by Susan Browning Cowing (Honolulu: East-West Center, University of Hawaii Press, 1968), p.137.

104. ดี.จี.อี. ฮอล์ล, *ประวัติศาสตร์เอเชียตะวันออกเฉียงใต้* เล่ม 1, หน้า 145.

105. *ชินกาลมาลีปกรณ์,* หน้า 95.

106. ฮันส์ เพนธ์, *ประวัติความเป็นมาของล้านนาไทย,* หน้า 11.

104. George **Cœdès**, *The Indianization States of Southeast Asia,* p. 161.

107. *ชินกาลมาลีปกรณ์,* หน้า 98-99.

108. ฮันส์ เพนธ์, *ประวัติความเป็นมาของล้านนาไทย,* หน้า 12.

109. *ชินกาลมาลีปรณ์,* หน้า 99.

110. ประเสริฐ ณ นคร, "สมัยไทยก่อนสุโขทัย" ใน *สารัตถคดีประเสริฐ ณ นคร,* หน้า 61.

111. *ตำนานมูลศาสนา,* หน้า 220.

112. ดูรายละเอียดใน สรัสวดี อ๋องสกุล, *เวียงกุมกาม: การศึกษาชุมชนโบราณในล้านนา,* หน้า 120.

113. "ตำนานพระธาตุลำปางหลวง ตำนานพระธาตุจุมพิตนครใน *ประชุมตำนานพระธาตุ* ภาคที่ 1 (พิมพ์เป็นที่ระลึกในงานศพ นางแข ฟูศักดิ์ 17 สิงหาคม, 2485), หน้า 61-87. และสงวน โชติสุขรัตน์ "ตำนานพระธาตุลำปางหลวง ตำนานพระธาตุแก้วดอนเต้า," ใน *ประชุมตำนานลานนาไทย* เล่ม 2, หน้า 329-380.

114. *คำแปลจามเทวีวงศ์ พงศาวดารหริภุญไชย,* หน้า 134.

115. โปรดดู คัมภีร์ใบลานเรื่อง "ตำนานเมืองเถิน," วัดแม่วะหลวง ตำบลแม่วะ อำเภอเถิน จังหวัดลำปาง รหัสไมโครฟิล์ม สถาบันวิจัยสังคม มหาวิทยาลัยเชียงใหม่ 81.094.01L.061-062, หน้าลานที่ 8 (คัมภีร์ผูกนี้มี 32 หน้าลาน)

116. *ชินกาลมาลีปกรณ์,* หน้า 102.

117. พระโพธิรังสี, *คำแปลจามเทวีวงศ์พงศาวดารเมืองหริภุญไชย* (กรุงเทพฯ: โรงพิมพ์รุ่งวัฒนา 2516), หน้า 136.

118. *ตำนานมูลศาสนา,* หน้า 153.

119. *ชินกาลมาลีปกรณ์,* หน้า 102.

120. ศรีศักร วัลลิโภดม "แคว้นหริภุญไชย," ใน *โบราณคดีไทยในทศวรรษที่ผ่านมา* (กรุงเทพฯ: สำนักพิมพ์เมืองโบราณ, 2524), หน้า 90.

121. ดู ภาสกร โทณะวณิก "การศึกษาเมืองโบราณเวียงพระธาตุลำปางหลวง," (วิทยานิพนธ์ศิลปศาสตร์มหาบัณฑิต สาขาวิชาโบราณคดีสมัยประวัติศาสตร์ ภาควิชาโบราณคดี คณะโบราณคดี บัณฑิตวิทยาลัย มหาวิทยาลัยศิลปากร 2529), หน้า 197.

122. ภาสกร โทณะวณิก "การศึกษาประวัติศาสตร์นครลำปาง จากหลักฐานทางโบราณคดี" ใน *ประวัติศาสตร์และโบราณคดีนครลำปาง,* หน้า 70.

123. สุณี หาญวงศ์ "การสำรวจชุมชนโบราณในจังหวัดลำปาง ใน *ประวัติศาสตร์และโบราณคดีนครลำปาง* (ลำปาง: วิทยาลัยครูลำปาง สหวิทยาลัยล้านนา, 2534), หน้า 112. และดู *สภาพสิ่งแวดล้อมแหล่งศิลปกรรมในจังหวัดลำปาง,* หน่วยอนุรักษ์สิ่งแวดล้อมศิลปกรรมท้องถิ่น ศูนย์วัฒนธรรมจังหวัดลำปาง, 2533, หน้า 116.

124. เรื่องเดียวกัน, หน้า 112.

125. ดู *ชินกาลมาลีปกรณ์* หน้า 102.

126. *ประชุมศิลาจารึก* ภาคที่ 3, คณะกรรมการจัดพิมพ์เอกสารทางประวัติศาสตร์ วัฒนธรรมและโบราณคดี สำนักนายกรัฐมนตรี 2508, หน้า 152.

127. เรื่องเดียวกัน, หน้า 228.

128. The *Chiang Mai Chronicle,* p. 50.

129. นวลศิริ วงศ์ทางสวัสดิ์, *ภูมิศาสตร์กายภาพภาคเหนือของประเทศไทย,* หน้า 30.

130. ศรีศักร วัลลิโภดม, *เมืองโบราณในอาณาจักรสุโขทัย,* หน้า 12.

131. ดูตำนานพระธาตุดอยปูภูทับ เมืองลองและแหลมลี่ ใน *ประชุมตำนานพระธาตุ* ภาคที่ 1, หน้า 99.

132. สงวน โชติสุขรัตน์ "ตำนานพระธาตุวัดศรีดอนคำ (ห้วยอ้อ)" ใน *ประชุมตำนานลานนาไทย* เล่ม 2, หน้า 384.

133. ศรีศักร วัลลิโภดม, *เมืองโบราณในอาณาจักรสุโขทัย,* หน้า 13, 233.

134. *จารึกล้านนา* ภาค 1, เล่ม 1, หน้า 246.

135. ดู "ตำนานพระธาตุลำปางหลวง" ใน *ประชุมตำนานพระธาตุ* ภาคที่ 1, หน้า 68-69.

136. ดู *ประชุมตำนานพระธาตุ* ภาคที่ 1, หน้า 104.

137. เรื่องเดียวกัน, หน้า 105.

138. *จารึกล้านนา* ภาค 1, เล่ม 1, หน้า 69-70.

139. พระยาประชากิจกรจักร์, *พงศาวดารโยนก,* พิมพ์ครั้งที่ 7 (2516), หน้า 235.

140. *ประชุมพงศาวดาร* ภาคที่ 61, หน้า 18.

141. *ประชุมตำนานพระธาตุ* ภาคที่ 1, หน้า 104.

142. สรัสวดี อ๋องสกุล, ปริวรรต, *พื้นเมืองน่าน* ฉบับวัดพระเกิด, หน้า 45-46.

143. *The Chiang Mai Chronicle,* p. 63.

144. เรื่องเดียวกัน หน้า 84-85.

145. ดู *เมืองน่าน: โบราณคดี ประวัติศาสตร์ และศิลปะ,* (กรุงเทพฯ: กรมศิลปากร, 2530, หน้า 333.

146. ดูรายละเอียดใน สรัสวดี อ๋องสกุล, ปริวรรต, *พื้นเมืองน่าน* ฉบับวัดพระเกิด

147. นวลศิริ วงศ์ทางสวัสดิ์, *ภูมิศาสตร์กายภาพภาคเหนือของประเทศไทย,* หน้า 31.

148. ดู แผนที่แสดงแหล่งที่ตั้งชุมชนโบราณในประเทศไทย จังหวัดน่าน

149. ตำนานกล่าวถึงฤาษีสร้างเมืองจันทบุรีให้ขุนนุ่น เมืองจันทบุรีหมายถึงเมืองเวียงจันทน์ แต่เมื่อพิจารณาตำแหน่งที่ตั้งเมืองของขุนนุ่น ตามบริบทที่ตำนานนางเกลือกล่าวถึงในพื้นเมืองน่านแล้ว พบว่าเมืองของขุนนุ่นควรเป็นหลวงพระบาง ดู สรัสวดี อ๋องสกุล, ปริวรรต, *พื้นเมืองน่าน* ฉบับวัดพระเกิด, หน้า 41, 50-51

150. เรื่องเดียวกัน, หน้า 2, 7.

151. *ประชุมศิลาจารึก* ภาคที่ 3, หน้า 62.

152. *ประชุมศิลาจารึก* ภาคที่ 7, หน้า 14-15.

153. สรัสวดี อ๋องสกุล, ปริวรรต, *พื้นเมืองน่าน* ฉบับวัดพระเกิด, หน้า 7.

154. ดูรายละเอียดใน ประพฤธิ์ ศุกลรัตนเมธี และวินัย พงศ์ศรีเพียร "บทบาทของล้านนาในวิกฤติการณ์การเมืองระหว่างรัฐในราชอาณาจักรลาว พ.ศ. 2002-2024," ใน *รวมบทความประวัติศาสตร์* ฉบับที่ 16, (2537): 98-110.

155. สรัสวดี อ๋องสกุล, ปริวรรต, *พื้นเมืองน่าน* ฉบับวัดพระเกิด, หน้า 47.

152. *ชินกาลมาลีปกรณ์,* หน้า 121.

CHAPTER 3
HISTORY OF THE KINGDOM (1296–1558)

1. ศักราชในสมัยพญามังราย ผู้เขียนใช้หลักฐานจากชินกาลมาลีปกรณ์ กล่าวคือ ประสูติ พ.ศ. 1782, อายุ 22 ปี ครองราชย์ พ.ศ. 1804, อายุ 23 ปี สร้างเชียงราย พ.ศ. 1805, ยึดครองเมืองเชียงของ พ.ศ. 1812, สร้างเมืองฝาง พ.ศ. 1816, ทำสัญญาเป็นมิตรไมตรีกับพญางำเมืองและพ่อขุนรามคำแหง พ.ศ. 1830, ยึดครองหริภุญไชย พ.ศ. 1835, สร้างเชียงใหม่ พ.ศ. 1839, สวรรคต พ.ศ. 1854, มีพระชนมายุ 72 ปี

2. ดี. จี. อี. ฮอล์ล, *ประวัติศาสตร์เอเชียตะวันออกเฉียงใต้* เล่ม 1, แปลโดย วรุณยุพา สนิทวงศ์ ณ อยุธยา และคณะ. กรุงเทพฯ: ไทยวัฒนาพานิช, 2522. หน้า 78.

3. "ประชุมพงศาวดารภาคที่ 10 พงศาวดารเมืองน่าน," ใน *ประชุมพงศาวดาร* เล่ม 9 (พระนคร: โรงพิมพ์ของคุรุสภา, 2507), หน้า 297.

5. *ตำนานสิบห้าราชวงศ์* เล่มที่ 1, ผูกที่ 1-2 (เชียงใหม่: สถาบันวิจัยสังคม มหาวิทยาลัยเชียงใหม่ 2524), หน้า 55.

5. ดี. จี. อี. ฮอล์ล, *ประวัติศาสตร์เอเชียตะวันออกเฉียงใต้* เล่ม 1, หน้า 78.

6. เรื่องเดียวกัน, หน้า 79.

7. อาคม พัฒิยะ และนิธิ เอียวศรีวงศ์, *ศรีรามเทพนคร: รวมความเรียงว่าด้วยประวัติศาสตร์อยุธยาตอนต้น*, นิธิ เอียวศรีวงศ์, บรรณาธิการ, (กรุงเทพฯ: สำนักพิมพ์เจ้าพระยา 2527), หน้า 81-86.

8. ศรีศักร วัลลิโภดม, "บ้านเมืองแถบนี้มีขึ้นมาได้อย่างไร?" ใน *เมืองพะเยา,* หน้า 64-65.

9. David K. Wyatt, Aroonrut Wichienkeeo, *The Chiang Mai Chronicle,* 2nd ed. (Chiang Mai: Silkworm Books, 1998), p. 19.

10. เรื่องเดียวกัน

11. การคมนาคมระหว่างฝางกับหริภุญไชย ส่วนหนึ่งคงอาศัยเดินทางเลียบตามแม่น้ำปิง ซึ่งเป็นเส้นทางสำคัญ ส่วนการคมนาคมระหว่างฝางกับเชียงรายใช้วิธีล่องแม่น้ำกก

12. *The Chiang Mai Chronicle,* p. 19.

13. ศักราชที่พญามังรายยึดหริภุญไชยได้แตกต่างกัน ตำนานพื้นเมืองเชียงใหม่ระบุเป็น พ.ศ. 1824 ส่วนชินกาลมาลีปกรณ์ระบุเป็น พ.ศ. 1835 ผู้เขียนเห็นว่า พ.ศ. 1835 ตามชินกาลมาลีปกรณ์น่าจะถูกต้อง เพราะเกิดขึ้นหลังจากการทำสัญญามิตรภาพ (พ.ศ. 1830) ระหว่างพญามังราย พญางำเมือง และพ่อขุนรามคำแหง และหลักฐานจากจีน (Yuan-Shih) กล่าวถึงจักรพรรดิมองโกลส่งกองทัพมาโจมตีอาณาจักรปาไป่ซีฟู (Pa-pai-hsi-fu, Ba Bai Xifu Kingdom) เป็นชื่อที่จีนเรียกอาณาจักรล้านนา) เป็นครั้งแรกใน พ.ศ. 1835 แต่หลักฐานจีนไม่กล่าวถึงสาเหตุของสงคราม ผู้เขียนเข้าใจว่าสาเหตุหนึ่งอาจเป็นเพราะพญามังรายขยายอำนาจเข้าครอบครองหริภุญไชย ดู *ชินกาลมาลีปกรณ์,* หน้า 101. และดู G. H. Luce, "The Early Syam in Burma's History," *Journal of the Siam Society* SLVI pt. 2 (November 1958): 123-214.

14. ตำนานทุกฉบับกล่าวตรงกันว่าพญามังรายครองหริภุญไชย 2 ปี ส่วนสาเหตุที่พญามังรายไม่ประทับที่หริภุญไชย มีตำนานสิงหนวติกุมารเท่านั้นอธิบายว่าเพราะเป็นเมืองพระธาตุและ "แม่น้ำ

ก็ผ่ากลางเวียงบ่ดีแล" ดูใน *ประชุมพงศาวดาร* ภาคที่ 61, หน้า 140.

15. โปรดดูรายละเอียดใน สรัสวดี อ๋องสกุล, *เวียงกุมกาม: การศึกษาประวัติศาสตร์ชุมชนโบราณในล้านนา,* หน้า 120.

16. *จดหมายเหตุการตรวจสอบและสืบค้นดวงเมือง* "นพบุรีศรีนครพิงค์เชียงใหม่" (เชียงใหม่: โรงพิมพ์ ส.ทรัพย์การพิมพ์ 2537), หน้า 3-10.

17. *The Chiang Mai Chronicle,* p. 45. และ *ชินกาลมาลีปกรณ์,* หน้า 104.

18. ดู คณะกรรมการดำเนินงานจัดทำหนังสือกำแพงเมืองเชียงใหม่ *กำแพงเมืองเชียงใหม่,* (เชียงใหม่: ทิพย์เนตรการพิมพ์ 2529), หน้า 243.

19. *ตำนานพื้นเมืองลานนาเชียงใหม่,* หน้า 16-20.

20. *ชินกาลมาลีปกรณ์,* หน้า 102

21. ดู อุษณีย์ ธงไชย "ความสัมพันธ์ระหว่างอยุธยาและลานนาไทย พ.ศ. 1839-2310," (วิทยานิพนธ์ปริญญามหาบัณฑิต ภาควิชาประวัติศาสตร์ บัณฑิตวิทยาลัย จุฬาลงกรณ์มหาวิทยาลัย, 2526), หน้า 27, 84-98.

22. *The Chiang Mai Chronicle,* p. 41-42.

23. G. H. Luce, *The Early Syam in Burma's History,* p. 149-152.

24. การยกทัพไปช่วยเหลือหัวหน้าไทยใหญ่สามพี่น้องคงได้ชัยชนะกลับมา เพราะมีข้อความกล่าวถึงการนำช่างเงิน ช่างทอง ช่างเหล็ก กลับมาด้วย ดู *The Chiang Mai Chronicle,* p. 39.

25. ตามหลักฐานจีนไม่ระบุถึงสาเหตุที่จักรพรรดิกุบไลข่านยกทัพมาโจมตี ดู G .H. Luce. *The Early Syam in Burma's History,* p. 146.

26. เรื่องเดียวกัน และดู หม่องทิน อ่อง, *ประวัติศาสตร์พม่า,* แปลโดย เพ็ชรี สุมิตร (กรุงเทพฯ: ไทยวัฒนาพานิช 2519), หน้า 45-46.

27. นิธิ เอียวศรีวงศ์, *ศรีรามเทพนคร: รวมความเรียงว่าด้วยประวัติศาสตร์อยุธยาตอนต้น* หน้า 69.

28. *ตำนานมูลศาสนา,* หน้า 184

29. *The Chiang Mai Chronicle,* p. 44.

30. โปรดดูรายละเอียดใน สรัสวดี อ๋องสกุล "วัดเจ็ดยอดในฐานะอายุเมืองเชียงใหม่," *ศิลปากร* ปีที่ 35, ฉบับที่ 3 (2535), หน้า 20-33.

31. ดูรายละเอียดเรื่องนี้ในสรัสวดี อ๋องสกุล และคณะ ใน "อ่างเก็บน้ำโบราณในมหาวิทยาลัยเชียงใหม่," *ศึกษาศาสตร์สาร* ปีที่ 17, ฉบับที่ 2 (ตุลาคม 2535), หน้า 78-88.

32. โปรดดู นิธิ เอียวศรีวงศ์ "ความสำคัญด้านประวัติศาสตร์ ศาสนา และวัฒนธรรมของดอยสุเทพ-ปุย" *รายงานการประชุมปฏิบัติการเรื่อง อุทยานแห่งชาติดอยสุเทพ-ปุย: การจัดการและการอนุรักษ์* 14-15 มีนาคม 2534 (เชียงใหม่: สันติการพิมพ์ 2536), หน้า 10-14.

33. จดหมายเหตุการสอบค้นดวงเมือง, *นพบุรีศรีนครพิงค์เชียงใหม่,* คณะกรรมการตรวจสอบและสืบค้นดวงเมืองและตำนานพื้นเมืองเชียงใหม่ 2527, หน้า 58.

34. *The Chiang Mai Chronicle,* p. 206.

35. สรัสวดี อ๋องสกุล, *หลักฐานประวัติศาสตร์ล้านนาจากเอกสารคัมภีร์ใบลานและพับหนังสา,* หน้า 106.

36. *The Chiang Mai Chronicle,* p. 111.

37. เรื่องเดียวกัน, หน้า 54-55.

38. ทวี สว่างปัญญางกูร, ปริวรรต, *ตำนานเมืองเชียงตุง* (เชียงใหม่: แผนกอนุรักษ์และเผยแพร่วรรณกรรมล้านนา ธรรมสถาน มหาวิทยาลัยเชียงใหม่ 2527), หน้า 44-51. (อัดสำเนา). และดู "ตำนานสิงหนวติ" ใน *ประชุมพงศาวดาร* ภาคที่ 61, หน้า 131.

39. ประเสริฐ ณ นคร, ปริวรรต, *มังรายศาสตร์* (กรุงเทพฯ: ภาควิชาประวัติศาสตร์ มหาวิทยาลัยศรีนครินทรวิโรฒ ประสานมิตร), 2521.

40. *The Chiang Mai Chronicle,* p. 35.

41. ฮันส์ เพนธ์, *ประวัติความเป็นมาของล้านนาไทย,* หน้า 210.

42. David K. Wyatt, *Thailand: A Short History,* (Bangkok: Thai Wattana Panich Press, 1984). p. 49

43. *ตำนานมูลศาสนา,* หน้า 189.

44. *The Chiang Mai Chronicle,* p. 56-58.

45. พระยาประชากิจกรจักร์, *พงศาวดารโยนก,* หน้า 283.

46. *ชินกาลมาลีปกรณ์,* หน้า 104.

47. พระยาประชากิจกรจักร์, *พงศาวดารโยนก,* หน้า 284-285.

48. *The Chiang Mai Chronicle,* p. 63.

49. เรื่องเดียวกัน, หน้า 66.

50. เรื่องเดียวกัน

51. เรื่องเดียวกัน

52. เรื่องเดียวกัน

53. ปริญญา กายสิทธิ์ "ประวัติศาสตร์พุทธศาสนาในล้านนาไทยตั้งแต่ พ.ศ. 1912 ถึง พ.ศ. 2101," (วิทยานิพนธ์ปริญญามหาบัณฑิต ภาควิชาประวัติศาสตร์ บัณฑิตวิทยาลัย มหาวิทยาลัยศรีนครินทรวิโรฒ ประสานมิตร, 2528), หน้า 82.

54. "ตำนานพระธาตุดอยสุเทพ" ใน *ประชุมตำนานพระธาตุ* ภาคที่ 2 (พระนคร: โรงพิมพ์พระจันทร์, 2510. พิมพ์เป็นอนุสรณ์ในงานพระราชทานเพลิงศพ พ.ต.ท. สลับ เกียรติสุต 2 ธันวาคม, 2510), หน้า 49.

พระสุมนเถรตามประวัติได้ไปศึกษาพุทธศาสนาที่เมืองพัน (เมาะตะมะ) โดยขออุปสมบทใหม่ในสำนักพระมหาสวามีอุทุมพร พระสุมนเถรศึกษาอยู่ 5 พรรษา จึงเดินทางกลับสุโขทัย พระสุมนเถรจึงสามารถกระทำสังฆกรรมได้

55. *ตำนานมูลศาสนา ฉบับวัดป่าแดง* (เชียงใหม่: ภาควิชาสังคมวิทยาและมานุษยวิทยา คณะสังคมศาสตร์ มหาวิทยาลัยเชียงใหม่, 2519), หน้า 9-10. (อัดสำเนา)

56. วัดบุปผาราม หรือวัดสวนดอกไม้ หรือวัดบุปผารามสวนดอกไม้หลวง

57. ศักราชนี้ยังไม่ยุติ เพราะแต่ละตำนานกล่าวไว้ไม่ตรงกัน

58. David K. Wyatt, *Thailand: A Short History,* p. 76.

59. *ชินกาลมาลีปกรณ์,* หน้า 114. และสงวน โชติสุขรัตน์, ผู้รวบรวม, "ตำนานวัดบุปผารามสวนดอกไม้," ใน *ประชุมตำนานลานนาไทย* เล่ม 2, หน้า 177-178.

60. *ตำนานมูลศาสนา ฉบับวัดป่าแดง,* หน้า 9-10.

61. *The Chiang Mai Chronicle,* p. 66.

62. ดู "ตำนานติดส่วยห้อ," ใน สรัสวดี อ๋องสกุล, *พื้นเมืองน่าน ฉบับวัดพระเกิด,* หน้า 59.

63. *คำให้การชาวกรุงเก่า คำให้การขุนหลวงหาวัด และพระราชพงศาวดารกรุงเก่าฉบับหลวงประเสริฐอักษรนิติ์* (นครหลวงกรุงเทพธนบุรี: คลังวิทยา 2515), หน้า 445.

64. David K. Wyatt, *Thailand: A Short History,* p. 76.

65. *ชินกาลมาลีปกรณ์,* หน้า 115.

66. เรื่องเดียวกัน, หน้า 48.

67. ลพ./9 "ศิลาจารึกกษัตริย์ราชวงศ์มังราย," ใน *ศิลปากร* 2 (พฤษภาคม 2523): 47.

68. เรื่องเดียวกัน, หน้า 48.

69. *The Chiang Mai Chronicle,* p. 72.

70. พระยาประชากิจกรจักร์, *พงศาวดารโยนก,* หน้า 316-319.

71. เรื่องเดียวกัน, หน้า 316.

72. *The Chiang Mai Chronicle,* p. 78.

73. เรื่องเดียวกัน, หน้า 80-81.

74. *คำให้การชาวกรุงเก่า คำให้การขุนหลวงหาวัด และพระราชพงศาวดารกรุงเก่าฉบับหลวงประเสริฐอักษรนิติ์,* หน้า 447.

75. ประเสริฐ ณ นคร "พระธรรมราชาที่สองถวายบังคม," ใน *สารัตถคดี ประเสริฐ ณ นคร* (กรุงเทพฯ: โรงพิมพ์พิฆเณศ, 2527), หน้า 88-89.

76. ต่อมาภายหลังพระยาเชลียงเอาใจออกห่างพระเจ้าติโลกราช จึงถูกส่งไปครองเมืองห้างหลวง ส่วนพระยายุทธิษเฐียรมีความชอบ ได้รับการแต่งตั้งให้เป็นเจ้าสี่หมื่นครองเมืองพะเยาใน พ.ศ. 2017 และยังมีอำนาจดูแลเมืองงาว เมืองแพร่ และเมืองน่านอีกด้วย ดู ประสาน บุญประคอง และ ประเสริฐ ณ นคร, "คำอ่านศิลาจารึกอักษรและภาษาไทยที่ใช้ในลานนาไทย," *ศิลปากร* 4 (พฤศจิกายน 2512): 77-79.

77. *คำให้การชาวกรุงเก่า คำให้การขุนหลวงหาวัด และพระราชพงศาวดารกรุงเก่าฉบับหลวงประเสริฐอักษรนิติ์,* หน้า 449.

78. *The Chiang Mai Chronicle,* p. 97-98.

79. *คำให้การชาวกรุงเก่า คำให้การขุนหลวงหาวัด และพระราชพงศาวดารกรุงเก่าฉบับหลวงประเสริฐอักษรนิติ์,* หน้า 449.

80. ประพฤทธิ์ ศุกลรัตนเมธี และ วินัย พงศ์ศรีเพียร "บทบาทล้านนาในวิกฤตการณ์การเมืองระหว่างรัฐในราชอาณาจักรลาว พ.ศ. 2002-2024," *รวมบทความประวัติศาสตร์* ฉบับที่ 16, พุทธศักราช 2537, หน้า 109.

81. *The Chiang Mai Chronicle,* p. 102.

82. เรื่องเดียวกัน, หน้า 85.

83. เรื่องเดียวกัน, หน้า 87.

84. นิกายสีหล หรือลัทธิวัดป่าแดง หรือลังกาวงศ์ใหม่ เป็นคณะสงฆ์ลัทธิลังกาวงศ์รุ่นล่าสุดที่เข้ามาเผยแผ่ในล้านนา มีพระมหาญาณคัมภีร์เป็นหัวหน้า นำเข้ามาในเชียงใหม่สมัยพญาสามฝั่งแกน

(ใน พ.ศ. 1973) เหตุที่เกิดนิกายสีหลนั้นเป็นผลมาจากการเผยแผ่ลัทธิลังกาวงศ์ของพระสุมนเถระ ซึ่งทำให้เกิดการตื่นตัวศึกษาพุทธศาสนากันกว้างขวาง และนำไปสู่ความคิดเกี่ยวกับพุทธศาสนาที่บริสุทธิ์ พระภิกษุชาวล้านนาต้องการพระพุทธศาสนาที่ถูกต้องตามพระธรรมวินัย จึงเดินทางไปศึกษาและอุปสมบทใหม่ที่ลังกาโดยตรง หลังจากกลับมาถึงเชียงใหม่ก็เผยแผ่หลักการและแนวปฏิบัติออกไปอย่างกว้างขวาง ในลักษณะที่มีความคิดขัดแย้งกับนิกายรามัญ (วัดสวนดอก) นิกายสีหลและนิกายรามัญขัดแย้งกันหลายสิบปีจนถึงสมัยพญาเมืองแก้วจึงยุติลง

85. วัดป่าแดง วัดป่าแดงหลวง วัดป่าแดงมหาวิหาร เมื่อพิจารณาจากชินกาลมาลีปกรณ์แล้ว เข้าใจว่าเป็นวัดเดียวกัน แต่ส่วนใหญ่ใช้วัดป่าแดงมหาวิหาร

86. *ชินกาลมาลีปกรณ์,* หน้า 144.

87. เรื่องเดียวกัน, หน้า 128.

88. เรื่องเดียวกัน, หน้า 130.

89. *The Chiang Mai Chronicle,* p. 108.

90. *ชินกาลมาลีปกรณ์,* หน้า 130.

91. เรื่องเดียวกัน, หน้า 163.

92. *คำให้การชาวกรุงเก่า คำให้การขุนหลวงหาวัด และพระราชพงศาวดารกรุงเก่าฉบับหลวงประเสริฐอักษรนิติ์,* หน้า 453.

93. *The Chiang Mai Chronicle,* p. 110. และ *ชินกาลมาลีปกรณ์,* หน้า 159-160

94. *ชินกาลมาลีปกรณ์,* หน้า 140.

95. *The Chiang Mai Chronicle,* p. 110.

96. *ชินกาลมาลีปกรณ์,* หน้า 130.

97. "ศิลาจารึก ชม. 25" วัดศรีสุพรรณ จ.ศ. 862

98. "ศิลาจารึกหลักที่ 71," ใน *ประชุมศิลาจารึก* ภาคที่ 3, หน้า 185-194.

99. *ชินกาลมาลีปกรณ์,* หน้า 135-151.

100. เรื่องดียวกัน หน้า 142-143.

101. วรรณกรรมล้านช้างมีลักษณะคล้ายกับวรรณกรรมล้านนา เพราะได้รับอิทธิพลจากวรรณกรรมล้านนา โดยพญาแก้วส่งพระไตรปิฎกและพระสงฆ์ล้านนาไปเผยแผ่ศาสนาในล้านช้างใน พ.ศ. 2066 ดู อานาโตล แป็ลติเยร์, "ความสัมพันธ์ระหว่างล้านนากับล้านช้างในด้านวรรณกรรม," ใน *ล้านนาไทย* (เชียงใหม่: ทิพย์เนตรการพิมพ์, 2526-2527), หน้า 149-156.

102. ลิขิต ลิขิตานนท์, "ยุคทองแห่งวรรณกรรมพุทธศาสนาของลานนาไทย," ใน *ล้านนาไทย,* หน้า 90-95.

103. ปริญญา กายสิทธิ์, "ประวัติศาสตร์พุทธศาสนาในล้านนาไทย," หน้า 269-270.

104. ลิขิต ลิขิตานนท์, "ยุคทองแห่งวรรณกรรมพุทธศาสนาของลานนาไทย," หน้า 97.

105. *The Chiang Mai Chronicle,* p. 112.

106. เรื่องเดียวกัน

107. เรื่องเดียวกัน

108. เรื่องเดียวกัน

109. มานิต วัลลิโภดม *ตำนานสิงหนวติกุมาร* ฉบับสอบค้น, หน้า 97.

110. ดูรายละเอียดใน "สมุดตราช ประเพณี 6 ประการ," ศูนย์ส่งเสริมการศึกษาและวัฒนธรรมลานนาไทย วิทยาลัยครูเชียงใหม่, 2524, หน้า 36. (อัดสำเนา)

111. เรื่องเดียวกัน, หน้า 2.

112. *ตำนานมูลศาสนา* (พิมพ์เป็นอนุสรณ์งานพระราชทางเพลิงศพ มล. เดช สนิทวงศ์, 17 ธันวาคม, 2518), หน้า 188-189.

113. *คำสอนพระยามังราย* ภาคปริวรรต, ลำดับที่ 11 ภาควิชาสังคมวิทยาและมานุษยวิทยา คณะสังคมศาสตร์ มหาวิทยาลัยเชียงใหม่ 2519.

114. *The Chiang Mai Chronicle,* p. 85. และ *ชินกาลมาลีปกรณ์,* หน้า 144.

115. ดู ธิดา สาระยา "สร้างบ้านแปงเมืองระบบเมืองคู่สถาบันเมืองลูกหลวง," *เมืองโบราณ* ปีที่ 9, (เมษายน-กรกฎาคม 2526): 13-26.

116. *The Chiang Mai Chronicle,* p. 101-102.

117. พระยาประชากิจกรจักร์, *พงศาวดารโยนก,* หน้า 330-333.

118. *The Chiang Mai Chronicle,* p. 85. และดู ทวี สว่างปัญญางกูร *ปริวรรตตำนานเมืองยอง* (เชียงใหม่: ทรัพย์การพิมพ์, 2527), หน้า 37-43.

119. *The Chiang Mai Chronicle,* p. 109.

120. *The Chiang Mai Chronicle,* p. 116

121. *คำสอนพระยามังราย,* หน้า 3.

122. *The Chiang Mai Chronicle,* p. 60.

123. เรื่องเดียวกัน, หน้า 79.

124. ศิลาจารึกเลขทะเบียน ชร./6 "คำอ่านศิลาจารึกวัดพระเกิด จ.ศ. 875," *ศิลปากร,* ฉบับที่ 3 (กันยายน 2518): 66-68 และ "ศิลาจารึกเลขทะเบียน ชร./16 คำอ่านศิลาจารึกวัดศรีอุโมงคำ จ.ศ. 845," *ศิลปากร,* ฉบับที่ 2 (กรกฎาคม 2518): 110-112.

125. *The Chiang Mai Chronicle,* p. 23-24.

126. หวญ., ศิลาจารึกเลขทะเบียน ลพ./22 "คำอ่านศิลาจารึกวัดวิสุทธาราม จ.ศ. 868"

127. *The Chiang Mai Chronicle,* p. 53.

128. เรื่องเดียวกัน, หน้า 48.

129. มณี พยอมยงค์, ปริวรรต, *ธรรมศาสตร์และกฎหมายพระยามังราย,* เอกสารงานวิจัย การถ่ายทอดคัมภีร์ใบลาน โครงการไทยศึกษา จุฬาลงกรณ์มหาวิทยาลัย, 2518, หน้า 26-29.

130. ศิลาจารึกเลขทะเบียน ลป. /1 หลักที่ 65 "ศิลาจารึกวัดพระธาตุลำปางหลวง จ.ศ. 838," ใน *ประชุมศิลาจารึก* ภาคที่ 3, หน้า 152-155.

131. หวญ., ศิลาจารึกเลขทะเบียน ชร./1 คำอ่านศิลาจารึกวัดจันทรอาราม จ.ศ. 830.

132. ประเสริฐ ณ นคร, ปริวรรต, *มังรายศาสตร์,* (พิมพ์เป็นอนุสรณ์งานพระราชทานเพลิงศพหลวงโหตรกิตยานุพัทธ์ (อาสา โหตระกิตย์), 4 เมษายน 2514), หน้า 109-110.

133. *คำสอนพระยามังราย,* หน้า 9.

134. ประเสริฐ ณ นคร, ปริวรรต, *มังรายศาสตร์,* หน้า 5.

135. เรื่องเดียวกัน, หน้า 2.

136. *กฎหมายพระเจ้าน่าน,* ศูนย์ส่งเสริมและศึกษาวัฒนธรรมลานนาไทย วิทยาลัยครูเชียงใหม่ 2533, หน้า 12. (อัดสำเนา)

137. สุเทพ สุนทรเภสัช “ประวัติศาสตร์ท้องถิ่นในล้านนา: ข้อวิจารณ์และเสนอแนะแนวการศึกษา,” เอกสารประกอบการสัมมนา “ล้านนาคดีศึกษา: ประวัติศาสตร์และโบราณคดี,” ณ วิทยาลัยครูเชียงใหม่ 28-31 มกราคม 2528, เอกสารเลขที่ 10-001, หน้า 10.

138. *สมุดตราช* ศูนย์ส่งเสริมและศึกษาวัฒนธรรมลานนาไทย วิทยาลัยครูเชียงใหม่ 2524, หน้า 34-35. และ *กฎหมายลานนา* ภาคปริวรรต, ลำดับที่ 2, ภาควิชาสังคมและมานุษยวิทยา คณะสังคมศาสตร์ มหาวิทยาลัยเชียงใหม่ 2518, หน้า 1.

139. ส่วยประกอบไปด้วยสิ่งของต่างๆ มากมายหลายชนิด เช่น ข้าว เหล็ก เงิน ทอง เกลือ ของป่า สัตว์ป่า แต่ที่มีมูลค่าสูงใช้เป็นสินค้าออกคือ ของป่า และผลิตภัณฑ์จากสัตว์ป่า

140. ไพร่ส่วยคงเกิดขึ้นในล้านนามานานแล้ว และคงมีเรื่อยมาจนถึงสมัยรัชกาลที่ 5 จึงเลิกระบบไพร่ในล้านนา ดู เสถียร ลายลักษณ์ และคนอื่นๆ, รวบรวม, “พระราชบัญญัติการเก็บเงินแทนการเกณฑ์มณฑลตะวันตกเฉียงเหนือ ร.ศ. 119,” *ประชุมกฎหมายประจำศก* เล่ม 17, หน้า 293

141. *The Chiang Mai Chronicle,* p. 61.

142. *กฎหมายพระเจ้าน่าน,* หน้า 10.

143. หลักฐานนี้แสดงว่าสมัยพญาสามฝั่งแกนหัวเมืองต้องส่งส่วยให้เมืองราชธานี ดู *ตำนานพื้นเมืองเชียงใหม่,* หน้า 80.

144. เรื่องเดียวกัน, หน้า 106.

145. มณี พยอมยงค์, ปริวรรต, *ธรรมศาสตร์และกฎหมายของพระยามังราย,* หน้า 44.

146. *คำสอนพระยามังราย,* หน้า 14.

147. เรื่องเดียวกัน, หน้า 21.

148. *The Chiang Mai Chronicle,* p. 79.

149. ดู ศิลาจารึกเลขทะเบียน ลพ. /9 “ศิลาจารึกลำดับกษัตริย์ราชวงศ์มังราย,” *ศิลปากร* ฉบับที่ 2, (พฤษภาคม 2523): หน้า 42-54.

150. ระวิวรรณ ภาคพรต “การกัลปนาในลานนาไทยตั้งแต่กลางพุทธศตวรรษที่ 20 ถึงต้นพุทธศตวรรษที่ 22,” (วิทยานิพนธ์ปริญญามหาบัณฑิต ภาควิชาประวัติศาสตร์ บัณฑิตวิทยาลัย จุฬาลงกรณ์มหาวิทยาลัย, 2526), หน้า 122-124.

151. *The Chiang Mai Chronicle,* p. 120.

152. นิธิ เอียวศรีวงศ์ “ลักษณะการปกครองประเทศสยามแต่โบราณ: พื้นฐานทางเศรษฐกิจ,” *สายธารแห่งความคิด* (กรุงเทพฯ: บริษัทพิมพ์สวยจำกัด, 2532), หน้า 32-33.

153. *The Chiang Mai Chronicle,* p. 69.

154. *มังรายศาสตร์* ฉบับวัดไชยสถาน, ศูนย์วัฒนธรรมจังหวัดเชียงใหม่ และศูนย์ศิลปวัฒนธรรมสหวิทยาลัยล้านนา วิทยาลัยครูเชียงใหม่, เอกสารลำดับที่ 12 มกราคม 2529 หน้า 66.

155. คาร์ล บ็อค, *สมัยพระปิยมหาราช,* หน้า 60.

156. อรุณรัตน์ วิเชียรเขียว “แนวคิดทางการเมือง: ความสัมพันธ์ระหว่างระบบพันนาและระบบนายสิบและระบบชลประทาน” เอกสารประกอบการสัมมนาทางวิชาการ *ล้านนาคดีศึกษา: โลกทัศน์ล้านนา* จัดโดยสหวิทยาลัยล้านนา วิทยาลัยครูเชียงใหม่, 11-14 กันยายน, 2532, เอกสารหมายเลข1/1 หน้า 5.

157. สุรสิงห์สำรวม ฉิมพะเนาว์, ปริวรรต, “บันทึกการตัดสินคดีโบราณล้านนา 60 คดี (คลองเจือแห่งพระเจ้ากือนา),” 2528, หน้า 65. (อัดสำเนา)

158. ประเสริฐ ณ นคร, ปริวรรต, *มังรายศาสตร์* ฉบับวัดเสาไห้, หน้า 2.

159. นิธิ เอียวศรีวงศ์ "ลักษณะการปกครองประเทศสยามแต่โบราณ...," หน้า 28.

160. *สมุดตราช ประเพณี 6 ประการ,* หน้า 7 อนึ่งใน *หัตถกัมมวินิจฉัยบาฬีฎีกาอมสมมุตราช,* หน้า 53 ระบุว่า "หื้อผ่าเปน 8 ส่วรแล้วเอามาหื้แก่กู 2 ส่วร ล้ำนั้นไว้ให้แก่สูเทอะ"

161. ประเสริฐ ณ นคร, ปริวรรต, *มังรายศาสตร์* ฉบับวัดเสาไห้, หน้า 27.

162. เรื่องเดียวกัน, หน้า 6.

163. อรุณรัตน์ วิเชียรเขียว และ ศรีธน คำแปง, ปริวรรต, "ธรรมศาสตร์หลวง และธรรมศาสตร์ราชกือนา," หนังสือปริวรรตจากคัมภีร์ใบลานชุด "ตำนานเมืองและกฎหมายล้านนา," เอกสารลำดับที่ 5 และ 6 คณะสังคมศาสตร์ มหาวิทยาลัยเชียงใหม่ และศูนย์ส่งเสริมและศึกษาวัฒนธรรมล้านนา วิทยาลัยครูเชียงใหม่, หน้า 4. (อัดสำเนา)

164. *The Chiang Mai Chronicle,* p. 48.

165. เรื่องเดียวกัน, หน้า 75.

166. *สมุดตราช ประเพณี 6 ประการ* หน้า 29-30 อนึ่งใน *หัตถกัมมวินิจฉัยบาฬีฎีกาอมสมมุติราช* หน้า 75. ระบุว่าให้ทุกหมู่บ้านแจ้งจำนวนไพร่ชาวลัวะทุกปี

167. อรุณรัตน์ วิเชียรเขียว และศรีธน คำแปง, ปริวรรต, *หัตถกัมมวินิจฉัยบาฬีฎีกาอมสมมุติราช,* หนังสือปริวรรตจากคัมภีร์ใบลานชุด "ตำนานเมืองและกฎหมายล้านนา," เอกสารลำดับที่ 3 และ 4 คณะสังคมศาสตร์ มหาวิทยาลัยเชียงใหม่ และศูนย์ส่งเสริมและศึกษาวัฒนธรรมล้านนา วิทยาลัยครูเชียงใหม่, หน้า 28. (อัดสำเนา)

168. สมหมาย เปรมจิตต์, ปริวรรต, "ประเพณี 6 ประการ ภาคปริวรรต," ลำดับที่ 17 (ภาควิชาสังคมวิทยาและมานุษยวิทยา คณะสังคมศาสตร์ มหาวิทยาลัยเชียงใหม่, 2521), หน้า 10. (อัดสำเนา)

169. ประเสริฐ ณ นคร, ปริวรรต, *มังรายศาสตร์* ฉบับวัดเสาไห้, หน้า 2-3.

170. นิธิ เอียวศรีวงศ์ *ศรีรามเทพนคร: ความเรียงว่าด้วยประวัติศาสตร์อยุธยาตอนต้น,* หน้า 58.

171. Archibald Ross Colquhoun, *Amongst the Shans,* p. 257.

172. *The Chiang Mai Chronicle,* p. 63.

173. สุรสิงห์สำรวม ฉิมพะเนาว์, ปริวรรต, *บันทึกการตัดสินคดีโบราณล้านนา 60 คดี (คลองเจือแห่งพระเจ้ากือนา),* หน้า 30.

174. อุษณีย์ ธงไชย "อาณาจักรล้านนาไทย: พ.ศ. 1839-2310," เอกสารประกอบการสัมมนา "ล้านนาคดีศึกษา: ประวัติศาสตร์และโบราณคดี," 18-21 มกราคม, 2528 ณ วิทยาลัยครูเชียงใหม่ เอกสารเลขที่ 01-002, หน้า 14.

175. สุรสิงห์สำรวม ฉิมพะเนาว์, *บันทึกการตัดสินคดีโบราณล้านนา* 60 คดี, หน้า 42-43.

176. เรื่องเดียวกัน, หน้า 58.

177. อรุณรัตน์ วิเชียรเขียว และสุรพล ดำริห์กุล, "วัดร้างในเวียงเชียงใหม่," สถาบันวิจัยสังคม มหาวิทยาลัยเชียงใหม่ 2529, หน้า 78. (อัดสำเนา)

178. อรุณรัตน์ วิเชียรเขียว และ ศรีธน คำแปง ปริวรรต, *หัตถกัมมวินิจฉัยบาฬีฎีกาอมสมมุติราช,* หน้า 1.

179. อุษณีย์ ธงไชย, "อาณาจักรล้านนาไทย...," หน้า 14-15.

180. เรื่องเดียวกัน

181. หวัง จี้ หมิน "ความสัมพันธ์ระหว่างเมืองเชอหลี่กับเมืองปาไป่ซีฟู ในพุทธศตวรรษที่ 19," (วิทยานิพนธ์ปริญญาอักษรศาสตร์มหาบัณฑิต ภาควิชาประวัติศาสตร์ บัณฑิตวิทยาลัย จุฬาลงกรณ์มหาวิทยาลัย, 2531), หน้า 72-80.

182. *The Chiang Mai Chronicle,* p. 70.

183. เจีย เยน จอง "ความเป็นมาของวัฒนธรรมโบราณในล้านนา-สิบสองพันนา," *แถลงงานประวัติศาสตร์ เอกสารโบราณคดี* ปีที่ 21, (มกราคม-ธันวาคม, 2531), หน้า 13.

184. สงวน โชติสุขรัตน์ แปล "ตำนานพระยามังรายสร้างเมืองเชียงตุง" *รวมสารนิยายไทย,* (นครหลวง กรุงเทพธนบุรี: โอเดียนสโตร์, 2515) หน้า 42.

185. ทวี สว่างปัญญางกูร, ปริวรรต, "ตำนานเมืองเชียงตุง," แผนกอนุรักษ์และเผยแพร่วรรณกรรมล้านนา ธรรมสถาน มหาวิทยาลัยเชียงใหม่, 2527, หน้า 51. (อัดสำเนา)

186. หัวข้อนี้สรุปจากสรัสวดี อ๋องสกุล "ไทลื้อเมืองยองในแดนพม่า: ข้อสังเกตเบื้องต้น," บทความเสนอเสวนาไทศึกษา ครั้งที่ 3 จัดโดยศูนย์ส่งเสริมศิลปวัฒนธรรม มหาวิทยาลัยเชียงใหม่

187. James George Scott, *Gazetteer of Upper Burma and Shan States* Part 2. (Rangoon: Superintendent, Government Printing, 1901) p. 500.

188. ทวี สว่างปัญญางกูร, ปริวรรต, *ตำนานเมืองยอง,* (เชียงใหม่: ศูนย์หนังสือเชียงใหม่, 2527), หน้า 25.

189. เรื่องเดียวกัน, หน้า 27.

190. เรื่องเดียวกัน, หน้า 32-33.

191. *The Chiang Mai Chronicle,* p. 87.

192. ทวี สว่างปัญญางกูร, *ตำนานเมืองยอง,* หน้า 43.

193. *The Chiang Mai Chronicle,* p. 55.

194. สงวน โชติสุขรัตน์ แปล, "ตำนานว่าด้วยล้านนา," *รวมสารนิยายไทย,* หน้า 62.

195. *The Chiang Mai Chronicle,* p. 116.

196. ดู อานาโตล แป็ลติเยร์ "ความสัมพันธ์ระหว่างล้านนากับล้านช้างในด้านวรรณกรรม," *ล้านนาไทย* อนุสรณ์พระราชพิธีเปิดพระบรมราชานุสาวรีย์สามกษัตริย์ เชียงใหม่, 2526-2527, หน้า 149-154.

197. *The Chiang Mai Chronicle,* p. 19.

198. โปรดดูคัมภีร์ใบลาน เรื่อง "ตำนานเมืองเชียงใหม่," ฉบับวัดเชียงมั่น ตำบลศรีภูมิ อำเภอเมือง จังหวัดเชียงใหม่ รหัสไมโครฟิล์มสถาบันวิจัยสังคม มหาวิทยาลัยเชียงใหม่ 78 012 05 006-008, หน้าลานที่ 6 (คัมภีร์ผูกนี้มี 34 หน้าลาน)

199. "พับหนังสาเรื่องประวัติศาสตร์ กฎหมายโบราณ," วัดป่าลาน ตำบลทุ่งต้อม อำเภอสันป่าตอง จังหวัดเชียงใหม่

200. *The Chiang Mai Chronicle,* p. 115.

CHAPTER 4
LAN NA UNDER BURMESE RULE (1558–1774)

1. สุเนตร ชุตินธรานนท์, *พม่ารบไทย* (กรุงเทพฯ: สำนักพิมพ์มติชน, 2537) หน้า 117.

2. นิธิ เอียวศรีวงศ์, *การเมืองไทยสมัยพระเจ้ากรุงธนบุรี* (กรุงเทพฯ: ศิลปวัฒนธรรม, 2529), หน้า 8.

3. *The Chiang Mai Chronicle,* p. 120-121.

4. *ประชุมพงศาวดาร* ภาคที่ 61, หน้า 177.

5. ดี.จี.อี. ฮอล์ล. *ประวัติศาสตร์เอเชียตะวันออกเฉียงใต้* เล่ม 1, หน้า 332.

6. *ประชุมพงศาวดาร* ภาคที่ 61, หน้า 177-178.

7. *Relationship with Burma* Part 1, p. 21.

8. หวญ. "ตำนานเมืองเชียงแสน," เลขที่ 9/ญ หน้า 7.

9. สรัสวดี อ๋องสกุล ปริวรรต, *พื้นเมืองน่าน* ฉบับวัดพระเกิด, หน้า 13.

10. *ราชวงศาพื้นเมืองเชียงใหม่* ภาคปริวรรต, ลำดับที่ 4 ภาควิชาสังคมวิทยาและมานุษยวิทยา คณะสังคมศาสตร์ มหาวิทยาลัยเชียงใหม่, สิงหาคม 2518, หน้า 38.

11. เรื่องเดียวกัน, หน้า 40.

12. เรื่องเดียวกัน

13. เรื่องเดียวกัน, หน้า 39-40.

14. ปริศนา แสงนาม "ความสัมพันธ์ระหว่างไทยและประเทศราชในหัวเมืองลานนาไทย สมัยรัตนโกสินทร์ตอนต้น," (วิทยานิพนธ์ปริญญามหาบัณฑิต ภาควิชาประวัติศาสตร์ บัณฑิตวิทยาลัย วิทยาลัยวิชาการศึกษา ประสานมิตร, 2516), หน้า 72.

15. *Relationship with Burma* Part 1, p. 18.

16. *The Chiang Mai Chronicle,* p. 124.

17. เรื่องเดียวกัน

18. ฮันส์ เพนธ์, *คำจารึกที่ฐานพระพุทธรูปในนครเชียงใหม่,* (กรุงเทพฯ: โรงพิมพ์สำนัก-นายกรัฐมนตรี 2519), หน้า 98-102

19. หวญ. "พงศาวดารเชียงใหม่ (เจ้ามังธาประทานเครื่องยศแก่ท้าวพระยา)," เลขที่ 1 มัดที่ 1 (16/กึ), หน้า 2.

20. ฮันส์ เพนธ์, *คำจารึกที่ฐานพระพุทธรูปในนครเชียงใหม่,* หน้า 5-7.

21. *ราชวงศาพื้นเมืองเชียงใหม่,* หน้า 38.

22. เรื่องเดียวกัน, หน้า 42.

23. เรื่องเดียวกัน, หน้า 38.

24. เรื่องเดียวกัน, หน้า 42.

25. เรื่องเดียวกัน

26. หม่อง ทิน อ่อง, *ประวัติศาสตร์พม่า,* แปลโดย เพ็ชรี สุมิตร, หน้า 76.

27. หวญ. "พงศาวดารเชียงใหม่ (เจ้ามังธาประทานเครื่องยศแก่ท้าวพระยา)," เลขที่ 1 มัดที่ 1 (16/กึ).

28. *Relationship with Burma* Part 1, p. 18.

29. *The Royal Order of Burma, A.D. 1598-1885,* Part 1, p. 4.

30. *The Royal Order of Burma, A.D. 1598-1885,* Part 1, p. 126.

31. *โคลงมังทรารบเชียงใหม่,* หน้า 17, 19. และดู *ประชุมพงศาวดาร* ภาคที่ 61, หน้า 180.

32. ดู *ประชุมศิลาจารึก* ภาค 3, จารึกหลักที่ 76 "ศิลาจารึกวัดเชียงมั่น," จังหวัดเชียงใหม่ จ.ศ. 943, คณะกรรมการจัดพิมพ์เอกสารทางประวัติศาสตร์ สำนักนายกรัฐมนตรี, 2508, หน้า 211-212. และดู "ศิลาจารึกวัดเกตการาม," ตำบลวัดเกต อำเภอเมือง จังหวัดเชียงใหม่, *วารสารศิลปากร* ปีที่ 16, (กันยายน 2515): 92-102.

33. ไกรศรี นิมมานเหมินท์ "ตราหลวงหลาบเงินของพระนางวิสุทธิเทวี," รวมบทความล้านนาคดีสัญจร: ตามรอยโคลงมังทรารบเชียงใหม่, ชมรมล้านนาคดี 2533, หน้า 18. (อัดสำเนา)

34. ฮันส์ เพนธ์, บรรณาธิการ, *ประวัติพระธาตุดอยตุง (*กรุงเทพฯ: มูลนิธิแม่ฟ้าหลวงและธนาคารไทยพาณิชย์, 2536) หน้า 123.

35. *หนังสือพื้นเมืองน่าน,* เอกสารลำดับที่ 9 ศูนย์วัฒนธรรมจังหวัดเชียงใหม่ วิทยาลัยครูเชียงใหม่, มกราคม 2528, หน้า 5-6. (อัดสำเนา)

36. พระครูชินวงศานุวัตร์ (สิงโต ชินว์โส) และหนานปวงคำ ตุ้ยเขียว *วัดปราสาทและบันทึกพระยาหลวงสามล้าน,* พระครูชินวงศานุวัตร์จัดพิมพ์, 2528, หน้า 12.

37. ฮันส์ เพนธ์, *คำจารึกที่ฐานพระพุทธรูปในนครเชียงใหม่,* คณะกรรมการจัดพิมพ์เอกสารทางประวัติศาสตร์ สำนักนายรัฐมนตรี 2519, หน้า 101.

38. ชร. 8 "จารึกฐานพระพุทธรูปพระเจ้าล้านทอง พ.ศ. 2269," *จารึกล้านนา* ภาค 1, เล่ม 1, "จารึกจังหวัดเชียงราย น่าน พะเยา แพร่," หน้า 20-21.

39. หม่อง ทิน อ่อง, *ประวัติศาสตร์พม่า,* แปลโดย เพ็ชรี สุมิตร, หน้า 76.

40. *Relationship With Burma* Part 1, p. 20.

41. เรื่องเดียวกัน. ตำนานพื้นเมืองเชียงใหม่กล่าวว่า ท้าวแม่กุได้เดินทางไปกับกองทัพพม่าเพื่อจัดการกับปัญหาการต่อต้านอำนาจพม่า เป็นเวลา 2 เดือน 29 วัน, ดูหน้า 79.

42. *Relationship with Burma* Part 1, p. 35.

43. หวญ. "พงศาวดารเชียงใหม่ (เจ้ามังธาประทานเครื่องยศแก่ท้าวพระยา)," เลขที่ 1 มัดที่ 1 (16/กึ), หน้า 4.

44. Than Tun, "Administration under King Thalun 1629-48," Essays on the History and Buddhism of Burma by Professor Than Tun, edited by Paul Strachan (Whiting Bay, Isle of Arran, Scotland: Kiscadale Publications, 1988), p. 118.

45. สิงฆะ วรรณสัย ถอดความ, *โคลงมังทรารบเชียงใหม่* (กรุงเทพฯ: โรงพิมพ์มิตรนราการพิมพ์, 2522) หน้า 16. กล่าวว่า พี่เลี้ยงชื่อโลกาสนับสนุนให้กินเมืองลำปางก่อน

46. คัมภีร์ใบลานเรื่อง "พื้นเมืองเชียงราย, เชียงแสน," วัดเมธังกราวาส ตำบลในเวียง อำเภอเมือง จังหวัดแพร่ รหัสไมโครฟิล์ม สถาบันวิจัยสังคม มหาวิทยาลัยเชียงใหม่ 81 088 05 082-082, หน้า 63.

47. เรื่องเดียวกัน, หน้า 75.

48. *The Chiang Mai Chronicle,* p. 130.

49. เรื่องเดียวกัน, หน้า 130.

50. *ประชุมพงศาวดาร* ภาคที่ 61, หน้า 183.

51 หม่อง ทิน อ่อง, *ประวัติศาสตร์พม่า,* แปลโดย เพ็ชรี สุมิตร, หน้า 93-94.

52. Than Tun, *Administration under King Thalun 1629-48*, pp. 120-121.

53. *The Royal Order of Burma, A.D. 1598-1885,* Part 1, pp. 85-127.

54. เรื่องเดียวกัน, หน้า 132-133.

55. สรัสวดี อ๋องสกุล, ปริวรรต, *พื้นเมืองเชียงราย,* หน้า 44.

56. หม่อง ทิน อ่อง, *ประวัติศาสตร์พม่า*, แปลโดย เพ็ชรี สุมิตร, หน้า 94-95.

57. *พระราชพงศาวดารกรุงศรีอยุธา* ฉบับพันจันทนุมาศ, (พระนคร: คลังวิทยา, 2507) หน้า 393-404.

58. หวญ. "ตำนานเมืองเชียงแสน" เลขที่ 9/ญ, หน้า 13-14.

59. เรื่องเดียวกัน หน้า 14.

60. "หนังสือพื้นนาเมืองน่าน," เอกสารลำดับที่ 9 ศูนย์วัฒนธรรมจังหวัดเชียงใหม่ วิทยาลัยครูเชียงใหม่ (มกราคม, 2528) หน้า 4. (อัดสำเนา)

61. หวญ. "ตำนานเมืองเชียงแสน," เลขที่ 9/ญ, หน้า 12.

62. *The Chiang Mai Chronicle,* p. 139

63. สรัสวดี อ๋องสกุล ปริวรรต, *พื้นเมืองน่าน ฉบับวัดพระเกิด,* หน้า 17-18.

64. สรัสวดี อ๋องสกุล ปริวรรต, *พื้นเมืองเชียงราย,* หน้า 43-44.

65. หวญ. "ตำนานเมืองเชียงแสน ฉบับวัดป่ารวก," เลขที่ 11/ง, หน้า 8-10.

66. เรื่องเดียวกัน, หน้า 10-11.

67. *The Chiang Mai Chronicle,* p. 136.

68. *ประชุมพงศาวดาร* ภาคที่ 61, หน้า 192.

69. สรัสวดี อ๋องสกุล, ปริวรรต, *พื้นเมืองเชียงราย,* หน้า 50.

70. หวญ. "ตำนานเมืองเชียงแสน" เลขที่ 9/ญ หน้า 12.

71. คัมภีร์ใบลานเรื่อง "พื้นเมืองเชียงราย, เชียงแสน," วัดเมธังกราวาส ตำบลในเวียง อำเภอเมือง จังหวัดแพร่ รหัสไมโครฟิล์ม สถาบันวิจัยสังคม มหาวิทยาลัยเชียงใหม่ 81 088 05 082-082, หน้า 25.

72. *The Royal Order of Burma,* Part 2, p. 66.

73. หนังสือพื้นนาเมืองน่าน, หน้า 3.

74. หวญ. "คำค่าวซอจดหมายเหตุการณ์สงครามอโยธิยา-ม่าน," เลขที่ 27 /ก ปี จ.ศ. 1047

75. เรื่องเดียวกัน

76. หวญ. "ตำนานเมืองเชียงแสน," เลขที่ 9/ญ, หน้า 12

77. เรื่องเดียวกัน, หน้า 19.

78. *The Chiang Mai Chronicle,* p. 138.

79. หวญ. "ตำนานเมืองเชียงแสน," เลขที่ 9/ญ, หน้า 19.

80. หวญ. "ตำนานเมืองเชียงแสน," ฉบับวัดป่ารวก เลขที่ 11/ง, หน้า 13.

81. สรัสวดี อ๋องสกุล, ปริวรรต, *จดหมายเหตุล้านนา: บันทึกเหตุการณ์ประวัติศาสตร์ พ.ศ. 2271-2397.*

82. *The Chiang Mai Chronicle,* p. 135.

83. หวญ. "ตำนานเมืองเชียงแสน," เลขที่ 9/ญ, หน้า 21

84. เรื่องเดียวกัน, หน้า 26.

85. เรื่องเดียวกัน, หน้า 90.

86. เรื่องเดียวกัน, หน้า 91.

87. หวญ. "ตำนานเมืองเชียงแสน," เลขที่ 9/ญ, หน้า 27.

88. หม่อง ทิน อ่อง, *ประวัติศาสตร์พม่า,* หน้า 116.

CHAPTER 5
A TRIBUTARY STATE OF THE SIAMESE KINGDOM (1774–1899)

1. ฮันส์ เพนธ์ อ่าน, "จารึกพระบรมธาตุจอมทอง," *สังคมและวัฒนธรรมลานนาไทย* มหาวิทยาลัยเชียงใหม่ (พิมพ์เนื่องในงานกฐินพระราชทาน วัดพระสิงห์วรมหาวิหาร 7 พฤศจิกายน, 2513), หน้า 161-163.

2. David K. Wyatt, Aroonrut Wichienkeeo, *The Chiang Mai Chronicle,* 2nd Ed. (Chiang Mai: Silkworm Books, 1998), p. 144-145.

3. เรื่องเดียวกัน

4. เรื่องเดียวกัน, หน้า 141.

5. สงวน โชติสุขรัตน์, ปริวรรต, *ตำนานเจ้าเจ็ดตน,* ฉบับ สิงฆะ วรรณสัย (เชียงใหม่: สงวนการพิมพ์, 2511), หน้า 20.

6. หวญ. "พงศาวดารเมืองเถิน," เลขที่ 7 มัดที่ 10

7. ฮันส์ เพนธ์ อ่าน, "จารึกพระบรมธาตุจอมทอง," *สังคมและวัฒนธรรมลานนาไทย,* มหาวิทยาลัยเชียงใหม่ (พิมพ์เนื่องในงานกฐินพระราชทานวัดพระสิงห์วรมหาวิหาร 7 พฤศจิกายน, 2513), หน้า 161-163.

8. พระราชพงศาวดารกรุงธนบุรีและจดหมายเหตุรายวันทัพสมัยกรุงธนบุรี ใน *ประชุมพงศาวดาร* เล่มที่ 40, ภาคที่ 65-66 (พระนคร: องค์การค้าคุรุสภา, 2512), หน้า 67.

9. เรื่องเดียวกัน, หน้า 69-70.

10. พระยาประชากิจกรจักร์, *พงศาวดารโยนก,* หน้า 450-451.

11. สรัสวดี อ๋องสกุล, ปริวรรต, *พื้นเมืองน่าน,* หน้า 19-23.

12. *The Chiang Mai Chronicle*, p. 162.

13. เรื่องเดียวกัน, หน้า 153.

14. เรื่องเดียวกัน, หน้า 135.

15. เรื่องเดียวกัน, หน้า 98.

16. ดู ไกรศรี นิมมานเหมินท์, "เก็บผักใส่ซ้า เก็บข้าใส่เมือง," ใน *ลานนาไทยคดี,* ประคอง นิมมานเหมินท์ และ ทรงศักดิ์ ปรางค์วัฒนากุล, บรรณาธิการ, (เชียงใหม่: สำนักพิมพ์ศูนย์

หนังสือเชียงใหม่, 2521), หน้า 48-62. และ ฟอลเกอร์ กราบ็อฟสกี้ "เก็บผักใส่ซ้า เก็บข้าใส่เมือง," *ศิลปวัฒนธรรม* (มกราคม 2538): 103-114.

17. ดู ฟอลเกอร์ กราบ็อฟสกี้, เรื่องเดียวกัน, หน้า 105.

18. *The Chiang Mai Chronicle,* p. 162.

19. เรื่องเดียวกัน, หน้า 192.

20. เรื่องเดียวกัน, หน้า 194.

21. ดูพับหนังสาเรื่อง "เอกสารประวัติศาสตร์ล้านนา," ไมโครฟิล์มสถาบันวิจัยสังคม มหาวิทยาลัยเชียงใหม่ หมายเลข 80 047 05 028-028 หน้า 22-23 ของวัดป่าสา ตำบลสันทราย อำเภอสารภี จังหวัดเชียงใหม่ (จำนวน 1 ผูกมี 24 หน้า)

22. เรื่องเดียวกัน, หน้าพับที่ 24.

23. *The Chiang Mai Chronicle,* p. 202.

24. เรื่องเดียวกัน, หน้า 171.

25. สัมภาษณ์ ถิ่น รัตนกนก, *คนบ้านฮ่อม,* 12 พฤศจิกายน 2535.

26. ดู ฟอลเกอร์ กราบ็อฟสกี้, "เก็บผักใส่ซ้า เก็บข้าใส่เมือง," หน้า 109.

27. สรัสวดี อ๋องสกุล, ปริวรรต, "รวมเรื่องเมืองเชียงใหม่: หลักฐานประวัติศาสตร์," *หลักฐานประวัติศาสตร์ล้านนาจากเอกสารคัมภีร์ใบลานและพับหนังสา,* หน้า 109.

28. เรื่องเดียวกัน, หน้า 121.

29. พระยาประชากิจกรจักร์, *พงศาวดารโยนก,* หน้า 454.

30. *The Chiang Mai Chronicle,* p. 203.

31. เรื่องเดียวกัน

32. เรื่องเดียวกัน, หน้า 204.

33. เรื่องเดียวกัน, หน้า 210.

34. Daniel McGilvary, "Half a Century among the Siamese and the Lao: An Autobiography," แปลโดย จิตราภรณ์ ตันรัตนกุล, หน้า 134, 217-218.

35. *หนังสือประวัติเจ้านครเชียงใหม่แลเจ้าเชียงใหม่* (เชียงใหม่: โรงพิมพ์บำรุงเจริญประเทศ บ้านฮ่อ นครเชียงใหม่), ไม่ปรากฏปีที่พิมพ์, หน้า 9.

36. หจช., ร.5 ม. 58 / 143 "ประวัติเจ้าอินทวโรรสสุริยวงษ์ เจ้าผู้ครองนครเชียงใหม่"

37. *The Chiang Mai Chronicle,* p. 201, 208-209.

38. เรื่องเดียวกัน, หน้า 208.

39. เรื่องเดียวกัน, หน้า 207-208.

40. พระยาประชากิจกรจักร์, *พงศาวดารโยนก,* หน้า 482.

41. *ตำนานพื้นเมืองเชียงใหม่,* หน้า 210.

42. พระยาประชากิจกรจักร์, *พงศาวดารโยนก,* หน้า 485.

43. เจ้าพระยาทิพากรวงศ์, *พระราชพงศาวดารกรุงรัตนโกสินทร์รัชกาลที่ 3* เล่ม 2 (พระนคร: องค์การค้าของคุรุสภา, 2504), หน้า 154.

44. "ประชุมพงศาวดาร ภาคที่ 3," ใน *ประชุมพงศาวดารฉบับหอสมุดแห่งชาติ* เล่ม 2, (พระนคร: ก้าวหน้า, 2507), หน้า 2.

45. เรื่องเดียวกัน, หน้า 4.

46. เรื่องเดียวกัน, หน้า 5.

47. หวญ. จดหมายเหตุ ร.4 จ.ศ. 1227 เลขที่ 13 คัดบอกเมืองตาก

48. หวญ. จดหมายเหตุ ร.4 จ.ศ. 1227 เลขที่ 15 คัดบอกเมืองเชียงใหม่

49. *ประชุมพงศาวดารฉบับหอสมุดแห่งชาติ* เล่ม 2, หน้า 307-308.

50. เรื่องเดียวกัน

51. หจช., ร.5 ม.58/191

52. คาร์ล บอค, *สมัยพระปิยมหาราช,* แปลโดย เสถียร พันธรังสี และ อัมพร จุลานนท์ (พระนคร: โรงพิมพ์เฟื่องอักษร, 2505), หน้า 307-308.

53. ดู สรัสวดี อ๋องสกุล, ปริวรรต, "อาณาจักรหลักคำ," *หลักฐานประวัติศาสตร์ล้านนาจากเอกสารคัมภีร์ใบลานและพับหนังสา*

54. เรื่องเดียวกัน, หน้า 87-91.

55. McGilvary, หน้า 71-76.

56. หจช. ร.5 ม. 58/193 "หนังสืออาญาเก็บเงินค่านา ออกอาญา," ณ วันเสาร์เดือน 3 ขึ้น 5 ค่ำ ปีวอก ฉศกศักราช 1246.

57. เรื่องเดียวกัน

58. หจช. ร.1 จ.ศ. 1164 เลขที่ 1 "ร่างพระบรมราชโองการตั้งเจ้าพระยาเชียงใหม่," จ.ศ. 1164

59. หวญ. ร.1 จ.ศ. 1164 เลขที่1 "ร่างพระบรมราชโองการตั้งเจ้าพระยาเชียงใหม่," จ.ศ. 1164

60. ปริศนา ศิรินาม, "ความสัมพันธ์ระหว่างไทยและประเทศราชในหัวเมืองล้านนาไทยตั้งแต่ พ.ศ. 1912 ถึง พ.ศ. 2101," (วิทยานิพนธ์ปริญญามหาบัณฑิต ภาควิชาประวัติศาสตร์ บัณฑิตวิทยาลัย วิทยาลัยการศึกษา ประสานมิตร, 2516), หน้า 126.

61. หลังจากตั้งตำแหน่งเจ้าเมืองเชียงราย พะเยา และงาว ได้โปรดเกล้าพระราชทานทินนามเจ้าเมืองเชียงรายคือ พระยารัตนเขต (ดูประวัติตั้งเมืองเชียงราย) เจ้าเมืองพะเยาคือ พระยาประเทศอุดรทิศ เมืองงาวคือ พระยาฤทธิภิญโญยศ ให้พะเยากับงาวขึ้นต่อเมืองลำปาง ดู หวญ. ร.3 จ.ศ. 1205 เลขที่ 21 "บัญชีเครื่องยศหัวเมืองต่างๆ" และหวญ., ร.3 จ.ศ.1209 เลขที่ 30 เรื่องพระยานครลำปางกับพระยาฤทธิภิญโญยศประพฤติการชั่วร้าย

62. หวญ., ร.3 จ.ศ. 1204 เลขที่ 15 สำเนาใบบอกเมืองเชียงใหม่ และ หวญ., ร.3 จ.ศ. 1210 เลขที่ 16 "ร่างสารตราถึงพระยาลำพูน เรื่องตั้งพระยาราชวงษ์เป็นที่พระยาอุปราชเมืองลำพูน"

63. ในสมัยรัชกาลที่ 4 นอกจากเจ้าขัน 5 ใบแล้ว มีหลักฐานว่าทรงพระราชทานสัญญาบัตรและเครื่องยศให้แก่พระยาสามล้าน และพระยาไชยสงคราม ดู หวญ., ร.4 เลขที่ 17 "ร่างศุภอักษรถึงเจ้านครเชียงใหม่," และ หวญ., ร.4 จ.ศ. 1222 เลขที่ 17 ร่างศุภอักษรถึงเจ้านครลำปาง"

64. หวญ., ร.3 ร.ศ. 1209 เลขที่ 13 "เรื่องสารตราถึงเจ้าเมืองเชียงใหม่"

65. หวญ., ร.3 ร.ศ. 1209 เลขที่ 17 "เรื่องสารตราถึงเจ้าเมืองเชียงใหม่ นครลำพูน นครลำปาง เรื่องตั้งพระยาอุปราช," และหวญ., ร.4 จ.ศ. 1222 เลขที่ 10 "ร่างพระบรมราโชวาท"

66. เจ้าพระยาทิพากรวงศ์, *พระราชพงศาวดารกรุงรัตนโกสินทร์รัชกาลที่ 1*, หน้า 140.

67. หวญ., ร.4 จ.ศ.1213 เลขที่ 107 "บัญชีเจ้าเมืองลาวพุงดำพุงขาวส่งเครื่องบรรณาการประจำปี"

68. ปริศนา ศิรินาม, เรื่องเดียวกัน, หน้า 105. (อ้างจาก หวญ., ร.3 จ.ศ. 1197 เลขที่ 5 "บัญชีรายวันเรื่องส่งไม้ขอนสักหัวเมืองต่างๆ เข้ามาถวาย")

69. หวญ., ร.4 จ.ศ. 1221 เลขที่ 196 "ร่างตราน้อยเจ้าพระยานิกรบดินทร์เรื่องเจ้าเมืองน่านของดส่งไม้ ฯลฯ"

70. หวญ., ร.3 จ.ศ. 1204 เลขที่ 13 "สารตราถึงเจ้าเมืองเชียงใหม่เรื่องตอบรับเครื่องยศของนายหนานมหาเทพ"

71. ปริศนา ศิรินาม, *ความสัมพันธ์ระหว่างไทย...*, หน้า 10. (อ้างจาก หวญ., ร.2 จ.ศ. 1171 เลขที่ 1 "ศุภอักษรถึงเจ้าประเทศราชฯ และเกณฑ์กระดาษเพลา ป่าน ใช้ในการพระบรมศพ ฯลฯ")

72. หวญ., ร.4 จ.ศ. 1218 เลขที่ 69 "ตราใหญ่ถึงนครลำปางให้จัดหาไม้ขอนสักพันต้น"

73. หวญ., ร.1 จ.ศ. 1164 เลขที่ 1 "ร่างพระบรมราชโองการเรื่องตั้งเจ้าพระยาเชียงใหม่ จ.ศ. 1164"

74. หวญ., ร.3 จ.ศ. 1209 เลขที่ 13 "สารตราเมืองเชียงใหม่ เรื่องตอบรับเครื่องยศของนายหนานมหาเทพ"

75. หจช. ร.5 "สารบาญสมุดพิเศษ" เล่ม 10, หน้า 233-234.

76. เรื่องเดียวกัน, หน้า 440-441.

77. เรื่องเดียวกัน

78. หวญ., ร.3 จ.ศ. 1209 เลขที่ 17 "สารตราถึงเจ้าเมืองเชียงใหม่ นครลำพูน นครลำปาง เรื่องตั้งพระยาอุปราช"

CHAPTER 6
BURMESE INVASIONS, SIAM'S EXPANSION OF POWER, AND THE CHIANG TUNG WARS

1. เจ้าพระยาทิพากรวงศ์, *พระราชพงศาวดารกรุงรัตนโกสินทร์* รัชกาลที่ 1, หน้า 113-114.

2. เรื่องเดียวกัน, หน้า 140.

3. หวญ. จดหมายเหตุรัชกาลที่ 1 จ.ศ. 1159 เลขที่ 2 "หนังสือเจ้าเมืองเมาะตะมะถึงเสนาบดีผู้ใหญ่ไทยให้ส่งพระยาเจ่ง พระยาทวายคืน," (อ้างใน ปริศนา ศิรินาม, "ความสัมพันธ์ระหว่างไทยและประเทศราชในหัวเมืองล้านนาไทยตั้งแต่ พ.ศ. 1912 ถึง พ.ศ. 2101," (วิทยานิพนธ์ปริญญามหาบัณฑิต ภาควิชาประวัติศาสตร์ บัณฑิตวิทยาลัย วิทยาลัยการศึกษา ประสานมิตร, 2516), หน้า 161).

4. *ตำนานพื้นเมืองเชียงใหม่*, หน้า 110.

5. เจ้าพระยาทิพากรวงศ์, *พระราชพงศาวดารกรุงรัตนโกสินทร์* รัชกาลที่ 1

6. เรื่องเดียวกัน, หน้า 277.

7. การเจรจาความเมืองระหว่างไทยกับพม่าสมัยรัตนโกสินทร์ มี 7 ครั้ง ครั้งแรก พ.ศ. 2327

ครั้งที่ 2 พ.ศ. 2336 ครั้งที่ 3 พ.ศ. 2345 ครั้งที่ 4 พ.ศ. 2349 ครั้งที่ 5 พ.ศ. 2351 ครั้งที่ 6 สมัยรัชกาลที่ 2 พ.ศ. 2356 ครั้งที่ 7 สมัยรัชกาลที่ 4 พ.ศ. 2399 ในการเจรจาไทยกับพม่าขอเป็นไมตรีก่อนทุกครั้ง บางครั้งมีหนังสือต่างโต้ตอบกัน บางครั้งไทยขับไล่ทูตโดยไม่ยอมเจรจา แต่ทุกครั้งไม่ประสบผลสำเร็จ เพราะความเป็นศัตรูกันมาช้านานทำให้ฝ่ายไทยระแวงพม่าไม่จริงใจ ซึ่งก็มักปรากฏว่าหลังจากที่เจรจาความเมือง พม่าก็ยกทัพมา จนเป็นลักษณะทำสงครามสลับกับเจรจาเป็นไมตรีกัน ดู *ประชุมพงศาวดารฉบับหอสมุดแห่งชาติ* เล่ม 6, ภาคที่ 21 (พระนคร: สำนักพิมพ์ก้าวหน้า, 2507), หน้า 129-210.

8. หวญ., ร.1 จ.ศ. 1170 เลขที่ 1 "สำเนาแปลหนังสือเสนาบดีเมืองอังวะถึงอัครมหาเสนาบดีไทย เรื่อง พระเจ้าเมืองเชียงใหม่ส่งศุภอักษรกับเครื่องราชบรรณาการไปถวายพระเจ้าอังวะ"

9. *ประชุมพงศาวดารฉบับหอสมุดแห่งชาติ* เล่ม 6, ภาคที่ 21, หน้า 151-159.

10. ในช่วงที่ไทยขยายอำนาจ นับเป็นโอกาสดีของไทยเพราะพม่าอยู่ในระหว่างทำสงครามกับอังกฤษ ซึ่งสงครามมี 3 ครั้ง ครั้งแรก พ.ศ. 2369 อังกฤษชนะพม่า ยึดแคว้นยะไข่ ตะนาวศรี และแคว้นอัสสัม ครั้งที่ 2 พ.ศ. 2395-2398 อังกฤษได้เมืองหงสาวดีและดินแดนพม่าตอนใต้ ครั้งที่ 3 พ.ศ. 2426 อังกฤษครอบครองพม่าทั้งประเทศ

11. *The Chiang Mai Chronicle,* p. 179.

12. เรื่องเดียวกัน, หน้า 194.

13. หวญ., ร.3 จ.ศ. 1205 เลขที่ 21 "บัญชีเครื่องยศเมืองต่างๆ"

14. หวญ., จดหมายเหตุรัชกาลที่ 3 จ.ศ. 1206 เลขที่ 43 "สารตราเจ้าพระยาจักรีถึงเมืองเชียงใหม่ เรื่องจัดการตั้งเมืองเชียงแสนและให้คอยระวังกองทัพพม่า"

15. เจ้าพระยาทิพากรวงศ์, *พระราชพงศาวดารกรุงรัตนโกสินทร์* รัชกาลที่ 3 เล่ม 2 (พระนคร: องค์การค้าคุรุสภา 2505), หน้า 140-143.

16. เรื่องเดียวกัน, หน้า 148.

17. เจ้าพระยาทิพากรวงศ์, *พระราชพงศาวดารกรุงรัตนโกสินทร์* รัชกาลที่ 4 (พระนคร: องค์การค้าคุรุสภา, 2504), หน้า 98-99.

18. หวญ., จดหมายเหตุ ร. 4 จ.ศ. 1214 เลขที่ 76 (ก) "พระบรมราชโองการถึงกรมหลวงวงศาธิราชสนิท เรื่องราชการทัพเมืองเชียงตุง," อ้างใน บัณฑิต อินทรชัยศรี, "พระบรมราโชบายด้านการปกครองที่เกี่ยวกับการสร้างความมั่นคงภายในพระราชอาณาจักร ของพระบาทสมเด็จพระจอมเกล้าเจ้าอยู่หัว (พ.ศ. 2394-2411)," (วิทยานิพนธ์ปริญญามหาบัณฑิต ภาควิชาประวัติศาสตร์ บัณฑิตวิทยาลัย มหาวิทยาลัยศรีนครินทรวิโรฒ ประสานมิตร, 2521), หน้า 156.

19. เจ้าพระยาทิพากรวงศ์, *พระราชพงศาวดารกรุงรัตนโกสินทร์* รัชกาลที่ 4, เล่ม 1, หน้า 114.

20. บัณฑิต อินทรชัยศรี, "พระบรมราโชบายด้านการปกครอง...," หน้า 159-160.

21. หวญ., ร. 4 จ.ศ. 1215 เลขที่ 7 "พระราชดำรัสรัชกาลที่ 4 ถึงกรมหลวงวงศาธิราชสนิท เรื่องเมืองเชียงตุง"

22. หวญ. ร. 4 จ.ศ. 1216 เลขที่ 54 "ร่างศุภอักษรถึงนครเชียงใหม่"

23. หวญ., ร. 4 จ.ศ. 1216 เลขที่ 115 "จดหมายเหตุพระเจ้าน้องยาเธอกรมหลวงวงศาธิราชสนิท เรื่องเมืองเชียงตุง"

24. เจ้าพระยาทิพากรวงศ์, *พระราชพงศาวดารกรุงรัตนโกสินทร์* รัชกาลที่ 4, เล่ม 1, หน้า 114-115.

25. เรื่องเดียวกัน, หน้า 121-122.

26. หวญ., ร. 4 จ.ศ. 1216 เลขที่ 55 “ร่างสารตราเมืองเชียงใหม่”

27. หวญ., ร. 4 จ.ศ. 1216 เลขที่ 70 “ร่างสารตราถึงพระยาสีหราชฤทธิไกร”

28. เรื่องเดียวกัน

29. สรัสวดี ประยูรเสถียร “การปฏิรูปการปกครองมณฑลพายัพ (พ.ศ. 2436-2476),” (วิทยานิพนธ์ปริญญาการศึกษามหาบัณฑิต มหาวิทยาลัยศรีนครินทรวิโรฒ ประสานมิตร, 2523), หน้า 87-88.

30. ดู เจ้าทิพวรรณ ณ เชียงตุง, *อนุสรณ์พระราชทานเพลิงศพ เจ้าทิพวรรณ ณ เชียงตุง* (27 มกราคม, 2533), หน้า 204.

CHAPTER 7
THE IMPACT OF WESTERN IMPERIALISM

1. เอกสารการสอนชุดวิชา *ประวัติศาสตร์ไทย,* สาขาวิชาประวัติศาสตร์ มหาวิทยาลัยสุโขทัยธรรมาธิราช หน่วยที่ 1-8, พิมพ์ครั้งที่ 2, 2534, หน้า 389.

2. เจ้าพระยาทิพากรวงศ์, *พระราชพงศาวดารกรุงรัตนโกสินทร์* รัชกาลที่ 3 เล่ม 1, หน้า 197

3. หวญ., ร.3 จ.ศ. 1200 เลขที่ 19/2 “ร่างตราเจ้าพระยาจักรีถึงพระยาเชียงใหม่ เรื่องให้ชำระเงินที่ลูกค้าอังกฤษว่ายังติดอยู่กับราษฎร”

4. หวญ., ร.3 จ.ศ. 1204 เลขที่ 14 “ร่างตราเจ้าพระยาจักรีถึงพระยาเชียงใหม่ เรื่องบอกข่าวเมืองอังวะรบกับอังกฤษ”

5. A.C. Pointon, *The Bombay Burmah Trading Corporation Ltd., 1863-1963* (Southampton: The Millbrook Press, 1964) หน้า 34. อ้างใน พรพรรณ จงวัฒนา, เรื่องเดียวกัน, หน้า 44.

6. หจช., ร.5 ม. 16 /10 “รายงานพระองค์เพ็ญฯ เสด็จตรวจการป่าไม้ ลงวันที่... พฤษภาคม ร.ศ. 112”

7. เรื่องเดียวกัน

8. หจช., ร.5 ม.58/88 “รายงานกรมหมื่นพิชิตปรีชากรเรื่องจัดราชการเชียงใหม่ลำพูน และ*ลำปาง* ลงวันที่... พฤษภาคม ร.ศ. 103”

9. 1 รูปี (แถบ) ขณะนั้นมีค่าประมาณ 80 สตางค์

10. กระทรวงเกษตร, *ประวัติกรมป่าไม้ในรอบ 72 ปี,* (พิมพ์เป็นอนุสรณ์ในงานพระราชทานเพลิงศพ พระยาดรุพันธุ์พิทักษ 30 ธันวาคม, 2511), หน้า 2.

11. หวญ., ร.4 จ.ศ. 1216 เลขที่ 153 “คำฟ้องและคำให้การเรื่องเจ้าราชบุตรเมืองเชียงใหม่ริบไม้สักมองสวยนิจ”

12. พรพรรณ จงวัฒนา, "การพิพาทระหว่างเจ้าเมืองเชียงใหม่กับคนบังคับในอังกฤษ อันเป็นเหตุให้รัฐบาลสยามจัดการปกครองมณฑลภาพัย (พ.ศ. 2401-2445)," (วิทยานิพนธ์ปริญญามหาบัณฑิต ภาควิชาประวัติศาสตร์ มหาวิทยาลัยศรีนครินทรวิโรฒ ประสานมิตร), หน้า 62-68.

13. สงวน โชติสุขรัตน์, *คนดีเมืองเหนือ* (นครหลวงกรุงเทพธนบุรี: สำนักพิมพ์โอเดียนสโตร์, 2515), หน้า 89.

14. สมเด็จกรมพระยาดำรงราชานุภาพ และพระยาราชเสนา, *เทศาภิบาล,* หน้า 3.

15. หจช., ร.5 ต. 40/3 ปึกที่ 2 "รายงานหลวงประชาคดีกิจ เรื่องภูมิประเทศเขตแดนฝ่ายตะวันตกเฉียงเหนือนครเชียงใหม่," สำเนาที่ 6229 ลงวันที่ 11 สิงหาคม ร.ศ. 109.

16. นคร พันธุ์ณรงค์, "การเจรจาและข้อตกลงระหว่างรัฐบาลสยามกับรัฐบาลอังกฤษเกี่ยวกับหัวเมืองชายแดนลานนาไทยพม่า สมัยพระบาทสมเด็จพระจุลจอมเกล้าเจ้าอยู่หัว ระยะ พ.ศ. 2428-2438," (วิทยานิพนธ์ปริญญาการศึกษามหาบัณฑิต วิทยาลัยวิชาการศึกษา ประสานมิตร, 2516), หน้า 22. (อ้างจาก กองบรรณสาร กระทรวงการต่างประเทศ แฟ้มที่ 8.2 ตอนที่ 6 "รายงานหลวงวิชิตสรศาสตร์ หลวงรอนอริราช กราบทูลเรื่องเมืองแจะ")

17. โปรดดู ธงชัย วินิจจะกูล, "ประวัติศาสตร์การสร้าง 'ตัวตน'," *อยู่เมืองไทย,* รวมบทความทางสังคมการเมือง เพื่อเป็นเกียรติแด่ศาสตราจารย์เสน่ห์ จามริก ในโอกาสครบรอบ 60 ปี สมบัติ จันทรวงศ์ ชัยวัฒน์ สถาอานันท์, บรรณาธิการ (กรุงเทพฯ: สำนักพิมพ์มหาวิทยาลัยธรรมศาสตร์, 2530) หน้า 148-157.

18. หจช., ร.5 ต. 40/3 ปึกที่ 2 "รายงานหลวงประชาคดีกิจ เรื่องภูมิประเทศเขตแดนฝ่ายตะวันตกเฉียงเหนือนครเชียงใหม่," สำเนาที่ 6229 ลงวันที่ 11 สิงหาคม ร.ศ. 109.

19. หจช., ร.5 สารบาญสมุดพิเศษ เล่ม 6, หน้า 420.

20. หจช., ร.5 ต. 40/3 "พระราชหัตถเลขารัชกาลที่ 5 ถึงกรมหมื่นดำรงราชานุภาพ," ลงวันที่ 14 กันยายน ร.ศ. 111.

21. นคร พันธุ์ณรงค์, "การเจรจาและข้อตกลง...," หน้า 134.

22. เรื่องเดียวกัน, หน้า 141.

23. หจช., ร.5 ม 40/5 "สารตราเจ้าพระยาจักรีฯ ถึงพระยาไกรโกษา," ลงวันที่ 27 ตุลาคม 2435

24. สรัสวดี อ๋องสกุล ปริวรรต "อาณาจักรหลักคำ," *หลักฐานประวัติศาสตร์ล้านนา จากเอกสารคัมภีร์ใบลานและพับหนังสา,* หน้า 91-93.

25. หจช., ร.5 ฝ. 18.2/5 "คำแปลร่างหนังสือสัญญาครั้งที่ 3 นายวิเลร์ถึงกรมหลวงเทวะวงษ์วโรปการ," ลงวันที่ 2 กันยายน ร.ศ. 112.

26. หจช., ร.5 กต. 40.11/8 "กรมหลวงดำรงราชุนุภาพถึงกรมหลวงเทวะวงษ์วโรปการ สำเนาที่ 6592 ที่ 551/15590," ลงวันที่ 4 สิงหาคม ร.ศ. 114.

27. หจช., ร.5 ฝ.20/3 "กรมหลวงดำรงราชานุภาพกราบบังคมทูลรัชกาลที่ 5," ที่ 80/14755 ลงวันที่ 27 กรกฎาคม ร.ศ. 114.

28. หจช., ร.5 ฝ.20/3 "ข้าหลวงเมืองน่านถึงข้าหลวงใหญ่มณฑลลาวเฉียง," สำเนาที่ 89/804 ลงวันที่ 1 กรกฎาคม ร.ศ. 117.

29. หจช., ร.5 กต. 40.11/15 "กรมหลวงดำรงราชานุภาพถึงกรมหลวงเทวะวงษ์วโรปการ," สำเนาที่ 1326 ที่ 10/3473 ลงวันที่ 30 เมษายน ร.ศ. 115.

30. หจช., ร.5 ฝ.20/4 "ข้าหลวงนครน่านกราบทูลกรมหลวงดำรงราชานุภาพ," ที่ 1/32 ลงวันที่ 11 เมษายน ร.ศ. 121.

31. หจช., ร.5 ฝ.20/3 "กรมหลวงดำรงราชนุภาพกราบบังคมทูลรัชกาลที่ 5," ที่ 80/14755 ลงวันที่ 27 กรกฎาคม ร.ศ. 114.

32. หจช., ร.5 กต.40.11/3 "กรมหลวงเทวะวงษ์วโรปการถึงพระยาสุริยานุวัตร," ที่ 64/2540 ลงวันที่ 12 สิงหาคม ร.ศ. 116.

33. หจช., ร.5 ฝ.20/3 "กรมหลวงดำรงราชานุภาพถึงกรมหมื่นสมมตอมรพันธ์," ที่ 415/12367 ลงวันที่ 16 กรกฎาคม ร.ศ. 115.

34. หจช., ร.5 ฝ.20/3 "พระราชกระแสรับสั่งรัชกาลที่ 5 ทรงตอบรับบอกกรมหลวงดำรงราชานุภาพ," ลงวันที่ 20 มกราคม ร.ศ. 120.

35. หจช., ร.5 ฝ.20/3 "กรมหลวงดำรงราชานุภาพกราบบังคมทูลรัชกาลที่ 5," ที่ 680/115591 ลงวันที่ 4 สิงหาคม ร.ศ. 114.

36. กองบรรณสาร กระทรวงการต่างประเทศ แฟ้มที่ 2.7 แผนกสนธิสัญญาระหว่างสยาม-ฝรั่งเศส ปี ร.ศ. 122

CHAPTER 8
UNIFICATION WITH BANGKOK UNDER THE ABSOLUTE MONARCHY

1. โปรดดู นิธิ เอียวศรีวงศ์, *ปากไก่และใบเรือ ความเรียงว่าด้วยวรรณกรรมและประวัติศาสตร์ต้นรัตนโกสินทร์,* (กรุงเทพฯ: อมรินทร์การพิมพ์, 2527), หน้า 422.

2. สุเทพ สุนทรเภสัช "จากบรรณาการสู่ศูนย์รวมอำนาจ: วิเคราะห์การเปลี่ยนแปลงทางสังคมและอุดมการณ์ในยุครัตนโกสินทร์ (พ.ศ. 2325-2475)" *สังคมศาสตร์* ปีที่ 6, ฉบับที่ 1 (เมษายน-กันยายน 2525), หน้า 140-142.

3. นิธิ เอียวศรีวงศ์, *ปากไก่และใบเรือ,* หน้า 213.

4. เรื่องเดียวกัน, หน้า 369.

5. ดูรายละเอียดสนธิสัญญาเชียงใหม่ใน สรัสวดี ประยูรเสถียร "การปฏิรูปการปกครองมณฑลพายัพ (2436-2476)," (วิทยานิพนธ์การศึกษาปริญญามหาบัณฑิต บัณฑิตวิทยาลัย มหาวิทยาลัยศรีนครินทรวิโรฒ ประสานมิตร, 2523), หน้า 332-337.

6. หจช., ร.5 บ.1.2/5 รัชกาลที่ 5 "ทูลสมเด็จพระเจ้าบรมวงษ์เธอ เจ้าฟ้ามหามาลาบำราบปรปักษ์" ร. ที่ 284/44.

7. พระยาประชากิจกรจักร์, *พงศาวดารโยนก,* หน้า 508.

8. หจช., ร.5 บ.1.1ก/8 "รัชกาลที่ 5 ถึงพระยาราชสัมภาราก," ลงเดือน 8 จ.ศ. 1245

9. "พระราชบัญญัติสำหรับข้าหลวงชำระความหัวเมือง," ราชกิจจานุเบกษา เล่ม 1, ลงวันอาทิตย์ เดือน 12 แรม 6 ค่ำ จ.ศ. 1236, หน้า 274-276. และ หจช., ร. 5 "ข้อบังคับให้อำนาจกับข้าหลวงเมืองเชียงใหม่ในความที่เกี่ยวข้องกับคนในบังคับอังกฤษ," *สารบาญสมุดพิเศษ* เล่ม 10, หน้า 194-195.

10. แถมสุข นุ่มนนท์ "อิทธิพลทางการเมืองและเศรษฐกิจของอังกฤษในเชียงใหม่" ใน รายงานสัมมนาประวัติศาสตร์และโบราณคดี, มหาวิทยาลัยเชียงใหม่ คณะมนุษยศาสตร์ 20-23 ตุลาคม 2510, หน้า 141.

11. หจช., ร.5 "สารบาญสมุดพิเศษ" เล่ม 10, หน้า 79.

12. เรื่องเดียวกัน

13. รายละเอียดเรื่องนี้ดู สรัสวดี อ๋องสกุล, "การปฏิรูปการศึกษาในล้านนา: การสร้างเอกภาพแห่งชาติ," *ศึกษาศาสตร์สาร* ปีที่ 10, ฉบับที่ 2-4 (ตุลาคม 2524, กันยายน 2525), หน้า 29-48.

14. หจช., ร.5. บ.1ก/7 "พระบาทสมเด็จพระจุลจอมเกล้าเจ้าอยู่หัวถึงสมเด็จพระเจ้าบรมวงษ์เธอ เจ้าฟ้ามหามาลาบำราบปรปักษ์" ที่ ร. 468/45 ลงเดือน 2 จ.ศ. 1245 (มกราคม พ.ศ. 2426)

15. หจช., ร.5 ม 58/88 "กรมหมื่นพิชิตปรีชากรกราบบังคมทูลรัชกาลที่ 5," ลงวันที่ 6ฯ$_{1}$8 ค่ำ จ.ศ. 1246.

16. กองบรรณสาร กระทรวงการต่างประเทศ หมวดจดหมายเหตุ เล่ม 2 ทูตลอนดอน จ.ศ. 1246 ม.ป.ป.

17. หจช., ร.5 ต.40/3 "หนังสือประกาศพระยาสัมภารากรข้าหลวง," ปี จ.ศ. 1246, ม.ป.ป.

18. หชจ., ร.5 ม.2.12 ก/17 เลขที่ 88 "หนังสือพระศรีธรรมสาสน์ถึงสมุหนายก," ม.ป.ป.

19. หจช., ร.5 ม.58/88 "รายงานกรมหมื่นพิชิตปรีชากร เรื่องจัดราชการเชียงใหม่ ลำพูน และลำปาง สำเนาหนังสือถึงกรมหมื่นเทวะวงษ์," ม.ป.ป.

20. กองบรรณสาร กระทรวงการต่างประเทศ หมวดจดหมายเหตุหมู่อังกฤษ เล่ม 2 ทูตลอนดอน ปี 1246 "หนังสือกราบทูลในกรมหมื่นนเรศวรฤทธิ์," ลงวันที่ 20 ตุลาคม พ.ศ. 2427.

21. หจช., ร.5 ม.58/89 "หนังสือนายแย้มมหาดเล็กผู้ช่วยราชการหกตำแหน่งเมืองนครเชียงใหม่ถึงพระยาเพชรพิไชย ข้าหลวงใหญ่รักษาการหัวเมือง ณ เมืองนครเชียงใหม่," ลงวันที่ 12 กรกฎาคม พ.ศ. 2431 และ หจช., ร.5 บ.10/35 "แบบตั้งตำแหน่งของกรมหลวงพิชิตปรีชากร".

22. หจช., ร.5 ม. 99/3 "รายงานหลวงอนุรักษ์ภูเบศกราบทูลเจ้าฟ้ามหามาลา กรมพระบำราบปรปักษ์" ลงวันที่ 6ฯ^{1}3 ค่ำ ปีวอก จ.ศ. 1246 (16 มกราคม 2427).

23. หจช., ร.5 ม.58/193 "พิกัดภาษีอากรมณฑลพายัพ," (ร.ศ. 103-104).

24. ชมัยโฉม สุนทรสวัสดิ์ *"การศึกษาเชิงประวัติศาสตร์...,"* หน้า 11.

25. เฉลิม ศิริวรรณ, *นโยบายการป่าไม้และประวัติกรมป่าไม้ของประเทศไทย,* หน้า 74-75.

26. หจช., ร.5 ม.58/88 "กรมหมื่นพิชิตปรีชากรกราบบังคมทูลรัชกาลที่ 5 เรื่องจัดราชการเชียงใหม่ ลำพูน ลำปาง," ลงวันที่ 4ฯ$_{5}$6 ค่ำ ปี 1246 (14 พฤษภาคม พ.ศ. 2427)

27. ตำแหน่งข้าหลวงห้าหัวเมืองคือ ข้าหลวงที่ดูแลในเขตเมืองเชียงใหม่ ลำพูน ลำปาง แพร่ น่าน ซึ่งแต่เดิมคือตำแหน่งข้าหลวงสามหัวเมืองคือ เชียงใหม่ ลำพูน ลำปาง ข้าหลวงสามหัวเมืองปฏิบัติหน้าที่ตามสนธิสัญญาเชียงใหม่ พ.ศ. 2416 ซึ่งครอบคลุมพื้นที่สามเมืองดังกล่าว แต่ต่อมาตามสนธิสัญญาเชียงใหม่ ฉบับที่ 2 พ.ศ. 2426 ได้ขยายขอบเขตออกไปครอบคลุมพื้นที่ด้านล้านนาตะวันออก โดยรวมเมืองแพร่ เมืองน่าน ด้วย ตำแหน่งข้าหลวงจึงขยายขอบเขตไปด้วย จึงเรียกว่า "ข้าหลวงห้าหัวเมือง"

28. สรัสวดี ประยูรเสถียร, *"การปฏิรูปมณฑลพายัพ...,"* หน้า 99.

29. หจช., ร.5 มท. จ.ศ. 1247-1248, เล่ม 31, หน้า 308.

30. หจช., ร.5 ม.58/89 "พระเจ้าอินทวิชยานนท์กราบทูลราชการเมืองเชียงใหม่," ลงวันที่ 3ฯ^{9}10 ค่ำ ปีชวด จ.ศ. 1250 (11 กันยายน 2431).

31. หจช., ร.5 ม.58/93 "เจ้าพระยารัตนบดินทร์กราบบังคมทูลรัชกาลที่ 5," ลงวันที่ 3 เมษายน ร.ศ. 108-24 มิถุนายน ร.ศ. 108.

32. หจช., ร.5 มท. จ.ศ. 1250, เล่ม 36, หน้า 194-198.

33. ชูสิทธิ์ ชูชาติ "กบฏพญาผาบ (ปราบสงคราม): กบฏชาวนาในภาคเหนือ," *วารสารสังคมศาสตร์,* 2 (ตุลาคม 2522-มีนาคม 2523) ชูสิทธิ์เน้นปัญหาเศรษฐกิจและพยายามชี้ว่าพญาผาบ (ปราบสงครามเป็นชาวนาธรรมดา ไม่มีตำแหน่งทางราชการเลย และวัลลภา รุ่งศิริแสงรัตน์, "กบฏไทยเขินเมืองเชียงใหม่ปี พ.ศ. 2432," *แถลงงานประวัติศาสตร์ เอกสารโบราณคดี* 1 (มกราคม-มิถุนายน 2523), หน้า 5-71. วัลลภาตีความในแนวทางปัญหาการเมืองระหว่างประเทศ โดยเน้นว่าอังกฤษมีส่วนรู้เห็นเป็นใจด้วยกับการช่วยเหลือพระยาปราบสงคราม เพราะเจ้าเมืองเชียงตุงและอังกฤษต้องการขยายอิทธิพลทางการเมืองในล้านนา

34. ในปัจจุบัน 3 แขวงดังกล่าวเป็นส่วนหนึ่งของอำเภอสันทราย อำเภอดอยสะเก็ด และอำเภอสันกำแพง จากการสำรวจมีบริเวณกว้างขวางเทียบได้กับอำเภอหนึ่ง

35. หจช., ร.5 ม.58/1 พระยาพลเทพกราบบังคมทูลรัชกาลที่ 5 ลงวันที่ 20 มีนาคม ร.ศ. 108.

36. เรื่องเดียวกัน

37. สัมภาษณ์ ลุงหนาน นันตา, อายุ 51 ปี บ้านสันทรายหลวง อำเภอสันทราย จังหวัดเชียงใหม่, 15 พฤศจิกายน 2523.

38. หจช., ร.5 ม.58/98 "พระยามหาเทพกราบเรียน ฯพณฯ สมุหนายก," ที่ 23/108 ลงวันที่ 19 มกราคม ร.ศ. 108.

39. เรื่องเดียวกัน

40. หจช., ร.5 ต40/3 "รายงานหลวงประชาคดีกิจกราบบังคมทูลพระองค์เจ้าโสณบัณฑิตย์ เรื่องปราบกบฏพระยาปราบสงคราม," ลงวันที่ 28 มีนาคม ร.ศ. 108.

41. หจช., ร.5 ม.58/98 "พระยามหาเทพกราบเรียน ฯพณฯ สมุหนายก," ที่ 23/108 ลงวันที่ 19 มกราคม ร.ศ. 108.

42. ศึกษารายละเอียดใน สรัสวดี อ๋องสกุล, "กบฏประยาปราบสงครามแม่ทัพเมืองเชียงใหม่ พ.ศ. 2432" ใน *ความเชื่อพระศรีอาริย์และกบฏผู้มีบุญในสังคมไทย,* พรเพ็ญ ฮั่นตระกูล อัจฉราพร กมุทพิสมัย, บรรณาธิการ (กรุงเทพฯ: สำนักพิมพ์สร้างสรรค์, 2527), หน้า 123-147.

43. หจช., ร.5 บ.1.1ก/7 "พระราชหัตถเลขารัชกาลที่ 5 ถึงพระเจ้าบรมวงศ์เธอกรมพระบำราบปรปักษ์"

44. หจช., ร.5 ม.58/33 "พระยาศรีสหเทพกราบทูลกรมหลวงดำรงราชานุภาพ," ลับที่ 10/1352 ลงวันที่ 2 เมษายน ร.ศ. 119.

45. หจช., ร.5 ม.58/109 "พระยาศรีสหเทพกราบทูลกรมหมื่นสมมตอมรพันธ์," ที่ 43/3631 ลงวันที่ 8 กันยายน ร.ศ. 111.

46. หจช., ร.5. ม.58/177 "กรมหลวงดำรงราชานุภาพถึงพระยาทรงสุรเดช," ตราลับที่ 63 ลงวันที่ 7 กุมภาพันธ์ ร.ศ. 111.

47. หจช., ร.5 ม.58/53 "กรมหลวงดำรงราชานุภาพกราบทูลกรมหมื่นสมมตอมรพันธ์," ลงวันที่ 30 เมษายน ร.ศ. 114.

48. หจช., ร.5 ม.58/171 "ภาษีอากรและเรื่องตั้งตำแหน่งเมืองแพร่," 22 มิถุนายน-7 ตุลาคม ร.ศ. 115.

49. หจช., ร.5 ม.58/63 "เรื่องนักเรียนฝึกหัดราชการมณฑลลาวเฉียง," ลงวันที่ 17 ตุลาคม ร.ศ. 115.

50. หจช., ร.5 ย.11/49 "เรื่องนายน้อยหมิวกล่าวโทษต่อศาลเมืองเชียงใหม่," ลงวันที่ 16 กุมภาพันธ์ ร.ศ. 116.

51. หจช., ร.5 ม.58/37 "พระยาทรงสุรเดชกราบทูลกรมหลวงดำรงราชานุภาพ," ที่ 27/503 ลงวันที่ 18 เมษายน ร.ศ. 114.

52. หจช., ร.5 ม.58/40 "เรื่องจัดระเบียบเก็บเงินค่าราชการแลผลประโยชน์ในมณฑลพายัพ," ลงวันที่ 5 สิงหาคม ร.ศ. 115.

53. หจช., ร.5 ค.14.4/2 "กรมหลวงเทวะวงษ์วโรปการกราบบังคมทูลรัชกาลที่ 5," ที่ 40/3534 ลงวันที่ 23 พฤษภาคม ร.ศ. 111.

54. หจช., ร.5 ม.58/59 "เรื่องภาษีต่างๆ ทางลาวเฉียง," ลงวันที่ 11 พฤษภาคม ร.ศ. 112.

55. หจช., ร.5 ค.14.2ก/12 "พระยาทรงสรุเดชกราบทูลกรมหลวงดำรงราชานุภาพ," ลงวันที่ 10 ธันวาคม ร.ศ. 114.

56. ดูรายละเอียดใน สรัสวดี ประยูรเสถียร "การปฏิรูปมณฑลพายัพ...," หน้า 145-152.

57. ชมัยโฉม สุนทรสวัสดิ์, "การศึกษาเชิงประวัติศาสตร์เกี่ยวกับกิจการป่าไม้ทางเหนือของไทยตั้งแต่ พ.ศ. 2439 ถึง พ.ศ. 2475," (วิทยานิพนธ์ปริญญาอักษรศาสตรบัณฑิต ภาควิชาประวัติศาสตร์ บัณฑิตวิทยาลัย จุฬาลงกรณ์มหาวิทยาลัย, 2521), หน้า 103-104.

58. หจช., ร.5 ม.58/33 "กรมหลวงดำรงราชานุภาพกราบทูลกรมหมื่นสมมตอมรพันธ์," ที่ 584/8225 ลงวันที่ 26 มีนาคม ร.ศ. 118.

59. ปราณี ศิริธร, "คุ้มเจ้าเชียงใหม่," เอกสารประกอบการสัมมนาเรื่อง แหล่งท่องเที่ยวทางประวัติศาสตร์ในจังหวัดเชียงใหม่ 17-20 มิถุนายน, 2530, ณ สหวิทยาลัยล้านนา วิทยาลัยครูเชียงใหม่.

60. หจช., ร.5 ม.58/42 "พระยาศรีสหเทพกราบทูลกรมหลวงดำรงราชานุภาพ," ที่ 583/8224 ลงวันที่ 26 มีนาคม ร.ศ. 118.

61. หจช., ร.5 ม.58/45 "ยกเว้นเก็บเงินค่าราชการในมณฑลพายัพ," ลงวันที่ 3 พฤษภาคม ร.ศ.120 และ วันที่ 24 ธันวาคม ร.ศ. 120.

62.หจช., ร.5 ม.58.1/4 "เงินสำหรับผู้ครองเมืองประเทศราช," ลงวันที่ กุมภาพันธ์ ร.ศ. 127.

63. หจช., ร.5 ม.58/129 "ไปรเวตเรื่องพม่าเงี้ยวลาวจีนจะคิดการประทุษร้ายต่อเมืองเชียงใหม่," ลงวันที่ 19 สิงหาคม ร.ศ. 119.

64. *เมืองพะเยา,* สุจิตต์ วงษ์เทศ, บรรณาธิการ (กรุงเทพฯ: สำนักพิมพ์มติชน, 2527, หน้า 169-170.

65. *ประวัติมหาดไทยส่วนภูมิภาคจังหวัดเชียงใหม่,* สำนักงานจังหวัดเชียงใหม่จัดพิมพ์ 2529, หน้า 123.

66. หจช., ร.5 ม.58/21 "ราษฎรขัดขืนไม่ยอมทำตามคำสั่งราชการ," ลงวันที่ 2 มิถุนายน ร.ศ. 121.

67. เรื่องเดียวกัน

68. กระทรวงมหาดไทย "พระราชหัตถเลขารัชกาลที่ 5 ที่เกี่ยวกับภารกิจของกระทรวงมหาดไทย," เล่ม 2, หน้า 122.

69. หจช., ร. 5 ศ.2/10 "พระบรมราโชบายการเล่าเรียนเมืองเชียงใหม่," ลงวันที่ 7 กุมภาพันธ์ ร.ศ. 124.

70. หจช., ร. 6 ศธ. 43/14 "พระยาไพศาลศิลปศาสตร์ตรวจราชการมณฑลพายัพ," ลงวันที่ 26 พฤษภาคม 2456

71. สรัสวดี อ๋องสกุล "การปฏิรูปการศึกษาในล้านนา: การสร้างเอกภาพแห่งชาติ," *ศึกษาศาสตร์สาร* ปีที่ 10, ฉบับที่ 2-4 (ตุลาคม 2524-กันยายน 2525): 29-48.

72. ดู "พระราชบัญญัติการปกครองคณะสงฆ์ มาตรา 4," *ประชุมกฎหมายประจำศก* เล่ม 18, กฎหมาย ร.ศ. 120-121, หน้า 370-373.

73. ดูรายละเอียดใน โสภา ชานะมูล, "ครูบาศรีวิชัย ตนบุญแห่งล้านนา (พ.ศ. 2421-2481)," (วิทยานิพนธ์ศิลปศาสตรมหาบัณฑิต สาขาวิชาประวัติศาสตร์ มหาวิทยาลัยธรรมศาสตร์, 2534)

CHAPTER 9
SOCIETY AND ECONOMY (1774–1933)

1. ไม่นับพระมหากษัตริย์ที่กรุงเทพฯ ซึ่งมีฐานะเป็นมูลนายที่เหนือเจ้าเมืองต่างๆ ในล้านนา

2. ผู้เขียนใช้หลักการแบ่งมูลนายของ อัญชลี สุสายัณห์ เพื่อจะได้เปรียบเทียบระหว่างสังคมไทยภาคกลางกับล้านนา ดู อัญชลี สุสายัณห์, "ความเปลี่ยนแปลงของระบบไพร่ และผลกระทบต่อสังคมไทยในรัชสมัยพระบาทสมเด็จพระจุลจอมเกล้าเจ้าอยู่หัว," (วิทยานิพนธ์ปริญญามหาบัณฑิต ภาควิชาประวัติศาสตร์ บัณฑิตวิทยาลัย จุฬาลงกรณ์มหาวิทยาลัย, 2524), หน้า 55-59.

3. อานันท์ กาญจนพันธุ์ "การขัดแย้งและการเปลี่ยนแปลงในสังคมลานนาไทย (พ.ศ. 2398-2520)" *สังคมศาสตร์* ปีที่ 3, ฉบับที่ 2 (ตุลาคม 2522-มีนาคม 2523), หน้า 1-23.

4. คาร์ล บ็อค, *สมัยพระปิยมหาราช*, เสถียร พันธรังษี และ อัมพร จุลานนท์, แปล (พระนคร: โรงพิมพ์เฟื่องอักษร, 2505), หน้า 115.

5. *The Chiang Mai Chronicle*, p. 181.

6. เรื่องเดียวกัน, หน้า 182.

7. เรื่องเดียวกัน, หน้า 196.

8. หวญ., ร.4 จ.ศ. ไม่มี เลขที่ 137 "เมืองเชียงใหม่ ลำปาง ลำพูน ถือน้ำ ฯลฯ"

9. หจช., ร.5 ม.58/170 "เรื่องธรรมเนียมถือน้ำมณฑลพายัพ" (15 มิ.ย. ร.ศ. 115-18 ก.ค. ร.ศ. 115).

10. หวญ., ร.4 จ.ศ. ไม่มี เลขที่ 137 "เมืองเชียงใหม่ ลำปาง ลำพูน ถือน้ำ ฯลฯ"

11. *The Chiang Mai Chronicle*, p. 16-17.

12. เรื่องเดียวกัน, หน้า 178.

13. คาร์ล บ็อค, *สมัยพระปิยมหาราช,* หน้า 239.

14. เรื่องเดียวกัน, หน้า 336.

15. *The Chiang Mai Chronicle,* p. 182.

16. หจช., ร.5 ม.58/170 "เรื่องธรรมเนียมถือน้ำมณฑลพายัพ," (15 มิถุนายน ร.ศ. 115-118 กรกฎาคม ร.ศ. 115)

17. แสงดาว ณ เชียงใหม่, *พระประวัติ พระราชชายาดารัศมี,* ม.ป.ท., ม.ป.ป., หน้า 25.

18. เดเนียล แมคกิลวารี, *กึ่งศตวรรษในหมู่คนไทยและคนลาว,* จิตราภรณ์ ตันรันตกุล แปล, หน้า 159.

19. ความประพฤติที่ถือว่าไม่เหมาะสมสำหรับภิกษุ เช่น เล่นการพนัน เที่ยวกลางคืน กินเหล้า กินข้าวมื้อเย็น เที่ยวหาซื้อของในตลาด เป็นต้น ดูรายละเอียดใน "หนังสือโอวาทคำสอน," สมหมาย เปรมจิตต์, ปริวรรต, ใน *วารสารมนุษยศาสตร์* 2, (กันยายน 2518), หน้า 41-47.

20. หวญ., ร.4 จ.ศ. 1217 เลขที่ 151 "บัญชีรายชื่อคนและเครื่องราชบรรณาการเมืองน่านที่ลงมาเผ้าทูลลอองฯ"

21. ประเสริฐ ณ นคร, ปริวรรต, *มังรายศาสตร์หรือกฎหมายพระเจ้ามังราย,* (กรุงเทพฯ: ภาควิชาประวัติศาสตร์ มหาวิทยาลัยศรีนครินทร์วิโรฒ ประสานมิตร, 2521), หน้า 8.

22. *The Chiang Mai Chronicle,* p. 138.

23. มณี พยอมยงค์, ปริวรรต, *ธรรมศาสตร์และกฎหมายพระเจ้ามังราย,* (กรุงเทพฯ: ภาควิชาประวัติศาสตร์ มหาวิทยาลัยศรีนครินทร์วิโรฒประสานมิตร, 2521) หน้า 8.

24. เดเนียล แมคกิลวารี, *กึ่งศตวรรษในหมู่คนไทยและคนลาว,* และ หวญ., ร.4 จ.ศ. 1217 เลขที่ 20 "สำเนาแปลใบบอกพระยามงคลยศ จ.ศ. 1217."

25. อัญชลี สุสายัณห์, "ความเปลี่ยนแปลงของระบบไพร่...," หน้า 103, 104, 110.

26. หวญ., ร.4 จ.ศ. 1217 เลขที่ 74 "ร่างตราถึงพระยามหาอำมาต ฯลฯ เรื่องส่งหนังสือนำกราบทูลแล้ว" อ้างใน นันทิยา สว่างวุฒิธรรม, "การควบคุมกำลังคนในสมัยรัตนโกสินทร์ก่อนการจัดการเกณฑ์ทหาร (พ.ศ. 2325-2448)," (วิทยานิพนธ์ปริญญามหาบัณฑิต ภาควิชาประวัติศาสตร์ บัณฑิตวิทยาลัย จุฬาลงกรณ์มหาวิทยาลัย, 2526), หน้า 26.

27. ไพร่ที่ขึ้นสังกัดต่อกรมกองนั้นมีในสังคมไทยภาคกลางเรียกว่า "ไพร่หลวง" ดู อัญชลี สุสายัณห์, "ความเปลี่ยนแปลงของระบบไพร่...," หน้า 90.

28. ลักษณะไพร่ของล้านนานี้จะคล้ายกับไพร่ของอยุธยาตอนต้น ดู นิธิ เอียวศรีวงศ์, *ศรีรามเทพนคร: ความเรียงว่าด้วยประวัติศาสตร์อยุธยาตอนต้น* (กรุงเทพฯ: สำนักพิมพ์เจ้าพระยา, 2527), หน้า 56.

29. ลักษณะของการแบ่งไพร่ของเจ้าเมืองคนเก่าดังกล่าวเหมือนกับการแบ่งป่าไม้ ซึ่งจะต้องนำป่าไม้ของเจ้าเมืองคนเก่ามาให้แก่เจ้าเมืองคนใหม่ โดยเจ้าเมืองคนใหม่จะเก็บไว้ส่วนหนึ่ง และแบ่งให้บุตรหลานของตนและบุตรหลานของเจ้าเมืองคนเก่าด้วย เป็นการแบ่งให้ตามความเหมาะสม ดู หจช., ร.5 ม.58/88 "รายงานกรมหมื่นพิชิตปรีชากร เรื่องจัดราชการเชียงใหม่ ลำพูน ลำปาง" ณ วัน 4ฯ6 ค่ำ ปี 1246
5

30. หวญ., ร.4 จ.ศ. 1218 เลขที่ 13 "ร่างสารตราถึงพระยารัตน์อาณาเขตร์"

31. หวญ., ร.4 จ.ศ. 1218 เลขที่ 21 "บัญชีรายชื่อคน"

32. *The Chiang Mai Chronicle,* p. 162-163. และ หวญ., ร.4 จ.ศ. 1218 เลขที่ 13 "ร่างสารตราถึงพระยารัตน์อาณาเขตร์"

33. ในบางครั้งเจ้าเมืองจะนำไพร่ที่ถูกกวาดต้อนมาได้จากการทำสงครามไปถวายพระมหากษัตริย์ที่กรุงเทพฯ พระมหากษัตริย์จะโปรดคืนไพร่พระราชทานแก่แม่ทัพนายกองเป็นบำเหน็จความชอบ อย่างไรก็ตาม มีบางครั้งที่ทรงรับไว้ส่วนหนึ่ง ซึ่งแล้วแต่จะทรงพระกรุณาเป็นสำคัญ ดู หวญ., ร.1 จ.ศ. 1164 เลขที่ 1 "ร่างพระบรมราชโองการเรื่องตั้งเจ้าพระยาเชียงใหม่" จ.ศ. 1164

34. นิธิ เอียวศรีวงศ์, *ศรีรามเทพนคร...,* หน้า 55-56.

35. ในสมัยพระเจ้ากาวิละเป็นเจ้าเชียงใหม่ (พ.ศ. 2325-2356) อาณาเขตของเมืองเชียงใหม่ด้านใต้ถึงเมืองระแหง บ้านตาก บ้านเชียงเงิน และเมืองเถิน ดู *The Chiang Mai Chronicle,* p. 162-163.

36. เรื่องเดียวกัน, หน้า 164.

37. ไพร่เมืองเชียงใหม่ 28 คนนี้ลงมาค้าขายที่เมืองตาก ต่อมาได้บุตรภรรยาอยู่ที่เมืองตาก ไพร่เมืองเชียงใหม่ 28 คนจึงมีฐานะเป็น "เลกเขยสู่" ซึ่งตามกฎหมายแล้ว ถ้ามาเป็นเขยสู่พ้น 3 เดือนแล้วมูลนายเดิมไม่ติดตามมา ให้ถือว่าเป็นเลกเมืองนั้นก่อน แต่เมื่อมูลนายติดตามขอคืน เลกเขยสู่ก็ต้องกลับเป็นเลกเมืองนั้นตามเดิม ดู หวญ., ร.4 จ.ศ. 1221 เลขที่ 164 "ร่างตราน้อยของเจ้าพระยานิกรบดินทร์ฯ ถึงเจ้าเมืองและกรมการ"

38. *ตำนานพื้นเมืองเชียงใหม่,* หน้า 102.

39. หวญ., ร.3 จ.ศ. 1209 เลขที่ 17 "ชื่อสารตราถึงเมืองเชียงใหม่, นครลำพูน, นครลำปาง เรื่องตั้งพระยาอุปราช" และ หวญ., ร.3 จ.ศ. 1210 เลขที่ 20 "หนังสือเจ้าพระยาจักรีมาถึงพญาวังซ้าย, พญาวังขวา, พระพิไชยราชา, พญานาขวา บุตรหลานแสนท้าวพญาลาว"

40. หวญ., ร.4 จ.ศ. 1218 เลขที่ 13 "ร่างสารตราถึงพระยารัตน์อาณาเขตร์"

41. การติดตามไพร่เมืองลำปางในช่วง พ.ศ. 2393-2394 ไม่ได้ผล เพราะปีนั้นลำปางแห้งแล้งมาก มีไพร่พากันย้ายไปอยู่เชียงใหม่ ลำพูน กันหลายระลอก และปัญหาที่ติดตามไพร่กลับคืนไม่ได้นี้ เมื่อเจ้านายบุตรหลานเมืองลำปาง นำผ้าขาวและน้ำรักไปถวายได้กราบบังคมทูลรัชกาลที่ 4 ถึงเรื่องนี้ด้วย ดู หวญ., ร.4 จ.ศ. 1214 เลขที่ 153 "พระยาละคอนลำปางจัดผ้าขาว ฯลฯ"

42. หจช., ร.5 ม.58/88 "รายงานกรมหมื่นพิชิตปรีชากรเรื่องการจัดราชการเชียงใหม่ ลำพูน ลำปาง" ณ วันที่ 4ฯ6 ค่ำ ปี 1246
5

43. เรื่องเดียวกัน

44. หวญ., ร.3 จ.ศ. 1210 เลขที่ 20 "ชื่อร่างสารตรา"

45. หวญ., ร.4 จ.ศ. 1218 เลขที่ 27 "คัดบอกพระยาพิไชย"

46. อุดม รุ่งเรืองศรี, *วรรณกรรมล้านนา* (หน่วยส่งเสริมศิลปศึกษาและวัฒนธรรมลานนา คณะมนุษยศาสตร์ มหาวิทยาลัยเชียงใหม่, 2526), หน้า 301.

47. หจช., ร.5 ม.58/33 "พระราชบัญญัติการเก็บเงินค่าแรงแทนเกณฑ์มณฑลตะวันตกเฉียงเหนือ, ร.ศ. 119"

48. หวญ., ร.4 จ.ศ. 1217 เลขที่ 20 "สำเนาแปลงใบบอกพระยามงคลยศ"

49. *The Chiang Mai Chronicle,* p. 202-203.

50. หวญ., ร.4 จ.ศ. 1127 เลขที่ 13 "คัดบอกเมืองตาก"

51. ตัวอย่างการนำช้างเผือกไปถวายใน พ.ศ. 2409 พระเจ้ากาวิโลรสสั่งให้ขุนนางเกณฑ์ไพร่ 50 คน คุมช้างเผือกไป และระยะทางที่พักตามจุดต่างๆ ไพร่ซึ่งอยู่ในตำบลเส้นทางผ่านจะต้องถูกเกณฑ์มาสร้างโรงช้างและที่พักของขุนนางและไพร่ที่คุมช้างด้วย พระเจ้ากาวิโลรสกำชับว่าต้องทำให้เรียบร้อย มิฉะนั้นแคว่นและแก่บ้านจะถูกลงโทษหนัก นับว่าการนำเข้าช้างเผือกไปถวายเป็นงานใหญ่ที่เดียว ดู หวญ., ร.4 จ.ศ. 1228 "สำเนาแปลจดหมายเจ้านครเชียงใหม่"

52. ตัวอย่างเช่น ใน พ.ศ. 2408 พระเจ้ากาวิโลรสให้นายน้อยทนันไชยคุมไพร่ 80 คน ไปติดตามจับกุมผู้ร้ายที่เมืองตาก ดู หวญ., ร.4 จ.ศ. 1227 เลขที่ 30 "คัดบอกพระสกลบุรินท์"

53. ไพร่กองด่านจะเป็นคนตามหมู่บ้านที่อยู่ในหัวเมืองชายแดน เช่น เชียงแสน เชียงราย เชียงของ ยวม ดู หวญ., ร.3 จ.ศ. 1204 เลขที่ 13 "สารตราถึงเจ้าเมืองเชียงใหม่ เรื่องตอบรับเครื่องยศของนายหนานมหาเทพผู้ถึงแก่กรรม" หจช., ร.5 ม. 99/18 "พระยาทรงสุรเดชถึงเจ้าไชยสงคราม" ลงวันที่ 8 กรกฎาคม ร.ศ. 112 และ หจช., ร.5 ม.58/85 "เรื่องตั้งด่านเมืองเชียงแสน เมืองเชียงราย เชียงของ" 14 กรกฎาคม ร.ศ. 112-1, กันยายน ร.ศ. 117.

54. คาร์ล บ็อค, *สมัยพระปิยมหาราช,* หน้า 199.

55. เรื่องเดียวกัน, หน้า 339-340.

56. ดาเนียล แมคกิลวารี, *เมืองไทยที่ข้าพเจ้ารู้จัก,* (กรุงเทพฯ: สำนักพิมพ์สุริยธรรม, 2525), หน้า 60.

57. อุดม รุ่งเรืองศรี, *วรรณกรรมล้านนา,* หน้า 334.

58. รายละเอียดเกี่ยวกับวรรณกรรมคำสอนเรื่องโคลงเจ้าวิฑูรสอนหลาน ดู ทรงศักดิ์ ปรางค์วัฒนากุล, "วิเคราะห์วรรณกรรมลานนาไทยเรื่อง เจ้าวิฑูรสอนหลานและพระลอสอนโลก," (วิทยานิพนธ์ปริญญามหาบัณฑิต ภาควิชาภาษาไทย บัณฑิตวิทยาลัย มหาวิทยาลัยศรีนครินทรวิโรฒ ประสานมิตร, 2519)

59. ทาสที่ส่งเงินส่วยแก่นายเงินเป็นรายปี เรียกว่าทาสขอผูกดอก หรือผูกดอก

60. สมหมาย เปรมจิตต์, ปริวรรต, *กฎหมายโคสาราษฎร์* ภาคปริวรรต, ลำดับที่ 16 (โครงการตำรา คณะสังคมศาสตร์ มหาวิทยาลัยเชียงใหม่, 2520), หน้า 14, 15.

61. ดังมีหลักฐานว่ามีการลักพาทาสจากเมืองเชียงรายไปขายที่เมืองหลวงพระบาง ผู้พาทาสไปขายถูกจับตัวนำไปลงโทษตามอาญาบ้านเมือง ดู คาร์ล บ็อค, *สมัยพระปิยมหาราช,* หน้า 428. ส่วนเจ้าของเรือนที่ให้ที่พักพิงแก่ทาสที่หลบหนีนายเงินอยู่นั้นจะถูกปรับ 300 เงิน ดู *กฎหมายโคสาราษฎร์,* หน้า 12.

62. Nigel J. Brailey, "The Origins of the Siamese Forward Movement in Western Laos 1850-92," Ph.D. Dissertation, University of London, 1968, P. 27.

63. พรรณนิภา อพิญชพงศ์ "เจ้า ไพร่ กับความเปลี่ยนแปลงในสังคมล้านนา ระหว่าง พ.ศ. พ.ศ. 2427-2476," (ปริญญานิพนธ์การศึกษามหาบัณฑิต สาขาประวัติศาสตร์ มหาวิทยาลัยศรีนครินทรวิโรฒ ประสานมิตร, 2535), หน้า 42.

64. หลักฐานที่แสดงให้เห็นว่าทาสเชลยมีจำนวนน้อย เช่น ทาสเชลยเมืองแพร่มีจำนวนน้อย พระยาแพร่ และกรมการขอยกเลิกน้อมเกล้าถวายพระบาทสมเด็จพระเจ้าอยู่หัว ดู หจช., ร.5 ม.58/42 "กรมหมื่นดำรงราชานุภาพกราบทูลกรมหมื่นสมมตอมรพันธุ์ราชเลขานุการ" ลงวันที่ 30

มกราคม ร.ศ. 118 นอกจากนั้นจากคำกราบบังคมทูลรัชกาลที่ 5 ของพระองค์เจ้าระพีพัฒนศักดิ์ ก็แสดงให้เห็นว่า พระองค์สงสัยว่าในล้านนามีแต่ทาสสินไถ่ ทาสเชลยคงไม่มี เพราะเชลยนั้นเป็นไพร่สม (เลกสม) ไปหมดแล้ว "ทาสเชลยมีปัญหามากในคำนำของพระราชบัญญัติ อธิบายคำที่เรียกว่า ทาสเชลยไว้ว่า เป็นทาสที่ได้มาจากการศึก ความรู้สึกของคนธรรมดาพื้นเมืองสงสัยว่า ทาสนอกจาก ทาสสินไถ่จะไม่ใช่ทาสดังไทยเข้าใจกันจะเป็นเลกสมแล้ว" ดู หจช., ร.5 ม.13/8 "พระราชบัญญัติ เลิกทาส คำกราบบังคมทูลพระองค์เจ้าระพีพัฒน์ศักดิ์เสนาบดียุติธรรม" ลงวันที่ 17 กรกฎาคม ร.ศ. 123. อ้างใน พงษ์เนียน ทองพงษ์เนียม, "การศึกษาเรื่องทาสในสมัยรัตนโกสินทร์," (วิทยานิพนธ์ ปริญญามหาบัณฑิต ภาควิชาประวัติศาสตร์ บัณฑิตวิทยาลัย จุฬาลงกรณ์มหาวิทยาลัย, 2526), หน้า 113).

65. พรรณนิภา อพิญชพงศ์, "เจ้า ไพร่ กับความเปลี่ยนแปลง...," หน้า 44.

66. โปรดดู เสถียร ลายลักษณ์ และคนอื่นๆ ผู้รวบรวม, "พระราชบัญญัติการเก็บเงินแทน เกณฑ์มณฑลตะวันตกเฉียงเหนือ ร.ศ. 119," ใน *ประชุมกฎหมายประจำศก,* เล่ม 17 หน้า 293.

67. "พระราชบัญญัติลักษณะทาสมณฑลตะวันตกเฉียงเหนือ," *ราชกิจจานุเษกษา* เล่ม 17, (มิถุนายน ร.ศ. 119), หน้า 134.

68. หจช., ร.5 ก.13.2/28 "จัดการทหารมณฑลพายัพ," ลงวันที่ 5 กันยายน ร.ศ. 112.

69. หจช., ร.6 ค.11/8 "เงินเดือนเจ้าจักคำขจรศักดิ์ เจ้าผู้ครองนครลำพูน" ลงวันที่ 1 ตุลาคม พ.ศ. 2462.

70. หจช., ร.7 ม.1/34 "บัญชีรายงานการเก็บเงินรัชชูปการทั่วพระราชอาณาจักร พ.ศ. 2469-2470," ลงวันที่...ตุลาคม พ.ศ. 2469.

71. นันทิยา สว่างวุฒิธรรม, "การควบคุมกำลังคนในสมัยรัตนโกสินทร์...," หน้า 305.

72. อัญชลี สุสายัณห์, "ความเปลี่ยนแปลงของระบบไพร่...," หน้า 302-303.

73. อานันท์ กาญจนพันธุ์, "พัฒนาการเศรษฐกิจของหมู่บ้านในล้านนา (2350-2490)," ใน *พัฒนาการของชีวิตและวัฒนธรรมล้านนา,* (เชียงใหม่: ศูนย์หนังสือเชียงใหม่, 2527), หน้า 85.

74. นวลศิริ วงศ์ทางสวัสดิ์, *ภูมิศาสตร์กายภาพไทยภาคเหนือ,* หน้า 11.

75. สุเทพ สุนทรเภสัช, "ประวัติศาสตร์ท้องถิ่นในล้านนา: ข้อวิจารณ์และเสนอแนะแนวทาง การศึกษา," เอกสารประกอบการสัมมนาล้านนาคดีศึกษา: ประวัติศาสตร์และโบราณคดี ณ วิทยาลัย ครูเชียงใหม่ 28-31 มกราคม, 2528 (เอกสารเลขที่ 10-001), หน้า 9.

76. คาร์ล ซี, ซิมเมอร์แมน, *การสำรวจเศรษฐกิจในชนบทสยาม,* ซิม วีระไวทยะ, แปลและ เรียบเรียง (กรุงเทพฯ: มูลนิธิโครงการตำราสังคมศาสตร์และมนุษยศาสตร์: 2525), หน้า 26, 32.

77. หจช., ร.5 ม.58/126 "เรื่องตลาดที่เมืองเชียงใหม่ กรมหมื่นดำรงราชานุภาพกราบบังคม ทูลรัชกาลที่ 5," วันที่ 24 เมษายน ร.ศ. 119.

78. Holt S. Hallett., *A Thousand Miles on an Elephant in the Shan States,* p. 100. และ คาร์ล บ็อค, *สมัยพระปิยมหาราช,* หน้า 313-314.

79. เรื่องเดียวกัน

80. อุดม รุ่งเรืองศรี, ปริวรรต, *คร่าวกาวิละและตำนานเมืองเชียงแสน* (เชียงใหม่: ศูนย์ วัฒนธรรมจังหวัดเชียงใหม่และศูนย์ศิลปวัฒธรรม วิทยาลัยครูเชียงใหม่, 2528), หน้า 18-19.

81. ฉัตรทิพย์ นาถสุภา, *เศรษฐกิจหมู่บ้านไทยในอดีต* (กรุงเทพฯ: สำนักพิมพ์สร้างสรรค์, 2527), หน้า 42 และ ดู สุเทพ สุนทรเภสัช, "ประวัติศาสตร์ท้องถิ่นในล้านนา...," หน้า 8.

82. ชูสิทธิ์ ชูชาติ, *พ่อค้าวัวต่าง: ผู้บุกเบิกการค้าขายในหมู่บ้านภาคเหนือของประเทศไทย* (พ.ศ. 2398-2503) รายงานการวิจัยกรมการฝึกหัดครู, 2525, หน้า 69.

83. มาร์โก ทาเก-แมคมอร์แรน, "ประวัติและพัฒนาการของการค้าขายในลำปาง ตั้งแต่ปลายคริสต์ศตวรรษที่ 19 ถึง ค.ศ. 1939," แปลโดย เครือมาศ วุฒิการณ์ *วารสารมนุษยศาสตร์* 1, (กรกฎาคม-ธันวาคม 2526), หน้า 1-7.

84. ชูสิทธิ์ ชูชาติ, *พ่อค้าวัวต่าง...*, หน้า 47.

85. คาร์ล บ็อค, *สมัยพระปิยมหาราช*, หน้า 257-258, 366.

86. ฉัตรทิพย์ นาถสุภา, *เศรษฐกิจหมู่บ้านไทยในอดีต,* หน้า 75.

87. หวญ., ร.3 จ.ศ. 1209 เลขที่ 29 "ใบบอกเชียงใหม่เรื่องกระบือและช้างสีปลาด เรื่องเจ้าอังวะตั้งเจ้าอุปราช"

88. Holt S. Hallett, *A Thousand Miles on an Elephant in the Shan States.*

89. อุดม รุ่งเรืองศรี, ปริวรรต, *คร่าวกาวิละและตำนานเมืองเชียงแสน,* หน้า 19.

90. ชูสิทธิ์ ชูชาติ, *พ่อค้าวัวต่าง...*, หน้า 29.

91. หจช., ร.5 ม.58/177 "เจ้านรนันทไชยชวลิต เจ้านครลำปาง กราบทูลกรมหมื่นดำรงราชานุภาพ" ลงวันที่ 31 มกราคม ร.ศ. 111

92. ชมัยโฉม สุนทรสวัสดิ์, "การศึกษาเชิงประวัติศาสตร์เกี่ยวกับกิจกรรมป่าไม้ทางภาคเหนือของไทย ตั้งแต่ พ.ศ. 2439 ถึง พ.ศ. 2475," (วิทยานิพนธ์ปริญญามหาบัณฑิต ภาควิชาประวัติศาสตร์ บัณฑิตวิทยาลัย จุฬาลงกรณ์มหาวิทยาลัย, 2521), หน้า 225.

93. พรพรรณ จงวัฒนา, "การพิพาทระหว่างเจ้านครเชียงใหม่กับคนในบังคบอังกฤษ อันเป็นเหตุให้รัฐบาลสยามจัดการปกครองมณฑลพายัพ (พ.ศ. 2401-2455)," (วิทยานิพนธ์ปริญญามหาบัณฑิต ภาควิชาประวัติศาสตร์ จุฬาลงกรณ์มหาวิทยาลัย, 2517), หน้า 88-90.

94. จ94. หจช., ร.5 ม.16.2/58 "กรมหมื่นดำรงราชานุภาพกราบทูล กรมหมื่นสมมตอมรพันธุ์" ที่ 130/1954 ลงวันที่ 27 มิถุนายน ร.ศ. 118

95. ดูรายละเอียดใน ชมัยโฉม สุนทรสวัสดิ์, "การศึกษาเชิงประวัติศาสตร์เกี่ยวกับกิจกรรมป่าไม้ทางภาคเหนือของไทย," หน้า 154-178.

96. หจช., ร.7 กษ. 5/6 "บริษัทบอมเบย์เบอร์มา ขอพระกรุณาเรื่องหนี้สินที่เกี่ยวกับเจ้าบุญวาทย์ในการทำป่าไม้แม่ต้า เมืองลอง," ลงวันที่ 1 สิงหาคม พ.ศ. 2470

97. วรรณชลีย์ บุญมี, "ความสัมพันธ์กับอังกฤษในบางลักษณะสมัยพระบาทสมเด็จพระจุลจอมเกล้าเจ้าอยู่หัว: การป่าไม้และการเหมืองแร่," (วิทยานิพนธ์ปริญญามหาบัณฑิต ภาควิชาประวัติศาสตร์ บัณฑิตวิทยาลัย มหาวิทยาลัยศรีนครินทรวิโรฒ ประสานมิตร, 2520), หน้า 141-142.

98. หจช. ร.5 ม.58/72 "ราชการหัวเมืองเรื่องขมุ" ลงวันที่ 25 กุมภาพันธ์ ร.ศ. 109

99. วรรณชลีย์ บุญมี, "ความสัมพันธ์กับอังกฤษ...," หน้า 254.

100. ปลายอ้อ ชนะนนท์, "บทบาทนายทุนพ่อค้าที่มีต่อการก่อและขยายตัวของทุนนิยมภาคเหนือของประเทศไทย," (วิทยานิพนธ์ปริญญามหาบัณฑิต ภาควิชาเศรษฐศาสตร์ บัณฑิตวิทยาลัย จุฬาลงกรณ์มหาวิทยาลัย, 2529), หน้า 40.

101. อานันท์ กาญจนพันธุ์, *ประวัติศาสตร์เศรษฐกิจภาคเหนือ,* หน้า 7.

102. ชูสิทธิ์ ชูชาติ, *วิวัฒนาการเศรษฐกิจหมู่บ้าน...*, หน้า 57.

103. มาร์โก ทาเกะ แมคมอร์แรน, *ประวัติและพัฒนาการของการค้าขาย...*, หน้า 4.

104. ชูสิทธิ์ ชูชาติ, *วิวัฒนาการเศรษฐกิจหมู่บ้าน...*, หน้า 58. (อ้างจาก หจช., ร.6 คค. 5.3/2 "มิสเตอร์แอล. ไวเลอร์ เจ้ากรมรถไฟ กราบทูลพระเจ้าบรมวงศ์เธอ กรมหลวงนเรศ์วรฤทธิ์" ที่ 111 ป. ลงวันที่ 20 พฤศจิกายน พ.ศ. 2455)

105. อานันท์ กาญจนพันธุ์, *ประวัติศาสตร์เศรษฐกิจภาคเหนือ,* หน้า 11.

106. เรื่องเดียวกัน, หน้า 4.

107. หจช., ร.5 ม.58/193 "พิกัดภาษีอากรมณฑลพายัพ" (ร.ศ. 103-104)

108. อานันท์ กาญจนพันธุ์, *ประวัติศาสตร์เศรษฐกิจภาคเหนือ,* หน้า 11.

109. หจช., ร.5 ค.14.4/7 "เรื่องจีนเต็งทำภาษีอากร เกี่ยวด้วยราชการทางเมืองนครเชียงใหม่," ลงวันที่ 27 ธันวาคม ร.ศ. 113.

110. หจช., ร.5 ค.14.4/1 "ภาษีอากรแลการพนันหัวเมืองในมณฑลลาวเฉียง" ลงวันที่ 3 มีนาคม ร.ศ. 110.

111. หจช., ร.5 ค.14.4/2 "เรื่องภาษีอากรหัวเมืองในมณฑลลาวเฉียง" 8 ธันวาคม ร.ศ. 109 ถึง 25 มกราคม ร.ศ. 111.

112. หจช., ร.5 ม. 58/59 "ภาษีอากรต่างๆ ทางลาวเฉียง" ลงวันที่ 21 กรกฎาคม ร.ศ. 112

113. ชูสิทธิ์ ชูชาติ, "กำเนิดระบบเศรษฐกิจทุนนิยมกับผลกระทบที่มีต่อสังคมชาวนาในภารเหนือ," *วารสารสังคมศาสตร์* ปีที่ 5, (เมษายน-กันยายน 2524), หน้า 38-63.

114. พรรณนิภา อพิญชพงศ์, "เจ้า ไพร่ กับความเปลี่ยนแปลงในสังคมล้านนา," หน้า 124 (อ้างจาก หจช., ร.7 สบ. 2.46/9 เจ้าราชวงศ์กราบบังคมทูล สมเด็จพระเจ้าบรมวงศ์เธอ กรมพระยาดำรงราชานุภาพ ลงวันที่ 27 มิถุนายน พ.ศ. 2474)

115. เรื่องเดียวกัน

116. เรื่องเดียวกัน, หน้า 130.

117. ปลายอ้อ ชนะนันท์, "บทบาทนายทุนพ่อค้า...," หน้า 85.

118. พรรณนิภา อพิญชพงศ์, "เจ้า ไพร่ กับความเปลี่ยนแปลงในสังคมล้านนา," หน้า 134.

119. คาร์ล ซี. ซิมเมอร์แมน, *การสำรวจเศรษฐกิจในชนบทสยาม,* หน้า 161-162.

120. มาร์โก ทาเกะ แมคมอร์แรน, "ประวัติและพัฒนาการของการค้าขาย...," หน้า 13.

121. ปลายอ้อ ชนะนันท์, *บทบาทนายทุนพ่อค้า...*, หน้า 55.

122. อานันท์ กาญจนพันธุ์, *ประวัติศาสตร์เศรษฐกิจภาคเหนือ,* หน้า 13.

123. Anan Ganjanapan, *The Partial Commercialization of Rice Production in Northern Thailand.,* p. 154.

124. อานันท์ กาญจนพันธุ์, *ประวัติศาสตร์เศรษฐกิจภาคเหนือ,* หน้า 14.

125. คาร์ล ซี. ซิมเมอร์แมน, *การสำรวจเศรษฐกิจในชนบทสยาม,* หน้า 117.

126. ฉัตรทิพย์ นาถสุภา, *เศรษฐกิจหมู่บ้านไทยในอดีต,* หน้า 78-79.

127. คาร์ล ซี. ซิมเมอร์แมน, *การสำรวจเศรษฐกิจในชนบทสยาม,* หน้า 66.

BIBLIOGRAPHY

1. เอกสารชั้นต้น (Primary Sources)

1.1 เอกสารชั้นต้นที่ยังไม่ได้พิมพ์ (Unpublished Primary Sources)

คัมภีร์ใบลานเรื่อง "ตำนานเมืองเชียงใหม่." ฉบับวัดเชียงมั่น ตำบลศรีภูมิ อำเภอเมือง จังหวัดเชียงใหม่. รหัสไมโครฟิล์ม สถาบันวิจัยสังคม มหาวิทยาลัยเชียงใหม่ 78 012 05 006-008, หน้าลานที่ 6.

คัมภีร์ใบลานเรื่อง "พื้นเมืองเชียงราย, เชียงแสน." วัดเมธังกราวาส ตำบลในเวียง อำเภอเมืองแพร่ รหัสไมโครฟิล์ม สถาบันวิจัยสังคม มหาวิทยาลัยเชียงใหม่ 81 088 05 082-082.

คัมภีร์ใบลานเรื่อง "พื้นเมืองพะเยา, จดหมายเหตุน้ำท่วมเมืองพะเยา และการกลับมาตั้งอยู่ใหม่." วัดศรีโคมคำ จังหวัดพะเยา รหัสไมโครฟิล์ม ศูนย์ส่งเสริมศิลปวัฒนธรรม มหาวิทยาลัยเชียงใหม่ พย 01 14 010 00, หน้าลานที่ 1.

คัมภีร์ใบลานเรื่อง "ตำนานพะเยา." วัดศรีโคมคำ จังหวัดพะเยา รหัสไมโครฟิล์ม ศูนย์ส่งเสริมศิลปวัฒนธรรม มหาวิทยาลัยเชียงใหม่ พย 01 140 02 00, หน้าลานที่ 55-56.

คัมภีร์ใบลานเรื่อง "ตำนานเมืองเถิน." วัดแม่วะหลวง ตำบลแม่วะ อำเภอเถิน จังหวัดลำปาง รหัสไมโครฟิล์ม สถาบันวิจัยสังคม มหาวิทยาลัยเชียงใหม่ 81.094.01L.061-062.

คัมภีร์ใบลานเรื่อง "อวหาร 25 ประการ." วัดบ้านปิง อำเภอเมือง จังหวัดเชียงใหม่ รหัสไมโครฟิล์ม สถาบันวิจัยสังคม มหาวิทยาลัยเชียงใหม่ 78.021.03.033-033, หน้าลานที่ 1-4.

พับสาเรื่อง "ประวัติศาสตร์ กฎหมายโบราณ." วัดป่าลาน ตำบลทุ่งต้อม อำเภอสันป่าตอง จังหวัดเชียงใหม่ รหัสไมโครฟิล์ม สถาบันวิจัยสังคม มหาวิทยาลัยเชียงใหม่ 82.113.03.017.-017, หน้าพับที่ 29 (จำนวน 1 พับ มี 194 หน้า).

พับสาเรื่อง "ประวัติศาสตร์ล้านนา." วัดป่าสา ตำบลสันทราย อำเภอสารภี จังหวัดเชียงใหม่ รหัสไมโครฟิล์ม สถาบันวิจัยสังคม มหาวิทยาลัยเชียงใหม่ 80.047.05.028-028, หน้าพับที่ 22-23 (จำนวน 1 พับ มี 24 หน้า).

หวญ. "คำค่าวซอจดหมายเหตุการณ์สงครามอโยธิยา-ม่าน" เลขที่ 27/ก ปี จ.ศ. 1047.

หวญ. "ตำนานเมืองเชียงแสน." ฉบับวัดป่ารวก เลขที่ 9/ญ.

หวญ. "ตำนานเมืองเชียงแสน." ฉบับวัดป่ารวก เลขที่ 11/ง.

หวญ. "พงศาวดารเมืองเชียงใหม่ (เจ้ามังธาประทานเครื่องยศแก่ท้าวพระยา)." เลขที่ 1 มัดที่ 1 (16/ก).

หวญ. จดหมายเหตุรัชกาลที่ 1 จ.ศ. 1159 เลขที่ 2 "หนังสือเจ้าเมืองเมาะตะมะถึงเสนาบดีผู้ใหญ่ฝ่ายไทยให้ส่งพระยาแจ่งพระยาทวายคืน"

———ร.1 จ.ศ. 1164 เลขที่ 1 "ร่างพระบรมราชโองการเรื่องการแต่งตั้งเจ้าพระยาเชียงใหม่ จ.ศ. 1164".

———ร.1 จ.ศ. 1170 เลขที่ 1 "สำเนาแปลหนังสือเสนาบดีเมืองอังวะถึงอัครมหาเสนาบดีไทยเรื่องพระเจ้าเชียงใหม่ส่งศุภอักษรกับเรื่องราชบรรณาการไปถวายพระเจ้าอังวะ"

———ร.2 จ.ศ. 1172 เลขที่ 1 "ศุภอักษรถึงเจ้าประเทศราชและเกณฑ์กระดาษเพลาป่านใช้ในการพระราชบรมศพ ฯลฯ"

———ร.3 จ.ศ. 1197 เลขที่ 5 "บัญชีรายวันเรื่องส่งไม้ขอนสักหัวเมืองต่างๆ เข้ามาถวาย"

———ร.3 จ.ศ. 1200 เลขที่ 19/1 "ร่างตราเจ้าพระยาจักรีถึงเมืองเชียงใหม่ เรื่องห้ามขายโคกระบือให้พ่อค้าชาวอังกฤษ"

———ร.3 จ.ศ. 1200 เลขที่ 19/2 "ร่างตราเจ้าพระยาจักรีถึงเจ้าพระยาเชียงใหม่ เรื่องให้ชำระเงินที่ลูกค้าอังกฤษว่ายังติดอยู่กับราษฎร"

———ร.3 จ.ศ. 1204 เลขที่ 13 "ตราสารถึงเจ้าเมืองเชียงใหม่ เรื่องตอบรับเรื่องยศของนายหนานมหาเทพผู้ถึงแก่กรรม"

———ร.3 จ.ศ. 1204 เลขที่ 14 "ร่างตราเจ้าพระยาจักรีถึงเจ้าพระยาเชียงใหม่ เรื่องบอกข่าวเมืองอังวะรบกับอังกฤษ"

———ร.3 จ.ศ. 1204 เลขที่ 15 "สำเนาใบบอกเมืองเชียงใหม่"

———ร.3 จ.ศ. 1205 เลขที่ 21 "บัญชีเครื่องยศหัวเมืองต่างๆ"

———ร.3 จ.ศ. 1206 เลขที่ 43 "สารตราเจ้าพระยาจักรีถึงเมืองเชียงใหม่ เรื่องการจัดตั้งเมืองเชียงแสน และให้คอยระวังกองทัพพม่า"

———ร.3 จ.ศ. 1209 เลขที่ 13 "สารตราเมืองเชียงใหม่ เรื่องตอบรับเครื่องยศของนายหนานมหาเทพ"

———ร.3 จ.ศ. 1209 เลขที่ 17 "สารตราถึงเมืองเชียงใหม่ นครลำพูน นครลำปาง เรื่องตั้งพระยาอุปราช"

———ร.3 จ.ศ. 1209 เลขที่ 29 "ใบบอกเชียงใหม่เรื่องกระบือและช้างสีปลาด เรื่องเจ้าอังวะตั้งเจ้าอุปราช"

———ร.3 จ.ศ. 1209 เลขที่ 30 "เรื่องพระยานครลำปางกับพระยาฤทธิภิญโญยศประพฤติการชั่วร้าย"

———ร.3 จ.ศ. 1210 เลขที่ 16 "ร่างตราสารถึงพระยาลำพูน เรื่องตั้งพระยาราชวงศ์เป็นที่พระยาอุปราชเมืองลำพูน"

———ร.3 จ.ศ. 1210 เลขที่ 20 "หนังสือเจ้าพระยาจักรีถึงพญาวังซ้าย พญาวังขวา พระพิไชยราชา พญานาขวา บุตรหลานแสนท้าวพญาลาว"

———ร.3 จ.ศ. 1212 เลขที่ 6/ก "สำเนาแปลจดหมายเมืองนครลำปาง เมืองตากเรื่องยกทัพไปตีเมืองเชียงตุง"

———ร.4 จ.ศ. ไม่ปรากฏ เลขที่ 137 "เมืองเชียงใหม่ ลำปาง นครลำพูน ถือน้ำ ฯลฯ"

———ร.4 จ.ศ. 1127 เลขที่ 13 "คัดบอกเมืองตาก"

———ร.4 จ.ศ. 1127 เลขที่ 107 "บัญชีเจ้าเมืองลาวพุงดำ พุงขาวส่งเครื่องบรรณาการประจำปี"

———ร.4 จ.ศ. 1214 เลขที่ 72(ก) "พระบรมราชโองการถึงกรมหลวงวงศาธิราชสนิท เรื่องราชการทัพเมืองเชียงตุง"

———ร.4 จ.ศ. 1214 เลขที่ 153 "พระยาละคอนลำปางจัดผ้าขาว"

———ร.4 จ.ศ. 1215 เลขที่ 87 "พระราชดำรัสรัชกาลที่ 4 ถึงกรมหลวงวงศาธิราชสนิท"

———ร.4 จ.ศ. 1216 เลขที่ 54 "ร่างศุภอักษรถึงนครเชียงใหม่"

———ร.4 จ.ศ. 1216 เลขที่ 55 "ร่างสารตราถึงเมืองน่าน"

———ร.4 จ.ศ. 1216 เลขที่ 67 "ร่างตราสารถึงพระยายมราช"

———ร.4 จ.ศ. 1216 เลขที่ 70 "ร่างตราสารถึงพระยาสีหะราชฤทธิไกร"

———ร.4 จ.ศ. 1216 เลขที่ 115 "จดหมายเหตุพระเจ้าน้องยาเธอกรมหลวงวงศาธิราชสนิทยกทัพไปเชียงตุง"

———ร.4 จ.ศ. 1216 เลขที่ 153 "คำฟ้องและคำให้การเรื่องเจ้าราชบุตรเมืองเชียงใหม่ ริบไม้สักมองสวยนิจ"

———ร.4 จ.ศ. 1217 เลขที่ 20 "สำเนาแปลใบบอกพระยามงคลยศ จ.ศ. 1217"

———ร.4 จ.ศ. 1217 เลขที่ 63 "ใบบอกเมืองลำปางเรื่องราษฎรทำนาได้เต็มที่ ตัวบุ้งกัดต้นข้าวเสียหายมาก"

———ร.4 จ.ศ. 1217 เลขที่ 74 "ร่างตราถึงพระยามหาอำมาตฯ ฯลฯ เรื่องส่งหนังสือนำกราบทูลแล้ว"

———ร.4 จ.ศ. 1217 เลขที่ 151 "บัญชีรายชื่อคนและเครื่องราชบรรณาการเมืองน่านที่มาเฝ้าทูลละออง"

———ร.4 จ.ศ. 1218 เลขที่ 13 "ร่างสารตราถึงพระยารัตน์อาณาเขตร์"

———ร.4 จ.ศ. 1218 เลขที่ 21 "บัญชีรายชื่อคน"

———ร.4 จ.ศ. 1218 เลขที่ 27 "คัดบอกพระยาพิไชย"

———ร.4 จ.ศ. 1218 เลขที่ 69 "ตราใหญ่ถึงนครลำปางให้จัดหาไม้ขอนสักพันต้น"

———ร.4 จ.ศ. 1219 เลขที่ 26 "ศุภอักษรเมืองเชียงใหม่"

———ร.4 จ.ศ. 1219 เลขที่ 158 "คัดบอกเมืองลำพูน เมืองแพร่ เรื่องส่งไม้สัก ต้นไม้ทองเงิน"

———ร.4 จ.ศ. 1220 เลขที่ 17 "ร่างศุภอักษรถึงเจ้านครเชียงใหม่"

———ร.4 จ.ศ. 1221 เลขที่ 164 "ร่างตราน้อยเจ้าพระยานิกรบดินทร์ ถึงเจ้าเมืองและกรมการ"

———ร.4 จ.ศ. 1221 เลขที่ 196 "ร่างตราน้อยเจ้าพระยานิกรบดินทร์ เรื่องเจ้าเมืองน่านของดส่งไม้ ฯลฯ"

———ร.4 จ.ศ. 1221 เลขที่ 210 "สารตราถึงเจ้าเมืองแพร่ พิษณุโลก และเมืองกำแพงเพชร"

———ร.4 จ.ศ. 1222 เลขที่ 10 "ร่างพระบรมราชโชวาท"

———ร.4 จ.ศ. 1222 เลขที่ 17 "ร่างศุภอักษรถึงเจ้านครลำปาง"

———ร.4 จ.ศ. 1227 เลขที่ 13 "คัดบอกเมืองตาก"

———ร.4 จ.ศ. 1227 เลขที่ 15 "คัดบอกเมืองเชียงใหม่"

———ร.4 จ.ศ. 1227 เลขที่ 30 "คัดบอกพระยาสกุลบุรินทร์"

———ร.4 จ.ศ. 1228 "สำเนาแปลจดหมายเจ้านครเชียงใหม่"

———ร.4 จ.ศ. 1277 เลขที่ 125 "ถึงเจ้านครเชียงใหม่เรื่องจับเงี้ยวตองซู่ที่เอาปืนไปขายพงศาวดารเมืองเถิน." เลขที่ 79 มัดที่ 10.

หอจดหมายเหตุแห่งชาติ, กอง. "เอกสารรัชการที่ 5 กต. 40.11/3 กรมหลวงเทวะวงษ์วโรปการถึงพระยาสุริยานุวัตร." ที่ 64/5240 ลงวันที่ 12 สิงหาคม ร.ศ. 116.

———ร.5 กต. 40/8 "กรมหลวงดำรงราชานุภาพถึงกรมหลวงเทวะวงษ์วโรปการ." สำเนาที่ 6592 ที่ 551/15590 ลงวันที่ 4 สิงหาคม ร.ศ. 114.

_____ร.5 กต. 40.10/14 "กรมหลวงดำรงราชานุภาพถึงกรมหลวงเทวะวงษ์วโรปการ." สำเนาที่ 1326 ที่ 109/3473 ลงวันที่ 30 เมษายน ร.ศ. 115.

_____ร.5 ค. 14.4/1 "ภาษีอากรและการพนันหัวเมืองในมณฑลลาวเฉียง." (8 ธันวาคม ร.ศ. 109-25 มกราคม ร.ศ. 111).

_____ร.5 ค. 14.4/2 เรื่อง "ภาษีอากรและการพนันหัวเมืองในมณฑลลาวเฉียง."

_____ร.5 ค. 14.4/7 เรื่อง "จีนเต็งทำภาษีอากรเกี่ยวด้วยราชการทางเมืองนครเชียงใหม่." ลงวันที่ 27 ธันวาคม ร.ศ. 113.

———ร.5 ค. 40/3 ปึกที่ 2 "รายงานหลวงประชาคดีกิจ เรื่องภูมิประเทศเขตแดนฝ่ายตะวันตกเฉียงเหนือเมืองนครเชียงใหม่." สำเนาที่ 6229 ลงวันที่ 11 สิงหาคม ร.ศ. 109.

———ร.5 บ. 11 ก/8 "รัชกาลที่ 5 ถึงพระยาราชสัมภากร." ลงเดือน 8 จ.ศ. 1245.

———ร.5 บ. 12/5 "รัชกาลที่ 5 ทูลสมเด็จพระเจ้าบรมวงศ์เธอเจ้าฟ้ามหามาลา กรมพระบำราบปรปักษ์." ร. ที่ 284/88.

———ร.5 บ. 10/35 "แบบแต่งตั้งตำแหน่งกรมหลวงพิชิตปรีชากร."

———ร.5 ฝ. 11/11 "จดหมายเรื่องภูมถานของบ้านเมืองที่เกี่ยวข้องกับนานาประเทศ กรมหลวงเทววงศ์โรปการกราบบังคมทูลรัชการที่ 5." ไม่ปรากฏวันเดือนปี

———ร.5 ฝ. 18.2/5 "คำแปลร่างหนังสือสัญญาครั้งที่ 3 นายวิเลร์ถึงกรมหลวงเทวะวงศ์วโรปการ" ลงวันที่ 29 กันยายน ร.ศ. 113.

———ร.5 ฝ. 19/4 "พระยาสุริยานุวัตรกราบทูล กรมหลวงเทวะวงศ์วโรปการ." ที่ 75 ลงวันที่ 16 ตุลาคม ร.ศ. 121.

———ร.5 ฝ. 19/11 "สำเนาประกาศเจ้าพระยาสุริยพงษ์ผลิตเดช เจ้าเมืองน่าน เรื่องมอบเมืองที่ยกให้ฝรั่งเศสตามสัญญา." ลงวันที่ 13 กุมภาพันธ์ ร.ศ. 112. ลงวันที่ 9 ธันวาคม ร.ศ. 123.

———ร.5 ฝ. 20/3 "กรมหลวงดำรงราชานุภาพถึงกรมหมื่นสมมตอมรพันธ์ ที่ 145/12367." ลงวันที่ 16 กรกฎาคม ร.ศ. 115.

———ร.5 ฝ. 20/4 "ข้าหลวงนครน่านกราบทูลกรมหลวงดำรงราชานุภาพ." ที่ 1/32 ลงวันที่ 11 เมษายน ร.ศ. 121.

———ร.5 ม. 2.21 ก/41 เล่ม 21 "ศุภอักษรพระเจ้าอินทรวิชยานนท์ กราบทูลสมเด็จพระเจ้าบรมวงศ์เธอเจ้าฟ้ามหามาลา กรมพระยาบำราบปรปักษ์."

———ร.5 ม. 2.21 ก/11 เล่ม 3 "พระยาราชสัมภาราก กราบทูลสมเด็จพระเจ้าบรมวงศ์เธอเจ้าฟ้ามหามาลา กรมพระบำราบปรปักษ์."

———ร.5 ม. 13/8 "พระราชบัญญัติเลิกทาส คำกราบบังคมทูลพระองค์เจ้าระพีพัฒนศักดิ์ เสนาบดียุติธรรม." ลงวันที่ 17 กรกฎาคม ร.ศ. 123.

———ร.5 ม. 13.2/28 "จัดการทหารมณฑลพายัพ." ลงวันที่ 13 ตุลาคม ร.ศ. 112.

———ร.5 ม. 16/10 "รายงานพระองค์เพ็ญฯ เสด็จตรวจการป่าไม้." ลงวันที่...พฤษภาคม ร.ศ. 112.

———ร.5 ม. 16.2/58 "กรมหมื่นดำรงราชานุภาพกราบทูลกรมหมื่นสมมตอรพันธ์." ที่ 130/1954 ลงวันที่ 17 มิถุนายน ร.ศ. 118.

———ร.5 ม. 28.1/4 "เงินสำหรับเจ้าผู้ครองเมืองประเทศราช." ลงวันที่...กุมภาพันธ์ ร.ศ. 127.

———ร.5 ม. 40/5 "สารตราเจ้าพระยาจักรีถึงเจ้าพระยาไกรโกษา." ลงวันที่ 7 ตุลาคม พ.ศ. 2435.

———ร.5 ม. 58/1 "พระยาปราบสงครามคิดก่อการกำเริบ." (สิงหาคม ร.ศ. 108-20 มีนาคม ร.ศ. 108).

———ร.5 ม. 58/21 "ราษฎรขัดขืนไม่ยอมทำตามคำสั่งทางราชการ." (28 มีนาคม ร.ศ. 121-27 พฤศจิกายน ร.ศ. 121).

———ร.5 ม. 58/32 "ราชการหัวเมืองเรื่องขมุ." ลงวันที่ 25 กุมภาพันธ์ ร.ศ. 109.

———ร.5 ม. 58/33 "พระยาศรีสหเทพออกไปจัดราชการทางมณฑลตะวันตกเฉียงเหนือ และมีพระราชบัญญัติอากรที่ดินด้วย." (30 มกราคม ร.ศ. 118-30 มิถุนายน ร.ศ. 119).

———ร.5 ม. 58/40 "เรื่องจัดระเบียบเก็บเงินค่าราชการ และผลประโยชน์ในมณฑลพายัพ." ลงวันที่ 5 สิงหาคม ร.ศ. 115.

———ร.5 ม. 58/42 "พระยาศรีสหเทพตรวจจัดราชการต่างๆ ในมณฑลพายัพ." ลงวันที่ 3 พฤษภาคม ร.ศ. 118.

———ร.5 ม. 58/45 "ยกเว้นเก็บเงินค่าราชการในมณฑลพายัพ." ลงวันที่ 3 พฤษภาคม ร.ศ. 120.

———ร.5 ม. 58/59 "ภาษีอากรต่างๆ ทางลาวเฉียง." ลงวันที่ 21 กรกฎาคม ร.ศ. 112.

———ร.5 ม. 58/85 "เรื่องตั้งค่าด่านเมืองเชียงแสน เมืองเชียงราย เชียงของ." (14 กรกฎาคม-1 กันยายน ร.ศ. 117).

———ร.5 ม. 58/88 "รายงานกรมหมื่นพิชิตปรีชากร." ลงวันที่ 6 ๆ 8 ค่ำ จ.ศ. 1246.

———ร.5 ม. 58/89 "เบ็ดเตล็ดเรื่องราชการเมืองเชียงใหม่ปีระกา สัปตศก 1247." (มิถุนายน ร.ศ. 104-ธันวาคม ร.ศ. 107).

———ร.5 ม. 58/93 "เจ้าพระยารัตนบดินทร์ กราบบังคมทูลรัชกาลที่ 5." (3 เมษายน-25 มิถุนายน ร.ศ. 108).

———ร.5 ม. 58/98 "หนังสือราชการฝ่ายเมืองนครเชียงใหม่." (5 มิถุนายน ร.ศ. 108-26 มีนาคม ร.ศ. 108).

———ร.5 ม. 58/103 "พระองค์เจ้าโสณบัณฑิตย์กราบบังคมทูลรัชกาลที่ 5." ที่ 18/119 ลงวันที่ 21 มีนาคม ร.ศ. 108.

———ร.5 ม. 58/126 "เรื่องตลาดที่เมืองเชียงใหม่กรมหมื่นดำรงราชานุภาพกราบบังคมทูลรัชกาลที่ 5." ลงวันที่ 24 เมษายน ร.ศ. 119.

———ร.5 ม. 58/143 "ประวัติเจ้าอินทวโรรสสุริยวงษ์ เจ้าผู้ครองนครเชียงใหม่."

———ร.5 ม. 58/170 "เรื่องธรรมเนียมถือน้ำมณฑลพายัพ." ลงวันที่ 15 มิถุนายน-18 กรกฎาคม ร.ศ. 115.

———ร.5 ม. 58/177 "เจ้านรนันทไชยชวลิตเจ้านครลำปาง กราบทูลกรมหมื่นดำรงราชานุภาพ." ลงวันที่ 31 มกราคม ร.ศ. 111.

———ร.5 ม. 58/181 "รายงานต่างๆ จัดราชการเมืองลำปาง." (20 ธันวาคม ร.ศ.116-เมษายน ร.ศ. 127).

———ร.5 ม. 58/191 "หนังสือสัญญาว่าด้วยการที่เจ้านครเชียงใหม่จะรักษาบ้านเมืองให้เรียบร้อย." ร.ศ. 92.

———ร.5 ม. 58/193 "พิกัดภาษีอากรมณฑลพายัพ." (ร.ศ. 103-104).

———ร.5 ม. 99/3 "รายงานหลวงอนุรักษ์ภูเบศกราบทูลเจ้าฟ้ามหามาลากรมพระบำราบปรปักษ์. ลงวันที่ 6ฯ13 ค่ำ ปีวอก จ.ศ. 1426.

———ร.5 "สารบาญสมุดพิเศษ." เล่ม 6 หน้า 420.

———ร.5 "สารบาญสมุดพิเศษ." เล่ม 8 หน้า 83.

———ร.5 "สารบาญสมุดพิเศษ." เล่ม 10 หน้า 78-82.

———ร.6 ก.1/27 "รายงานตรวจราชการกรมหลวงพิษณุโลกประชานาถ." ลงวันที่ 27 มกราคม พ.ศ. 2458.

———ร.6 ค.11/1 "เงินเดือนเจ้าแก้วนวรัฐ เจ้าผู้ครองนครเชียงใหม่." ลงวันที่ 21 สิงหาคม พ.ศ. 2463.

———ร.6 ค.11/8 "เงินเดือนเจ้าจักรคำขจรศักดิ์ เจ้าผู้ครองนครลำพูน." ลงวันที่ 1 ตุลาคม พ.ศ. 2462.

———ร.6 ค.5.3/2 "มิสเตอร์ แอล.ไวเลอร์ เจ้ากรมรถไฟกราบทูลพระเจ้าบรมวงศ์เธอกรมหลวงนเรศวรวรฤทธิ์." ที่ 1111 ป. ลงวันที่ 20 พฤศจิกายน พ.ศ. 2455.

———ร.6 กษ.5/6 "บริษัทบอมเบย์เบอร์มา ขอพระกรุณาเรื่องหนี้สินที่เกี่ยวกับเจ้าบุญวาทย์ในการทำป่าไม้ แม่ต้าเมืองลอง." ลงวันที่ 1 สิงหาคม พ.ศ. 2470.

———ร.7 ม.1/34 "บัญชีรายการเก็บเงินรัชชูปการทั่วพระราชอาณาจักร พ.ศ. 2469-2470." ลงวันที่...ตุลาคม พ.ศ. 2469.

———ร.7 รล.2/6 "รายงานประชุมสภา. ครั้งที่ 7/2469 ลงวันที่ 17 พฤษภาคม พ.ศ. 2469." บรรณาสาร, กอง, กระทรวงต่างประเทศ เอกสารแฟ้มที่ 2.7 แผนกสนธิสัญญา ระหว่างสยามฝรั่งเศส ปี ร.ศ. 122.

———เอกสารแฟ้มที่ 8.1 ตอนที่ 2 "หนังสือมิสเตอร์กูลด์กราบบังคมทูลหลวงเทวะวงษ์วโรประการ." ลงวันที่ 25 มิถุนายน พ.ศ. 2431.

1.2 เอกสารชั้นต้นที่ตีพิมพ์แล้ว [Published Primary Sources]

กฎหมายโคสาราษฎร์ ภาคปริวรรต, ลำดับที่ 16. ปริวรรตโดย สมหมาย เปรมจิตต์. โครงการตำรา คณะสังคมศาสตร์ มหาวิทยาลัยเชียงใหม่, 2520.

"กฎหมายพระเจ้าน่าน." ศูนย์ส่งเสริมและศึกษาวัฒนธรรมลานนาไทย วิทยาลัยครูเชียงใหม่. 2533. (อัดสำเนา)

กฎหมายล้านนา ภาคปริวรรต, ลำดับที่ 2. ภาควิชาสังคมวิทยาและมานุษยวิทยา คณะสังคมศาสตร์ มหาวิทยาลัยเชียงใหม่, 2518.

คร่าวกาวิละและตำนานเมืองเชียงแสน. อุดม รุ่งเรืองศรี ปริวรรต. ศูนย์วัฒนธรรมจังหวัดเชียงใหม่ และศูนย์ศิลปวัฒนธรรม วิทยาลัยครูเชียงใหม่, 2528.

คำสอนพระยามังราย ภาคปริวรรต, ลำดับที่ 11. ภาควิชาสังคมวิทยาและมานุษยวิทยา คณะสังคมศาสตร์ มหาวิทยาลัยเชียงใหม่, 2519.

คำอ่านศิลาจารึกเลขทะเบียน ชร./16 “คำอ่านศิลาจารึกวัดศรีอุโมงคำ.” จ.ศ. 845 *ศิลปากร,* ฉบับที่ 2, (กรกฎาคม, 2518).

จารึกในประเทศไทย เล่ม 2. กรุงเทพฯ: หอสมุดแห่งชาติ กรมศิลปากร, 2529.

“จารึกลานทองสมเด็จพระมหาเถรจุฑามุณี พุทธศักราช 1919.” *จารึกสมัยสุโขทัย.* กรุงเทพฯ: กรมศิลปากร, 2527.

“จารึกวัดป่าแดง หลักที่ 9.” ใน *จารึกสุโขทัย.* ศูนย์สุโขทัยศึกษา มหาวิทยาลัยศรีนครินทรวิโรฒ พิษณุโลก, 2520. (อัดสำเนา)

จำปา เยื้องเจริญ และคนอื่นๆ. *ศิลาจารึกในพิพิธภัณฑ์สถานแห่งชาติหริภุญไชย.* กรุงเทพฯ: กรมศิลปากร, 2522.

ชร. 8 “จารึกฐานพระพุทธรูปพระเจ้าล้านทอง พ.ศ. 2269.” *จารึกล้านนา* ภาค 1, เล่ม 1. “จารึกจังหวัดเชียงราย น่าน พะเยา แพร่”.

ตำนานเจ้า 7 พระองค์เชียงใหม่. ปริวรรตโดย ทอง ไชยชาติ. (พิมพ์เป็นที่ระลึกในงานศพนางจินดา อินทเคหะ เชียงใหม่ 13 กุมภาพันธ์, 2517).

ตำนานเจ้าเจ็ดตน ฉบับสิงฆะ วรรณสัย. ปริวรรตโดย สงวน โชติสุขรัตน์. เชียงใหม่: สงวนการพิมพ์, 2511.

ตำนานนพบุรีเมืองพิงค์เชียงใหม่. ปริวรรตโดย เทิม มีเต็ม. คัมภีร์ใบลานอักษรธรรมล้านนาสยามสมาคม. มัดที่ 50 เลขที่ 506, หน้าลานที่ 37.

“ตำนานพระธาตุดอยสุเทพ” *ประชุมตำนานพระธาตุ,* ภาคที่ 2. พระนคร: โรงพิมพ์พระจันทร์, 2510. (พิมพ์เป็นอนุสรณ์งานพระราชทานเพลิงศพ พันตำรวจโท สลับ เกียรติสุต 2 ธันวาคม, 2510).

ตำนานพื้นเมืองเชียงใหม่. ปริวรรตโดย ทน ตนมั่น. คณะกรรมการจัดพิมพ์เอกสารทางประวัติศาสตร์ สำนักนายกรัฐมนตรี, 2514.

ตำนานพื้นเมืองลานนาเชียงใหม่. เชียงใหม่: สถาบันวิจัยสังคม มหาวิทยาลัยเชียงใหม่, 2524.

ตำนานพระธาตุหริภุญชัย. (พิมพ์เป็นอนุสรณ์งานพระราชทานเพลิงศพ พระพิจิตรโอสถ (รอด สุตันตานนท์) 29 พฤษภาคม, 2505).

ตำนานมูลศาสนา. (พิมพ์เป็นอนุสรณ์งานพระราชทานเพลิงศพ ม.ล. เดช สนิทวงศ์ ณ อยุธยา 17 ธันวาคม, 2518).

ตำนานมูลศาสนา ฉบับวัดป่าแดง. เชียงใหม่: ภาควิชาสังคมวิทยาและมานุษยวิทยา คณะสังคมศาสตร์ มหาวิทยาลัยเชียงใหม่, 2519.

ตำนานเมืองเชียงตุง. ปริวรรตโดย ทวี สว่างปัญญางกูร. เชียงใหม่: แผนกอนุรักษ์และเผยแพร่วรรณกรรมล้านนา ธรรมสถาน มหาวิทยาลัยเชียงใหม่, 2527.

ตำนานเมืองพะเยาและค่าวซอเล่นคำเป็นแท้. ปริวรรตโดย อรุณรัตน์ วิเชียรเขียว และจินตนา มัธยมบุรุษ. เชียงใหม่: ศูนย์วัฒนธรรมจังหวัดเชียงใหม่ วิทยาลัยครูเชียงใหม่.

“ตำนานสุวรรณโคมคำ” ใน *ประชุมพงศาวดาร* ภาคที่ 72, เล่ม 45. พระนคร: องค์การค้าของคุรุสภา, 2512.

“ตำนานสิงหนวติ” ใน *ประชุมพงศาวดาร* ภาคที่ 61. (พิมพ์เป็นอนุสรณ์งานพระราชทานเพลิงศพ พลตรีเจ้าราชบุตร (วงษ์ตวัน ณ เชียงใหม่) 12 มกราคม, 2516).

ตำนานสิบห้าราชวงศ์ เล่ม 1, ผูกที่ 1-2. เชียงใหม่: สถาบันวิจัยสังคม มหาวิยาลัยเชียงใหม่, 2524.

ธรรมศาสตร์และกฎหมายพระยามังราย. ปริวรรตโดย มณี พยอมพงค์. เอกสารงานวิจัยการถ่ายทอดคัมภีร์โบราณ, โครงการไทยศึกษา จุฬาลงกรณ์มหาวิทยาลัย 2518. (อัดสำเนา)

ทวี สว่างปัญญางกูร, ปริวรรต. *ตำนานเมืองเชียงตุง.* แผนกอนุรักษ์และเผยแพร่วรรณกรรมล้านนา ธรรมสถาน มหาวิทยาลัยเชียงใหม่, 2527. (อัดสำเนา).

———, ปริวรรต. *ตำนานเมืองยอง.* เชียงใหม่: ศูนย์หนังสือเชียงใหม่, 2527.

ประชุมตำนานพระธาตุ, ภาคที่ 1. (พิมพ์เป็นที่ระลึกในงานศพ นางแข ฟูศักดิ์ 17 สิงหาคม, 2485).

ประชุมศิลาจารึก ภาคที่ 3. คณะกรรมการจัดพิมพ์เอกสารทางประวัติศาสตร์ วัฒนธรรมและโบราณคดี สำนักนายกรัฐมนตรี, 2508.

ประชุมศิลาจารึก ภาคที่ 4. คณะกรรมการจัดพิมพ์เอกสารทางประวัติศาสตร์ วัฒนธรรมและโบราณคดี สำนักนายกรัฐมนตรี, 2513.

ประชุมศิลาจารึก ภาคที่ 7. คณะกรรมการจัดพิมพ์เอกสารทางประวัติศาสตร์ วัฒนธรรมและโบราณคดี สำนักนายกรัฐมนตรี, 2535.

ประดิษฐ์ มนูธรรม, หลวง (ปรีดี พนมยงค์) ผู้รวบรวม. *ประชุมกฎหมายไทย.* ภาคเพิ่มเติม กรุงเทพฯ: สำนักพิมพ์นิติสาส์น, 2473.

ประสาน บุญประคอง และ ประเสริฐ ณ นคร. "คำอ่านศิลาจารึกและอักษรภาษาไทยที่ใช้ในลานนาไทย" ใน *ศิลปากร* 4. (พฤศจิกายน 2512): 77-79.

ประเสริฐ ณ นคร, ปริวรรต. *มังรายศาสตร์.* (พิมพ์เป็นอนุสรณ์งานพระราชทานเพลิงศพหลวงโหตรกิตยานุพัทธ์ (อาสา โหตระกิตย์) 4 เมษายน, 2514).

"พระราชบัญญัติลักษณะทาสมณฑลตะวันออกเฉียงเหนือ" *ราชกิจจานุเบกษา* เล่มที่ 17. มิถุนายน ร.ศ. 119, หน้า 134.

"พระราชบัญญัติสำหรับข้าหลวงชำระความหัวเมือง." *ราชกิจจานุเบกษา* เล่ม 1. ลงวันอาทิตย์ เดือน 12 แรม 6 ค่ำ จ.ศ. 1276, หน้า 274-276.

เพนธ์, ฮันส์. "คำจารึกที่ฐานพระพุทธรูปจากวัดกลางเวียงเชียงราย (พ.ศ. 2280)." ใน *ศิลปากร* 4. (พฤศจิกายน 2519).

———. *คำจารึกที่ฐานพระพุทธรูปในนครเชียงใหม่.* กรุงเทพฯ: โรงพิมพ์สำนักนายกรัฐมนตรี, 2519.

มังรายศาสตร์. ปริวรรตและเรียบเรียงโดย ประเสริฐ ณ นคร. กรุงเทพฯ: ภาควิชาประวัติศาสตร์ มหาวิทยาลัยศรีนครินทรวิโรฒ ประสานมิตร, 2521.

มังรายศาสตร์ ฉบับวัดไชยสถาน. ศูนย์วัฒนธรรม จังหวัดเชียงใหม่ และศูนย์ส่งเสริมศิลปวัฒนธรรม สหวิทยาลัยล้านนา, เอกสารลำดับที่ 12 มกราคม 2529.

มานิต วัลลิโภดม. *ตำนานสิงหนวติกุมาร* ฉบับสอบค้น. คณะกรรมการจัดพิมพ์เอกสารทางประวัติศาสตร์ สำนักนายกรัฐมนตรี, 2516.

เดเนียล แมคกิลวารี ดี.ดี. *กึ่งศตวรรษในหมู่คนไทยและคนลาว.* แปลโดย จิตราภรณ์ ตันรัตนกุล. กรุงเทพฯ: สำนักพิมพ์สยามประเทศ, 2538.

รัตนปัญญาเถระ, พระภิกษุ. *ชินกาลมาลีปกรณ์.* แปลโดย ศ. ร.ต.ท. แสง มนวิทูร. (พิมพ์เป็นอนุสรณ์ในงานพระราชทานเพลิงศพ ศ. ร.ต.ท. แสง มนวิทูร 20 เมษายน, 2517).

ราชวงศาพื้นเมืองเชียงใหม่ ภาคปริวรรต ลำดับที่ 4. ปริวรรตโดย สมหมาย เปรมจิตต์. เชียงใหม่: ภาควิชาสังคมวิทยาและมานุษยวิทยา คณะสังคมศาสตร์ มหาวิทยาลัยเชียงใหม่, 2518.

ศิลาจารึกในพิพิธภัณฑ์แห่งชาติหริภุญไชย. กรุงเทพฯ: กรมศิลปากร, 2522.

ศิลาจารึกเลขทะเบียน ชร./6 "คำอ่านศิลาจารึกวัดพระเกิด จ.ศ. 875." *ศิลปากร,* ฉบับที่ 3 (กันยายน 2518.

ศิลาจารึกเลขทะเบียน ลพ./9 "ศิลาจารึกลำดับกษัตริย์ราชวงศ์มังราย." *ศิลปากร,* ฉบับที่ 2 (พฤษภาคม 2529).

"ศิลาจารึกวัดเกตการาม" ตำบลวัดเกต อำเภอเมือง จังหวัดเชียงใหม่. *ศิลปากร,* ปีที่ 16, (กันยายน 2515).

สงวน โชติสุขรัตน์. *ประชุมตำนานลานนาไทย* เล่ม 1. พระนคร: สำนักพิมพ์โอเดียนสโตร์, 2515.

———. *ประชุมตำนานลานนาไทย* เล่ม 2. พระนคร: สำนักพิมพ์โอเดียนสโตร์, 2515.

———. "ตำนานพระยามังรายสร้างเมืองเชียงตุง." *รวมสารนิยายไทย.* นครหลวงกรุงเทพธนบุรี: โอเดียนสโตร์, 2515.

สิงฆะ วรรณสัย. ถอดความ. *โคลงมังทรารบเชียงใหม่.* กรุงเทพฯ: โรงพิมพ์มิตรนราการพิมพ์, 2522.

———, ปริวรรต. *พุทธตำนานพระเจ้าเลียบโลก.* ผูกที่ 9 ลานที่ 10.

เสถียร ลายลักษณ์ และคนอื่นๆ, ผู้รวบรวม. *ประชุมกฎหมายประจำศก,* เล่ม 17, 26, 28. กรุงเทพฯ: โรงพิมพ์เดลิเมล์, 2477.

สมุตตราช ประเพณี 6 ประการ. ศูนย์ส่งเสริมและศึกษาวัฒนธรรมลานนาไทย วิทยาลัยครูเชียงใหม่ 2524. (อัดสำเนา)

สมหมาย เปรมจิตต์, ปริวรรต. *ประเพณี 6 ประการ.* ภาคปริวรรต ลำดับที่ 17 ภาควิชาสังคมวิทยาและมานุษยวิทยา คณะสังคมศาสตร์ มหาวิทยาลัยเชียงใหม่, 2521. (อัดสำเนา)

สรัสวดี อ๋องสกุล, ปริวรรต. *หลักฐานประวัติศาสตร์ล้านนา จากเอกสารคัมภีร์ใบลานและพับหนังสา.* 2534. (อัดสำเนา)

———, ปริวรรต. *พื้นเมืองน่าน.* ฉบับวัดพระเกิด 2537. (อัดสำเนา)

หนังสือพื้นเมืองน่าน. เอกสารอันดับที่ 9 ศูนย์วัฒนธรรมเชียงใหม่ วิทยาลัยครูเชียงใหม่, มกราคม 2528. (อัดสำเนา)

สมหมาย เปรมจิตต์. "หนังสือโอวาทคำสอน" *วารสารมนุษยศาสตร์ 2,* (กันยายน 2518), หน้า 41-47. (อัดสำเนา)

อรุณรัตน์ วิเชียรเขียว, ปริวรรต. *มังรายธรรมศาสตร์.* ฉบับวัดช้างค้ำ อำเภอเมือง จังหวัดน่าน, 2526.

อรุณรัตน์ วิเชียรเขียว และ ศรีธน คำแปง, ปริวรรต. *ธรรมศาสตร์หลวงและธรรมศาสตร์ราชก็อนา.* หนังสือปริวรรตจากคัมภีร์ใบลานชุด *ตำนานเมืองและกฎหมายล้านนา,* เอกสารลำดับที่ 3 และ 4. คณะสังคมศาสตร์ มหาวิทยาลัยเชียงใหม่ และศูนย์ส่งเสริมการศึกษาวัฒนธรรมล้านนาวิทยาลัยครูเชียงใหม่, 2528. (อัดสำเนา)

——— และ ศรีธน คำแปง, ปริวรรต. *หัตถกัมมวินิจฉัยบาฬีฎีกาสมมุติราช.* หนังสือปริวรรตจากคัมภีร์ใบลานชุด *ตำนานเมืองและกฎหมายล้านนา,* เอกสารลำดับที่ 3 และ 4. คณะสังคมศาสตร์ มหาวิทยาลัยเชียงใหม่ และศูนย์ส่งเสริมการศึกษาวัฒนธรรมล้านนาวิทยาลัยครูเชียงใหม่ 2527. (อัดสำเนา)

2. เอกสารชั้นรอง (Secondary Sources)

2.1 หนังสือ, เอกสารประกอบการสัมมนา [Books and Articles]

กรมพระนราธิปประพันธ์พงศ์, พระเจ้าบรมวงศ์เธอ. *พระราชพงศาวดารพม่า,* เล่ม 1. พระนคร: องค์การค้าคุรุสภา, 2505.

กรรณิการ์ วิมลเกษม. *อักษรฝักขามที่พบในศิลาจารึกภาคเหนือ.* ภาควิชาภาษาตะวันออก คณะโบราณคดี มหาวิทยาลัยศิลปากร 2526. (อัดสำเนา)

เกษตร, กระทรวง. *ประวัติป่าไม้ในรอบ 72 ปี.* (พิมพ์เป็นอนุสรณ์งานพระราชทานเพลิงศพพระยาดรุพันพิทักษ์ 30 ธันวาคม, 2511).

ไกรศรี นิมมานเหมินท์. "ความรู้พื้นฐานด้านลานนาคดี: ด้านศาสนาและวัฒนธรรม" ใน *ลานนาปริทัศน์.* (พิมพ์เนื่องในวาระครบรอบปีคล้ายวันมรณะ นางกิมฮ้อ นิมมานเหมินท์, 2525).

———. *ลายคราม.* (หนังสืออนุสรณ์เฉลิมฉลองอายุครบ 6 รอบ นายไกรศรี นิมมานเหมินท์ 24 ธันวาคม, 2527).

———. "ตราหลวงหลาบเงินของพระนางวิสุทธิเทวี." *รวมบทความล้านนาคดีสัญจร: ตามรอยโคลงมังทรารบเชียงใหม่.* ชมรมล้านนาคดี 2533. (อัดสำเนา)

ขจร สุขพานิช. "การเสียดินแดน ใน ร.ศ. 111." ใน *ข้อมูลประวัติศาสตร์บางกอก.* กรุงเทพฯ: ภาควิชาประวัติศาสตร์ มหาวิทยาลัยศรีนครินทรวิโรฒ ประสานมิตร, 2518.

———. *ประวัติศาสตร์ไทย พ.ศ. 1600-2310.* กรุงเทพฯ: ภาควิชาประวัติศาสตร์ คณะสังคมศาสตร์ มหาวิทยาลัยศรีนครินทรวิโรฒ ประสานมิตร, 2521.

คณะกรรมการจัดทำหนังสืออนุสรณ์พระราชพิธีเปิดพระบรมราชานุสาวรีย์สามกษัตริย์. *ล้านนาไทย.* เชียงใหม่: ทิพย์เนตรการพิมพ์, 2526-2527.

คณะกรรมการดำเนินงานจัดทำหนังสือกำแพงเมืองเชียงใหม่. *กำแพงเมืองเชียงใหม่.* เชียงใหม่: ทิพย์เนตรการพิมพ์, 2529.

คำให้การชาวกรุงเก่า. คำให้การขุนหลวงหาวัด และพระราชพงศาวดารกรุงเก่าฉบับหลวงประเสริฐอักษรนิติ์. นครหลวงกรุงเทพธนบุรี: คลังวิทยา, 2515.

เคดี้, จอห์น เอฟ. *ไทย พม่า ลาว และกัมพูชา.* แปลและเรียบเรียงโดย ภรณี กาญจนัษฐิติ และชื่นจิตร อำไพพรรณ. กรุงเทพฯ: โรงพิมพ์พิฆเณศ, 2520.

โครงการศึกษาวิจัยใบลานในภาคเหนือ สถาบันวิจัยสังคม มหาวิทยาลัยเชียงใหม่. *รายชื่อหนังสือโบราณล้านนา,* เอกสารไมโครฟิล์มของสถาบันวิจัยสังคม มหาวิทยาลัยเชียงใหม่ พ.ศ. 2521-2523. 2534. (อัดสำเนา)

จดหมายเหตุการตรวจสอบและการสืบค้นดวงเมือง "นพบุรีนครพิงค์เชียงใหม่." เชียงใหม่: ส. ทรัพย์การพิมพ์, 2527.

จิตร ภูมิศักดิ์. *ข้อเท็จจริงว่าด้วยชนชาติขอม.* กรุงเทพฯ: สำนักพิมพ์ไม้งาม, 2525.

———. *คำเป็นมาของคำสยาม ไทย ลาว และขอม และลักษณะทางสังคมของชื่อชนชาติ.* กรุงเทพฯ: โครงการตำราสังคมศาสตร์และมนุษยศาสตร์, 2519.

จุลสารคลังข้อมูลจารึกล้านนา, ฉบับที่ 5 สถาบันวิจัยสังคม มหาวิทยาลัยเชียงใหม่ เชียงใหม่: บุญชัยการพิมพ์, 2534.

ฉัตรทิพย์ นาถสุภา. *เศรษฐกิจหมู่บ้านไทยในอดีต.* กรุงเทพฯ: สำนักพิมพ์สร้างสรรค์, 2527.

ชูสิทธิ์ ชูชาติ. *พ่อค้าวัวต่าง: ผู้บุกเบิกการค้าขายในหมู่บ้านภาคเหนือของประเทศไทย* (พ.ศ. 2398-2503). รายงานการวิจัยกรมการฝึกหัดครู, 2525. (อัดสำเนา)

ซิมเบอร์แมน, คาร์ล ซี. *การสำรวจเศรษฐกิจในชนบทสยาม.* แปลและเรียบเรียงโดย ซิม วีระไวทยะ. กรุงเทพฯ: มูลนิธิโครงการตำราสังคมศาสตร์และมนุษยศาสตร์, 2525. (อัดสำเนา)

ดำรงราชานุภาพ, สมเด็จกรมพระยา และพระยาราชเสนา. *เทศาภิบาล.* (อนุสรณ์งานพระราชทานเพลิงศพพระยาอรรถกวีสุนทร (สงวน ศตรัตอรรถกวีสุนทร) 9 พฤษภาคม, 2503).

ต้วน ลี เชิง. "ประวัติศาสตร์ไทยก่อนสมัยกรุงศรีอยุธยา" *พลิกต้นตระกูลไทย.* กรุงเทพฯ: สำนักพิมพ์เคล็ดไทย, 2529.

แถมสุข นุ่นนนท์. "อิทธิพลทางการเมืองและเศรษฐกิจของอังกฤษในเมืองเชียงใหม่." ใน *รายงานสัมมนาประวัติศาสตร์และโบราณคดี.* ครั้งที่ 1 คณะมนุษยศาสตร์ มหาวิทยาลัยเชียงใหม่, 2510.

ทิน อ่อง, หม่อง. *ประวัติศาสตร์พม่า.* แปลโดย เพ็ชรี สุมิตร. กรุงเทพฯ: ไทยวัฒนาพานิช, 2519.

ทิพากรวงศ์, เจ้าพระยา. *พระราชพงศาวดารกรุงรัตนโกสินทร์* รัชกาลที่ 2. พระนคร: องค์การค้าคุรุสภา, 2503.

———. *พระราชพงศาวดารกรุงรัตนโกสินทร์* รัชกาลที่ 3. พระนคร: องค์การค้าคุรุสภา, 2505.

———. *พระราชพงศาวดารกรุงรัตนโกสินทร์* รัชกาลที่ 4. พระนคร: องค์การค้าคุรุสภา, 2505.

นราธิปประพันธ์พงศ์, พระเจ้าบรมวงศ์เธอ กรมพระ. *พระราชพงศาวดารพม่า,* เล่ม 1 กรุงเทพฯ: องค์การค้าคุรุสภา, 2505.

นรินทรเทวี, กรมหลวง. *จดหมายเหตุความทรงจำ.* กรุงเทพฯ: องค์การค้าคุรุสภา, 2516.

นิธิ เอียวศรีวงศ์. *การเมืองไทยสมัยพระเจ้ากรุงธนบุรี.* กรุงเทพฯ: ศิลปวัฒนธรรม, 2529.

———. "ความสำคัญด้านประวัติศาสตร์ ศาสนา และวัฒนธรรมของดอยสุเทพ-ปุย." *อุทยานแห่งชาติดอยสุเทพ-ปุย: การจัดการและการอนุรักษ์.* เชียงใหม่: โครงการศูนย์ส่งเสริมศิลปวัฒนธรรม มหาวิทยาลัยเชียงใหม่, 2536.

———. "ปัญหาการศึกษาและการประยุกต์ใช้ประวัติศาสตร์ไทย." เอกสารการสอนชุดวิชา *สังคมศึกษา* 5 (ประวัติศาสตร์ไทยสำหรับครู). มหาวิทยาลัยสุโขทัยธรรมาธิราช, 2529.

———. "ลักษณะการปกครองประเทศสยามแต่โบราณ: พื้นฐานทางเศรษฐกิจ." *สายธารแห่งความคิด.* กรุงเทพฯ: บริษัทพิมพ์สวยจำกัด, 2532.

นวลศิริ วงศ์ทางสวัสดิ์. *ชุมชนโบราณในล้านนา.* เชียงใหม่: ภาควิชาภูมิศาสตร์ คณะสังคมศาสตร์ มหาวิทยาลัยเชียงใหม่, 2528. (อัดสำเนา)

———. *ภูมิศาสตร์กายภาพภาคเหนือของประเทศไทย.* พิมพ์ครั้งที่ 3. ภาควิชาภูมิศาสตร์ มหาวิทยาลัยเชียงใหม่ 2534. (อัดสำเนา)

นัยนา โปร่งธุระ. *อักษรธรรมล้านนา.* ภาควิชาภาษาตะวันออก คณะโบราณคดี มหาวิทยาลัยศิลปากร, 2527. (อัดสำเนา)

บ็อค, คาร์ล. *สมัยพระปิยมหาราช.* แปลโดย เสถียร พันธรังสี และอัมพร จุลานนท์. พระนคร: โรงพิมพ์เฟื่องอักษร, 2505.

บุญเสริม สาตราภัย. *ลานนาไทยในอดีต.* เชียงใหม่: โรงพิมพ์ช้างเผือกการพิมพ์, 2522.

——— และสังคิต จันทนโพธิ์. *อดีตลานนา.* กรุงเทพฯ: สำนักพิมพ์เรืองศิลป์, 2525.

ประชากิจกรจักร์, พระยา. *พงศาวดารโยนก.* สำนักพิมพ์คลังวิทยา, 2516.

"ประชุมพงศาวดารภาคที่ 10 พงศาวดารเมืองน่าน." ใน *ประชุมพงศาวดาร* เล่ม 9. พระนคร: คุรุสภา, 2507.

ประเสริฐ ณ นคร. "ประวัติศาสตร์ล้านนาจากจารึก." *งานจารึกและประวัติศาสตร์ของ ประเสริฐ ณ นคร.* (พิมพ์เนื่องในโอกาสฉลองอายุ 6 รอบ ศ. ดร. ประเสริฐ ณ นคร 21 มีนาคม, 2534).

———. "สัมพันธภาพระหว่างราชวงศ์พระร่วงกับราชวงศ์น่าน." *งานจารึกและประวัติศาสตร์ ของ ประเสริฐ ณ นคร.* (พิมพ์เนื่องในโอกาสฉลองอายุ 6 รอบ ศ. ดร. ประเสริฐ ณ นคร 21 มีนาคม, 2534).

———. *สารัตถคดีประเสริฐ ณ นคร.* กรุงเทพฯ: โรงพิมพ์พิฆเนศ, 2517.

ผ่องศรี วนาสิน และ ทิวา ศุภจรรยา. *เมืองโบราณบริเวณชายฝั่งทะเลเดิมของที่ราบภาคกลางประเทศไทย: การศึกษาตำแหน่งที่ตั้งและภูมิศาสตร์สัมพันธ์.* กรุงเทพฯ: โครงการเผยแพร่ผลงานวิจัยฝ่ายวิจัยจุฬาลงกรณ์มหาวิทยาลัย, 2524.

พจนานุกรมล้านนา-ไทย. ฉบับแม่ฟ้าหลวง (จัดทำในวโรกาส "แม่ฟ้าหลวง" เจริญพระชนมายุครบรอบ 90 พรรษา, 2533).

พระครูชินวงศานุวัตร์ (สิงโต ชินวโส) และหนานปวงคำ ตุ้ยเขียว. *วัดปราสาทและบันทึกพระยาหลวงสามล้าน.* พระครูชินวงศานุวัตร์จัดพิมพ์, 2528.

พระราชพงศาวดารกรุงธนบุรี และจดหมายเหตุรายวันทัพสมัยกรุงธนบุรี ใน *ประชุมพงศาวดาร* เล่ม 40. พระนคร: องค์การค้าคุรุสภา, 2512.

พระราชพงศาวดารกรุงศรีอยุธยา ฉบับพระจักรพรรดิพงศ์. พระนคร: คลังวิทยา, 2507.

พระราชพงศาวดารกรุงศรีอยุธยา ฉบับพันจันทนุมาศ. พระนคร: คลังวิทยา, 2507.

พิริยะ ไกรฤกษ์. *พิพิธภัณฑ์สถานแห่งชาติหริภุญไชย.* กรุงเทพฯ: กรมศิลปากรจัดพิมพ์, 2522.

โพธิรังสี, พระภิกษุ. *คำแปลจามเทวีวงศ์ พงศาวดารเมืองหริภุญไชย.* กรุงเทพฯ: โรงพิมพ์รุ่งวัฒนา, 2516.

เพนธ์, ฮันส์. *ประวัติความเป็นมาของล้านนาไทย.* เชียงใหม่: ทิพย์เนตรการพิมพ์, 2526.

———, บรรณาธิการ. *ประวัติพระธาตุดอยตุง.* กรุงเทพฯ: มูลนิธิแม่ฟ้าหลวง และธนาคารไทยพาณิชย์, 2536.

เพ็ญพักตร์ ลิ้มสัมพันธ์. *อักษรธรรมอีสาน.* ภาควิชาภาษาตะวันออก คณะโบราณคดี มหาวิทยาลัยศิลปากร, 2532.

ภาสกร โทณะวณิก. "การศึกษาประวัติศาสตร์นครลำปางจากหลักฐานทางโบราณคดี." *ประวัติศาสตร์และโบราณคดีนครลำปาง.* ลำปาง: สหวิทยาลัยล้านนา วิทยาลัยครูลำปาง, 2524.

มารุต อัมรานนท์. *วัดเจ็ดยอด (มหาโพธาราม) ศิลปยุคทองของล้านนา.* เชียงใหม่: โครงการวิจัยสถาปัตยกรรมล้านนา สถาบันวิจัยสังคม มหาวิทยาลัยเชียงใหม่, 2527.

รุจยา อาภากร, ม.ร.ว. "พัฒนาการทางประวัติศาสตร์และสังคม: สถานภาพของการศึกษาประวัติศาสตร์และสังคม." เอกสารประกอบการสัมมนาเรื่อง "สถานภาพล้านนาคดีศึกษา," จัดโดยศูนย์ส่งเสริมศิลปวัฒนธรรม มหาวิทยาลัยเชียงใหม่ 22-24 สิงหาคม, 2529.

ศรีศักร วัลลิโภดม. "แคว้นหริภุญไชย" ใน *โบราณคดีไทยในทศวรรษที่ผ่านมา.* กรุงเทพฯ: สำนักพิมพ์เมืองโบราณ, 2524.

ศิลปากร, กรม. "ประชุมพงศาวดารภาค 3." *ประชุมพงศาวดาร* ฉบับหอสมุดแห่งชาติ, เล่ม 2. พระนคร: สำนักพิมพ์ก้าวหน้า, 2507.

———. *ประชุมพงศาวดาร ฉบับหอสมุดแห่งชาติ,* เล่ม 4. พระนคร: สำนักพิมพ์ก้าวหน้า, 2507.

———. *ประชุมพงศาวดาร ฉบับหอสมุดแห่งชาติ,* เล่ม 6. พระนคร: สำนักพิมพ์ก้าวหน้า, 2507.

———. "พงศาวดารเมืองเงินยางเชียงแสน." *ประชุมพงศาวดาร* ภาคที่ 61. พระนคร: คุรุสภา, 2507.

———. "พงศาวดารเมืองน่าน" *ประชุมพงศาวดาร* ภาคที่ 10. พระนคร: คุรุสภา, 2507

สงวน โชติสุขรัตน์. *คนดีเมืองเหนือ.* พระนคร: โอเดียนสโตร์, 2515.

สภาพสิ่งแวดล้อมแหล่งศิลปกรรมในจังหวัดลำปาง. หน่วยอนุรักษ์สิ่งแวดล้อมศิลปกรรมท้องถิ่น ศูนย์วัฒนธรรมจังหวัดลำปาง, 2533.

สรัสวดี อ๋องสกุล. *ประวัติศาสตร์ล้านนา.* เชียงใหม่: โครงการข้อสนเทศล้านนาคดีศึกษา โครงการศูนย์ส่งเสริมศิลปวัฒนธรรม มหาวิทยาลัยเชียงใหม่, 2529.

———. "พญางำเมือง: บทวิเคราะห์ใหม่จากตำนานเมืองน่าน." *พะเยา-วิถีชีวิตและภูมิปัญญา.* กรุงเทพฯ: สำนักงานคณะกรรมการวัฒนธรรมแห่งชาติ, 2537.

———. *เวียงกุมกาม: การศึกษาประวัติศาสตร์ชุมชนโบราณในล้านนา.* เชียงใหม่: โรงพิมพ์มิ่งเมือง, 2537.

สวาท เสนาณรงค์. *ภูมิศาสตร์ประเทศไทย.* พระนคร: ไทยวัฒนาพานิช, 2512.

สุรสิงห์สำรวม ฉิมพะเนาว์, ปริวรรต. *บันทึกคำตัดสินคดีโบราณล้านนา* 60 คดี (คลองเจือแห่งพระเจ้ากือนา), 2528. (อัดสำเนา)

สุเนตร ชุตินธรานนท์. *พม่ารบไทย.* กรุงเทพฯ: สำนักพิมพ์มติชน, 2535.

สุณี หาญวงค์. "การสำรวจชุมชนโบราณในจังหวัดลำปาง." ใน *ประวัติศาสตร์และโบราณคดีนครลำปาง.* ลำปาง: วิทยาลัยครูลำปาง สหวิทยาล้านนา, 2524.

สุเทพ สุนทรเภสัช. "ประวัติศาสตร์ท้องถิ่นในล้านนา: ข้อวิจารณ์และเสนอแนะแนวการศึกษา" เอกสารประกอบการสัมมนาล้านนาคดีศึกษา: ประวัติศาสตร์และโบราณคดี ณ วิทยาลัยครูเชียงใหม่ 28-31 มกราคม, 2528.

สุลักษณ์ ศิวรักษ์, ผู้รวบรวม. *อัตชีวประวัติของหม่อมศรีพรหมา กฤษดากร.* กรุงเทพฯ: มูลนิธิจิม ทอมป์สัน, 2522.

สุวิทย์ ธีรศาศวัต. *ความสัมพันธ์ไทยฝรั่งเศส ร.ศ. 112-126.* คุณวรุณยุพา สนิทวงศ์ ณ อยุธยา และวุฒิชัย มูลศิลป์ บรรณาธิการ กรุงเทพฯ: ภาควิชาประวัติศาสตร์ มหาวิทยาลัยศรีนครินทรวิโรฒประสานมิตร, 2523.

สันติ เล็กสุขุม. "ประติมากรรมและสถาปัตยกรรมเมืองพะเยา." ใน *พะเยา-วิถีชีวิตและภูมิปัญญา.* กรุงเทพฯ: สำนักงานคณะกรรมการวัฒนธรรมแห่งชาติ, 2537.

———. *ศิลปะเชียงแสน (ศิลปะล้านนา) และศิลปะสุโขทัย.* นครปฐม: โรงพิมพ์มหาวิทยาลัยศิลปากร, 2534.

สามารถ สิริเวชพันธ์. *วิหารโถง ซุ้มโขง สกุลช่างลำปาง.* เชียงใหม่: โครงการศึกษาวิจัยศิลปสถาปัตยกรรมล้านนา งานล้านนาศึกษา, สถาบันวิจัยสังคม มหาวิทยาลัยเชียงใหม่, 2527.

แสงดาว ณ เชียงใหม่. *พระประวัติพระชายาเจ้าดารารัศมี.* ม.ป.ท., ม.ป.ป.

อาคม พัฒิยะ และนิธิ เอียวศรีวงศ์. *ศรีรามเทพนคร: รวมความเรียงว่าด้วยประวัติศาสตร์อยุธยาตอนต้น.* นิธิ เอียวศรีวงศ์, บรรณาธิการ. กรุงเทพฯ: สำนักพิมพ์เจ้าพระยา, 2527.

อานันท์ กาญจนพันธุ์, "บทนำ". *ตำนานพระยาเจือง*, เล่ม 1. เชียงใหม่: คณะสังคมศาสตร์ มหาวิทยาลัยเชียงใหม่ และศูนย์ส่งเสริมการศึกษาวัฒนธรรมลานนาไทย วิทยาลัยครูเชียงใหม่, 2524.

———. "พัฒนาการเศรษฐกิจของหมู่บ้านในล้านนา (พ.ศ. 2350-2490)" ใน *พัฒนาการของชีวิตและวัฒนธรรมล้านนา.* เชียงใหม่: ศูนย์หนังสือเชียงใหม่, 2527.

อุดม รุ่งเรืองศรี. *วรรณกรรมล้านนา.* เชียงใหม่: หน่วยส่งเสริมศิลปศึกษาและวัฒนธรรมล้านนา คณะมนุษยศาสตร์ มหาวิทยาลัยเชียงใหม่, 2526.

อรุณรัตน์ วิเชียรเขียว. "แนวคิดทางการเมือง: ความสัมพันธ์ระหว่างระบบพัฒนา ระบบนายสิบ และระบบชลประทาน." เอกสารประกอบการสัมมนาทางวิชาการล้านนาคดีศึกษา: โลกทัศน์ล้านนา จัดโดยสหวิทยาล้านนา วิทยาลัยครูเชียงใหม่ 11-14, กันยายน 2532. เอกสารหมายเลข 1/1

——— และสุรพล ดำริห์กุล. *วัดร้างในเวียงเชียงใหม่.* สถาบันวิจัยสังคม มหาวิทยาลัยเชียงใหม่ 2529. (อัดสำเนา)

อุษณีย์ ธงไชย. "อาณาจักรล้านนาไทย: พ.ศ. 1839-2310." เอกสารประกอบการสัมมนาล้านนาคดีศึกษา: ประวัติศาสตร์โบราณคดี 18-21 มกราคม 2528 ณ วิทยาลัยครูเชียงใหม่ เอกสารเลขที่ 01-002.

ฮอล์ล, ดี.จี.อี. *ประวัติศาสตร์เอเชียตะวันออกเฉียงใต้* เล่ม 1. แปลโดย วรุณยุพา สนิทวงศ์ ณ อยุธยา และคณะ. กรุงเทพฯ: ไทยวัฒนาพานิช, 2522.

2.2 วิทยานิพนธ์, สารนิพนธ์ [Thesis]

ชมัยโฉม สุนทรสวัสดิ์. "การศึกษาเชิงประวัติศาสตร์เกี่ยวกับกิจการป่าไม้ทางภาคเหนือของไทยตั้งแต่ พ.ศ. 2439 ถึง พ.ศ. 2475." วิทยานิพนธ์ปริญญามหาบัณฑิต ภาควิชาประวัติศาสตร์ บัณฑิตวิทยาลัย จุฬาลงกรณ์มหาวิทยาลัย, 2521.

ชูสิทธิ์ ชูชาติ. "วิวัฒนาการเศรษฐกิจหมู่บ้านในภาคเหนือของประเทศไทย (พ.ศ. 2394-2475)." วิทยานิพนธ์ปริญญามหาบัณฑิต ภาควิชาประวัติศาสตร์ บัณฑิตวิทยาลัย มหาวิทยาลัยศรีนครินทรวิโรฒ ประสานมิตร, 2523.

ทรงศักดิ์ ปรางค์วัฒนากุล. "วิเคราะห์วรรณกรรมล้านนาไทย เรื่องเจ้าวิทูรสอนหลาน และพระลอสอนโลก." วิทยานิพนธ์ปริญญามหาบัณฑิต ภาควิชาภาษาไทย บัณฑิตวิทยาลัย มหาวิทยาลัยศรีนครินทรวิโรฒ ประสานมิตร, 2523.

ธำรงค์ศักดิ์ ทำบุญ. "กำเนิดอาณาจักรลานนาไทย." วิทยานิพนธ์ปริญญามหาบัณฑิต ภาควิชาประวัติศาสตร์ จุฬาลงกรณ์มหาวิทยาลัย, 2529.

นคร พันธุ์ณรงค์. "การเจรจาข้อตกลงระหว่างรัฐบาลสยามกับรัฐบาลอังกฤษเกี่ยวกับหัวเมืองชายแดนลานนาไทยพม่า สมัยพระบาทสมเด็จพระจุลจอมเกล้าเจ้าอยู่หัว ระยะ 2428-2438." วิทยานิพนธ์ปริญญามหาบัณฑิต ภาควิชาประวัติศาสตร์ บัณฑิตวิทยาลัย วิทยาลัยวิชาการศึกษาประสานมิตร, 2516.

นันทิยา สว่างวุฒิธรรม. "การคุมกำลังคนในสมัยรัตนโกสินทร์ก่อนการจัดการเกณฑ์ทหาร (พ.ศ. 2325-2448)." วิทยานิพนธ์ปริญญามหาบัณฑิต ภาควิชาประวัติศาสตร์ จุฬาลงกรณ์มหาวิทยาลัย, 2524.

บัณฑิต อินทรชัยศรี. "พระบรมราโชบายด้านการปกครองที่เกี่ยวกับการสร้างความมั่นคงภายในพระราชอาณาจักรของพระบาทสมเด็จพระจอมเกล้าเจ้าอยู่หัว (พ.ศ. 2394-2411)." วิทยานิพนธ์ปริญญามหาบัณฑิต ภาควิชาประวัติศาสตร์ บัณฑิตวิทยาลัย วิทยาลัยวิชาการ ศึกษาประสานมิตร, 2521.

ประคอง นิมมานเหมินท์. "มหากาพย์เรื่องท้าวบาเจือง: การศึกษาเชิงวิเคราะห์." วิทยานิพนธ์ปริญญาดุษฎีบัณฑิต สาขาวิชาภาษาไทย บัณฑิตวิทยาลัย จุฬาลงกรณ์มหาวิทยาลัย, 2530.

ปริญญา กายสิทธิ์. “ประวัติศาสตร์พุทธศาสนาในล้านนาไทยตั้งแต่ พ.ศ. 1912 ถึง พ.ศ. 2101.” วิทยานิพนธ์ปริญญามหาบัณฑิต ภาควิชาประวัติศาสตร์ บัณฑิตวิทยาลัย มหาวิทยาลัยศรีนครินทรวิโรฒ ประสานมิตร, 2528.

ปริศนา ศิรินาม. “ความสัมพันธ์ระหว่างไทยและประเทศราชในหัวเมืองลานนาไทย สมัยรัตนโกสินทร์ตอนต้น.” วิทยานิพนธ์ปริญญามหาบัณฑิต ภาควิชาประวัติศาสตร์ บัณฑิตวิทยาลัย วิทยาลัยวิชาการศึกษา ประสานมิตร, 2516.

ปลายอ้อ ชนะนนท์. “บทบาทนายทุนพ่อค้าที่มีต่อการก่อและขยายตัวของทุนนิยมภาคเหนือของประเทศไทย พ.ศ. 2464-2523.” วิทยานิพนธ์ ภาควิชาเศรษฐศาสตร์ บัณฑิตวิทยาลัย จุฬาลงกรณ์มหาวิทยาลัย, 2529.

พงษ์เนียน ทองพงษ์เนียน. “การศึกษาเรื่องทาสในสมัยกรุงรัตนโกสินทร์.” วิทยานิพนธ์ปริญญามหาบัณฑิต ภาควิชาประวัติศาสตร์ จุฬาลงกรณ์มหาวิทยาลัย, 2517.

พรพรรณ จงวัฒนา. “การพิพาทระหว่างเจ้านครเชียงใหม่กับคนบังคับในอังกฤษ อันเป็นเหตุให้รัฐบาลสยามจัดการปกครองมณฑลพายัพ (พ.ศ. 2401-2445).” วิทยานิพนธ์ปริญญามหาบัณฑิต ภาควิชาประวัติศาสตร์ จุฬาลงกรณ์มหาวิทยาลัย, 2517.

พรรณิภา อพิญชพงศ์. “เจ้า ไพร่ กับความเปลี่ยนแปลงในสังคมล้านนา ระหว่าง พ.ศ. 2427-2476.” วิทยานิพนธ์ปริญญามหาบัณฑิต ภาควิชาประวัติศาสตร์ มหาวิทยาลัยศรีนครินทรวิโรฒ ประสานมิตร, 2535.

พรสวรรค์ อัมรานนท์. “ตำนานเชียงแสน: การศึกษาเชิงวิจารณ์.” วิทยานิพนธ์ปริญญามหาบัณฑิต ภาควิชาภาษาตะวันออก: บัณฑิตวิทยาลัย มหาวิทยาลัยศิลปากร, 2526.

ภาสกร โทณะวณิก. “การศึกษาเมืองโบราณเวียงพระธาตุลำปางหลวง.” วิทยานิพนธ์ศิลปศาสตร มหาบัณฑิต สาขาวิชาโบราณคดีสมัยประวัติศาสตร์ ภาควิชาโบราณคดี บัณฑิตวิทยาลัย มหาวิทยาลัยศิลปากร, 2529.

รวิวรรณ ภาคพรต. “การกัลปนาในลานนาไทยตั้งแต่กลางพุทธศตวรรษที่ 20 ถึงต้นพุทธศตวรรษที่ 22.” วิทยานิพนธ์ปริญญามหาบัณฑิต ภาควิชาประวัติศาสตร์ บัณฑิตวิทยาลัย จุฬาลงกรณ์มหาวิทยาลัย, 2526.

วรรณชลีย์ บุญมี. “ความสัมพันธ์กับอังกฤษในบางลักษณะ สมัยพระบาทสมเด็จพระจุลจอมเกล้าเจ้าอยู่หัว: การป่าไม้และการเหมืองแร่.” วิทยานิพนธ์ปริญญามหาบัณฑิต ภาควิชาประวัติศาสตร์ บัณฑิตวิทยาลัย มหาวิทยาลัยศรีนครินทรวิโรฒ ประสานมิตร, 2520.

วิบูลย์ ทานุชิต. “การปฏิรูปการศึกษาในมณฑลพายัพ (พ.ศ. 2442-2476).” วิทยานิพนธ์ปริญญามหาบัณฑิต ภาควิชาประวัติศาสตร์ บัณฑิตวิทยาลัย มหาวิทยาลัยศรีนครินทรวิโรฒ ประสานมิตร, 2528.

วราวุธ ศรีโสภาค. “การศึกษาวิเคราะห์ความสัมพันธ์ของกลุ่มเมืองโบราณที่มีคู-คันดินล้อมรอบในบริเวณเมืองพะเยา.” สารนิพนธ์ปริญญาศิลปศาสตรบัณฑิต (โบราณคดี) ภาควิชาโบราณคดี คณะโบราณคดี มหาวิทยาลัยศิลปากร, 2533

สรัสวดี ประยูรเสถียร. “การปฏิรูปการปกครองมณฑลพายัพ (พ.ศ. 2436-2476).” วิทยานิพนธ์ปริญญามหาบัณฑิต ภาควิชาประวัติศาสตร์ บัณฑิตวิทยาลัย มหาวิทยาลัยศรีนครินทรวิโรฒ ประสานมิตร, 2522.

โสภา ชานะมูล. “ครูบาศรีวิชัย ‘ตนบุญ’ แห่งล้านนา (พ.ศ. 2421-2481).” วิทยานิพนธ์ศิลปศาสตรมหาบัณฑิต สาขาประวัติศาสตร์ คณะศิลปศาสตร์ มหาวิทยาลัยธรรมศาสตร์, 2534.

หวัง จี้ หมิน. "ความสัมพันธ์ระหว่างเมืองเชอหลี่กับเมืองปาไปซีฟู." วิทยานิพนธ์ปริญญาอักษรศาสตรมหาบัณฑิต ภาควิชาประวัติศาสตร์ บัณฑิตวิทยาลัยจุฬาลงกรณ์มหาวิทยาลัย, 2531.

อัญชลี สุสายัณห์. "ความเปลี่ยนแปลงของระบบไพร่และผลกระทบต่อสังคมไทยในสมัยพระบาทสมเด็จพระจุลจอมเกล้าเจ้าอยู่หัว." วิทยานิพนธ์ปริญญามหาบัณฑิต ภาควิชาประวัติศาสตร์ บัณฑิตวิทยาลัย จุฬาลงกรณ์มหาวิทยาลัย, 2524.

อิศรา กันแตง. "การศึกษาลักษณะเฉพาะและพัฒนาการของโครงข่ายการสัญจรและพื้นที่ปลูกสร้างในบริเวณนครเชียงใหม่." วิทยานิพนธ์ปริญญามหาบัณฑิต ภาควิชาการวางแผนภาคและเมือง บัณฑิตวิทยาลัย จุฬาลงกรณ์มหาวิทยาลัย, 2533.

อุษณีย์ ธงไชย. "ความสัมพันธ์ระหว่างอยุธยาและลานนาไทย พ.ศ. 1839-2310." วิทยานิพนธ์ปริญญามหาบัณฑิต ภาควิชาประวัติศาสตร์ บัณฑิตวิทยาลัย จุฬาลงกรณ์มหาวิทยาลัย, 2526.

2.3 บทความ [Articles]

กิติ แก่นจำปี. "ความเชื่อเรื่องผีปู่แสะย่าแสะ." ใน *ศึกษาศาสตร์สาร.* (ตุลาคม 2525-กันยายน 2526): 121-133.

เจีย เยน จอง. "ความเป็นมาของวัฒนธรรมในล้านนา-สิบสองพันนา." *แถลงงานประวัติศาสตร์เอกสารโบราณคดี* ปีที่ 21, (มกราคม-ธันวาคม, 2531).

ชูสิทธิ์ ชูชาติ. "กำเนิดระบบเศรษฐกิจทุนนิยมกับผลกระทบที่มีต่อสังคมชาวนาในภาคเหนือ." ใน *วารสารสังคมศาสตร์* 5, (เมษายน-กันยายน 2524): 36-38.

———. "กบฏพญาผาบ (ปราบสงคราม): กบฏชาวนาภาคเหนือ." ใน *วารสารสังคมศาสตร์* 2, (ตุลาคม 2522-มีนาคม 2523): 24-25.

ธิดา สาระยา. "สร้างบ้างแปงเมืองระบบเมืองคู่สถาบันเมืองลูกหลวง." *เมืองโบราณ* ปีที่ 9, (เมษายน-กรกฎาคม, 2526).

นิธิ เอียวศรีวงศ์. "การศึกษาประวัติศาสตร์ไทยอดีตและอนาคต." *รวมบทความประวัติศาสตร์* ฉบับที่ 1, (กรกฎาคม, 2523).

———. "คนไทยมาจากโน่นด้วย และคนไทยอยู่ที่นี่ด้วย." *ศิลปวัฒนธรรม* ปีที่ 11, ฉบับที่ 12 (ตุลาคม, 2533).

ประพฤทธิ์ ศุกลรัตนเมธี และ วินัย พงศ์ศรีเพียร. "บทบาทของล้านนาในวิกฤตการณ์การเมืองระหว่างรัฐในราชอาณาจักรลาว พ.ศ. 2002-2024." *รวมบทความประวัติศาสตร์* ฉบับที่ 16, (2537).

______. 'ปอเล่อ' ใน "หมิงสือลู่กับการคลี่คลายของประวัติศาสตร์ไทย." *วารสารอักษรศาสตร์* ปีที่ 24, ฉบับที่ 1 (มกราคม-มิถุนายน, 2535).

ประสาน บุญประคอง และประเสริฐ ณ นคร. "คำอ่านศิลาจารึกและอักษรที่ใช้ในล้านาไทย." *ศิลปากร* 4. พฤศจิกายน 2512.

ผาสุข อินทราวุธ. "ผลการขุดค้นเมืองโบราณสมัยทวาราวดีที่จังหวัดสิงห์บุรีและนครปฐม." *เมืองโบราณ* ปีที่ 10, (ตุลาคม-ธันวาคม, 2527).

แม็คมอร์แกน, มาร์โก ทาเก. "ประวัติและพัฒนาการของการค้าขายในลำปาง ตั้งแต่ปลายคริสต์ศตวรรษที่ 19 ถึง ค.ศ. 1939." แปลโดย เครือมาศ วุฒิการณ์ ใน *วารสารมนุษยศาสตร์* 1. (กรกฎาคม-ธันวาคม, 2527): 1-7.

รัตนาภรณ์ เศรษฐกุล. "ความสัมพันธ์ทางการเมืองระหว่างเชียงใหม่และเชียงตุงจนถึงศตวรรษที่ 19." ใน *วารสารมนุษยศาสตร์* 1 (กรกฎาคม-ธันวาคม 2527): 18-41.

วัลภา รุ่งศิริแสงรัตน์ "กบฏไทยเขินเมืองเชียงใหม่ปี พ.ศ. 2432." ใน *แถลงงานประวัติศาสตร์ เอกสารโบราณคดี* 1 (มกราคม-มิถุนายน 2523): 59-71.

ศรีศักร วัลลิโภดม. "ขุนเจือง: ความสำนึกร่วมทางวัฒนธรรมของคนในลุ่มแม่น้ำโขงตอนบน." *เมืองโบราณ* ปีที่ 20, ฉบับที่ 1 มกราคม 2537.

———. "เมืองลูกหลวงกับการปกครองไทยโบราณ." *ข้อขัดแย้งเกี่ยวกับประวัติศาสตร์ไทย.* กรุงเทพฯ: สำนักพิมพ์เมืองโบราณ, 2524.

———. "เวียงมโน." *เมืองโบราณ* ปีที่ 4, (มกราคม-มีนาคม, 2521).

สมโชติ อ๋องสกุล. "ความเป็นมาของคำ 'ล้านนา-ลานนา' ในประวัติศาสตร์นิพนธ์ไทย." *แถลงงานประวัติศาสตร์ เอกสารโบราณคดี* ปีที่ 20, เล่ม 2 (กรกฎาคม-ธันวาคม, 2530).

สรัสวดี อ๋องสกุล. "กบฏพระยาปราบสงคราม แม่ทัพเมืองเชียงใหม่ พ.ศ. 2432." *ความเชื่อพระศรีอารย์ และกบฏผู้มีบุญในสังคมไทย.* พรเพ็ญ ฮั่นตระกูล อัจฉราพร กมุทพิสมัย บรรณาธิการ. กรุงเทพฯ: สำนักพิมพ์สร้างสรรค์, 2527.

———. "การปฏิรูปการศึกษาในล้านนา: การสร้างเอกภาพแห่งชาติ (พ.ศ. 2446-2475)." *ศึกษาศาสตร์สาร.* 2-4 (ตุลาคม-กันยายน 2525): 29-48.

———. "ไทลื้อเมืองยอง ในแดนพม่า: ข้อสังเกตเบื้องต้น." บทความเสนอในเสวนาไทยศึกษา ครั้งที่ 3 จัดโดยศูนย์ส่งเสริมศิลปวัฒนธรรม มหาวิทยาลัยเชียงใหม่.

———. และคณะ "อ่างเก็บน้ำโบราณคดีในมหาวิทยาลัยเชียงใหม่." *ศึกษาศาสตร์สาร.* 2536.

———. "วัดเจ็ดยอดในฐานะอายุเมืองเชียงใหม่" *ศิลปากร.* ปีที่ 35, ฉบับที่ 3/2535.

สายชล วรรณรัตน์. "ละโว้ก่อนสมัยอยุธยา." *รวมบทความประวัติศาสตร์* ปีที่ 2, มกราคม 2524.

อานาโตล แป็ลติเยอร์. "ความสัมพันธ์ระหว่างล้านนากับล้านช้างในด้านวรรณกรรม." *ล้านนาไทย.* อนุสรณ์พระราชพิธีเปิดพระบรมราชานุสาวรีย์สามกษัตริย์ เชียงใหม่, 2526-2527.

อานันท์ กาญจนพันธุ์. "ประวัติศาสตร์เศรษฐกิจภาคเหนือ (พ.ศ. 2420-2500)." *เอกสารประกอบการประชุมทางวิชาการ เรื่องเศรษฐกิจภาคเหนือปัจจุบันและอนาคต.* จัดโดยภาควิชาเศรษฐศาสตร์ คณะสังคมศาสตร์ มหาวิทยาลัยเชียงใหม่ ร่วมกับมูลนิธิโตโยต้า ณ ห้องประชุมโรงแรมสุริวงศ์ จังหวัดเชียงใหม่ 22-24 กุมภาพันธ์ 2528.

2.4 Books in English

Bock, Carl. *Temples and Elephants.* Bangkok: White Orchid Press, 1985.

Cœdés, George. *The Indianized State of Southeast Asia.* Translated by Susan Browning Cowing. Edited by Walter Vella. Honolulu: East-West Center Press, 1968.

Condominus, Georges. *From Lawa to Mon, From Saa to Thai: Historical and Anthropological Aspects of Southeast Asian Social Spaces.* Translated by Stephanie Anderson, Maria Magannon, and Gehan Wijeyewardene. Canberra: Department of Anthropology, Research School of Pacific Studies, Australian National University, 1990.

Hallette, Holt S. *A Thousand Miles on an Elephant in the Shan States.* 1890. Reprint. Bangkok: White Lotus, 1988.

Luce, G. H. *Old Burma-Early Pagan.* Vol. 1. Locust Valley, N.Y.: Augustin, 1968.

McGilvary, Daniel. *A Half Century among the Siamese and the Lao: An Autobiography.* New York: Fleming H. Revell Company, 1912.

Pointon, A. C. *The Bombay Burmah Trading Corporation Ltd., 1863-1963.* Southampton: Millbrook Press, 1964.

Siam Society. *Relationship with Burma.* 2 vol. Bangkok: Siam Society, 1959.

Scott, James George. *Gazetteer of Upper Burma and the Shan States,* Part 2. Rangoon: Superintendent, Government Printing, 1901.

Than Tun. "Administration under King Thalun 1629–48" Essay on the *History and Buddhism of Burma by Professor Tan Tun.* Edit by Paul Strachan. Kiscadale Publications, 1988.

Than Tun, ed. *The Royal Orders of Burma A.D. 1568–1885,* vol 1. Kyoto: Center for Southeast Asian Studies, Kyoto University, 1983.

Wyatt, David K. *Thailand: A Short History.* Bangkok: Thai Wattana Panich Press, 1984.

Wyatt, David K. and Aroonrut Wichienkeeo. The Chiang Mai Chronicle. Second Edition. Chiang Mai: Silkworm Books, 1998.

2.5 Dissertations and Articles in English

Anan Ganjanaphan. "The Partial Commercialization of Rice Production in Northern Thailand." Ph.D. Dissertation, Cornell University, 1984.

Brailey, Nigle J. "The Origins of the Siamese forward Movement in Western Laos 1850–92." Ph.D. Dissertation. University of London, 1968.

Ramsay, James Ansil. "The Development of a Bureaucratic Polity: The Case of Northern Siam." Ph.D. Dissertation. Cornell University, 1871.

Griswold A. B. and Prasert Na Nagara. "An inscription in Old Mon from Wiang Mano in Chiang Mai Province." *Journal of the Siam Society.* 59 (January 1971).

Luce, G. H. "The Early Sayam in Burma History," *Journal of the Siam Society* 56 (November 1968).

Macleod, T. E. "Abstract Journal of Expedition to Kiang Hung on the Chinese Frontier Starting From Moulmein on the 13th December 1836." *Journal of the Asiatic Society* 72 (December, 1837).

Siam Society. "Intercourse between Burma and Siam as Recorded in Hmannan Yazawindawggyi." In *Selected Articles from the Siam Society Journal.* Vol. 6. Bangkok: Siam Society 1959.

Than Tun. "Administration under King Thalun 1629–48." In *Essays on the History and Buddhism of Burma by Professor Than Tun.* Edited by Paul Strachan. Whiting Bay, Isle of Arran, Scotland: Kiscadale Publications, 1988.

Winai Pongsripian. "Traditional Thai Historiography and Its Nineteenth Century Decline," Ph.D. Dissertation. University of Bristol, 1983.

INDEX